TACKY'S REVOLT

TACKY'S REVOLT

The Story of an
Atlantic Slave War

VINCENT BROWN

THE BELKNAP PRESS OF
HARVARD UNIVERSITY PRESS

Cambridge, Massachusetts
London, England
2020

Third printing

Library of Congress Cataloging-in-Publication Data

Names: Brown, Vincent, 1967– author.
Title: Tacky's revolt : the story of an Atlantic slave war / Vincent Brown.
Description: Cambridge, Massachusetts : The Belknap Press of
Harvard University Press, 2020. | Includes bibliographical references and index.
Identifiers: LCCN 2019028500 | ISBN 9780674737570 (alk. paper)
Subjects: LCSH: Slave insurrections—Jamaica—History—18th century. |
Slavery—Jamaica—History—18th century. | Great Britain—Colonies—America.
Classification: LCC HT1096 .S 2019 | DDC 306.3 / 62097292—dc23
LC record available at https://lccn.loc.gov/2019028500

Contents

List of Illustrations

TACKY'S REVOLT

Prologue: The Path to Rebel's Barricade

And I will set the Egyptians against the Egyptians, and they shall fight everyone against his brother, and everyone against his neighbor; city against city and kingdom against kingdom.

—ISAIAH 19:2

WAGER, ALSO KNOWN by his African name, Apongo, was a leader of the largest slave rebellion in the eighteenth-century British Empire. But long before taking his part in the great Jamaican insurrection of 1760–1761, commonly called Tacky's Revolt, he had been on a remarkable odyssey. Apongo had been a military leader in West Africa during a period of imperial expansion and intensive warfare there. During this time, he had even been a notable guest of John Cope, a chief agent of Cape Coast Castle, Britain's principal fort on the Gold Coast. Captured and sold at some point in the 1740s, Apongo became the property of Captain Arthur Forrest of HMS *Wager*, who renamed him for the Royal Navy warship. Wager came in bondage to Forrest's plantation in Westmoreland Parish, Jamaica, where he again encountered John Cope, who had retired to his own Jamaican estate. Occasionally, Cope would entertain his acquaintance from the Old World, laying a table for weekend visits, treating the slave as a man of honor, and insinuating that Apongo would one day be redeemed and sent home. Whatever understanding there was between the two men did not outlast John Cope's death in 1756. In the ensuing years Wager began plotting and organizing a war against the whites, and awaiting an opportune moment to strike.[1]

Taking advantage of Britain's Seven Years' War against its European opponents, Wager and more than a thousand other enslaved black people on the island engaged in a series of uprisings, which began on April 7, 1760, and continued until October of the next year. Over those eighteen months the rebels managed to kill sixty whites and destroy tens of thousands of pounds' worth of property. During the suppression of the revolt and the repression that followed, over five hundred black men and women were killed in battle, executed, or driven to suicide. Another five hundred were transported from the island for life. Considering "the extent and secrecy of its plan, the multitude of the conspirators, and the difficulty of opposing its eruptions in such a variety of different places at once," wrote one planter who lived through the upheaval, this revolt was "more formidable than any hitherto known in the West Indies." According to two slaveholders who wrote histories of the conflict, the rebellion arose "at the instigation" of an African man named "Tacky, who had been a chief in Guinea," and was organized and executed principally by people called Coromantees (or Koromantyns) from the Gold Coast—the West African region stretching between the Komoe and Volta rivers—who had an established reputation for military prowess. Slaveholders knew these Africans to be rebellious, and their notoriety has endured to this day.[2]

Wager's involvement in the revolt might further justify this martial reputation, but it is also part of a less familiar story. Although we are accustomed to hearing about rebels reacting against their enslavement by rising up against their masters, and about elite people in Africa falling into the hands of slavers, rarely have these accounts acknowledged the complex patterns of alliance and antagonism over time and great distance that defined relationships like those among Apongo, John Cope, and Arthur Forrest.[3] Recognizing how life histories like theirs—stories of displacement, belonging, and political predicament—were intertwined helps us understand how the slave trade triggered the diasporic warfare that both created and convulsed the eighteenth-century Atlantic world.[4]

Apongo's Atlantic odyssey spans the martial geography of Atlantic slavery, highlighting the entanglement of African and European empires with the massive forced migrations of the eighteenth century—and suggesting a new way to understand slave insurrection.[5] Rather than a two-sided conflict between masters and slaves, the 1760–1761 revolt was the volatile admixture of many journeys and military campaigns. The people who took part in it traveled far and endured many turns of fortune, entangling their numerous episodes into a single story. In its causes and consequences, what we know as Tacky's Revolt combined the itineraries of many people: merchants, planters, imperial functionaries, soldiers and sailors from Europe, Africa, and the Caribbean, and enslaved men, women, and children, all engaged in life-and-death struggles to accumulate wealth, build state power, strike for freedom, or merely survive.

FIGURE 0.1. Attack on Fort Haldane. This depiction of Tacky's Revolt appeared in *The Story of Jamaica*, a graphic illustration of the island's history from the fifteenth century until its independence from the United Kingdom in 1962, by the great comic artist Robert Fujitani. The image and its caption helped to define the insurrection for generations of Jamaicans.

From *The Story of Jamaica* (Kingston, 1962). *Courtesy of The Gleaner Co. Limited.*

The transatlantic slave trade extracted people from a vast region of Atlantic Africa and spread them throughout the Americas. People who had been administrative or military leaders suddenly found themselves uprooted from sustaining landscapes, scattered by currents and trade winds, and replanted in strange territories where they labored to build new social lives and regain a level of influence. Inevitably, some of them concluded that only war could end their enslavement. Mostly it was common people who found themselves caught up in slaving raids and expansionary wars, cast across the ocean, and set down in alien lands where slaveholders exploited and brutalized them. When new conflicts promised to liberate them or offered rewards for serving their masters, slaves might take up arms for whichever faction presented the prospect of a better life.

This process of dispersal from a native land, transplantation, and adaptation to a new and strange one is familiar to students of cultural change, who pull African, American, and Atlantic history into one large, common frame to see large-scale patterns of transformation in African religion, expression, and identity.[6] A similarly expansive approach can reveal how the turmoil of enslavement and the daily hostilities of life in bondage ignited a militant response that erupted in widespread rebellions reverberating across the Americas and back to Europe. The effect when Africans from the Gold Coast staged a series of revolts and conspiracies in the seventeenth and eighteenth centuries—most dramatically in Cartagena de Indias, Surinam,

St. John, New York, Antigua, and Jamaica—was to form an archipelago of insurrection stretching throughout the North Atlantic Americas.[7] The Jamaican insurrections of 1760–1761, and further uprisings there in 1765 and 1766, were among the largest and most consequential of these.

The aims and tactics employed by the rebels made it clear to observers that many had been soldiers in Africa. As John Thornton has argued, "Africans with military experience played an important role in revolts, if not by providing all of the rebels, at least by providing enough to stiffen and increase the viability of revolts." Beyond one or two exceptional leaders, whole cadres of people had military training and discipline, or had at least gained knowledge of defensive tactics in Africa. Indeed, many American slave revolts might be seen as extensions of African wars. Casting them as such does more than assert the importance of Africa in the making of the Atlantic world; it helps to reveal how complex networks of migration, belonging, transregional power, and conflict gave the political history of the eighteenth century some of its distinctive contours. Recognizing slave revolt as a species of warfare is the first step toward a new cartography of Atlantic slavery.[8]

The former slave and veteran of the Seven Years' War Gustavus Vassa, now commonly known by his African name, Olaudah Equiano, famously defined slavery itself as a perpetual "state of war." This was not war in the conventional sense, however, involving disciplined armies directed by the rulers of states. Rather, it was the simmering violence inherent in mastery, by its nature a forceful assault, and the slaves' countervailing resentment of slaveholders' "fraud, rapine, and cruelty."[9] Equiano echoed the English philosopher John Locke, who argued in the late seventeenth century that the "perfect condition of slavery" was nothing "but the state of war continued, between a lawful conqueror, and a captive."[10] To be sure, while Locke extolled freedom as humankind's natural condition and consent as the basis of all government, his theory clashed with his practice; he invested in slave-trading and slaveholding enterprises, and looked upon war captives as a legitimate source of slaves who would remain outside of political society.[11] Equiano, by contrast, pointed directly at the practical, daily war that defined any society afflicted by slavery.

To the slaveholders, Equiano asked, "Are you not hourly in dread of an insurrection?" It was not a rhetorical question. Since the early years of Jamaica's slave society, slaveholders had often considered the enslaved as "Irreconcilable and yet Intestine Enemies," subjected to the colonists' will only by the rule of the whip. The prospect of slave rebellion was a perennial anxiety, "a War always the more terrible," one slaveholder wrote, "by how much there is no Quarter given in it."[12] Equiano visited Jamaica in

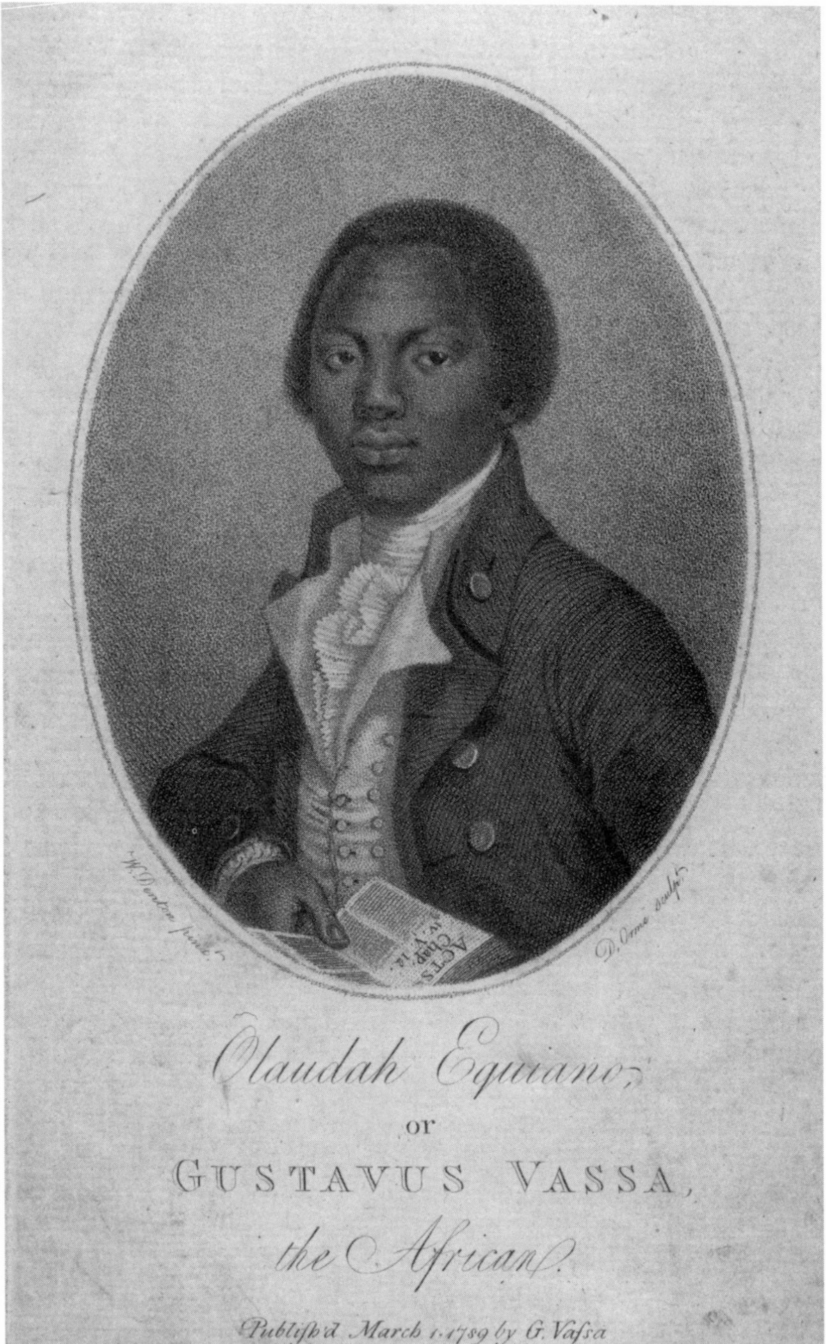
W. Denton pinx.
D. Orme sculpt.
ACTS Chap. IV. V. 12.
Olaudah Equiano,
or
GUSTAVUS VASSA,
the African.
Publish'd March 1. 1789 by G. Vassa

FIGURE 0.2. Olaudah Equiano.

Engraving by Daniel Orme, after a sketch by W. Denton. © *National Portrait Gallery, London.*

1772, as a free man, and he found the island still reeling from the slave uprisings of the previous decade. There he saw how an entire society could be organized around violence and counterattack on every level from the quotidian to the epic.[13] It was an observation shared by black people in other times and places; conditions of bondage were often characterized as a "permanent state of low-intensity war, with the enslaved regularly talking about how to wage that war."[14] The martial characteristics of Atlantic slavery deserve closer inspection.[15]

Acts of resistance to slavery are commonly thought of as falling along a single continuum: at one end of the struggle for freedom are everyday assertions of independent will and volition, such as malingering in the fields, breaking tools, or pilfering from masters, while violent collective uprisings like the ones led by Tacky and Apongo lie at the other end. There is some value in seeing these insurrections as different in scale but not in kind from less dramatic refusals of slaveholders' authority; it allows us to understand the variety and consistency of slaves' opposition to slaveholders. At the same time, however, this framing is too reductive. It masks the complexity of large revolts, glosses over the multiple aspirations of rebels, confines the contest to circumscribed locations, and forecloses important questions about planning, strategy, tactics, and claims to territory—the very questions we ask about wars.[16]

The Jamaican insurrections that began in 1760 clearly constituted resistance. More concretely, they were acts of war. They featured a kind of fighting that has become familiar to military theorists—the kind that involves improvised militias dispersed over wide areas taking up arms against great powers, with largely undefined battle lines and blurred distinctions between civilians and combatants.[17] Viewing the revolt as a war, as its combatants did, helps us to see connections and dynamics that signal far more than the insubordination and defiance of slave resistance. The struggle ranged well beyond the limits of plantations, colonies, or states to encompass and integrate entire regions. As much as it grew out of plantation slavery's inherent, everyday violence, it was sustained by imperial militarism and broader transformations of commerce, governance, and cultural belonging. It was more than a local outburst, more than a continuation of prior experience, and it involved a far larger and more diverse cast of players than studies of resistance normally feature. It was the kind of event best narrated as a war story.[18]

WARFARE migrates. This has never been more apparent than in the era when the violence of imperial expansion and enslavement transformed Europe, Africa, and the Americas as they interacted across the Atlantic Ocean.

European imperial conflicts extended the dominion of capitalist agriculture. African battles fed captives to the transatlantic trade in slaves. Masters and their captives struggled with one another continuously. These clashes amounted to borderless slave war: war to enslave, war to expand slavery, and war against slaves, answered on the side of the enslaved by war against slaveholders, and also war among slaves themselves. In this sense, the Jamaican slave revolt of 1760–1761 was a war within an interlinked network of other wars which had diverging and overlapping provocations, combat zones, political alliances, and enemy combatants. In effect, it was part of four wars at once: it was an extension of wars on the African continent; it was a race war between black slaves and white slaveholders; it was a struggle among black people over the terms of communal belonging, effective control of local territory, and establishment of their own political legacies; and it was, most immediately, one of the hardest-fought battles of that titanic global conflict between Britain and its European rivals that would come to be known as the Seven Years' War. Each of these four wars introduced different currents that converged and eddied in the Jamaican insurrections of the 1760s. To chart their flows, a new cartography of slave revolt is required—one that combines the histories of Europe, Africa, and America and makes room for new stories of place, territory, and movement.[19]

To map the hemispheric reach of a slave war, we must see the interlocking patterns of state, commerce, migration, labor, and militancy formed by a multitude of journeys. These patterns present themselves differently with changes in the scale and scope of our examination. A scale that encompasses large regions and historic transformations complements a narrower focus on the contingent experiences of individual captives, colonists, bureaucrats, soldiers, and seamen. Both are necessary if we are to understand how slaving raids, racial conflict, communal hostilities, and the Seven Years' War created a theater of combat as dynamic as the winds, currents, and weather patterns of the Atlantic Ocean itself.[20] Across vast distances, these wars within wars connected the constituent elements of empire, diaspora, and insurrection. An integrated history of slave revolt that considers its sources, circuits, and reverberations will take us far from the plantations, beyond relations between masters and slaves, and outside the conventional locations for observing racial violence. Vectors of slave war in Jamaica formed a knot in the intertwined itineraries of soldiers who fought in Europe, North America, and Africa; sailors who crisscrossed the Atlantic world for merchants and empires; and slaves who were swept up in many conflicts on both sides of the Atlantic Ocean. Mapping the movements of profiteers, warlords, workers, refugees, and ordinary fighters exposes the shape of a martial archipelago made up of peaks bearing witness to the great volcanic forces of world history operating below.[21]

Slave revolt was race war to the extent that it concerned relations between masters and their vassals. From the fifteenth century onward, skin color was used as a primary index of social status, with blackness becoming increasingly synonymous with slavery over time. By the eighteenth century, in British America especially, white people had come to expect that blacks existed to serve their material, sexual, and psychic desires. In slave societies like those in the Caribbean and southern North America, whites thought of themselves as collectively belonging to a ruling race. Often outnumbered by their desperate slaves, the colonists developed elaborate regimes of terror to keep them in submission. On rare occasions, when opportunities arose, slave rebels responded in kind.[22]

Slave revolts and conspiracies were usually put down quickly and brutally by slaveholders on the lookout for the total onslaught by angry black people they anticipated might come.[23] The 1760–1761 revolt in Jamaica was more exemplary than exceptional, because it represented the sum of their fears. Occurring three decades before the 1789–1804 Haitian Revolution destroyed Europe's most profitable colony in the Americas, neighboring French St. Domingue, this Jamaican conflict suspended life as colonists knew it, violating domestic order, halting business, and promising the end of their prestige. It threatened a remapping of colonial America as African territory where white rule would have no sway. The British devoted great energy and spent considerable sums to fortify their society against this prospect.

Enslaved Africans did indeed have their own designs on Jamaica's landscape, guided by their experiences of enslavement and their understanding of the possibilities for escape.[24] They envisioned moving freely through the terrain that lay beyond the slave masters' control, seeing in the forests and mountains a world apart from the plains and valleys stamped with agricultural estates, where communities of runaways might turn natural dangers to their defensive advantage. They also saw, even within the slaveholders' domain, chances to repurpose small spaces into places where they could protect their collective sense of self-worth from daily assault, and dreamed of building their own societies even on the sites of their bondage.[25] These visions for the island were shaped, as they were for whites, by the long history of violent transformations that attended the slave trade.

Wars were principal conduits and facilitators of Atlantic commerce, and created favorable conditions for proliferating aggression. Military conquests secured new markets and new captured and coerced labor forces, while troops guaranteed the viability of trade. The eminent scholar W. E. B. Du

Bois clearly recognized how war laid the foundations of commercial production systems with hidden costs of "sweat, blood, death, and despair."[26] Following Du Bois, historians writing on colonial slavery in the radical tradition—such as C. L. R. James, Eric Williams, and Walter Rodney—have insisted that the slave trade was the strongest cord binding the region together, the stimulus for economic growth, and a principal cause of enduring inequalities.[27] The slave trade linked European commerce and colonial development to the political history of African wars—which produced a majority of the captives sold on the coast, both by taking prisoners of war and by creating conditions such as drought, famine, and failed government that drove people from their homes and made them vulnerable to predation. Given this tight linkage of war, enslavement, and economic expansion, the history of Africa must be understood as an integral part of the development of European empires.[28]

To do their work, slave traders on the Gold Coast needed at least some knowledge of African political territory. Early in their trade with Atlantic Africa, Europeans who knew little more than the coastal silhouette of the continent produced speculative maps of the polities they encountered or heard about from informants. They tried to discover which rulers to flatter, who controlled access to the best trade routes, and who was preparing for battle, since wars yielded human commodities. As the Europeans vied for trade, they took turns ousting each other from their forts, raising a series of flags to signal their shifting possession to local African envoys and to the ships bobbing offshore. Making up a jagged line along the coast, these little garrisons were the sites where captives marched from the interior met their European incarceration. From there they were wedged into the holds of slave ships for their journeys to the Americas. Already victimized by slaving wars and torn from their ancestral communities, now they faced the challenges of forging new ways of belonging suited to the New World's race wars.

Black people's struggles to order their communities in the Americas often turned violent. Historians have commonly cast Coromantee slave revolts as the quintessential "African rebellions"—the most spectacular examples of "national" or "ethnic" revolt—because they were organized and executed principally by people from a single, broad linguistic region. But these uprisings featured dynamics more fraught and complicated than this characterization allows. Far from a unified African ethnic group with a clear sense of identity, Coromantees were divided along multiple lines. There were political struggles among those Gold Coast Africans who had been pitted against each other in Old World wars; among strangers thrown together into colonial slavery's crucible of misery; between black people born in Africa and those born in America; and among Coromantees with conflicting interests and beliefs.[29] Even in the context of a joint fight against enslavement, Coromantee insurrections featured all of these tensions. To assume the coherence of the Coromantee ethnic group is to obscure the internal turbulence that affected the course of their crusades.

All the Africans brought to America were shaped by past societies and experiences; understanding these helps us to trace the influences of African history on America, and of American history on Africans.[30] Among the strongest of these influences were their experiences of warfare, dislocation, and social regeneration, which continued in the American slave societies. Slaves differed from and resembled each other along multiple axes including not only their languages, spiritual beliefs and practices, ideals for gender relations, and contingent political allegiances, but also the ways in which they were subject to the prerogatives of slaveholders, the social roles required by the labor regime, and the operations of colonial security. No single facet of identity determined how people responded to enslavement. They adopted various and conflicting positions, leading to political conflict among slaves and between slaves and free blacks. To appreciate how the African rebels in Jamaica managed to mobilize a scattered array of "co-nationals" to wage war against their era's most powerful Atlantic empire—and why so many other black people stood against them or stood to the side—we must examine how they adjusted to their novel circumstances by making new identifications and affinities, regrouping together in new political communities.

Struggles over communal belonging were not only part of the larger enterprise of ethnic group formation, or what has been called ethnogenesis.[31] They were also present in intimate spaces and close interactions. In slave quarters and slaveholders' homes, at work and in the fields, in port towns and aboard ships, and along the pathways connecting parts of the island—in every place one could read and interpret signs of difference and similarity, of deference and disrespect—people created what the historian Stephanie Camp has termed "rival geographies," engaging in the "politics of place" that would attach meaning to their surroundings.[32] Across the island people maintained a "warring intimacy," in which adversarial claims relating to shared territory arose from individuals' deep and differing senses of privilege, morality, and justice.[33]

Much easier to map than these communal struggles are the land claims of nation-states and empires. Having been Spanish territory before 1655, Jamaica was captured in that year by the English, and became one of the kingdom's most valuable possessions. Throughout Britain's frequent wars against the Dutch, Spanish, and French, the island presented a tempting target and was thus heavily fortified against attack. Yet the most serious challenge to British sovereignty in Jamaica came not from European rivals but from Africans and their descendants. Black rebels fragmented the territory of colonial control throughout the seventeenth and eighteenth centuries, and were positioned to take the entire island during the Seven Years' War—or so the slaveholders feared.

The Seven Years' War was a global conflict with enormous consequences, but historians have barely noticed that the Jamaican insurrection was one of its major battles.[34] The most comprehensive accounts of the war focus mainly on the rivalry among Europeans, giving due consideration to Native American nations in North America but ignoring the Jamaican rebellion completely.[35] Historians of the British army during the period have expressed doubt that the military learned much from deployments in the Caribbean.[36] Even the most important interpretations of racial attitudes in Anglo-American warfare in the era neglect the suppression of slave uprisings.[37] The tendency is for chronicles to segregate the slaves' war from the British campaign for the West Indies.[38] The prodigious corpus of British military history includes scant reference to the suppression of slave revolts in Jamaica, despite the island's status as the most militarily significant colony in eighteenth-century British America.[39] Common combatants were more observant. Some of the very same soldiers, sailors, and marines who waged the most famous battles of the Seven Years' War in Quebec, Senegal, Martinique, and Guadeloupe went on to fight against Jamaica's rebels. There is nothing surprising about troops being deployed to multiple theaters, yet in this case the troops' experiences did not generate anything like a codified counterinsurgency strategy. Perhaps this is the reason that neither the military historians concerned with officially acknowledged wars nor the scholars of slave resistance focusing on local freedom struggles have devoted much attention to the way these small dirty wars epitomized the relationship between trade, labor, and imperial power.[40]

EVERY slave revolt drew a congeries of participants into close engagements, but the rebels' stories must be learned mainly from the records left by their enemies. The powerful people of the time and their scribes were quick to distinguish between legitimate and illegitimate combatants, and their documents treat slave insurgents with disdain. Likewise, the collecting practices of historical repositories, whether state- or family-owned, have traditionally been guided by patrons with settled understandings of the world; materials testifying to untidy popular politics rarely fit the established narratives of nations, peoples, and historic events. Slave revolts can look isolated and insignificant in retrospect because, with the exception of

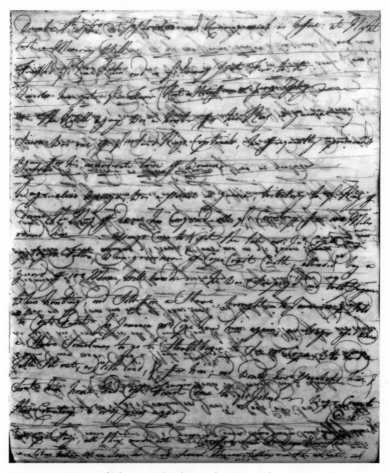

FIGURE 0.3. Diary of Thomas Thistlewood, 4 December 1760.
Courtesy of the Beinecke Library, Yale University.

the great uprising that created the nation-state of Haiti, they seem to have mattered mostly to local people on their estates or in their individual colonies, and to have been of little long-term consequence.[41]

This misimpression is partly due to the paucity of written sources produced by black people at the time. The government officials, slave-trading merchants, planter diarists, property-owning correspondents, colonial printers, and Christian missionaries whose inscriptions fill the archives were not primarily concerned with the politics of the enslaved. These writers discussed their own plans and maneuvers, competed with each other, and fretted over the great many things that could cause their endeavors to fail. Even where we find colonists writing directly about slave revolts, their comments betray an eagerness to move on to other topics. Black lives mattered mostly to the extent that they satisfied a desire for productivity, sexual gratification, or the magnification of personal status. Uprisings caused unfortunate interruptions in planting, trade, and travel, for which correspondents duly apologized to their creditors or supervisors—always promising a quick resumption of normal business—but few people paused to elaborate on the slaves' grievances and goals, or the connections among the various individuals and forces behind the insurrections.

Yet the content of a text is never limited to its author's agenda and purpose. Historical sources are never transparent reflections of what happened, how, and why; nor, in the case of the Jamaican uprisings, are they merely the literary phantasms of the colonists' imaginations. The story of Tacky's Revolt is forever entangled with their fears and fantasies, but these were stimulated by the stout militancy of rebellious blacks. As surely as wind and water change the contours of stone, slavery's archival sources have been shaped by the black people they rarely describe. Reading these records both against the grain, to investigate things the sources never meant to illustrate, and along the grain, to note how they constrain and shape our knowledge, we can tell plausible stories about the aspirations and strivings of the enslaved.[42]

These were never the stories that someone like the eighteenth-century historian Edward Long wanted to tell. And yet Long's account of the slave insurrections of the 1760s remained the standard text for nearly two hundred and fifty years. Long was a well-cultivated and erudite Englishman with deep connections to Jamaica, the great-great-grandson of Samuel Long, who had been Speaker of the island's House of Assembly in the 1670s and 1680s. The younger Long went to the island in 1757 while in his early twenties, spending twelve years there as a planter, a judge in the vice-admiralty court, and a secretary to his brother-in-law, Lieutenant Governor Henry Moore, before returning to England in 1769 to write his three-volume *History of Jamaica*. Long was a serious historian, gathering his sources diligently and interpreting them carefully. He also hated black people, especially Africans, and was an ardent defender of slavery. His work cannot be ignored; neither can it be taken at face value. Interrogating Long aggressively, subjecting his stories and motivations to exacting scrutiny, produces useful intelligence. This applies equally to the subsequent history of the British West Indies written by Long's fellow planter Bryan Edwards, and to the eyewitness reports of Edwards' uncle Zachary Bayly, who helped to suppress slave uprisings in 1760 and 1765. In each case, as with the records of military and government officials, merchants, and missionaries, we must discover the history of the enslaved through the unreliable narrations of their captors.[43]

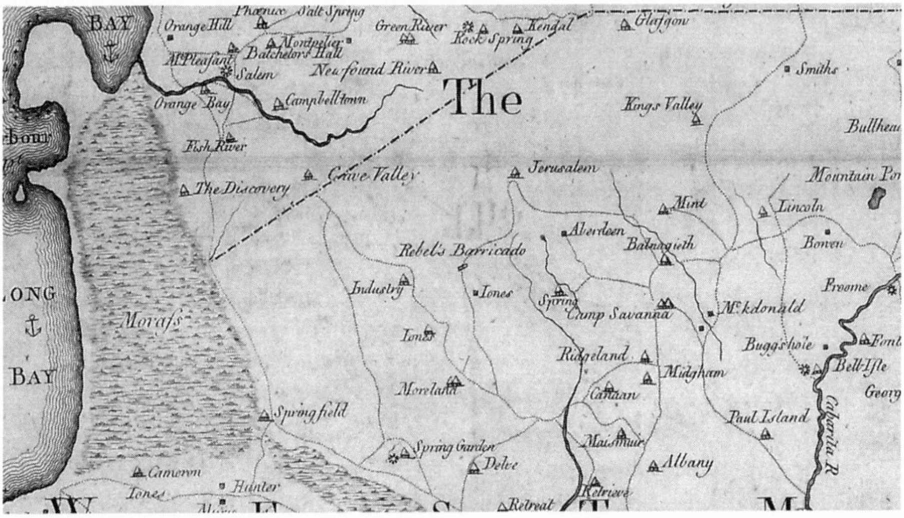

FIGURE 0.4. Rebel's Barricade. This detail from a 1763 Map of Jamaica shows the location of the Rebel's Barricade in Westmoreland Parish.

By Thomas Craskell, surveyor. *Courtesy of the UK National Archives.*

The bare outline of Wager's story, for example, was sketched by the overseer Thomas Thistlewood, whose personal diary is a catalog of brutal disciplinary tactics, casual cruelties, and sexual assaults over three decades. Thistlewood may not be a credible witness, but his brief mention of Apongo's time on the Gold Coast, enslavement in the Royal Navy, and execution on the public gibbet points toward the broader process of diasporic warfare.[44] By following the clues left by the diarist, we discover that Apongo was one of many persons of high status to fall prey to slavers, sail with other men from the Gold Coast, and labor alongside scores of other plantation slaves determined to fight the master class. Though he was an exceptional individual, his life was also full of experiences common to many. The slave trade forced all enslaved people to remake and renegotiate their sense of affiliation and belonging, while the massive dispersal of Africans across the Atlantic also scattered the seeds of military conflict throughout the Americas.

Like most slave insurrections, Tacky's and Wager's war ended badly for the rebels. The insurgents were killed or captured, publicly executed in grisly displays, or banished from the island—probably along with many bystanders who had taken no part in the fighting. Looking back with a historian's perspective, one can see that the outcome was never in doubt; the balance of forces doomed the rebellion from the start. The Coromantees would not win the colony from the British, as the North American colonists won their territory two and a half decades later, and as the Haitians in 1804 took Saint-Domingue from the French. But the rebels in Jamaica did not know they would fail. They acted with the hope of success, and their confidence demands a reassessment of the politics of slavery. Even amidst the business of war and enslavement in a colony garrisoned for battle with foreign and domestic enemies, they could find fissures in the landscape of planter power beyond the reach of the slaveholders' whips. They could even challenge the combined forces of the British Empire and find an enduring place in popular memory.

When they built a mountain stronghold for more than a thousand men, women, and children, the rebels forced their way onto the official map of Jamaica. In the midst of the Seven Years' War, surveyors were commissioned to produce the most detailed atlas of the island to date. Printed in 1763, it features large maps of the topography and estates in each of the colony's three counties. In Westmoreland Parish, in addition to the sites of the major towns built by former slaves called maroons, the map clearly marks the location of the "Rebel's Barricade." The concession of place name is a testament to the insurgents' ambition and a slave insurrection that could not go unnoticed, however much slaveholders might try to disavow and distort its history. Power is never total. Even the most subjugated peoples have dared to plan and fight for their own forbidden aims. The rebels' perspectives on empire and insurrection should inform our own. Their struggles illuminate cracks in the edifice of racial capitalism, reminding us that another world is not only possible, another world is inevitable.

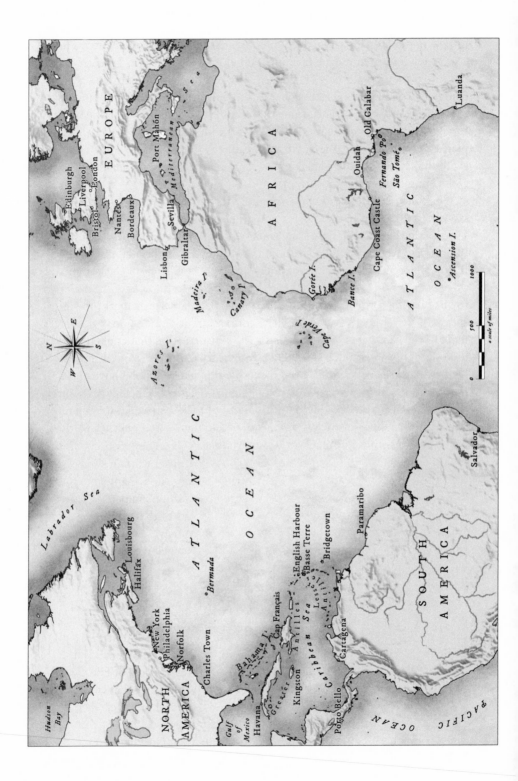

CHAPTER ONE

War's Empire

THE JAMAICAN SLAVE uprising of 1760–1761 did not begin in Africa, but that is where its story starts. Although the revolt was a response to the African rebels' predicament in Jamaica, they drew upon lessons learned long before they crossed the Atlantic Ocean. It is unclear exactly what they knew about white colonists, about the power of European empires, or about the best strategies and tactics for fighting them. Yet this uncertain aspect of the story suggests its most important point of departure: many Africans came to the Americas with firsthand experience of Europe's imperial expansion. African history was already joined to the history of the Americas.[1]

Beginning the story of American slave revolt with West Africa's entanglement with European empire allows a shift in perspective, taking in the wider geography that shaped the course of the insurgency and the political imagination of its participants. Starting with the image of slaves in Jamaica, or elsewhere in the Americas, encourages us to fixate on their suffering black bodies and see only their reactions to bondage. By contrast, recalling their roots in West Africa reminds us to consider their goals, initiatives, and maneuvers. This provides a different perspective on slaveholders, as well: their interactions with militant Africans highlight the failures of European command as much as mastery, the brittleness and insecurity that colonists could overcome only with massive displays of force. Slaveholders cited black militancy as a justification for their brutality. In response, late-eighteenth-century abolitionists would rally around the image of a kneeling supplicant begging to be recognized as a man and a brother, as if the condemnation of evil required the meek innocence of its victims. That icon of abjection has shaped the prevailing understanding of bondage and race to this day. But the caricature bore no resemblance to the black fighters who stood toe-to-toe with whites in encounters all across the war-torn world of Atlantic slavery, from West Africa to the Americas.

We can glimpse the outlines of this transatlantic struggle through the entangled lives of Wager (or Apongo, as he was originally named), John Cope, and Arthur Forrest, which embodied the nature of African insurrection in Jamaica as a war within a network of wars. Wager's enigmatic life story encompasses an unlikely journey from the administrative councils of Gold Coast statecraft and trade to the British Royal Navy at war, and from the sugar plantation fields of Jamaica to leadership of a massive slave uprising, and finally to his execution on the public gibbet. Cope spent a tumultuous few years in West Africa, taking the opportunity of internecine African strife to enhance his fortunes in the British slave trade. Then, after some years of financing the trade from London, he retired to an affluent life as a planter in Jamaica, Britain's most profitable colony. Arthur Forrest, a naval warrior and great planter, fought commendably in some of Britain's most celebrated military triumphs of the eighteenth century, even while his slaves staged the empire's greatest servile rebellion. Though we know Cope's and Forrest's stories with more certainty than Wager's, they are all in their way emblematic of various experiences, forces, and patterns. The story of the two white men's relations with Apongo, or Wager, uncertain as it is, illuminates the connective circuits of Atlantic slavery.

These men were all traveling the main arteries of Atlantic empire, but their divergent paths suggest other ways of seeing the Atlantic world beyond those of official plans and diagrams.[2] Their interconnected stories draw attention to the "intimacies" of intercontinental history, showing how the people who made empires work linked oceanic, imperial, and topographical scales of analysis that are often held apart.[3] From the intimacy of this shared social geography, characters such as Cope, Wager, and Forrest learned lessons that would guide their strategic decisions and tactical responses in the face of violence. Their experiential knowledge braided Europe, Africa, and America into a single region where almost everyone knew the traffic in human beings as integral to the business of war.

On a large map and an extended timeline, we can view the major transformations from the mid-seventeenth century to the mid-eighteenth century that set the stage for the three men's journeys. European empires expanded through military competition and trade, West Africa grew more violent to meet the European demand for enslaved captives, and the Caribbean emerged as a hotly contested region where slavery flourished. The conflicts that shaped these interlocking regions began long before Apongo, Cope, and Forrest crossed paths, and would continue long after. Battle by battle, across a century of imperial expansion on three continents, a succession of military actions connected the world of Atlantic empire to African slaving wars.

Transatlantic commerce in African bodies depended on a symbiotic relationship between war, slavery, and maritime empire. From the mid-sixteenth century, when African traders in the Senegambia and Angola first supplied slaves to the Europeans in significant numbers, the trade expanded dramatically through the eighteenth century, when it reached a new height and integrated more territories than in any previous time period. European enterprise in the Americas flourished whenever and wherever enslaved African labor was most exploited. Slaves were the region's most significant commodities and the most vital factor in the production of goods and services.[4]

Force defined the political economy of the Atlantic world, as European powers vied for territory with Native Americans and with each other, as the brutal discipline and terror of slavery sustained the expansion of plantation agriculture, and as the growth of the Atlantic system stimulated violent dislocations throughout the region.[5] Enslaved captives were herded into fortified ships built specifically to discourage uprisings.[6] The wealth of the Atlantic world traveled between garrisoned ports, and the consumption of goods was generally the fruit of some great or small conquest—of territories, of polities and peoples, or of individual wills. Interpersonal violence, like other forms of human interaction, scaled to the market and its routes of exchange. As the circuits grew and extended, so did the scope of warfare, mapping an archipelago of bloody conflict delineated by the movements of traders, soldiers, sailors, and slaves.

The integration of England, West Africa, and the Caribbean during the period shows the broad outlines of the pattern. In the eighteenth century, Great Britain (referring to England and Scotland after their 1707 union) fought an escalating series of wars, most famously with France, on the European continent and in the colonies. Over the same period that they were acquiring a global empire, the British emerged as the world's preeminent slave traders. Sociologist Orlando Patterson argues that slavery is a form of parasitism. The insight applies to slavery not only as an interpersonal relationship but as a principle of social geography. Great Britain's Caribbean colonies, overwhelmingly populated by enslaved workers from Africa, were far and away its most profitable. To staff the plantations, the slave trade fed upon inter-African rivalries and stimulated the regional appetite for violence. It thrived opportunistically on African wars, which ultimately added to European imperial wealth. As historians Jane Burbank and Frederick Cooper explain, "it was slavery that made empire pay and empire that made slavery possible."[7] At the same time, war made empire work, and the various slaving empires were entangled in a bellicose embrace.

War and slavery nourished each other as the histories of Europe, Africa, and America became increasingly intertwined. The routine violence of military occupation and the brutal exploitation of colonial workers precipitated murders, revolts, and massacres. More broadly, extensions in the scope and scale of commerce encouraged parallel expansions in the field of military competition. Dynastic conflicts on the European peninsula became Atlantic wars, in which a conflict in one theater often provoked retaliation in another across the ocean. Minor frontier incidents, raids, and mutinies grew into titanic struggles over the fate of empires. Traditional ritual combat intended to establish symbolic dominance and political tribute turned into more frequent armed conflicts aimed at exterminating the enemy. Naval competitions to control sea-lanes and establish strategic enclaves mushroomed into wars that reached multiple continents.

In fact, war nurtured and sapped empires at the same time. War in any particular location generally depressed trade by increasing its risks and driving up its costs, even if commercial competition had inspired the belligerence in the first place. On the other hand, war helped to expand the field of trade, despite being bad for most individual traders. In the context of African history, the intensification of political violence, which enabled the growth of an export market in slaves, disrupted societies wherever external trade was important. Yet suppliers of slaves needed their trading routes and mercantile relationships to be shielded from that violence. Sovereign powers and merchants resolved this seeming contradiction by separating commercial infrastructure from the direct violence of enslavement, creating safe zones for money and goods to change hands by consolidating independent trading networks that permitted the movement of slaves even as states fought each other incessantly.[8] This process of simultaneous disruption and integration worked beyond Africa, too; particular wars disrupted trade while imperial militarism made the growth of commerce possible and profitable. Under armed guard, within the firing range of a fortress, or in the wake of a warship, coercion created stable markets. Successful merchants required calm only for themselves, in the eye of the storm; everyone beyond the point of exchange could be damned.[9]

   The Caribbean became a pivot point for the relationships among England, Africa, and the Atlantic Ocean with the growth of agricultural plantations. By the 1640s, tobacco and sugar planting had begun to generate impressive wealth for some enterprising planters. During the same period that the Wars of the Three Kingdoms were ravaging England, Ireland, and Scotland, colonists on Barbados, first occupied by the English in 1627, were developing large-scale sugar plantations dependent on bonded labor. Tens of thousands of dislocated captives from the kingdoms were shipped to the colonies under fixed terms of compulsory service, usually for seven to ten years. This allowed Barbados planters to operate plantations with coerced white workers, in much the same way that sugar planters had been doing in the Atlantic islands and Brazil with enslaved Africans. English colonists carried this plantation model to other islands, including Jamaica after its capture from the Spanish in 1655. The tropical environment was deadly, and planters could keep up agricultural production only by importing laborers to replace those who died. When the English Civil Wars ended and the numbers of workers arriving from Europe dwindled, planters turned to Africa to fill the need. By 1672 England had established the Royal African Company to maintain the supply of slaves.[10]

   Already, England had committed to building its maritime strength in war and trade, investing heavily in the Royal Navy and merchant shipping. Scrambling to overtake the Dutch, its main competitor in the carrying trade, England fought a series of wars against the Netherlands in the second half of the seventeenth century, emerging stronger from each conflict. By the 1690s, England was a leading naval power and a persistent threat to the vast American empire claimed by Spain. Although English statesmen remained focused on Europe and the looming threat of invasion from France, which maintained the strongest army on the continent, England was gaining the advantage in overseas trade, a critical source of national power. Beginning in 1651, the Navigation Acts sought to confine as much of England's commercial trade as possible to English ships, and placed a priority on regulating commerce to enrich the nation. Policymakers of many persuasions saw commercial wealth and naval power as mutually reinforcing: customs revenues filled the coffers of state, shipping swelled the reserves of able seamen, and a powerful navy could guard England from attack and expand avenues for profitable traffic. The rapid extension of England's maritime range inspired an abiding interest in overseas empire.

   In the aftermath of the Glorious Revolution of 1688, the English Parliament gained the power of the purse, limiting royal prerogative to the consent of civil society. In the ensuing years of war with the French and Spanish, the English government became a powerful "fiscal-military state," generating high taxes, a well-organized civil administration, a standing army, and a militaristic outlook on world affairs. New financial arrangements supported denser networks of trade, more powerful militaries, more elaborate administrative regulation, and better communication. With the increasing significance of revenues from trade and the new compact between the Crown and the people's representatives in Parliament, a new commercial elite gained influence in the affairs of state, and could define rules of trade and finance more to their benefit.[11] Merchants waged a vigorous public campaign to dislodge the exclusive rights of monopoly concerns like the Royal African Company, shifting the slave trade to the "free market" by the second decade of the eighteenth century. With alluring incentives spurring private enterprise, the volume of the slave trade increased dramatically. For example, Jamaica alone received nearly four times the number of human cargos in 1729 as it had in 1687.[12]

In the Americas during the Nine Years' War from 1689 to 1698 and Queen Anne's War from 1702 to 1713 (the latter known in Europe as the War of Spanish Succession), the English, French, and Spanish worked to sap each other's commercial strength by pillaging plantations, seizing slaves, and burning buildings. Between such raids and the threat of piracy, the constant sense of vulnerability encouraged ever greater fortification of trade. The English established permanent naval squadrons at Port Royal, Jamaica, and English Harbour, Antigua, to maintain cruising forces capable of defending imperial commerce, which could be reinforced by larger fleets for more ambitious operations.[13] Although Queen Anne's War had temporarily slowed the slave trade, the 1713 Treaty of Utrecht, which ended the war, granted Britain the monopoly power via *asiento* contract to supply slaves to the Spanish Americas and entitled it to send one ship each year to engage in general trading at the great market fair at Porto Bello on the isthmus of Panama. This concession led to a further expansion of British slave purchasing in Africa and a lively reexport trade from Jamaica, which rapidly became the locus of slave trading in British America.

During the same period, in West Africa, violence escalated to meet the Atlantic demand for slave labor, as the growth of the Atlantic system fueled militarization of vast areas of Africa beyond the coast. Warfare increased in scale, and some societies came to celebrate militarism with great public displays of brutality. Military aristocracies dominated the most powerful slaving regimes, which in many cases had come to power by exploiting Atlantic commerce.[14] This was especially true on the Gold Coast, where Apongo resided before his captivity in Jamaica. War captives generally ranked highest among the sources of domestic slaves, outnumbering those provided through market supply, pawning, raids, kidnapping, and tribute, and minor sources such as gifts, convicts, and communal and private sales or deals. The French slave trader Jean Barbot noted in 1732 how "in times of war between the inland nations and those nearer the sea" the Gold Coast would "furnish great numbers of slaves of all sexes and ages; sometimes at one place and sometimes at another, according to the nature of the war, and the situation of the country between which it is waged."[15] Ransoms often spared people of significant social status from permanent bondage, but not always. Frequently, bounties were so high that friends and relations could not pay. As a result, another slave trader contended, the "most Potent Negroe can't pretend to be insured from Slavery."[16] People of any social station, including military leaders like Apongo, could find themselves sold to the Europeans alongside common soldiers, women, and children.[17]

By European calculations, slaves made up about half of Europe's trade with Africa in 1680, and by the second half of the eighteenth century they constituted ninety percent.[18] The trade in captives had taken hold in the four-hundred-mile stretch of West African coastline known to Europeans as the Gold Coast and Slave Coast, and was reaching ever deeper into the interior.

ALONG the coast, the British maintained a series of trading forts. They had originally been built to facilitate the gold trade and defend it from European competitors, but by the early eighteenth century slaves were the primary commodity. The Royal African Company had its headquarters at Cape Coast Castle, close by the Dutch command center at Elmina, and also maintained smaller outposts, including Dixcove, Sekondi, Komenda, Tantumkweri, Winneba, Anomabo (purpose-built for the slave trade in 1751), Accra, and Fort William at Ouidah. Interspersed with these were the trading forts of the Dutch, Portuguese, and French, and a few Danish stations near Accra. The primary purpose of these fortifications was to provide residence for company agents, soldiers, and workers, as they transacted business with African merchants and ever-increasing numbers of slave ships. They also offered storage for provisions and goods, and dungeons for captives awaiting sale. The forts were costly to maintain, but served as valuable indications of the company's presence and interest in regional affairs. The towns around the forts, which maintained uneasy alliances with the Europeans, supplied agricultural produce, fish, and daily labor, as well as residents willing to serve as soldiers and diplomats to address local tensions in the company's interests.[19]

Atlantic trade wasn't the African elites' only concern by any means, but as various merchants, middlemen, and enterprising renegades recognized

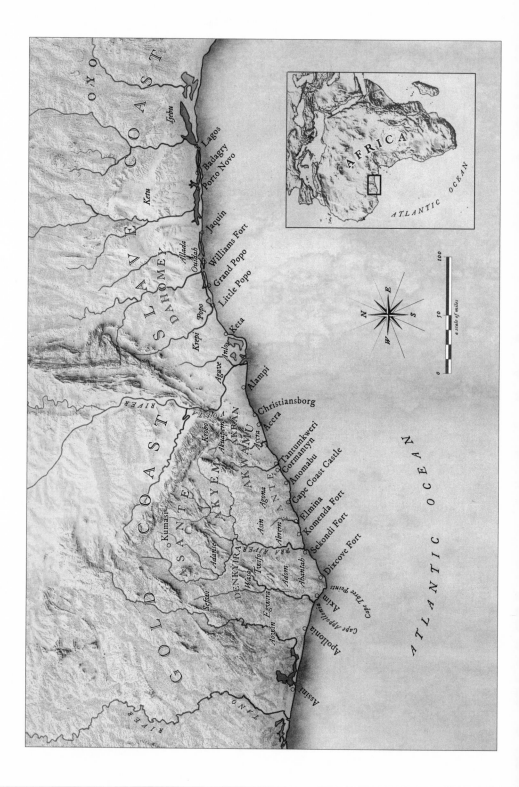

FIGURE 1.1. Cape Coast Castle, ca. 1720s.
From William Smith, *Thirty Different Drafts of Guinea* (London, 1727). *Courtesy of the Harvard Map Collection.*

the increasing scope of Atlantic opportunities, they found ways to turn the slave trade to their advantage.[20] The process was dramatically demonstrated by the highly centralized states—such as Oyo, Dahomey, and Asante inland from the Gold and Slave Coasts—that incorporated trade with Europeans into their wars of expansion. They valued firearms from Europe among the most useful commodities. Gold Coast traders had imported sizable numbers of guns beginning as early as the 1650s, but by 1730 an estimated 180,000 firearms a year were flooding into the Gold and Slave Coasts, facilitating the rise and reach of predatory slaving states.[21] These slaving regimes engaged in regular campaigns to plunder stateless societies for captives or to raid weakened polities that could no longer protect their people. Captives could be retained to swell armies and enlarge retinues or be sold to Europeans for goods and more guns, which only deepened the spiraling vortex of violence. Such predatory slaving states proliferated and gathered strength in the eighteenth century, and the privations and chaos attending their local wars made ever more refugees available for capture and sale abroad.

Far upcountry from the Bight of Benin, on the open grasslands south of the Sahara Desert, the kingdom of Oyo had imported horses from the north, and used that advantage to conquer a wide area on the edge of the forest belt that separated them from the shoreline. By the end of the seventeenth century, the Oyo were a dominant power in the region; they overwhelmed the small kingdoms in their path to the port of Ouidah, where they traded slaves for guns, textiles, metal goods, and the cowrie shells commonly used as currency.[22] On the coast, however, the Oyo—whose empire was still centered on the savannah—had to contend with the rising power of Dahomey, a highly centralized warrior state which had come to see territorial conquest as an end in itself. Slave trading was an outgrowth of Dahomey's frequent annexations, and as Dahomey's dominion expanded, it too sought direct access to European merchants. Under the eventful reign of King Agaja, from 1718 to 1740, Dahomey conquered coastal Allada in 1724 and Ouidah in 1727, eventually making it the most prolific slave-trading port on the African coast.[23]

West of the Bight of Benin lay the Gold Coast, where a number of states formed by powerful Akan families and clans vied to control trading in gold, ivory, kola nuts, and other local goods. Here captives worked in the mines and cleared forests for agriculture.[24] From the mid-seventeenth century, Akwamu, Denkyira, Akyem, and other powerful states in the region engaged in intermittent and inconclusive wars. It was the emergence of the state of Asante that finally upset the balance of power. Beginning with its 1701 conquest of Denkyira, Asante pursued a course of expansion that would accelerate under the rule of its king Nana Opoku Ware from 1720 to 1750 and continue for the rest of the century. Meanwhile, war between the states of Akyem and Akwamu ended in 1730 with the defeat of the Akwamu and their expulsion to an area east of the Volta River. In 1742, Akyem was in turn subdued by Asante. Having already conquered territories to the north, Asante pushed for northeast and northwest expansion in the 1740s. Behind all of these campaigns were political motivations that went well beyond the desire to export slaves to the Europeans. Yet never far from the minds of state rulers and private merchants were the Europeans' trade goods, and particularly the weapons on offer. Between 1700 and 1750, the Akan wars helped to contribute some 375,000 slaves to the transatlantic trade. One European agent called these "delightful times on the Coast," when traders could buy a slave for as little as a single bottle of brandy.[25]

These expansive wars in Africa were part of the pan-Atlantic trend toward the integration of smaller-scale conflicts into a transoceanic region. The greatest of the eighteenth-century slaving states, Great Britain, developed into a bellicose Atlantic maritime power capable of conducting overseas warfare on an unprecedented scale and marshaling the massive financial resources to pay for it. Cognizant of the synergy between war and commerce, Britain continued its belligerent campaign to make the world safe for its private traders.

The War of Jenkins' Ear (1739–1748), which took its name from the mutilation of a British merchant captain by sailors from the Spanish naval patrol, offered the British an excuse to expand trade to Spanish America beyond the strict terms of its *asiento,* the restrictive contract that allowed British merchants to sell slaves in the Spanish colonies. The war was popular in England at first, given growing recognition of the importance of Atlantic trade, and especially because of an audacious success in the 1739 Battle of

Porto Bello. But a costly, failed attempt on Cartagena a year later brought the war in the Caribbean to a stalemate. In 1742 the American conflict merged into the wider War of the Austrian Succession, which brought in France, Britain's most dangerous enemy. As in previous wars, the exchange of raids produced no significant territorial gains for either side. After a dramatic seizure of Louisbourg from the French in 1745, the 1748 Treaty of Aix-la-Chappelle largely restored the *status quo ante bellum*.[26] However, the war had the effect of drawing the Caribbean closer to the center of British imperial concerns. During the conflict, the British established a policy of dominating the Western Approaches to the British Isles, the so-called home waters, with a standing fleet that could simultaneously guard against invasion, protect maritime commerce, and interfere with enemy shipping. From this forward posture, the Royal Navy's Western Squadron gave Britain a formidable strategic advantage in West Indian war and trade.[27]

By 1750, the Caribbean had become a vital focus of British strategy.[28] Sugar, grown by armies of enslaved Africans, was by far Great Britain's largest import from the region.[29] Along with tobacco, rice, and other products from American plantations, sugar was central to imperial expansion, and its trade was protected by the Royal Navy. The colonies offered Great Britain its fastest-growing markets, contributed to some of the most readily apparent changes in daily life, and supported a broadly shared vision of commercial society.[30] Crucially, that vision depended upon the labors of Africans and their descendants. One gentleman with business interests in the colonies summed up the situation: "If the negro trade was lost, the Colonies must be lost."[31] Indeed, the unfortunate victims of the "negro trade" and their descendants made up about 85 percent of a British Caribbean population totaling some three hundred thousand persons.[32] The greatest number of these men, women, and children had been carried to the West Indies on the winds of war.

Seen from the perspective of statesmen, these wars were national efforts on a grand scale, involving royal and ministerial prerogatives, imperial military strategies, and the accumulation of national wealth. Missing from most accounts of these conflicts, with their focus on nation states, are considerations of the diasporas created by these incessant wars, the dislocations they caused, and the ensuing struggles of scattered peoples to remake communal belonging and territory for themselves. Beneath the kings, ministers, and merchants were soldiers, sailors, and slaves, whose travels along the violent conduits of empire traced multidimensional maps of social space.[33] While British officials thought about empire in terms of their nation's standing vis-à-vis Europe, and African rulers focused on rivalries with their own neighbors, overseas and overland traders paid closer attention to the territories of their commerce. Whereas military leaders took the fight to their enemies along elastic routes of imperial conflict, commoners and captives were alert to fugitive spaces—the shelters and safe havens within landscapes otherwise dominated by warlords and slaveholders.

In this endemically violent Atlantic world, all these itineraries, actual and imagined, threaded together and every dislocation caused by conflict raised urgent questions of belonging and affiliation. Where were the boundaries between insider and outsider? How and by whom were these boundaries made and enforced? Which people could enter alliances and under what circumstances? Europeans and Africans alike wrestled with these questions at the levels of state and society, peoples and bands, and intimate relations between individuals. Such struggles over belonging and affiliation marked territory and its shifting contours. Rather than allowing imperial or national boundaries to define their spatial imaginations, subject peoples indexed their own groupings in various ways, creating distinct, intersecting, and rival geographies. And these rival geographies formed the terrain of interlocking wars.[34]

In this way, slavery's violent conflicts integrated Europe, Africa, America, and the Atlantic Ocean. The movements of combatants, émigrés, and outcasts sketched the political outlines of the Atlantic world.[35] Their itineraries show how physical geography, territorial control, and social struggle unfolded in dynamic relation to each other, demonstrating that imperial spaces were often fragmented with porous or undefined borders. Despite vast territorial claims, empires exercised actual control over narrow and irregular stretches and enclaves. Transatlantic warfare highlighted this phenomenon, showing how geographical space reflected complicated lines of political contention across a vast theater of events.[36]

Militarized pathways—all around the shorelines, across the ocean, along rivers, through dense forests, and over mountains—marked the eighteenth-century Atlantic world's enclaves of association and corridors of control. Along these pathways traveled people whose aspirations, struggles, and practical knowledge created shared regions of experience, from which they learned to distinguish friend from foe and to negotiate across difference. This was an emergent knowledge, shaped by the intersection of personal and collective trajectories through the world of war and trade, and it often transcended received affiliations of race, nation, and empire. People like Apongo, John Cope, and Arthur Forrest knew less about the long history of transformation that had shaped the mid-eighteenth-century world of Atlantic slavery than they did about how, with whom, and where they needed to fight in order to survive it. On the Gold Coast, Cope would learn that profiting from the business of slaving wars required delicate negotiations, careful diplomacy, and ruthless personal ambition. Apongo would learn that white people's materialism could be exploited, and that they could be checked by the right combination of forces. Arthur Forrest, having risen through the British Royal Navy, one of the most effective military institutions of the period, would become convinced that slavery, war, and empire constituted a winning combination for national greatness and personal enrichment. The experiences of these three men predicted that large-scale regional trends would result in explosive local conflicts.

A LEARNED Englishman in his mid-thirties, John Cope traveled to West Africa in the service of the Royal African Company late in 1736, looking forward to a lucrative posting. Aboard the *Phenix,* he and the two other new chief agents for Cape Coast Castle, Jeremiah Tinker and Thomas Esson, traveled in the company of a surgeon, a scribe, and an apprentice. Demand for slaves was increasing in the West Indian plantations, and at this point the *asiento* contract to supply the Spanish Americas was still in the hands of the British. In the previous two decades, nearly a quarter of a million Africans had been shipped by British traders from the Gold Coast and the Bight of Benin. Cope surely knew from his predecessors that there were abundant opportunities for personal enrichment on the African coast. Yet he must also have felt some trepidation, for the coast was notoriously unhealthy for Europeans. Most died before they could make their fortunes.[37]

Diplomacy with African states was dangerous, too. Over the previous decade, two of the most powerful kings in eighteenth-century West Africa, Opoku Ware of Asante and Agaja of Dahomey, had expanded their influence in the region. They contended with others, such as Intsiful of Wassa at the western end of the Gold Coast and Owusu of Akyem to the east. As rulers of powerful militaristic states, these men were not to be bullied or trifled with by Europeans. Nearer to the company's forts on the Gold Coast and at Ouidah, a number of smaller but well-armed polities vied for power and for commercial trade. All the European nations with trading forts on the coast paid substantial rents for the privilege to operate there. They frequently doled out additional gifts and monetary payments to secure other concessions and favors. Disputes were settled by palaver—that is, long discussions among contending parties that could involve family or household members, communal groups, nations, and trading companies. Differences that could not be settled by palaver often ended in violence.[38]

Neither Cope nor any other company official could envision territorial sovereignty in Africa. Their dominion was limited to the cramped forts that dotted the coast, operating in the context of surrounding towns, confederations of people beyond, and the expansive powers of the major states. European traders looked narrowly down the pathways of trade that led to the interior and expectantly out upon the ocean, keeping watch for vessels anchored in the "roads" offshore, their conduits to imperial power. Yet these toeholds on the coast were by no means isolated, and nor were their administrators impotent. Employing African militias from the towns around the forts, company agents repeatedly exerted influence in African affairs to facilitate trade. During his time on the coast, Cope found it "necessary to have a Vessel at all times ready, to transport Men & Arms, as well as Provision & Goods" to troublesome areas where wars or palavers threatened trade or offered fresh opportunities.[39] The company hanged African and European pirates at the fort, and employed armed natives to capture and return deserting soldiers and sailors.[40] Although company agents grumbled, often with good reason, that they did not always get their way on the coast, that conditions were miserable, and that Africans wielded too much power, the broader political geography favored their interests. After all, Africans had no equivalent forts in Liverpool, Bristol, or London.

Landing at Cape Coast Castle in December, Cope was immediately embroiled in the combative politics of regional commerce.[41] The accounts from William's Fort, located down the coast at Ouidah, offered an introduction to coastal relations. Just a few months before, King Agaja of Dahomey had sent an army to the coast that "destroyed the Whydah Country" and took more than forty slaves belonging to the company. When the chief agent there, Alexander Spalding, went up to Dahomey's capital, Ardra, to recover the slaves, he was detained and held prisoner. Agaja claimed that the company's slaves had stolen a large quantity of coral, and demanded that Spalding make restitution. Wary of upsetting their trade, the British paid what amounted to ransom, and Spalding boarded the next ship for Barbados.[42]

Agaja's relationship with the British had been troubled for some time. In 1732, he had executed an English trader for reasons that remain obscure. Not long after that, the Royal African Company's chief agent at Ouidah, Charles Whitaker, had promised delivery of fine silks, guns, and a "rich coffin" to be imported from England—only to abscond with the king's prepayment of two hundred ounces of gold. The king was unforgiving. His mistrust only deepened in 1735 when one of the fort's great guns was accidentally fired, killing several of his men.[43] The British paid considerable sums to maintain their position at Ouidah, but by the time Cope and his colleagues took over at Cape Coast Castle, Spalding was gone and his successor was dead, too. The company complained of Agaja's wars and the "ill use" he made of "his absolute power," but they also supplied his army with gunpowder. War had unfortunate side effects, but for a time it also generated good business. Agaja had sacked nearby Jakin in 1732, producing some six thousand captives for sale to the British alone, but with the country subsequently "depopulated 2 or 300 miles up" from the coast, the slave trade had dwindled in the years since.[44] So the company's chief agents, choosing to focus on the Gold Coast trade instead, sent two low-level representatives down to Ouidah with 175 guns and powder, among other trade goods, and relieved themselves of responsibility for William's Fort.

More urgent than the situation at Ouidah was the management of affairs at and near Cape Coast. From their first arrival, Cope, Esson, and Tinker had differences with the people of the town and the surrounding country, and trade to Cape Coast Castle was slow. For the next few months they settled most palavers with strategic payments, hoping to "dash" their way to better commerce. Meanwhile, it was an unhealthy time for company personnel. Many of the company's soldiers had sickened and died for want of fresh provisions, which were expensive in and around Cape Coast Town. Cope raised their wages in the hope of "keeping alive" the "lower class of servants," thereby "saving the Company some expense in Equipments."[45] Cope fell ill himself not long after arriving in West Africa. He recovered, but Esson and Tinker soon died, the latter having allegedly "kill'd himself by very extravagant drinking." Having come to the fort as its accountant, Cope now assumed the additional office of warehouse-keeper, increasing his annual salary to £300. This was a violation of company policy, which forebade the official in charge of goods to act as his own accountant. As a key check on abuse, financial decisions had to be made by unanimous consent by a council of three chief agents—the treasurer, warehousekeeper, and accountant—but Cope had made himself, for the time being, a one-man council.[46]

Alone and in command of the company's operations, Cope proceeded to pursue his fortune. He found his opportunity by opening trade with the powerful inland kingdom of Asante. Taking command of the warehouse, he discovered four hundred chests of salt in it. He conveyed a small sample upcountry, and within a few weeks, traders from Asante had bought it all. Sending frequent inducements in the form of gifts to Asante's representatives, Cope continued to entice them to trade directly with the fort. He also attended to relations with the Fante down the coast at Anomabo, where a powerful local merchant had emerged, known to Europeans as John Currantee and to Africans as Eno Baisee Kurentsi.[47]

Not all of Cope's trade was for the company's benefit. Trading privately was a long-standing custom, though frowned upon by the company. Letters between coastal agents and officials in London were rife with accusations and defenses, and fingers seemed to point in every direction. Charles Whitaker protested innocence in the affair with King Agaja. Alexander Spalding avowed that he had done nothing wrong in fleeing Ouidah for Barbados. The sister of another agent claimed that agents in Africa had purloined his effects, rightfully hers by inheritance. For his part, Cope introduced a new custom at Cape Coast Castle by obliging all the agents at the outer forts to send an ounce of gold with their accounting reports every two months. The company looked upon the levy as an "act of downright oppression." Cope also held the company's vessel, the *Phenix* that had brought him to Africa, on the coast for a year and a half, conducting trade along the coast. Some of this was surely for his own profit. Company officials noted with suspicion that Cope had failed to send journals and commercial ledgers for the majority of his first eighteenth months on the coast.[48]

Cope yielded his unitary role when James Hope came out to assume the post of warehousekeeper and William Lea became treasurer in early 1738. This would be the most active year of slave trading during Cope's time in West Africa, as the British shipped more than twelve thousand people from the coast. But trouble within the new council was as common as disputes with the locals. And indeed, factional squabbling often created difficulties between the company and African leaders. Lea proved to be an especially incorrigible character. His fellow agents accused him of "rude insolent behaviour" not only to the local Africans but to his "Colleagues & Equals," and held a special meeting of the council to consider his "vile practices." He had been especially "abusive and tyrannical" to the company's lower rank of servants, making capricious demands and withholding their pay. He was a notorious cheat among the captains of private ships, and they consequently avoided all dealings with him. In short, his presence was bad for business. Before he had served two years, the company dismissed him with harsh words: "Your whole study ever since your arrival on the Coast has been to perplex and embarrass our Affairs, and to make yourself odious to every living soul about you, and that you mind nothing but by all the clandestine ways you can invent to make your own fortune upon the ruin of your employers." More exceptional, however, than Lea's corruption was the fact that he was dismissed for it.[49]

James Hope was no less self-serving, and his brief time on the coast was similarly chaotic, marked by disputes with other agents and with African elites. Despite Hope's official role as keeper of the warehouse, Cope continued to control the small trade in gold, leaving Hope with the challenge of paying to keep the garrison and visiting company ships supplied with provisions. Hope raised an objection in the council, but Cope rebuffed him. Meanwhile, Hope pursued his own scheme. Mrs. Phipps, a wealthy local woman, died a few weeks after Hope arrived at Cape Coast. The daughter of a Dutch soldier at Elmina and a native woman, she had been the widow of James Phipps, the former chief agent (from 1711 to 1722) of Cape Coast Castle. Her relatives buried her "according to the Custom of the Country" with gold and other valuable things. Hope had several of her servants and relations whipped and cruelly "abused" for information. Then, in secret, he plundered Mrs. Phipps' grave. Having learned of the affair from Cope, company officials in London worried that the theft might "occasion very troublesome Palavers with the Natives perhaps Twenty Years hence." Indeed, Mrs. Phipps had a son and daughter in England who were already hiring attorneys to secure their rightful inheritance. The company advised Hope to "give them all due Countinance and assistance" but "without imbroiling or interesting the Company therein in any manner whatsoever." But by the time Hope received their admonishment, he was already involved in a much more immediate palaver down the coast at Accra.[50]

In May 1738, a local leader, provoked by the British agent Hosey Besouth, attacked the British fort at Accra. In retaliation, Besouth burned down two-thirds of the surrounding town, sending its people to seek shelter from the nearby Danish and Dutch forts and to other native towns in the area. Without their labor, the fort would be ruined. The council at Cape Coast agreed to send Hope down to Accra, accompanied by the town *caboceer*, or chief. At great expense, Hope hosted meetings with the governors of the Danish and Dutch forts in October, prevailing upon them to help him recover the town's population. The Danes had recently suffered an uprising of slaves at Christiansborg Castle in August and were eager to quiet the region, though the Dutch disagreed among themselves about the virtue of helping other European traders. Hope managed to settle the dispute, and he confiscated Besouth's gold in order to help defray the company's expenses. This was too much for the other members of the council, who dispatched Besouth to stand before the Court of Assistants in England but returned to him his own gold. Hope then filed a protest with officials in London, his final formal complaint.[51]

At the end of July 1739, Hope died under mysterious circumstances. "By all assumptions," according to London officials, "his death was occasioned by Poison." Soon thereafter, with William Lea frozen out of the council at Cape Coast, John Cope again assumed the post of warehousekeeper, this time with the blessing of London. Having survived his competition, he would spend another two years on the coast watching company agents come and go. The summer months of 1741 were particularly morbid. "We have had a very Sickly time of it lately, and many of our people have died within these few months," he informed the company, naming a chief agent, four factors, two apprentices, and the surgeon among the dead, in addition to "most of our white soldiers." Cope endured and quit the coast the next year with his fortune secure, drawing more than £3,700 from the Royal African Company at his departure. He had done well for the company and for himself. In 1739, he had even shipped a little enslaved black boy home to his wife, adding one more to the men, women, and children—more than thirty-three thousand of them—who boarded British ships on the Gold Coast during Cope's years in West Africa, most of them destined, if they survived the journey, for enslavement in America.[52]

How exactly John Cope met Apongo remains a mystery. No one with precisely that name appears in Cope's records of the time he spent on the African coast. But there are various plausible scenarios in which they could have met given what is known of other Africans shipped from the Gold Coast to Jamaica in the same period—the people whose shared experiences would form the raw material for the rebellions of the 1760s. Most of the slaves and free black people who fought the era's slave wars were engaged in continuous struggles to create openings and possibilities across a landscape engulfed by violence, whether they had been leaders in formal militaries, followers in those militaries, or simply civilians swept up in the fighting.

The only explicitly biographical information about Apongo is found in the diary of Jamaica overseer Thomas Thistlewood. In it he wrote that, prior to arriving in Jamaica six or seven years before the insurrection of 1760, Apongo had been "a prince in guinea, tributary to the King off dorme: the King off dorme so Conquer'd all the Country ffor Miles round him."[53] At first glance, Thistlewood's description of Apongo as a prince evokes a stock character that was popular among the English in the eighteenth century. Periodicals, novels, and stage dramas routinely depicted stories of African nobility accidentally enslaved by some kind of treachery. The "royal slave" was just one of those idealized figures that helped Britons absorb and interpret their impressions as the expansion of their empire brought a disorienting array of exotic foreigners into view. Fables of native princes encouraged empathy for their predicament, while at the same time sharply distinguishing them from common slaves. When the princes rebelled in these stories, they did so as individuals in unfortunate circumstances, inherently unfit for slavery, not as revolutionaries seeking the overthrow of oppressive systems.[54]

Periodically, these stories seemed to be vindicated by events. Just before Thistlewood left England for Jamaica in 1750, the son of the Gold Coast merchant Eno Baisee Kurentsi had been feted in London. Having been sent by his father to be educated in England, young William Ansah Sessarakoo was tricked and sold into slavery on Barbados before being ransomed. When his father found out, he threatened to cut off trade with all British merchants, whereupon Sessarakoo traveled to England and was placed under the protection of the Earl of Halifax. In 1749, he made a celebrated appearance at a Covent Garden performance of *Oroonoko,* a sentimental play about the wrongful captivity, ill-fated romance, and doomed rebellion of a royal slave from the Gold Coast.[55]

Yet Thistlewood's diary entry was not playing at literary sentiment; he wasn't the type. If he described Apongo's background in a familiar way, he also meant to convey something widely known but rarely conceded. Stories about captive African elites offered the English a way of domesticating the threat of difference, but they also implicitly acknowledged that threat in the first place. There would be no need for fables of black princes if they had not represented an unsettling fact of imperial expansion: black people were not easily subjected to European command. It was easier to imagine Africans as inferiors than it was to control them. They fought back. For example, the name Tacky identified the rebel as belonging to a royal office or lineage in one of the Gold Coast's eastern kingdoms.[56]

Because Apongo doesn't appear in Cope's records, it is tempting to read this "prince" as a mere literary trope. Without the certainty suggested by documentation, the African remains a shadowy subject. But that may be just as well. It is best to understand Apongo's origins within the tension created by that uncertainty as both a real person and a sign of the struggles produced by Atlantic slavery. Viewed through Cope's tumultuous time on the Gold Coast, the possibilities for Apongo's life allow us to more easily see what he represents as a character in the story of slave war, historical and mythic, at once as real as death and as spectral as the hereafter. Apongo embodied the force of African military potential in both its material and its phantasmal effects. He was not just an unfortunate aristocrat or a rebellious slave. Like many others, including his fellow rebel Tacky, he was a soldier with his own reasons to fight, a subject and object of warfare who inspired his followers and who frightened his enemies—so much that they would spin wild tales about everyone like him.[57]

Among the several plausible scenarios for Apongo's encounter with Cope in West Africa, none of them conform wholly with what Thistlewood recorded in his diary, but all of them underscore how likely it would have been for an African in Jamaica to know what Apongo knew about the politics of war and trade, and to be able to draw upon that knowledge in a struggle against colonial slavery. Apongo might have been a subject of Dahomey, or perhaps of Adom, a smaller polity west of Cape Coast near the fort at Commenda; alternatively, he might have been Asante or Fante. Each of these possibilities turns on the sound of his name. Eighteenth-century European transcription of African names was inexact and inconsistent. The same name was often spelled in multiple variations, sometimes by the same scribe. Names that must have sounded like Apongo appear throughout the accounts of British trading operations during Cope's years at Cape Coast Castle between early 1737 and the middle of 1742.

Some have assumed that "dorme" was Dahomey, and that Apongo was a subject of that powerful inland kingdom well east of the Volta River with its capital far north of the coast.[58] "Apongo," then, could be a miscopying of "Aplogan," the title for Dahomey's provincial governor of Allada, which had been conquered in 1724. By 1727, the Dahomeans had expanded their empire to the trading town of Ouidah near the coast, but they found it difficult to consolidate their rule. Small skirmishes and major wars with a shifting series of enemies plagued Dahomey's southwestern frontier through the mid-eighteenth century.

In 1737, these conflicts extended nearly as far as the Gold Coast. Dahomey's King Agaja sent an expeditionary force of some thirteen thousand soldiers in pursuit of a renegade chief named Ashangmo from the town of Little Popo. After subduing him, the Dahomean army planned to continue its westward march to join forces with the Akwamu in a push to retake their homeland from the Akyem. Crossing the River Mono in a fleet of canoes, the Dahomeans besieged the Dutch fort at Keta, which they suspected of harboring their quarry. For nine days, there was a tense standoff. They implored the governor of the fort to make palaver with them, urging a negotiation to avoid violence. But after inducing the Dutchman to leave the fort, they put him in chains, along with several other white men. At the same time, they undermined one bastion of the fort, causing it to collapse, and simultaneously scaled the walls with ladders. Before his capture the governor had given orders to blow up the fort with fifty muskets and fifty barrels of gunpowder hidden under blankets in his quarters. The explosion killed many, but Dahomey's army stayed encamped at Keta for several days, combing the wreckage for valuables. One Dutch soldier escaped to a nearby village and relayed his story to Ashangmo's cousin, who happened to command the town. Seizing the advantage, Ashangmo and his allies surrounded the Dahomeans, burned their canoes to prevent their escape, and utterly destroyed them while taking at least thirteen hundred prisoners. "Not a single one escaped," according to a Dutch report. The white captives were recovered, except for the governor of Keta, "whose brains had been bashed out by a sergeant of the mentioned robbers with a cudgel when he saw that he did not longer have a chance to escape."[59]

Dahomey's many enemies rallied at news of its defeat, and the death of Agaja in 1740 encouraged them even more. The powerful Oyo attacked

Dahomey in the early 1740s, reducing Agaja's successor to tributary status at the conclusion of a peace in 1748. Then, in the early 1750s—about the time Apongo was supposed by Thistlewood to have been enslaved—a major series of battles erupted in Dahomey's continuing war with the confederated armies of Little Popo and Hueda, former rulers of Ouidah. Dahomey sent the Aplogan, described by British traders as a "General of War," down from Allada to "take care of the land." There is no evidence that Dahomey's Aplogan was captured and sold in these years—but it is certainly possible. If Apongo was indeed the Aplogan, or if he was a leader among Dahomey's many foes and was one of the estimated 673 Africans shipped from the Bight of Benin and delivered to Jamaica in 1753–1754, then somehow, either by force of character or habit of command, he managed to reconstitute his authority among the slaves of Westmoreland Parish within the few short years before 1760.[60] We cannot be too quick, however, in accepting this as the most likely scenario for Apongo's African background. To have met John Cope at Cape Coast Castle would have required a Dahomean official to make an unlikely journey through many hostile lands from the Bight of Benin all the way to the Gold Coast. And Cope never remarked on visits by Dahomean officials or subjects to Cape Coast Castle, or recorded any travel to Ouidah himself.

Given Apongo's eventual leadership of Akan-speakers during the Jamaica insurrection of 1760, it makes better sense to speculate that he was from the Gold Coast. Although Cope met with a great variety of local leaders, no one named Apongo appears in the company records for his time on the coast. Instead, there is an African trader named Attando, who came to pay his compliments at Cape Coast Castle in late 1740 after acceding to the post of caboceer of Komenda.[61] Komenda lay near the state of Adom— which might easily be misapprehended as "dorme"—labeled as a "powerful & kind of Republick" on a map of 1729. Stretched along both the Chama and the Arikobra rivers, Adom encompassed a significant territory. Rather than a kingdom, the polity was a "Common-wealth," as described by the Dutch trader Willem Bosman in the late seventeenth century, "governed by five or six of the Principal Men" with the capacity to "raise a Powerful Army to the Terror of their Neighbors."[62]

Attando could certainly have been part of a delegation to Cape Coast Castle from Adom, which is more likely than the long journey from Da-homey.[63] He appears in the expense accounts of Commenda fort, often as Tando, collecting "presents and dashees" through the early 1740s. Near the beginning of 1745, after Cope had departed from the coast, Attando fought against the British, who fired four rounds of cannon on his militia. The dispute continued for many months, depressing trade and requiring the company to expend significant resources to maintain its position. At one point, it gave £3 worth of goods to a man named Ancuma, "he having a Dispute with Tando[,] to let him see the company was ready to give him any assistance or protection on his deserting Tando's Cause and making proper Submission."[64] It is plausible, then, that Apongo was Attando, and that after clashing with the British he was, as Thistlewood learned, "Surprize'd and took prizoner when hunting, and Sold ffor a Slave." Kidnapping was endemic, with frequent conflict and disorder creating ample opportunities for bush traders to capture and sell people throughout the region. This might have happened no matter who Apongo was. But there is a problem with this interpretation, too, because Attando continues to appear in Royal African Company sources through 1747, by which time the man named Wager had appeared in a ship's muster on the far side of the Atlantic Ocean.[65]

There are still other possibilities for Cope and Apongo's meeting, for Apongo may have been a Fante or Asante warrior involved in a major confrontation in 1740. To the north and west of Cape Coast Castle, Asante's influence expanded rapidly, though it continued to face resistance even from defeated foes like Wassa, north of Cape Three Points. East of the fort, Akyem dominated the trade to Accra. But, like the other polities in the region, it kept a nervous watch on Asante, even as it looked out for attacks from Dahomey and the revanchist Akwamu, which Akyem had conquered in 1730. Meanwhile, a confederation of Fante peoples had coalesced to resist the incursions of Asante and to control the coastal trade.[66]

At Cape Coast Castle, Cope frequently received delegations from Asante. In 1738, he paid the Dey of Fetu £4 to settle palavers on the trading paths so that Asante traders could reach the coast unmolested, then sent a group of local caboceers to Asante's capital at Kumasi to inform Asante's King Opoku Ware that "the Chief Agents have Obliged the Fetues to give satisfaction for an Ashantee Man they had panyar'd [taken to be held for ransom]; and to permit the Ashantees to pass through their Country to this place unmolested, the path being now open."[67] Cope's diplomacy for the Royal African Company also took him east to Tantumkweri to settle a palaver in 1739 and to Anomabo in 1741, both deep in Fante territory.[68]

During this tense time in the region, Europeans were reminded not to trifle with local leaders, as Africans demonstrated their capacity to conduct major military operations while keeping the Europeans in their place. Agents like Cope learned that alliances with Africans were essential to the success of their ventures, and how catastrophic it could be when they broke down. Cope faced his most serious diplomatic challenge after the death of Director-General Martinus François Des Bordes of the Dutch West India and Guinea Company at Elmina in March 1740. The funeral of a dignitary was always a significant occasion, drawing great gatherings of people paying their respects, and at the same time conducting business and interstate mediation. As Cope made the short trip to Elmina in a canoe, he took the opportunity to press the Royal African Company's interest among the various representatives of the hinterland polities in attendance.[69] His political maneuvering resulted in a great meeting at Cape Coast Castle in June with representatives from countries surrounding the trade routes to the north, who came to the fort "in order to settle all Palavers and bring trade." Through July and August, Cope entertained various African visitors in the fort's chapel.[70] Among those who had paid their respects at Elmina were representatives sent by the great Asante king Opoku Ware, with whom all Europeans were eager for good relations. From promises made by the Asante, the Dutch expected to buy "at least 2,000 Ps. slaves besides the usual quantities of gold and ivory." A few months later, Cope would send the Asante king a present of madeira wine and fine sugar from his personal stores.[71] The British hoped to capitalize on the diplomatic failures of the Dutch, whose trade was in crisis.

The year before his death, Des Bordes had been involved in a bitter dispute with the residents of Elmina town. In 1738, he had learned that the peoples of Great Commenda and Abrambo, just north of Elmina, had entered an alliance with "a certain Negro of the Fantyn country" and were demanding tolls on the trading paths and allegiance from the people of Elmina town, which they resisted. Almost certainly, this was an effort by Anomabo's Kurentsi to extend his influence over the hinterland trading routes. The new tensions caused trouble on the roads, and traders from the interior avoided Elmina in favor of forts further west.[72] Frustrated at the lack of commerce, Des Bordes hoped that one side or the other would score a decisive victory and end the dispute. When the townspeople repelled an attack, he urged them to pursue the war into the interior, but they refused, "claiming that their ancestors never had had the habit of making war into the interior, and that they had always fought their wars on the coast." They would defend themselves vigorously, but they would not engage in military adventures.[73]

Resenting their refusal, Des Bordes declared that "he would see to it that they would be forced to fight." He sent an emissary to Great Commenda, letting them know that the Dutch had no quarrel with them and that they were free to enslave "as many Elmina Negroes as they would like." Then he prohibited Elmina's fishermen from putting to sea, confiscated food meant for the town, and had several of the town's fishermen and maize traders imprisoned. Now the townspeople took up arms against the fortress. On May 27, Des Bordes bombarded them from the fort and set fire to the town.[74] When the pastor Johan Hessing arrived to take up a mission in July, he found hundreds of the people's huts in ashes and the castle damaged on all sides from the constant firing of its own heavy guns. At a palaver in September, the Elmina people claimed that, in addition to the various indignities they had suffered from the company, they "mourned 414 dead, that 13 had been badly wounded and that their houses were burnt." The meeting was inconclusive.

Director-General Des Bordes was "angry and of a weak physical condition," but he was determined to ruin the town.[75] Through his chief agent at Cormantyn Fort to the east, Des Bordes sent for the Fante, promising money, more than a hundred casks of gunpowder, a quantity of gold, and two thousand pounds of lead if they would sack the town. To secure the deal, he accepted thirteen young people as pawns, to be returned to Kurentsi at the satisfactory end of the campaign.[76] In early January 1740, an army of more than thirty thousand Fante besieged the townspeople "in order to ruin them, if possible, totally and to make their wives and children their slaves."[77] Ensconced in the fort, Des Bordes continued to be "of a very bad temper." He drank great quantities of schnapps "any day he felt bored" and became increasingly ill.[78] In March, Des Bordes died, "leaving the country full of war and an indescribable confusion."[79]

With the Fante army encamped around the fort and the town under siege, Elmina was at a dangerous crossroads with few paths toward peace. As far away as Accra, Europeans heard that "on the Upper Coast everything is in an uproar." The Danish governor of Christiansborg thought that Des Bordes had "now done the Dutch Company such harm that another [director-general] will not be able to remedy it for the next 10–12 years."[80] Des Bordes had been unpopular among most Dutch West India Company agents, too; only the chief agent at Anomabo, aware of the virtues of an alliance with the increasingly powerful Kurentsi, fully approved his scheme. The remaining agents of the Dutch West India Company sent deputies to ask the Fante to stand down. Instead, the Fante pledged to continue the war, expecting that the company would honor the terms agreed to by the deceased director-general. The Dutch, however, now had other ideas, deciding to protect Elmina's townspeople, as they said, "rigorously with such power as we had, and to show this bribed army that the present Government had resolved to take the Noble Comp.'s prosperity at heart, and not its ruin." The Fante attacked but faced stiff resistance from the townspeople. Dutch cannon then broke the assault, and the Fante retreated "after having set fire to their camp leaving behind at least 70 canoes and various items of baggage." The Dutch had invited the Fante to war and then turned them back to Anomabo, and they knew there would be consequences for their treachery. "There was a general fear that after their defeat at Elmina the

Fantynen would immediately go to the Lower Coast in order to take there what the late D-G had promised them but not given." Indeed, when the governor of the Dutch fort at Cormantyn tried to return to his post, Kurentsi had him captured and held for ransom.[81]

The Fante remained confrontational, blockading trade and seizing (or *panyarring*) enemies all along the lower coast. The Dutch, cut off from communicating with their forts in the east, bemoaned the "unsafety of the paths and the poaching of the Fantynen." The English paid several caboceers to protect their workers in the bush against Fante kidnappers and contributed funds to the military defense of Fetu against a threatened Fante raid. Europeans commonly disparaged the Fante as a "thieving and haughty nation" with a tendency to "rob and despoil everyone underfoot."[82] The Fante, on the other hand, saw themselves as securing their independence, both from the powerful inland states like Asante and from the duplicitous arrangements made at the European forts. They preferred to sell their goods directly to the ships at Anomabo, where Kurentsi consolidated his position; he was soon to become Great Britain's most important trading partner in West Africa.

A year after the funeral at Elmina, John Cope traveled to Anomabo to treat with officials there. Apparently, he gained an understanding that not all Fante aggressors were acting on legitimate authority under state protection. When Cope returned to Cape Coast Castle, he paid some locals £6 "on their taking a Fanteen Prisoner & for their encouragement to take more." A few months later, three "Fanteen pirates" were hanged at Cape Coast Castle.[83]

Even as the Fante tested their power on the lower coast, King Intsiful's forces from Wassa threatened from the northwest. Wassa had been overrun by Asante in 1726, but Intsiful escaped with a large following and continued to harass and attack Asante allies such as Twifo. For the next several years Asante and Wassa fought a series of battles that brought trade at the western end of the Gold Coast to a standstill. Through the 1730s, despite several defeats, the Wassa army occupied many of the most important inland passages, stemming the flow of trade, and secured alliances among the states behind the coast to prevent guns and powder from reaching Asante.[84] By the late 1730s, they had designs on the Ahanta territory behind Cape Three Points, between the Pra and the Ankobra Rivers. When Cope came to West Africa, Intsiful offered "to defeat the Antase, and to give him the Dutch forts." Cope refused, but was happy to sell tobacco, cloth, and gunpowder to the Wassa. He sent a messenger to express his hope that, if Intsiful moved against the Ahanta, he would bypass the English fort at Sekondi and attack only the Dutch.[85]

FIGURE 1.2. The English and Dutch Forts at Sekondi, ca. 1720s.

From William Smith, *Thirty Different Drafts of Guinea* (London, 1727). *Courtesy of the Harvard Map Collection.*

The chaos at Elmina provided Intsiful with an opportunity. By November 1739, news had spread that "the Wassase Negroes have definitely the intention to make war on the Antase" and that the forts on the upper coast could not expect help from Elmina. At the end of the month, the entire area was "in commotion as the Wassase are marching down from their land and want to make war on the coast from Axim to Chama." Frightened civilians fled to nearby forts for protection, forming makeshift refugee camps surrounded with palisades.[86] The English fort at Sekondi took in women and children, but when company agents began to count them, the Africans feared they were being inventoried for sale.[87] Even as the Fante surrounded Elmina, the Wassa laid siege to the Dutch fort at Sekondi, "bringing it to very narrow straits."[88] The Dutch urged the English not to offer protection to Intsiful and to keep out of the palaver, but when the Wassa attacked the Ahanta near the Royal African Company's fort, the English supported the assault with cannon fire. The town militia managed to repel the Wassa, then nursed their grievance against the English with a declaration and a demand: "Our ancestors have built this fort, of which we expect protection, and we wish to know why the English have assisted our enemy." They began to harass and *panyar* English merchants in revenge.[89]

For the remainder of 1740, company agents were embroiled in the Ahanta Palavers, which preoccupied coastal residents from Sekondi to Dixcove. In August, company agent John Castries, newly arrived from England, sailed up from Cape Coast with a retinue of Cape Coast caboceers, guards, canoe men, and translators. Over several months, the company logged "extraordinary expenses for Liquor" and accommodations as they negotiated a settlement. The palaver even drew in Opoku Ware, who sent a high-level delegation to the meetings at Dixcove. Finally, the Royal African Company expended £120 in saluting Ahanta's king at Christmas, showering gifts upon the king and local caboceers. The palaver was formally settled, but tensions continued for well over a year.[90]

Such were the likely conditions of Cope and Apongo's meeting. Given the political circumstances, Apongo might well have been Asante. Perhaps he was among the Asante dignitaries who came to Elmina after the death of its director-general, or who came to Cape Coast Castle to meet with Cope about opening trade to the interior, or to settle the Ahanta Palavers. As a "prince in guinea," it is even possible that Apongo was named after the great Asante king Opoku Ware, which was often written as *Appocu* in company records. Perhaps, in the turbulence that followed Asante's defeat of Akyem in 1742, just after Cope left the coast, Apongo was panyarred by independent Fante "bush traders," traded quickly to the coast, and loaded directly onto a slave ship to avoid a diplomatic furor. Or indeed, the fact that he later worked as a sailor in the Royal Navy might suggest that he had been a coastal resident, perhaps even one among the thirty thousand to forty thousand Fante who encamped at Elmina in 1740.

All of these scenarios accept the likelihood that Thomas Thistlewood did not have perfect knowledge of Apongo's origins. The overseer could record only what he had heard from Cope, or from Cope's son, Thistlewood's employer, John Cope Jr., or from the rush of speculation that followed the slave uprising in 1760. What Thistlewood heard was undoubtedly muddled with rumor and legend. So Apongo's origins remain obscure. Instead, Thistlewood's brief profile points to something more illuminating than the biography of an individual. It offers an unexpected opportunity to imagine the variety of Apongo's plausible pathways to the Caribbean, leading to a more searching account of the slave trade's political context.[91] If any of these situations could have brought Apongo to Jamaica, any number of other Africans might have arrived in similar circumstances—or, at least, in circumstances that made them similarly familiar with the martial geography of Atlantic slavery. Uncertainty requires us to draw a larger picture of Apongo's possible worlds, highlighting the range of military experience that Africans might have carried to the Americas. Apongo could have been a Dahomean war chief, a subject of the great Opoku Ware, or a coastal headman with a vexed relationship with British traders. These were backgrounds for other future slave rebels, too. Any of these life histories would have given Apongo, and some unknown number of others, an aptitude for political and military leadership, and made them dangerous people to own.

CHAPTER TWO

The Jamaica Garrison

B Y THE TIME APONGO, Tacky, or any of their rebellion's other soldiers crossed the Atlantic, Jamaica was a fabulous commercial entrepôt and a potent military garrison. The island was Britain's most lucrative colony, its most formidable military base in America, and a pivotal place in the strategic considerations of the empire. Profitable and powerful, Jamaica was a militarized society from top to bottom, with a tense symbiosis of war and business. Military force kept the turbulent violence of Atlantic warfare at bay, while militant order allowed profit to accumulate without war's disruptions. From the garrison, the military projected force throughout the Caribbean region, directing sternly disciplined troops to treat Britain's enemies with entrepreneurial aggression. The commerce of empire accumulated amid the violence of everyday terror. Militarism operated on multiple scales, from interstate conflict that ranged across oceans and continents to quotidian assaults on the dignity of subordinates. Indeed, intimate social relations and imperial warfare were intertwined, whether in the formal military institutions of states or in the private wars necessitated by the daily reproduction of racial bondage: violent conflict in Jamaica stitched close personal contact into the operations of colonial government and imperial conquest. This violence was tremendously profitable, and it would continue as long as the world could be made safe for slavery.[1]

The riches of the West Indies presented tempting prizes to contending belligerents. Daring raids by the pirates of the Caribbean gripped the imaginations of contemporaries and became the stuff of legend. Imperial navies organized maneuvers and tactics to prey upon enemy trade and to protect their own maritime commerce during wartime. The smaller islands of the Antilles traded hands frequently, scrambling the affiliations and allegiances of their residents. International legal regimes that first recognized "no peace beyond the line"—the idea that the colonies existed in a marchland of unregulated violence—eventually came to carefully delineate the contours of amity and hostility in colonial territories.[2] These aspects of the history of war and trade in the West Indies are well-known. Less clear are the ways in which war shaped the contours of colonial plantation slavery itself, and the ways that slave society conditioned the operations of imperial military outposts. Few other colonies exemplified as neatly as Jamaica how the aggression of slavery, the battles the colonists fought to keep their slaves in subjection, and the conflicts to secure and extend British dominion linked the geography of war with human bondage.

From the mid-seventeenth century, the English ruled colonial Jamaica by "garrison government." Jamaica was a fortified commercial outpost, run by military veterans focused on order and security. A military governor presided over a centralized provincial administration, with an appointed council and an elected assembly made up of "men of business," most of them beneficiaries of the governor's patronage. "We shall be governed as an army," said one Jamaican colonist in the seventeenth century, acknowledging that military necessity would take precedence over the legislature and the law. Even when commercial imperatives began to overlay military considerations in the third decade of the eighteenth century, a garrison mentality prevailed, cultivating a tense but mutually sustaining relationship between armed authority and the prerogatives of private wealth. Governors rarely hesitated to invoke martial law when they felt the island was under internal or external threat.[3]

Martial sentiments were prevalent among the colonists, who viewed success in war as a paramount interest of the imperial and colonial state. But this militarism carried well beyond the state. It shaped habits of general belligerence that organized the island's society largely for the benefit of its white male population. Armed men occupied the island, and officers of the militia and regular military ranked high among the island's elite.[4] Slaveholding patriarchs applied force to bend the environment to their will, extorting profit from labor and nature. They put women's fertility to the task of reproducing their human property stocks and ensuring the continuity of racial status for successive generations. Masters generated and reinforced their sense of masculinity by sexual conquest and the humiliation of lesser men. These activities connected the broad-gauge power of armies, navies, and militias to more narrowly targeted assaults on personhood, bodily integrity, and dignity. The cultivation and direction of masculine brutality was crucial to the projection of imperial power. Customs of male domination pervaded every aspect of the colonists' community formation, ensuring that conflict between slaveholders and slaves was intensely personal. War suffused the landscape of plantation agriculture, the work routines of plantation production, and the sexual exploits of white men, whose everyday belligerence was underwritten by the legal regime, an armed population of slaveholders, and the formal British military.[5]

Garrison society mobilized frequently for both internal and external warfare. The result was a militarized landscape that overlaid Jamaica's topography and ecology. The colony's "intestine" wars, as the colonists called them, included the battles against the enslaved, whose labor made Jamaica so profitable, even as the island's situation in the Caribbean made it Britain's preeminent imperial outpost. By the first decades of the eighteenth century Jamaica's martial landscape had distinctive contours, noted in detail by early historians like James Knight. Having lived nearly three decades on the island as a merchant, royal official, and representative in the Jamaica Assembly, Knight described Jamaica from a perspective that combined careful research with deep personal experience. In the 1740s, he authored a two-volume history of Jamaica, paying special attention to the principal forts and their numbers of cannon, the barracks and their troop capacities, and the defensibility of the harbors. He was especially attentive to the vulnerability of the windward settlements on the eastern side of the island, dangerously "exposed to an Enemy in time of war, and to the Insults & Depredations of the Spanish Guarda Costas & Pyrates, in time of peace," while continuously "liable to the Incursions of the wild Negroes."[6] As with so many others, he conceived the plantation colony as a military fortification.

WARFARE from within and without had plagued Jamaica ever since its beginnings as an English colony. Following the English conquest in 1655, Spanish holdouts, accompanied in many cases by their slaves and by reinforcements from what is now Mexico, fled to the mountainous interior. From their unapproachable redoubts, they harassed the invaders, who soon began to succumb to starvation and disease. In 1657 Jamaica's governor at the time, Edward D'Oyley, invited buccaneers from nearby Tortuga to aid in the expulsion of the Spanish, and the holdouts finally surrendered on the north side of the island in 1660. By that time, an English occupation force of more than eight thousand men had diminished to some twenty-two hundred.

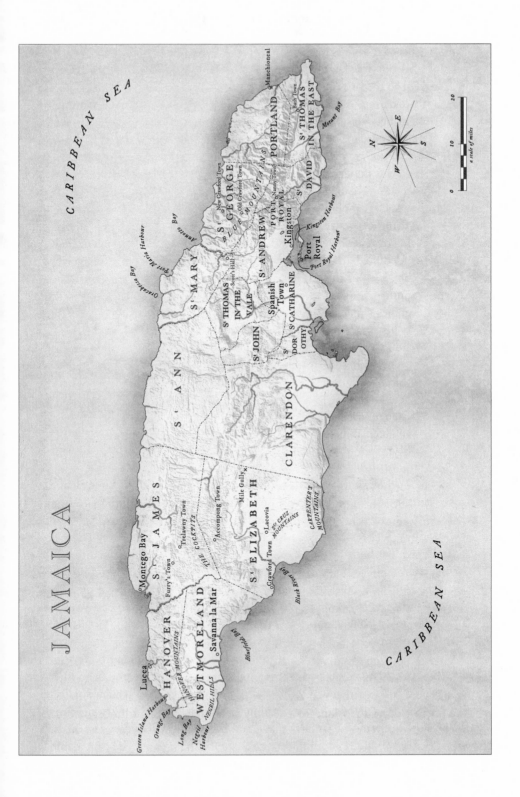

FIGURE 2.1. Port Royal Harbour. "View of Port Royal and Kingston Harbours, Jamaica," engraved by Peter Mazell, from Edward Long, *History of Jamaica*, vol. I (London, 1774).

Courtesy of the National Maritime Museum, Greenwich, London.

Swashbuckling opportunists continued to congregate at Port Royal, and the island quickly became a base for attacks on Spanish shipping. Recognizing the strategic advantage of Jamaica's position deep in the Caribbean with quick access to the Spanish mainland, the next governor, Thomas Modyford, continued to promote the attacks. When England went to war with France and the Netherlands in 1665, Modyford conducted a private war against Spain, sending the privateer Captain Henry Morgan on a series of daring raids. Between 1665 and 1671, Morgan sacked several Spanish towns around the Caribbean basin, bringing his loot back to Port Royal, which soon ranked as the most heavily fortified town in the English territories. Defended from the sea by four forts with a combined battery of ninety-four cannon, and from amphibious attack by a parapet with another sixteen guns, the garrison accommodated two companies of regular soldiers and a substantial contingent of militia, complementing the maritime mercenaries who harassed Jamaica's enemies. For the next two decades, the island hosted an impressive military base, a bustling commercial center, and a roiling pirate nest at Port Royal, becoming infamous for its plundered riches and freewheeling debauchery.[7]

Modyford, who served as governor between 1664 and 1671, also promoted Jamaica's agricultural settlement. When he arrived from Barbados in 1664, he brought about a thousand settlers with him. With two decades of experience as a sugar planter on Barbados, Modyford recognized Jamaica's potential as a plantation society. He used his royal prerogative to issue approximately eighteen hundred land patents comprising more than three hundred thousand acres, secured major capital investments from England, and prevailed upon the earliest planters to expand their operations and add more slaves to their estates. The development of the plantations overlapped with the maintenance of the garrison. Many holders of the largest land grants were military men. Even Henry Morgan became a substantial sugar planter and slave owner, taking his place among the island's emerging planter elite.[8]

Nevertheless, the relationship between planters and buccaneers was tense. While the planters benefited from the currency that buccaneering expeditions brought to the island, the buccaneers were difficult to control and their raids couldn't be confined to approved targets. In times of official peace, they sometimes disrupted the planters' favored commerce, adding an unwelcome degree of uncertainty into the planters' efforts to amass wealth. The more prominent planters, who were often merchants as well, bristled at the lack of order. As agricultural settlements spread around the island and the influence of the planters grew, they prevailed upon the imperial governors and the Royal Navy to brand the buccaneers as pirates and chase them from Jamaica.[9]

Port Royal's role as a pirate haven ended decisively with a massive earthquake on June 7, 1692, which inaugurated a series of disasters that befell the island in the 1690s. "In the space of two Minutes," a witness recalled, "all the Churches, the dwelling houses & sugar works of the whole island were thrown down," even as much of Port Royal was "swallowed up by the sea" and "all its Forts and Fortifications demolished and a great part of its Inhabitants Miserably either knockt on the head or drowned." The subsequent paucity of housing and the disruption of food supplies led to morbid conditions. Hundreds died, and chaos ensued, leaving the island "open and exposed to the Attempts of Enemys by seas as well as land." Between the earthquake and the calamities that followed, the stronghold at Port Royal was reduced from two thousand to two hundred fighting men.[10] In the years immediately following the earthquake, malaria and yellow fever epidemics swept away thousands of settlers.[11] The situation worsened, according to a report by Jamaica's governor at the time, William Beeston, as news about "the sickness and calamity of the place" frightened off commercial traffic and "terrified all that used to bring provisions to it," leading to famine.[12]

The Nine Years' War that followed England's Glorious Revolution (1689–1697) compounded the island's troubles. In 1694, the French invaded Jamaica with a force of three thousand men. Landing east of Port Royal at Cow's Bay in the parish of St. David, the French forces "plundered, burnt and Destroyed all before them" as they pushed through the parish of St. Thomas, killing livestock, pulling up cane, and cutting down fruit trees. They burned fifty sugar works and captured more than fifteen hundred slaves before the English could repulse them.[13] Governor Beeston complained that the French tortured and murdered settlers in cold blood, dug some corpses out of their graves, and "suffered the negroes to violate" some women. "There was never more inhumane Barbarities committed by Turks or Infidels in the world," he fulminated.[14] The two eastern parishes remained thinly populated for decades after the invasion, with colonists fearing their continued vulnerability. The French attackers were less successful on the southern coast west of Port Royal, where they lost nearly four hundred men to the English defense.[15]

Jamaica's exposure during the war exacerbated a decline in white settlement. On top of astonishingly high mortality rates in the late seventeenth century, colonial officials lamented a dearth of new arrivals. "The island hath been in a Declining condition for Seven Years last Past," read one report, "Especially the Inward parts of the Country Occasioned by the want of Importation of Servants." The number of white settlers on the island had increased from about 3,700 to 7,800 between 1662 and 1673, but by the mid-1690s the population had fallen back by several hundred, with the number of deaths greatly exceeding the number of births. This decline stood in dramatic contrast to the growth of the black population. Between 1671 and 1684, Jamaica imported 1,500 Africans a year, supplemented by small numbers of native peoples captured from North America, and though the numbers of blacks and whites were equal in 1673, by the 1690s Jamaica held more than forty thousand enslaved black people.[16]

Without white workers, Jamaica's political elite feared that it could not maintain the island's defenses or manage the burgeoning number of slaves. Though a large expeditionary force from England buttressed the garrison following the French invasion of 1694, and lawmakers banned soldiers from leaving the island during the war in the 1690s, yellow fever ravaged the troops, who generally had no immunity to the tropical disease. Between 1694 and 1700, militia lists showed an increase of some 1,400 men, from 1,774 to 3,156, but these were hardly sufficient for the security needs of the island.[17] The dearth of white immigrants was a grave concern to the colonists, who complained that they had been "brought so low" that they were "not of force to Secure ourselves from the Insurrection of slaves."[18] Desperate to attract white settlers who could help maintain the defense of slavery, in 1703 Jamaica passed the first of many laws that required planters to keep one white man for every twenty slaves on an estate. Initially, these "deficiency acts" stipulated that plantations which failed to maintain the requisite number of white servants could be compelled to provide quarter for regular troops, but after 1720, with the ratio reduced to one white man for every thirty slaves, the laws levied substantial duties for noncompliance. Through the middle of the eighteenth century, few planters maintained their quota, and the richest plantation regions of the island were populated overwhelmingly by black slaves whom the planters mistrusted and feared.[19]

Even as the colonists contended with external threats, they faced a growing danger from enemy encampments in the island's interior. When the Spanish departed the island, they left behind many of their former slaves, who had fought rearguard actions against English occupation. Called maroons, after the Spanish *cimarrones* (wild ones), they formed communities in the mountains, their numbers swelling from the continuous trickle of runaway slaves from English settlements, and continued to harry the new settlers. From their sanctuaries in the densely forested mountains, maroons raided the plantations for provisions, weapons, and new recruits. The presence of these free communities helped to inspire captives on the plantations, who staged several serious revolts between 1673 and 1694. Most of these occurred on the north coast, where large plantations were scattered far apart, although one took place just five miles from the seat of the colonial government in Spanish Town. In the first years of the eighteenth century, small bands of slaves continued to break away from the estates to join the maroons, who soon grew numerous and powerful enough to threaten the future of the colony. Through the 1720s and 1730s, the colonists and the maroons waged a protracted war, which caused many to doubt the prospects for continued British occupation of the island.[20]

Military governance thus turned simultaneously inward to suppress the frequent slave revolts and maroon raids and outward to harass and contest with imperial rivals. Patterns of settlement reflected the exigencies of conflict as well as the prospects afforded by the island's topography. Plantations hugged the coast at the lower elevations, clustering along rivers. The earliest settlements in the southeast became the densest, with the main artery of plantation society running between Port Royal and Spanish Town and extending west through the lowlands.[21] On the northeast side, some estates were scattered in the valleys, but colonists found more room on the broader plains at the northwest end of the island. The mountainous interior and uncleared forests remained the preserve of fugitives and maroon communities. As black slaves came to dominate plantation labor and the rural population, whites bundled together in the towns, where they felt secure in each other's presence and in the embrace of the imperial military. Here they could look to the forts, barracks, and military parade grounds for peace of mind, as these "theaters of power" offered reassurance to the colonists and warning to their slaves.[22]

The design and architecture of the plantations and their placement within the landscape reflected security concerns. Many whites' houses were fortified, especially in the remoter parts of the island. James Knight described dwellings "built with stone & made Defensible with Flankers, having loop holes for Fire Arms & Ports for small carriage Guns, the windows and Doors being made Musquet proof; so that they are capable of making a good defence with the Assistance of their white servants & Trusty Negroes against a Foreign or Intestine Enemy."[23] Throughout the island, planters placed overseers' houses with an eye to facilitating surveillance, elevating them above the slave quarters or placing them near the quarters, the fields, and the plantation's processing machinery. In mountainous regions, estates might situate the white people's houses high on the slopes, in view of each other, so they could communicate at a distance in case of any trouble.[24] Slaveholders relied upon the extent of the island itself to protect them against "any general Insurrection of the Negroes." With the estates spread out across Jamaica's dense woods and formidable mountains, they believed for a time that potential slave conspirators would find it impossible to "join to Execute Their Designs."[25]

By the mid-eighteenth century, England had claimed sovereignty over the island and was able to defend its plantations from other European powers. Still, it was in practice a highly uneven dominion, threatened by internal enemies who made deep impressions on the political landscape.

THIS perilous state of affairs persisted because, after the crises of the 1690s, Jamaica became the most profitable colony in British America. The most successful planters bought up large swaths of real estate, squeezing out smaller proprietors and consolidating lesser estates into ever larger landholdings. Despite the slow growth of the white population, the colony thrived by turning more and more plantations over to sugar production. Many of the less prosperous whites joined the emerging plantation society as overseers and managers, while others continued on as shopkeepers and artisans.[26] The fortunes of the island grew with its plantations. By the middle of the eighteenth century, the naturalist author Patrick Browne could justifiably claim that Jamaica was "not only the richest, but the most considerable colony at this time under the government of Great Britain."[27]

Browne was not exaggerating. The island burgeoned with more than one hundred thousand slaves "by whose labours and industry almost alone, the colony flourisheth, and its productions are cultivated and man-ufactured."[28] Alongside sugar, planters grew coffee, ginger, and other crops, and also cultivated livestock. On top of their agricultural and pas-toral pursuits, Jamaican planters speculated in a thriving land market, bought and sold slaves, and lent money to each other at advantageous rates.[29] Jamaica conducted an impressive trade from its commercial center in Kingston, shipping sugar, rum, and other tropical commodities to North America and Britain. Kingston was among the busiest slave-trading ports in the British Empire, receiving more than four hundred thousand captives from 1700 to 1760. As many as a third of these were reexported to the Spanish Americas, which maintained a lively trade with Jamaica even in times of war.[30] The ships arriving in Kingston Harbor from 1744 to 1746 averaged 342 per year. Wealthy merchants engaging in transatlantic com-merce shared the city with traders of more limited scope, combining with them to distribute a variety of goods throughout the island and across the Atlantic.[31]

Browne characterized the colony as rich, but the vast majority of its pop-ulation was made up of enslaved workers who were miserably poor. Beset by high rates of sickness and mortality, they spent much of their short lives hungry, ill, and exhausted. Jamaica's wealth accumulated in the tight fists of its big planters and merchants, who were among the richest men in the world. As in so many market economies, "the great wealth of the few depended on the poverty of the productive many."[32] The wealthiest of Jamaica's estate holders owned hundreds of slaves. William Beckford (1709–1770), whose grandfather and father had established the family in the first rank of Jamaica's elite, held more than 1,300 slaves at his death in 1770.[33] Zachary Bayly (1720–1769) left an estate valued at £114,743 sterling, in-cluding 2,010 slaves. In addition to being a sugar planter and fabulously successful merchant, Bayly served as a planting attorney for several ab-sentee owners, managing thousands more slaves for other estates. Beck-ford and Bayly were among the ten wealthiest Jamaicans alive between 1674 and 1784, but wealth in slaves was widespread. By the mid-eighteenth century, half of all personal property in Jamaica consisted of slaves, and few of the island's leading men owned less than fifty people.[34]

The wealthiest of Jamaica's planters and merchants bought entry into elite circles in Great Britain, brokering between West Indian and metropolitan interests. William Beckford's career offered a spectacular example. He was perhaps the most successful member of a substantial group of absentee planters and merchants who acted as agents of imperial exchange. Having entered boarding school at Westminster while still a boy in 1719, he mixed with the English upper classes and other notables with fortunes in the Americas. Traveling back and forth between 1736 and 1744, Beckford served in Jamaica's militia and assembly and used his metropolitan contacts to advocate successfully for war with Spain in 1739. Returning to England in 1744, he purchased a country estate in Wiltshire, then developed his political networks, won the post of London sheriff, and gained a parliamentary seat in 1747. In the mid-1750s, having become a member of Parliament representing London, he cultivated an alliance with William Pitt, helping to convince the new prime minister to launch a major expedition to the Caribbean during the Seven Years' War. He served in the House of Commons until his death, while also serving two terms as Lord Mayor of London.[35]

Zachary Bayly had immigrated to Jamaica with his family in the 1730s and kept up close connections with merchant houses and politicians in London. When his younger brother Nathaniel (1726–1798) moved to England in 1759, the two men managed a transatlantic family business, keeping slaves at work on the plantations, moving tropical staples to Great Britain, prudently investing their profits, and using political contacts to protect them. As a man of great fortune, Nathaniel was well connected, eventually serving in Parliament himself during the 1770s. Like the Beckfords, the Baylys worked to harmonize the transatlantic national interests in slavery and military security.[36]

Slave labor and property in persons made merchants and planters rich beyond reasonable expectations, notwithstanding the slaves' demonstrated threat to the colony. One might see the Baylys, the Beckfords, and others like them as the victors in a class war. And, given that the island's workers were overwhelmingly of African descent, this was also a race war. The violence of enslavement continued daily on the plantations, just as it did along the slaving routes that brought these workers to the Americas. As conflict between African polities produced captives for the slave trade, violence on the plantations produced commodities for export, and the everyday antagonisms inherent in plantation production connected slavery to imperial war. Even before the slaves on Bayly's Trinity and Beckford's Esher estates, on the north side of the island in St. Mary's Parish, rose up against the British Empire in 1760, they were as well trained by the militarism of Jamaican society as by the slaving wars of West Africa.

THE plantation economy was an assault on the enslaved, who labored under the constant threat of attacks ranging from personal humiliation to public terror. The work regime required for sugar cultivation demanded strict control by plantation supervisors. Their management practices both drew upon and reinforced imperial violence, extending garrison government to the organization of the economy. Slavery encouraged the society's militaristic tenets: a belief that violence offered a ready solution to social problems, a propensity to resort to force often and with little provocation, and the maintenance of sharp and invidious distinctions between friends and enemies. Among themselves, the whites were renowned for convivial hospitality; beyond the circle of fellowship, they were notoriously ready to attack. Violence and domination were vital elements of daily life, and black people bore the brunt of this aggression.

As the leading sector of the economy, sugar production occupied the greatest amount of land and employed the most slaves. Roughly half of Jamaica's slaves worked on sugar plantations, which were among the world's largest private agricultural enterprises. Slaves commonly lived on plantations of more than 150 people, and a quarter of the population lived on properties with more than 250 people. Operating at a scale that allowed the integration of all important elements of production, from planting, harvesting, and processing to cultivating provisions for the labor force, the Jamaican sugar industry enjoyed remarkable productivity.[37]

For the enslaved, these powerful engines of profit were devastating, and the plantations that grew sugar were among the more life-threatening places a worker could be. The physical demands of planting, tending, and refining the cane amplified the hazards of malnutrition and tropical disease. Modern researchers have confirmed what contemporaries knew all too well: enslaved workers were consumed by the cane fields. On Mesopotamia, a large and productive estate in Westmoreland Parish, inventories of slaves taken between the mid-1730s and early 1760s show twice as many deaths as births, with children, teenagers, and young adults making up a high proportion of the dead. As overwork "decimated the field gangs," the estates depended on constant importation of new slaves from Africa.[38]

Gang labor supplied the crucial element of the work regime for large-scale sugar production. Armies of slaves working six long days a week in tightly controlled teams rotated through a series of time-sensitive, interdependent tasks. Field gangs, divided into multiple contingents, employed the largest proportion of slaves on a large plantation. A gang of children carried grass to the livestock and did light hoeing work around the cane shoots. Another gang would weed the cane pieces, clean pastures, and assist the first gang of prime field hands at crop time. This first gang performed the hardest labor, digging deep cane holes for planting and cutting the ripe canes at harvest. There might be something of a respite during May and June, after the reaping and before the slaves began boring into the ground again for the next crop. To meet these demands, slaves were kept at their tasks in lockstep fashion on a rigid schedule. Such labor was obtained through compulsion, especially by the threat of the whip.[39]

Mid-eighteenth-century sugar estates demanded a hierarchical division of labor and maintained a brutal discipline, comparable to that of the military. Estate owners and their planting attorneys gave direction to overseers, who supervised several white managers, generally called bookkeepers, below them. Even the enslaved workers were highly stratified. Drivers, almost exclusively male, commanded the field gangs who performed the most grueling work. Presenting the front line of intimidation on behalf of the planters, drivers set the pace of fieldwork. For this they received special privileges: better clothing and food, and sometimes a house set apart from other workers. Their position gave them a tense and ambivalent relationship with overseers and their other immediate white supervisors, who depended on the drivers' ability to manage the slaves, yet feared their potential for independent leadership.[40]

A number of occupations required looser discipline and offered a modicum of social status. Boilers and distillers possessed indispensable technical skills and commanded some respect within the chain of command. There were also coopers, who constructed the hogsheads and puncheons for containing sugar and rum; carpenters, masons, and blacksmiths, who maintained buildings and machinery; keepers to tend the livestock; and carters, who conducted cargo around the island. These tradesmen and craft workers had more autonomy than the fieldworkers, and also tended to live longer, healthier lives. Domestic workers in households could seek favors and resources by virtue of their proximity to whites, but were more directly subject to their abuses, too.[41]

Gender and ethnicity helped to determine who performed particular roles on the plantations. Women worked disproportionately in the field and were largely excluded from the highly skilled and higher-status jobs. Very occasionally, they might be drivers of secondary gangs; more often, they worked as domestics. The higher-status jobs went mostly to men. Creoles, those born on the island and accustomed to the ways of plantation society, generally won the less taxing and autonomous occupations that required the trust and preference of the masters. Native Africans were overwhelmingly relegated to the fields. Yet some slaveholders were prejudiced in favor of Africans from particular regions, such as the Gold Coast. Likewise, a particular African's demonstrated ability to wield responsible authority might land him the position of driver, a potentially contradictory role as both enforcer of plantation order and leader of enslaved communities.[42]

Militarism set the customary pattern for white dominance in slave society, which encompassed a routinely brutal civil conflict. Many of the white men who staffed the plantations in the formative phases of Jamaica's development were military veterans, trained by service in the highly regimented and harshly disciplined armies and navies of the Nine Years' War and Queen Anne's War. Viewing Africans essentially as enemies, they had no compunction about terrorizing them into submission.[43]

As it applied to the enslaved, even the law itself served as a public declaration of war. The earliest slave codes described Africans as an "uncertain, dangerous, and brutish sort of people," to be governed as adversaries. Despite Jamaica's history of uprisings and war with the maroons, Beckford's friend James Knight insisted that "the Security of the White People is under providence owing to the Laws for the good Order & Government of Slaves." It was a capital crime for a slave to "compass or imagine the death of a White Person." A slave was neither permitted to keep firearms or other "dangerous Weapons" at home, "nor suffered to go out of the Plantation They belong to without a Certificate from the Master or Overseer, expressing the Time He has leave to be Absent, and upon what Occasion." Slaveholders used their discretion in applying these regulations, which were "sometimes winked at and not strictly put into Execution." Trusted slaves could even bear arms for their masters in the event of a foreign invasion or internal uprising. But slaveholders all understood the need to keep slaves "in awe."[44] When rebellions occurred, the whites' reactions were extreme. "No Country excels them in a barbarous Treatment of Slaves," wrote Charles Leslie of Jamaicans in 1739, "or in the cruel Methods they put them to Death."[45] The law treated rebel combatants simultaneously as traitors against legitimate authority and as enemies outside the protection of society. As "intestine enemies," rebels received gruesome exemplary punishments. They were beaten to pulp, suspended in cages to starve, drawn and quartered, and burned alive. Some were beheaded—and their skulls were used to adorn signposts dispersed across the landscape.[46]

Exemplary violence was not limited to sudden events like uprisings; it was woven into the everyday experience of slave society. In the late 1720s, one astute commentator noted the "Barbarity daily exercised on the Bodies of the miserable Negros; The piercing Cryes and dolefull Lamentations that every Day enters one's Ears both in Town and Country, being enough to terrify a meek natur'd Person just landed in those parts of the World." After some time on the island, however, most managed to become inured to "those

Barbarous Treatments, and at last become as cruel and hard hearted" as the native-born whites. The explanation for the "unmerciful Temper" of the locals was simple: "It is no wonder that Children born in the Country and brought up and educated among a perpetual Scourging, and by Degrees delighted with the clamour of those miserable Creatures, as well as with the Sight of their Bodies cover'd with Blood and the Flesh thereof perfectly dissected after Correction, should as they grow up not only be hardened to it, but make it one of their Diversions." Whites trained themselves to discipline slaves at a young age—and learned to enjoy it. "They are pleas'd in the West Indies with Scourging, and the first Play-Thing put into their hands is commonly a Whip with which they exercise themselves upon a Post, in Imitation of what they daily see perform'd on the naked Bodies of those miserable Creatures, till they are come to an Age that will allow them Strength enough to do it themselves."[47] This deliberate introduction to brutality trained whites in the practice of mastery, which required continuous assaults on the slaves' capacity for independent volition. Migrants to the island who wished to work in the sugar industry quickly learned to be pitiless soldiers in a war against the dignity of the enslaved.

The Englishman Thomas Thistlewood arrived in Jamaica in 1750 and kept a diary of his thirty-six years on the island until his death in 1786. He began his career as an overseer of a livestock pen in the parish of St. Elizabeth. Supervising forty-two slaves on an isolated tract of land, Thistlewood sometimes went weeks without seeing another white person. He secured his mastery through a liberal resort to violence and sexual dominance. In his one-year employment at the pen, he found occasions to whip three-quarters of the men and more than a third of the women under his charge. Thistlewood had sexual intercourse with ten of these seventeen women, taking one as a regular concubine. The next year he moved to neighboring Westmoreland Parish, where William Beckford and Arthur Forrest owned plantations, and took a job on the Egypt sugar estate owned by John Cope Jr., son of the former chief agent of Cape Coast Castle. There, as overseer of more than ninety slaves, Thistlewood turned decidedly more monstrous. He frequently threatened dismemberment and death as punishment for recalcitrance. He penetrated the women of his choice, copulating as frequently as two hundred times a year. He devised degrading tortures, several times forcing slaves to defecate in each other's mouths for small infractions. And Thistlewood was hardly unique in his rough treatment of black people. Indeed, his diary's descriptions of many other white men's methods make his own seem relatively disciplined and restrained.[48]

The personal domination required to manage a slave society facilitated a bellicose demeanor on the part of men looking to justify and direct their aggression. Soon after arriving on the island, Thistlewood was given advice: "In this Country it is highly necessary for a Man to fight once or twice, to keep Cowards from putting upon him." Jamaican white men were known to be haughty and "liable to sudden transports of anger."[49] Martial masculinity valorized violent self-assertion, absolute control over black subordinates, and sexual dominance of women. These were the prerogatives of mastery, akin to rights of conquest, and were apt expressions of a man's capacity to act forcefully upon his environment. The coercive power of slaveholders was seldom questioned, and slaves had little formal protection from punishment, rape, torture, or even murder. Lording over vast numbers of vulnerable people whom they could oppress without repercussion, whites turned belligerence toward blacks into a common custom. Blacks endured showers of insults and epithets, personal violations, physical assaults, and assorted humiliations while they dreamed of self defense.[50]

In their own company, one white judged another by his capacity to exert his will in the world, to possess people and things, and to acquire useful knowledge. Admired for their hospitality to those within the circle of amity, they were also intensely competitive in their pursuits—whether in business, in courtship, or in matters of social rank. Masculine rivalry even stirred their scientific curiosities. Thistlewood maintained interests in botany, physics, and astronomy, and collected a range of scientific instruments over his lifetime. As a capable amateur astronomer, he could not help being impressed by the "6 feet Acromatic Telescope" possessed by a friend: "Better than Mine, tho' not in proportion" to the difference in the amounts each had each paid for his. He later consoled himself that at least his telescope was bigger than Captain Arthur Forrest's.[51]

As with most white men of fighting age, Thomas Thistlewood served in the local militia, mustering some forty times through the 1750s.[52] The militia could protect against invasion, as it had during the French incursion of 1694, but its primary purpose was to defend against slave revolt. James Knight described Jamaica's public vigilance in this way: "Guards are constantly kept on Sundays & Holidays and the Troops of Horse in several Parishes or Precincts are obliged to Patrol in Their Respective Divisions, to prevent Conspiracies or disorders amongst the Negroes." Knight was confident in the militia's ability to intimidate slaves, especially when they exercised in combination with regular army troops. "When [the slaves] see the White People Muster or Exercise," he claimed, "it strikes an awe and terrour into Them." Slaves generally avoided anyone wearing a red coat, like those worn by grenadiers, he noted, and as a result, "some Gentlemen put on a Coat of that Colour when they Travell" to deter trouble on the roads.[53]

This was partly wishful thinking on Knight's part. He thought that Africans were more afraid of militiamen than black people born on the island were, the latter being more familiar with the sight of a muster and able to "make use of Fire Arms as well as the Militia." Certainly, despite not being trusted by whites to possess guns, many Africans were as able as creoles to use firearms. Moreover, not everyone shared Knight's belief in the militia's effectiveness. In 1730, Governor Robert Hunter disparaged the militia as "indifferent," worrying that most of its men were "not to be trusted with arms." Knight admitted that in the 1730s, Jamaicans were "not so well Disciplined as formerly," referring to past years when the militia had more war veterans experienced in imperial campaigns.[54]

A more precise portrayal of the Jamaican militia emerges in the writings of the Swiss naturalist and collector Pierre Eugène du Simitière, who arrived on the island in the late 1750s after a stay in the neighboring French colony of St. Domingue. In general, he found the Jamaican militias overrun with pride, pomp, and regalia. He was especially unimpressed by the countryside militias, like Thistlewood's in Westmoreland Parish, which were top-heavy with men of rank, he observed, having too many leaders in command of too few followers. The soldiers were mostly the overseers, bookkeepers, and other white servants of the plantations, with the estate owners and attorneys serving as officers. "No planter or owner of an Estate is willing to muster as a private man," du Simitière explained, "if he can for a dobloon purchase a commission from the governors secretary, which is seldom refused." Having easily bought an officer's rank, no matter for how long a term of service, a planter gained the pleasure of "hearing himself call'd all his life afterward Cap[tai]n Such a one[,] Major or Col[onel]." Indeed, the militia was littered with colonels because, once having held the commission, planters were "stiled Colonels forever after."[55] This system helped elite colonists maintain an exalted sense of self-worth, but it saddled the militia with proud men of no formal military training, skill, or virtue. Military rank merely reflected prevailing social hierarchies of property, race, and nationality.

Du Simitière had little more confidence in the Spanish Town units. These reflected social rank in the capital, a "mixture of high & low without any medium."[56] As in the countryside, the Spanish Town militia was made up of wealthy men holding officers' commissions and so-called private men of modest means. Du Simitière observed that "those that muster in the capacity of soldiers are little better in general than what is understood by common white men in that Island." The officers, though, were mostly lawyers, doctors, and a small number of planters, "whose Pride exceeds always their fortune."[57] The distinction showed up starkly in the militiamen's attire.

Divided into companies, each with their own coats, capes, and hats of distinctive colors, "the lower class of them looks ragged & despised," sniffed du Simitière, while the officers "cover themselves with Regimentals veneer'd all over with lace."[58]

Du Simitière also disapproved of the way Jews were "promiscuously mixt with the Christians & the blacks with the mulattoes." Spanish Town was home to a sizable population of Jewish and free black and brown people, the latter composing nearly a third of the town's 1,271 inhabitants in 1754. These groups were middlemen of sorts, brought into the militia to secure their allegiance to the dominant white Christians. Many of the Jews were descended from those who had fled the Iberian Peninsula during the Inquisition and continued to practice their religion secretly in the colonies. They engaged principally in shopkeeping and trade, and needed to maintain amicable relations with the planters, as did the free people of color, who worked mostly in service occupations. So-called mulattoes, having white as well as black ancestry, generally required white patrons to make their way in society. Some were granted the privileges of white people by acts of legislature. Free black people lacking the benefit of blood relations could also seek out patrons. Militia service offered each of these groups a way to demonstrate loyalty to the ruling race.

There were also many Jews and free black and brown people in Kingston, but its greater wealth supported the finer distinctions of an ascending social pyramid.[59] The Kingston militia was more formidable than Spanish Town's, in du Simitière's view. It comprised some one thousand men, including the free people of color, divided into eight companies that were each distinguished by regiments with their own distinctive uniforms. Du Simitière described these in detail from high social status to low: "a Scarlet regimental faced with Blue & metal Buttons" for the colonel's company, with officers donning a "Scarlet Coat faced with blue velvet without any lace but a gold one upon the Hat"; the merchant colonel's company sporting "blue faced [regimental] with red & gold-laced Hat"; the numerous "True Blues" with blue and red coats and plain hats; red with green capes for the major's company; blue with crimson velvet cape for the captain commandant's; a sizable Jewish company in red; a "mulattoe's company" with red and green colors; and the blacks' "Blue faced with Buff." Besides these there were horse troop units, one Jewish and two Christian, with their own colors and standards. The infantry regiment had "two Pair of Colours one of which is the union flag Such as it is used by all his majesty's & the other is white with the coat of arms of the Island as granted by King Charles II emblazoned in her proper colours upon it." The drummers of all these companies, including the drum majors, were black men, with "liverys Generally the Reverse of the Regimental of the Companys whom they belong to, adorned with a great deal of Rich livery lace." Kingston's wealth kept these units cohesive and well-decorated.[60] Drilling in the commercial capital, though, they had little deterrent effect on the great populations of enslaved Africans in the countryside.

A few white men received religious exemptions from militia service. In the mid-1750s, at the invitation of several absentee landholders, the Unitas Fratrum, or Moravian Church, established a chain of mission stations at estates in the parishes of Westmoreland and St. Elizabeth, where they proselytized among the enslaved. Begun by Zacharias George Caries late in 1754, the mission grew with the arrival in 1757 of Christian and Anna Rauch, Brother Nicolaus Gandrup, and their converts. As pacifists opposed to military service, they shunned the taking of oaths, the bearing of arms, and military service in any capacity. A parliamentary act of 1749 allowed them full liberty of conscience in the exercise of their religious beliefs, though they remained a scorned religious minority in a colony under the jurisdiction of the established Anglican Church.[61]

The Moravian missions had been approved by the property owners, but the attorneys, overseers, and bookkeepers who managed the sugar plantations disdained the brethren. Most slaveholders feared that converting slaves to Christianity might propagate dangerous notions of equality, weakening the sense of awe required to keep them in subjection.[62] They also resented the missionaries' refusal to take up arms, especially as they worked in parishes where the black population vastly outnumbered the whites. Despite the missionaries' best efforts to placate the slaveholders by preaching obedience and avoiding direct criticism of planter brutality, they took little part in the martial masculinity that underpinned the whites' sense of security. To most free men in a colony perpetually on alert, Moravian pacifism appeared fainthearted, perhaps disloyal. In a society committed to aggression as a way of life, the brethren were the exceptions that proved the rule of Jamaican militarism.

JAMAICA's internally violent system remained productive only insofar as it was not undermined by Great Britain's imperial conflicts. Wars between European empires interrupted trade and disrupted plantation output. As a military outpost, Jamaica was viewed in Great Britain as a fortress to protect British agriculture and commerce. But it was no remote bastion. Since maritime trade extended British interests along the lattice of sea lanes connecting Europe, Africa, and America, Jamaica was a key node in a network of military power that linked landscapes and seascapes across the Atlantic.

The combined forces of the British Empire—militia, army, navy, and marines—stood ready to protect shipping and defend plantation colonies against attack. When called upon to serve larger ambitions, they could also take ships and territory from rivals. Patrick Browne crowed that Jamaica was "so advantageously situated in regard to the main continent, that it has been considered for many years as a magazine for the neighbouring parts of America."[63] While the British concentrated their land forces in the more populous expanses of the North American continent, a report of 1748 counted 7,500 men on the island fit to bear arms, including the militia. Colonial governors often complained that militia men were not as well trained or strictly disciplined as regular imperial forces, yet the regulars often served as adjuncts to the militia's prosecution of the internal war against the enslaved. Through the 1720s and 1730s, British redcoats fought the maroons to a stalemate. At the end of 1743, the British raised a regiment from the eight independent companies of the regular army, placing it under the direct command of Governor Edward Trelawny, who was especially alert to the danger of slave revolt and maroon war. "Edward Trelawny's Regiment of Foot" was redesignated as the "Forty-ninth Regiment of Foot" in 1751, when a royal warrant reorganized the British infantry. The Seventy-fourth Regiment soon joined the Forty-ninth, and the primary purpose of these troops was to formally prosecute "intestine war."[64]

The Navy was crucial to this effort. Though much attention has been devoted to the Navy's outward engagements with foreign enemies and its practice of pressing unwilling men into service, another of its missions was to aid in the suppression of domestic revolts. The Royal Navy's well-deserved historical reputation as an antislavery organization in the nineteenth century has deflected attention from its active eighteenth-century role in the maintenance of slavery in the sugar colonies. James Knight lauded British maritime strength not only in imperial war and commerce but also for its value in intimidating the enslaved. "The Men of War that are constantly on the Station & the great Number of Shipping continually coming and going gives Them an Idea of the Strength & Power of the English Nation, & Strikes an awe and Terrour into Them," he contended. The Navy's role in protecting planters proved as vital as its defense of merchants.[65]

Without question, the Jamaica garrison relied upon the Royal Navy to fight its external wars. The island's location at some distance from Cuba and Hispaniola made it an excellent base for campaigns against the Spanish possessions in the Caribbean and the French in St. Domingue. From the time of Queen Anne's War, the Admiralty deployed a permanent squadron at Jamaica, keeping it there after the war to intercept Spanish galleons when

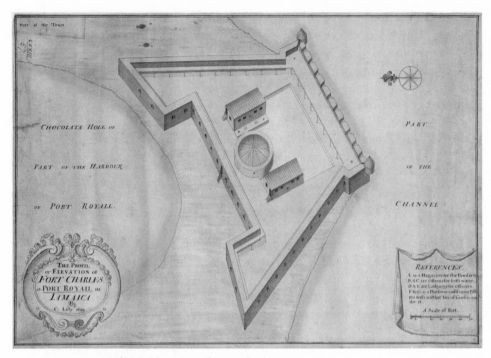

FIGURE 2.2. Profile or Elevation of Fort Charles, 1699.
Ink on paper by C. Lilly. *Courtesy of the British Library.*

possible and to take opportunistic advantage of trouble between Spain and her colonial subjects. During the War of Jenkins' Ear and the Seven Years' War, as the British reengaged the increasingly powerful French navy, the government committed more consistent naval firepower to the Caribbean than ever before.[66]

Although Port Royal had been destroyed in the 1692 earthquake, damaged by fire in 1702, and leveled again by successive hurricanes in the first two decades of the eighteenth century, in 1735 the Admiralty expended significant resources to rebuild and expand its wharves and dockyards. It remained, according to James Knight, an excellent harbor and a "Convenient Place for a Garrison, the Fortifications on which the Security of the Island, at least of the Trade and Navigation depend being chiefly here." An independent company of about one hundred regular army soldiers kept constant watch, accompanied by a regiment of militia, which kept a nightly guard. Military deputies oversaw the entrance and clearance of ships. Port Royal continued to maintain an impressive battery. Sixty-five cannon lined the fortifications at Fort Charles, thirty-four more constituted the Hanover

Line built in 1717, and forty heavy cannon and some mortars topped the wall running from the northeast to the south end of the town. More fortifications and batteries at Augusta Fort on Mosquito Point defended the passage into Kingston Harbour. In the 1720s, an additional, smaller naval base had been established at Lynch's Island off Port Antonio, to supplement the facilities at Port Royal.[67]

The size of the Jamaica squadron varied according to circumstances. The colonists had requested ten or twelve warships for the station during the early eighteenth century but seldom hosted so many. During the War of Jenkins' Ear, however, the squadron commonly included ten to fourteen warships of various sizes, including as many as seven ships of the line—heavy warships built to fire successive rounds of cannon alongside others—for major engagements. The Admiralty decided to keep eight ships of the line and eleven smaller craft at Jamaica in 1757. By 1760, at the height of the Seven Years' War in the Caribbean, there were sixteen British warships assigned to Jamaica, with 478 cannon and nearly 3,700 men between them, as compared to eighteen ships in the Leeward Islands and nineteen vessels assigned to the whole of the North American continent.[68]

Despite a chronic shortage of seamen, compounded by high death rates and frequent desertion, the Royal Navy maintained permanent squadrons in the West Indies while the French did not. Most importantly, British sailors with long-term residence in the region grew accustomed to the disease environment, which ravaged the large French flotillas sent to the Caribbean on special expeditions. North America provided abundant provisions, timber, and pitch, and the Caribbean dockyards at Port Royal, English Harbour, and Bridgetown allowed for most necessary repairs. Warships could stay in the West Indies for long periods of time, relieved periodically by those that accompanied commercial convoys from across the Atlantic once or twice a year. When a new admiral or commodore arrived to take command of the station, he generally brought a large company of ships with him. Station commanders therefore had the flexibility to send smaller ships on regular cruises to gather intelligence and intercept trade, while reserving their ships of the line for strategic attacks or defense against invasion.[69]

Adjunct to the Navy, the Royal Marines provided light infantry troops for amphibious warfare. Tracing their origins to the first maritime regiment of foot founded in 1664, His Majesty's Marine Forces formed three divisions under the control of the Admiralty in 1755.[70] Their establishment coincided with an increasing investment in "conjunct expeditions" of land and sea forces. While military planners developed grand plans for invasions of France and Spain, smaller expeditions in the colonies provided continuous experience, especially in the Caribbean, where amphibious fighting was the established way of war. In 1759, Thomas More Molyneux published a detailed analysis of all British amphibious expeditions carried out since the time of Queen Elizabeth, divided into great and small and successful and unsuccessful campaigns. Of the sixty-eight expeditions that he counted in Europe, Africa, the East Indies, and America, nearly a third took place in the Caribbean, and the West Indies accounted for more than eighty percent of the American campaigns.[71]

Among the failed ventures, the 1741 siege of Cartagena loomed large, and Molyneux's analysis would have been of special interest to veterans of that disaster. Admiral Thomas Cotes, who commanded the Jamaica station in 1760 and had led a group that included young Arthur Forrest in taking a Spanish battery at Cartagena, was surely well-versed in the latest wisdom on amphibious assaults when the slaves of St. Mary's Parish first rose up in revolt.[72] So, too, was his successor on the station, Rear Admiral Charles Holmes, who arrived during the rebellion soon after serving as Major General James Wolfe's third-in-command during the siege and capture of Quebec in September 1759. But despite railing against Britain's propensity to "flounder and flounce about" in the conduct of amphibious warfare because of a lack of systematic study, Molyneux said nothing about combined operations against rebellious slaves. Jamaica's military commanders would have to figure that out for themselves.[73]

In pursuit of its war aims, the Admiralty employed the most notorious system of discipline outside the slave plantation. British forces were bound by the rigor of martial law on land and at sea. Following some disappointing performances by naval officers during the early years of the War of the Austrian Succession in the 1740s, a powerful faction of the British government became convinced of the need for a more professional navy with a stronger sense of duty, tighter discipline, and greater courage in battle. These authoritarian Whigs sought naval reforms aimed at standardizing military regulations, reasserting hierarchy, and securing obedience to central authority. Accordingly, in 1749, Parliament revised the 1661 Articles of War and subsequent laws "relating to the Sea Service," which regulated the conduct of sailors.[74]

The new Articles of War ran like a cable throughout the Royal Navy, connecting, combining, and strengthening its exertions while promising punishment to the disobedient. The officers frequently read their provisions aloud to the crew, a ritual intended to incite fear of the naval command as much as of the enemy. Invoking the spiritual authority of the Anglican Church, the Articles of War compelled the performance of public piety aboard ships, "according to the Liturgy of the Church of England." Under the "good Providence of God," they also reaffirmed the Navy's jurisdiction over sailors on the "main Sea, or in great Rivers," and "beneath the Bridges of the said Rivers nigh to the Sea, or in any Haven, River, or Creek within the Jurisdiction of the Admiralty." Crew members in "actual Service and full Pay of his Majesty's Ships and vessels of War" could not escape the Admiralty's justice by committing crimes on shore.[75]

One special concern of the reform was a tendency by those in the officer corps to use status and connections to influence outcomes of courts martial. It addressed this by limiting the courts' power to reduce punishments for particular crimes.[76] Twenty-one of the thirty-six articles threatened the death sentence, which was expressly mandated for murder or "holding illegal correspondence with the enemy," but could also be fitting punishment for "uttering seditious words," concealing "mutinous Practice or Design," striking a superior officer, or committing buggery or other offenses.

Most of all, the Articles of War were designed to stimulate aggression against the enemy. Yielding or crying for quarter in a treacherous or cowardly manner was punishable by death. So, too, was "Cowardice or Neglect of Duty during a time of Action," as British subjects discovered when the rich and well-connected Admiral John Byng was famously executed for failing to "do his utmost" to defend the British fortress at Minorca, taken by the French in the spring of 1756. Article XIII promised death to "Every Person in the Fleet, who through Cowardice, Negligence, or Disaffection, shall forbear to pursue the Chace of any Enemy, Pirate, or Rebel, beaten or flying." Sailors were similarly discouraged "upon pain of death" from "relieving an enemy or rebel" with money, munitions, food and drink, "or any other supplies whatsoever." The common problem of desertion or inciting others to desert invited "death, or other such punishments as the Circumstances of the Offence shall deserve." Most offenses and punishments remained vaguely defined; courts martial still had broad discretion in most cases, and the death penalty was infrequently imposed. But the ascendancy of the Articles of War fulfilled its intention to intimidate, and an anxiously observant officer class led to more browbeaten common seamen as the coercion cascaded downward. Officers made liberal use of public flogging to punish "Other Crimes not Capital," according to the "Laws and Customs in such Cases used at Sea." With hierarchy, discipline, and bellicosity reasserted, the Articles of War strengthened Britain's capacity to subdue its enemies, both foreign and domestic.[77]

WAGER, the enslaved man from the Gold Cost owned by Captain Arthur Forrest, fought in Great Britain's foreign wars before he became an internal enemy. Prior to being a driver on Forrest's estate, Wager labored for more than a year aboard a Royal Navy warship, but what little we know of

Captain *Arthur Forrest, of his* MAJESTY'S *Ship* Augusta;
Senior Officer *in that memorable* Action *with the* FRENCH *off* Cape Francois 21.st *October,* 1757.

May ev'ry gallant TARR, *like him maintain,*
BRITANNIA'S *Title* —— EMPRESS *of the* MAIN.
Printed for Cha.s Bakewell & Henry Parker, opposite Birchin-lane, in Cornhill.

FIGURE 2.3. Arthur Forrest.

Engraving by Richard Purcell, after Johan van Diest, published ca. 1758. © *National Portrait Gallery, London.*

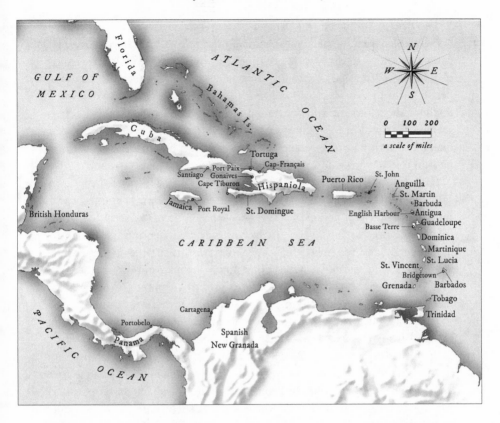

his military service emerges obliquely through the story of his master. Born in Edinburgh, Scotland, Arthur Forrest moved to London as an adolescent and went to sea at an early age. He was working as a master of a merchant ship in the Jamaica trade when war broke out between England and Spain in 1739. Captain Charles Knowles and Vice-Admiral Edward Vernon recruited him to join the expedition to Porto Bello as a pilot. The capture of Porto Bello made Vernon a national hero, and Forrest shared in the glory of the victory, ascending to the rank of Lieutenant in the Royal Navy the next year.[78] At Jamaica, Vernon planned his next campaign, sending Forrest to scout the route to Santiago, Cuba, before deciding instead upon Cartagena, the commercial and military hub of Spanish New Granada, a great swath of South America that was rich in precious minerals, agricultural products, and timber. Forrest sailed from Jamaica aboard HMS *Burford*, in the company of some 186 vessels, including twenty-nine ships of the line. He was one of fifteen thousand sailors, and about twenty-nine thousand men in total, the largest military force that had ever been assembled in the Caribbean.[79]

The British laid siege to Cartagena for over a month, but yellow fever ravaged the troops as their commanding officers squabbled over tactics. The campaign ended in disaster. More than eight thousand soldiers and sailors died in less than two months at Cartagena; another thousand-plus would perish within a few weeks of the fleet's return to Jamaica. Yet Forrest had distinguished himself during the amphibious assault, leading a party of seamen that took a four-cannon Spanish battery while capturing six prisoners. He and the other seamen in the operation personally received a financial token from Admiral Vernon as a reward for their "gallantry."[80]

Credited for courage in battle, Forrest accelerated in his rise through the ranks, commanding three different vessels before being promoted to the rank of post captain on HMS *Wager* on March 9, 1745.[81] Around this time, too, he acquired an enslaved African with a name that sounded something like Apongo, and renamed him Wager to mark this significant career milestone. If he had learned anything of Apongo's background, Forrest might even have seen the new appellation as a way of subsuming Apongo's formerly exalted status by making him a mascot. During the insurrection of 1760 it was rumored that Wager had sailed in this ship, which Forrest commanded from 1744 to 1748, and indeed, one able seaman named James Wager mustered aboard at Port Royal on April 13, 1746.[82] It was common for slaves serving on Royal Navy ships to receive generically Christian forenames such as James, John, or Peter, attached to the single designations, of African or European origin, that the enslaved usually carried. Wager sailed alongside at least three other black men listed on the same musters. Judging by their Akan names, at least two of these were probably from the Gold Coast: John Quaco, an able seaman who served from January 9, 1746, to June 14, 1747; and Peter Quamina, a servant to the ship's carpenter, who mustered on July 18, 1746, and left the ship on May 3, 1747. They accompanied able seaman John Primus, who arrived November 16, 1746, and served until July 3, 1747.[83] These men joined dozens of other black seamen employed at Jamaica, who constituted about a quarter of the crews plying the island's shipping lanes at the time.[84]

After James Wager joined the crew, HMS *Wager* spent the next fourteen months patrolling Jamaica's coastal shoreline and cruising its eastern waters to the French colony of St. Domingue. He had been aboard only six days when the *Wager* chased, attacked, and captured a Spanish privateer off the east end of Jamaica. Less than two weeks after that, the crew pursued two vessels off Cape Tiberon. The *Wager* quickly caught up to the smaller of them, a sloop, and sent out a barge and canoe "Man'd & Arm'd" with a boarding party. Alarmingly, the sailors "found her to be a French Privateer of Great Force," and they aborted their attempt, rowing away as fast as they could under fire from cannon and small arms. When a bigger ship, and likely a better prize, appeared on the horizon, the *Wager* broke off and gave chase. The next night, with a brief exchange of cannon fire, Forrest captured his prize—a French warship bound for home from the colonies—and took sixty-five prisoners. Forrest sent the French prisoners to shore at Port Royal a few days later, and Wager might have noted that they were not to be sold as slaves as African captives generally were.[85]

The French cannon fire had torn up the *Wager's* rigging and shot through the main and mizzen masts, and the ship had to spend the next two weeks undergoing repairs in Port Royal Harbour. Watching the comings and goings in a naval port at war, Wager surely reflected on British power. The waterfront was busy and growing. In the previous decade, workers had constructed a careening wharf, storehouses, officers' quarters, and a wall to surround the naval yard. Another new wharf had just come into service in 1744. He would have noted the polyglot composition of the military's workforce. Black people performed much of the basic labor on the station: a report of 1748 listed fifty-three caulkers, two sawyers, six smiths, and fifty-one laborers, all paid five shillings a day. Alongside these were fourteen more black laborers and seven boat crewmen earning less than two shillings a day, as well as ten "King's Negroes," slaves owned by the Navy. Listening to the guttural commands and urgent translations among multiple languages, he must have become aware of the chronic shortage of seamen, made acute by sudden death and desertion.[86]

Wager also probably paid close attention to the rituals of hierarchy, the stern discipline, and the eager aggression that made the Royal Navy such a capable force. Yet, having seen sailors repelled in a battle and the *Wager* wounded even in victory, he would have known that the British military was not invulnerable. And he would have heard from other crewmembers the story of the *Wager's* deadly dispute in Boston, less than six months before he mustered, when Captain Forrest had caused a fracas with the locals there by pressing some men into service. Two men died in the skirmish and the *Wager's* boatswain was arrested, charged with murder, and sentenced to die, although it appears he escaped the hangman. The story of this recent conflict might have been Wager's earliest lesson on imperial compulsion and local rebellion in the Americas.[87] More directly, he would have seen that the Navy's role in fighting the French and Spanish was not distinct from the maintenance of colonial slavery. At least once, the *Wager's* crew helped to police the enslaved population, as in September 1746, when they captured a canoe carrying "two English Negros" who had escaped from Spanish Town.[88]

Several months later, Wager participated in a major engagement. In company with two other warships on June 6, 1747, HMS *Wager* chased two French ships of twenty-four and thirty-six guns between the St. Domingue coast and the small island of Tortuga toward the forts overlooking the bay at Port Paix. Arranging into a line of battle, the English ran by the bay firing upon the ships and forts, but then came too close to the shore and had to bear away before they could get within cannon range. Brisk return fire from the French did little damage. The forts above the bay had made the difference, something Wager might have remembered years later when he gathered with fellow African rebels at a barricade high above the Westmoreland plain.[89]

James Wager was discharged as "unserviceable" on July 3, 1747, before the *Wager* made its return voyage to Great Britain via North America.[90] He may have been ill, like most sailors so listed in the muster. Just as likely, Forrest may have discharged him as part of a general practice of employing black sailors, often enslaved, in Caribbean waters and then leaving them behind when the ships returned to England. Ships' crews carried more black men in the Caribbean than elsewhere, even though the Admiralty generally discouraged slavery within its ranks. Following regional expectations, captains often took on black sailors in the slave colonies and discharged them before going home, as Forrest also did with John Quaco and John Primus.[91]

Captain Forrest himself had no disagreement with Caribbean slavery. Indeed, he had deep roots among Jamaica's local elite. His family had owned property on the island from the late seventeenth century, and his many years of service in the region had acclimated him physically and culturally. Having recently inherited sugar plantations from his father, Thomas, in 1747 Forrest married the daughter of another wealthy Jamaica planter. By the time Forrest left for Great Britain with his new wife, in August 1747, he was sole or part owner of nearly three thousand acres in the parishes of Westmoreland and St. Elizabeth. He had also added commercial assets to his landed wealth, investing heavily in prize cargos captured from Britain's enemies. In England, Captain and Mrs. Forrest purchased a country estate called the Grove at Emmer Green, north of Caversham in Oxfordshire. Still, Forrest's friends thought Jamaica was "the place most agreeable to him." Since he was an accomplished naval officer, a great planter, and a war profiteer, there were no tensions between Forrest's military service to the British Empire, his zeal in the protection of its trade, and his personal interest in slavery. He knew as well as anyone that slavery thrived as the fruit of war, even if he did not acknowledge, as his fellow mariner Olaudah Equiano did, that slavery itself was a form of war.[92]

With Forrest away from the island from 1748 through 1755, Wager's next encounter with the captain probably occurred upon Forrest's return to the island in 1756 aboard the *Rye*. John Cope had died on February 3 of that same year, only weeks before the *Rye* anchored at Port Royal Harbour.[93] Would Cope have made good on his promise to Apongo to "have purchased him and sent him home had Capt. Forest come to the island" sooner, as Thistlewood surmised?[94] There is no way to know. Yet, given what we do know of their travels and experiences, we might imagine a palaver between Cope, Forrest, and Wager to decide the African's fate. In their arguments, each might have drawn upon how he understood the relationship between war and slavery.

Cope might have impressed upon Forrest that Africans, as he knew them, could easily be the equals or even the superiors of Europeans. On the Gold Coast, he had learned the need to resolve conflicting interests and discovered that the black-white racial distinction was rarely the most salient division among contending parties. In Africa, the British jockeyed with the Dutch, the Danish, and the French, even as they negotiated seriously with various African polities. To play all these parties off against each other to one's own advantage, one had to recognize the differences and various status hierarchies among them. That might allow one to maintain an advantageous position from a cramped and undermanned fort, just as one might occupy a plantation's great house in Jamaica surrounded by armies of slaves. Cope had seen the cost of the Ahanta Palavers at Sekondi and Dixcove. Surely, too, he must have agreed with the Danish perspective on the calamitous actions of Director-General Des Bordes at Elmina, who had "set an example to all Whites how not, without reason, to provoke the Blacks into trying their own strength."[95]

Having learned over decades in the Caribbean that war and slavery were a lucrative pairing, Forrest might have countered that Wager was his property by right of commerce and conquest. Having purchased him legitimately, he held a fair title. Like most American slaveholders, he would have felt certain that skin color was the surest indication of rank. Plus, he had mastered Wager twice, as owner and as military commander. Subordinates took orders; they did not negotiate terms. If Cope wanted to make such an altruistic purchase, perhaps Forrest would have considered it. But it would have been a business transaction between propertied white men, not a diplomatic palaver.

Wager had also known war. In 1756, he would have had fresh memories of Asante's expansion, of the swelling power of the Fante along the coast, and of the deadly struggles around the European forts. He, too, had developed a habit of command and was not in awe of Europeans, either as a free man or as a slave. If he was painfully aware of how precarious his own status had become, he would also have known that force worked against Europeans as well as any other people.

Of course, few slaves in Jamaica could have imagined such a meeting. Wager's story, as imprecise as it is, seems exceptional. By the time of his rebellion, Apongo had been an adult man of elite status and a captive, with a sense of the world that encompassed coastal West Africa, the greater islands of the Caribbean Sea, and life on a sugar plantation. He had played multiple roles and occupied several positions in this geography, but always with a capacity to soldier. And he was not alone in this, even if most enslaved migrants moved through worlds of more limited scope.

Though few shared Apongo's exalted status, most slaves engaged in a fluid struggle that compelled them to make unbearable decisions about when to yield, how to protect themselves and others from harm, whom to align with, and when and how to fight back, if at all.[96] In these decisions, the matrices of movement traced by soldiers, slavers, and their captives made political histories of space, connecting the expansive to the intimate as small wars kindled within larger wars. Jamaican slave society was therefore not only the commercial and military heart of the British Empire, but also a constant battleground at the intersection of the seascapes and landscapes that formed the martial geography of Atlantic slavery.

Whether or not a palaver would have resolved the dispute over Wager's freedom, the issue remained unsettled, and four years hence he would lead a West African war in Jamaica even as the island was embroiled in a European world war.

GIVEN Jamaica's capacity to wage war within and beyond its shores, the importance of the garrison was not in doubt on the eve of the Seven Years' War. In 1754, with British colonial settlements pushing ever deeper into the North American continent, a territorial dispute with the French and their Indian allies in the Ohio backcountry sparked a conflict that would last until 1763 and would eventually encompass the globe, with theaters in North America, the Caribbean, South America, West Africa, India, and the Philippine Islands. The war ended with the Treaty of Paris and an overwhelming victory for Great Britain, including the formal recognition of Britain's dominance in eastern North America. But this outcome was far from certain when the war began.

The conflict elevated to power William Pitt, Earl of Chatham, who maintained an aggressive outlook on European rivalries and a firm conviction that American trade and sea power were crucial to national fortune. Having been an influential member of the Board of Trade, Pitt emerged as an advocate for the interests of West Indian planters and merchants. When he assumed the position of secretary of state and the *de facto* leadership of the government in 1756, he doubled the size of the naval squadrons at

Jamaica and the Leeward Islands, though the West Indies remained ancillary to Britain's strategic considerations in continental Europe and North America for the first several years of the war.[97]

Meanwhile, Jamaica was ripe with the expectation of a French invasion. In November 1756, colonists received news that a French expedition of six warships had arrived in the Caribbean. The Navy's squadron commander called his ships of the line back to station, and merchants and planters fretted over the consequences for their trade. Vessels had been scarce at Jamaica all year, and the principal shippers could not fix the price of freight for the following year for fear that their cargos would be taken by the French. The governor declared martial law, putting a stop to the ordinary business of the courts and obliging all white men of fighting age to report for militia duty. The islanders anxiously awaited the arrival of more ships from England, worried that they might be intercepted by the French cruising off Cape Tiberon.[98]

Well into 1758, the colonists complained of the bad fortune caused by the war. One described the situation to a colleague in London in dire terms: "There is no business to be done here with any pleasure as the Planters in general are greatly distressed for money. The Guinea Trade is in a very languid situation, and nothing has been done in that branch for many Months past, neither are the Merchants desirous of doing any more 'til they have collected their outstanding debts. I am afraid that the long credit, and bad pay, will be the ruin of this country, the scarcity of money never was known to be so great as it is here at present."[99] Importations of Africans had decreased nearly 60 percent between 1755 and 1758, down from a twenty-five-year high of nearly fifteen thousand to fewer than 5,600.[100] The decline in the slave trade betokened a decrease in business across the board. Because the British government required colonists to supplement the costs of housing, feeding, and equipping the army, this dip strained Jamaica's defenses.[101] Zachary Bayly noted how the slumping slave trade hindered Jamaica's military readiness, despite the news of promised relief from England: "We are big with Expectation of our new Governor, and another Regiment; but few Negroes having arrived this Year it's a difficult Task to find money, out of all our Friends, to maintain the Regiment we have here."[102] As the war dragged on, Jamaica's colonists desperately hoped that their lobby in Great Britain would convince the government to pay closer attention to the West India interest.

In London, Pitt was indeed preparing a strategy that would bring the Caribbean more directly into the war. He maintained that British sea power could break the stalemate in Europe by stripping France of its colonial possessions. In August 1758, he learned of the capture of France's North

American stronghold at Louisbourg, a crucial step toward the conquest of Montreal. But if Canada remained the biggest territorial prize, the richer nodes of Atlantic trade to the south offered other opportunities to utilize British naval superiority. France's wealth, like that of Great Britain, was greatly enhanced by African labor in the sugar islands, making West African slaving forts a military priority. In Senegal, the French had monopolized access to the trade in gum arabic, a crucial raw ingredient in silk manufacture, and they commanded the labor of a large population of "slave sailors" who plied their trade along the river. In the Lesser Antilles of the Caribbean, Martinique and Guadeloupe were as prodigiously profitable as Jamaica and Barbados; in fact, Pitt believed that Guadeloupe was worth more to Britain than the whole of Canada. Naval victories against the French in West Africa and their plantations in the Caribbean would sap their finances and make it more difficult for them to continue the war elsewhere.[103]

Pitt received advice from William Beckford, who had enlisted with Pitt's faction of the government: "In the militia of Jamaica I was no more than a common soldier," he declared. "In our present political warfare, I intend to act as one of your private soldiers without commission." Beckford counseled Pitt that an attack on the French island of Martinique would bring an easy victory and laudable spoils. "The negroes and stock of that island are worth above four millions sterling," he claimed. "For God's sake," Beckford urged, "attempt it without delay."[104] British West Indian planters did not hope to bring more sugar colonies into the fold—the competition would lower the price of their own commodities—but they did want to bring more British armaments into the region and more slaves to their own estates. Pitt was persuaded that capturing one of France's most profitable possessions would give the British considerable leverage in diplomatic bargaining when the war ended. Successful operations in Africa and the Caribbean might force the French to sue for peace on favorable terms and would serve West Indian interests, as well.[105]

MILITARY strategists in London must have been encouraged by Captain Arthur Forrest's success during the war. Forrest had lived on a well-appointed countryside estate in England from 1748 until he earned his next command in May 1755, of HMS *Rye,* a twenty-four-gun frigate. By March 1756, he was back in Jamaica. A year later, he transferred his command to the sixty-gun ship of the line HMS *Augusta,* and embarked on what would be his most celebrated tour of duty.[106]

In October 1757, off the coast of St. Domingue, Forrest led the *Augusta,* the *Dreadnought,* and the *Edinburgh* into an engagement with a far superior French fleet of seven ships—four ships of the line and three well-armed frigates. By this time, the news that Admiral John Byng had been shot on his own quarterdeck in March for failing to fight the enemy had circulated around the officer corps, stimulating what naval historian Nicholas Rodger has called a "culture of aggressive determination which set British officers apart from their foreign contemporaries, and which in time gave them a steadily mounting psychological ascendancy."[107] According to several accounts, the war council between Forrest and the two captains of the accompanying ships was brief and direct: despite their numerical disadvantage, the three captains were eager to fight.[108]

In the "furious action" that commenced on October 21, the ships under Forrest's command crippled the French squadron, though the British ships were themselves so damaged by the fighting that they were unable to take any prizes. By one estimate, the French had between five hundred and six hundred men killed and wounded. The *Augusta* had nine men killed, and twenty-nine wounded, adding to the fourteen killed and sixty wounded between the other two British warships. Forrest's bold action made his reputation and epitomized the new spirit of gallantry among naval captains. What came to be called the Battle of Cap François was soon one of the Royal Navy's most widely known actions, even memorialized a few years later in a Church of England hymn. Just one month later, off the coast of Gonaïves, Forrest single-handedly captured a convoy of nine French ships carrying 112 guns and 415 men, and laden with sugar, indigo, and cotton valued at £170,000. That feat, too, was reported throughout the empire, but the news was especially celebrated in Jamaica, where Forrest brought the prizes to harbor.[109] His success in taking French prizes continued into the new year.

In the meantime, Forrest's slave Wager labored as a driver on Masemure estate. He had missed the Battle of Cap François and the Tiberon Cruise off Gonaïves, though at least three other black sailors—James Cudjoe, Jupiter Anon., and John Fortune—had mustered from the *Rye* to the *Augusta* along with Forrest. It is almost certain that when these men were discharged at Port Royal on December 31, 1757, they eagerly told their stories to other black sailors and to slaves. The deeds of their crew were the talk of the station, and it is safe to assume that the news reached Wager in Westmoreland Parish even before Forrest came to visit his plantation. This was less than two short years after John Cope, Wager's potential patron, died in 1756, and with him Wager's hope of manumission. Through 1758 and 1759, while Forrest became the hero of the Jamaica squadron and the toast of the empire, Wager contemplated his dwindling prospects for freedom.[110]

FIGURE 2.4. The Battle of Cap François, 21 October 1757.

"The Glorious Action off Cape Francois Octr. 21, 1757, between three English, and seven French Ships of War wherein the latter were entirely defeated," in Francis Swaine, *Twelve Prints of Sea Engagements*, ca. 1760. Painting by John Cleveley, after an engraving by Francis Swaine. *Courtesy of the Collections of the National Maritime Museum, Greenwich, London.*

It is impossible to know with any certainty what the news of the triumphs meant to Wager, at once Forrest's mascot, former crew member, and one of the "principal men" on his Jamaican estate. But it is likely that at least some of his sentiments revolved around the relationship between martial masculinity and mastery. In part because Africans from the Gold Coast often had experience in military campaigns, Jamaican slaveholders thought of them as a superior but difficult-to-manage species of property; like wild horses broken to domesticity, they conferred prestige upon the master. One can imagine that Arthur Forrest felt pride in enslaving another military man, absorbing him into his self-image as a conqueror—and that Forrest's martial achievements galled Wager all the more. How this weighed in his decision to plot a slave revolt we cannot know, though he probably began planning soon after Forrest left the island again in August 1759.

Forrest returned to England as a rich man made wealthier by war. He moved his family to a sumptuous estate, where he fashioned several additions and improvements to the house. The centerpiece of the renovation was a suite of rooms connected to the original house by a splendid picture gallery, a spacious drawing room, a salon, and an octagonal music room lighted by an overhead dome. Along the walls he hung large paintings to commemorate his various naval battles, most conspicuously the Battle of Cap François. In April 1760, on the eve of the slave insurrection in Jamaica, he commissioned the *Centaur,* a seventy-four-gun ship of the line, captured from France the previous year. Forrest would not return to Jamaica until early 1761, after his slaves had risen up to destroy his plantation.[111]

As England pursued its campaigns in West Africa and the West Indies, its ships, sailors, and soldiers traced the connections between the Jamaica garrison and the wider war. By their movements and actions, these instruments of empire bound the disparate regions of the Atlantic world to the slaving economy. The belligerent cruise of HMS *Harwich* offers a telling example. The *Harwich's* Captain, William Marsh, is known for the capture of Senegal in 1758, which preceded and prepared the way for the more celebrated conquest of Goree by Augustus Keppel later the same year.[112] Yet Marsh's conquest may be the least illuminating event in the ship's deployment.

Representing more than a single victory in a global imperial struggle, the *Harwich's* eventful mission along the Guinea coast and in the Caribbean highlights the inextricable link between soldiering and the geography of slavery during the Seven Years' War. The actions in Senegambia became a template for future marine operations during the period. At Senegal, the *Harwich's* marines proved the Navy's ability to project British sea power ashore and to seize strategically valuable assets without the help of the army.[113] Crucially, the campaign prepared the marines to fight Africans in close quarters, an experience they would call upon when suppressing the slave insurrection in Jamaica two years later.

Commissioned by the Royal Navy in 1756, the *Harwich* was a fourth-rate ship of the line bearing fifty heavy guns. In 1758, Captain Marsh assumed command of a small expedition under Pitt's orders to attack "any French forts and settlements on the River Senegal or the Coast of Africa" and to take stock of armaments and manpower at the British trading forts along the littoral.[114] Aboard the ship were one hundred fifty sailors and two hundred marines, prepared to bombard the French forts, land for close combat, and carry away prize ships and cargos. The *Harwich* sailed in company with HMS *Nassau,* sixty-four guns, Arthur Forrest's former ship HMS *Rye,* and three smaller vessels. The fleet arrived at the mouth of the Senegal River on April 23.

For the next few days, they transferred marines, munitions, and provisions to the smaller ships for landing, and then began to work their way past the dangerous sandbar bordering the harbor toward Fort Saint-Louis, the strongest post on the river, situated on an island about twelve miles within the bar. The French fired on the British from several small ships while their African allies "kept up a continual fire with small arms," but by April 29, with the ships of the line bombarding the shore, the British had landed seven hundred seamen and marines with their artillery. On May 1, the French formally capitulated, yielding "all the forts, storehouses, vessels, arms, provision, and every thing belonging to the company, upon the River Senegal." Between the spoils in the fort and the sixteen prizes in the harbor, the British took ninety-two pieces of cannon, four hundred tons of gum, a great quantity of gold dust, nearly fifty thousand dollars, and a year's supply of goods for barter, in addition to fifty slaves and more than two hundred other prisoners.[115]

Leaving a large contingent of marines to occupy the fort, the fleet sailed on to the French naval station and slave barracoon at Goree Island, considered the key to French West Africa. On May 21, under fire from the fort's batteries, the warships anchored in Goree Road and prepared their assault on the fort. The smaller vessels took soundings of the water's depth between the island and mainland, but musket fire from African soldiers in canoes slowed their work. The *Harwich* anchored close to the shore, near one of the smaller ships, to prevent the canoes passing from the mainland to the island. By May 25, the crew were "making all clear for attacking Goree." Before daybreak the next morning, the *Harwich* formed a line of battle with the *Nassau* and the *Rye*. The British and French exchanged cannon fire for more than two hours, after which Captain Marsh found the *Harwich* badly damaged, its "mast & Rigging so much Shattered & Cutt," the main mast and main topsail yard "Shott in Pieces," and the foremast and rigging "very much Shattered." He ordered a retreat, but before they could sail out of range the French guns blasted the *Harwich's* stern, wounding many of its crew with flying shards of wood. Anchoring a safe distance from the fort, the officers counted their casualties: nine wounded from the *Harwich*, twelve killed and fourteen wounded on the *Nassau*, two killed and several wounded on the *Rye*, and one killed and several more wounded on one of the smaller ships.[116] The invasion had stalled.

The fleet retreated to the adjacent Gambia River, where the British secured the local trade from their fort at James Island. On May 30, the *Harwich* parted company with the *Nassau* and most of the rest of the fleet, who had been ordered home to England; it remained only with the *Rye* and one smaller ship. Casualties mounted as several sailors and marines died of their wounds, including a seaman who had "Lost his Leggs at Goree," but the campaign continued. The rump squadron's next target was Allbreda, a small outpost two miles up the Gambia River from James Fort. Allbreda was isolated from France's other positions on the Senegal River but had strong support from the local African polity. On June 6, before Marsh had a decided plan of attack, the *Harwich's* crew "saw the *Rye* and Brigantine firing at the natives and French factory." They learned that the "Officers of Marines & some of their People was Stop'd by the Natives," and the *Harwich* ran upriver to join the battle. On the morning of June 9, a force of more than two hundred sailors and marines went ashore "to Distroy the French Factory," while the *Harwich* and *Rye* bombarded the fort to cover the landing. The British fought a "close engagement" on the coast, but the Africans heavily outnumbered them and forced the invaders to retreat to the ships. Before leaving, the troops set fire to the factory. Nine men from the *Harwich* had been "dangerously wounded and several slightly." Three men from the *Rye* had been killed and "a great many wounded in Bush fighting."[117] Several of the wounded sailors and marines died as the ships worked their way down the coast. For the next several months, the *Harwich* attended to protecting the slave trade on the Gold Coast—once engaging in "very Hott" battle with a French warship—before departing Africa for the Caribbean.[118]

The *Harwich* arrived within sight of Jamaica on December 1. Soon after, a black pilot came aboard and "took Charge of the Ship," steering it safely into Port Royal Harbour. Here, Marsh came under the orders of Admiral Thomas Cotes in HMS *Marlborough,* the flagship of the Jamaica station, where the *Harwich* would be based for the next two years and where its campaigns against the French and their African allies would inform the Jamaica garrison's war against the enslaved.[119]

IN 1758 and 1759, the Seven Years' War turned decisively in Britain's favor. London received good news from the European continent as well as from India, Africa, North America, and the Caribbean. The United Kingdom's combination of superior sea power and trade, inventive financing, and military fortune had enabled a string of victories that brought the British to the verge of global supremacy. In the Atlantic theater, the conquest of Quebec led to the fall of Canada. Along with the capture of Guadeloupe, this secured an advantage for Britain that it never relinquished and heralded the defeat of France, though the war would drag on for several more years.[120] The reverberations of these battles came to Jamaica with the soldiers, marines, and sailors who fought them.

The war brought militant slaves to the island, too, as captives. Black people were employed on both sides of the conflict, but the French employed more blacks in arms, both free people of color and slaves. One naval lieutenant, who had resided for a time at Martinique, noted that there were 60,000 black people on that island, "many of whom are dextrous in Shooting, and all know the Use of small Arms, tho' not of Artillery." Something similar could be said of Guadeloupe. Some of these combatants were slaves promised freedom in exchange for service in the militia; others formed private armies for planters.[121]

Early in 1759, after a failed attempt on Martinique, the British attacked the island of Guadeloupe with a fleet that included HMS *Cambridge,* which would become the flagship of the Jamaica station a year later. Jamaica's governor-elect, General George Haldane, commanded an army brigade on the expedition. Heavy bombardment set fire to the island's main town, Basse Terre. The French abandoned their fort, broke into smaller detachments, and retreated to the hillside plantations around the town and to the clefts in the mountains. In these enclaves, they could "fortify themselves on the Hills, putting their Negroes in a Situation of Defence," making them "capable of disputing the Ground, at every Gully where the Troops should appear."[122] The British landed marines and soldiers, who encountered small parties of French soldiers firing from the cover of the sugarcane fields and entrenchments rapidly constructed by their slaves. The British burned nearby villages and fields in response, and continued fighting all around the forested hills. In one battle, they came under attack from a woman named Madame Ducharmey and her "armed Negroes," who had built fortifications on an opposing hill. According to Marine Captain Richard Gardiner, this slave militia, commanded in person by their mistress, killed twelve and wounded thirty British troops. Ten of the armed slaves died fighting, and a number were taken prisoner. Such skirmishes continued for several weeks, with the French continuing to occupy strongholds in the mountains and woods, while thousands of British troops succumbed to disease. The British did not take the island until the end of April.[123]

In the meantime, on March 21, George Haldane sailed to Jamaica aboard HMS *Renown* to take up his position as governor.[124] Black prisoners of war went to Jamaica, as well. In the conquest of Guadeloupe the British captured scores, perhaps hundreds, of slaves and free blacks. Free people of color were not supposed to be sold as slaves, but this was a difficult policy to enforce.[125] Before leaving Jamaica for England in August, Arthur Forrest bought some of these war captives for his Masemure estate. Hearing the stories of the blacks' resistance on Guadeloupe, perhaps Captain Forrest congratulated himself on completing their defeat by making them his vassals. Perhaps, too, the new captives learned from Wager that Forrest had a taste for enslaving military men.

More British troops and sailors made their way to Jamaica from Guadeloupe in the ensuing months. Among them, a year later, were the marines aboard HMS *Cambridge.*[126] Admiral Charles Holmes had assumed command of the *Cambridge* upon its brief return to England following the campaigns against the French. He had been a member of the court martial that tried and convicted Admiral Byng in 1757, was a recently elected Member of Parliament for Newport on the Isle of Wight, and was a veteran of Wolfe's Quebec conquest. A military grandee and an acknowledged hero of the war effort, Holmes arrived at Jamaica on May 13, 1760, with a complement of marines celebrating their triumph in Guadeloupe. Their next mission would be to aid in the suppression of a slave revolt.

THE Seven Years' War was, first and foremost, a global conflict between the powers of Europe. But within this war was another struggle that aimed to secure the benefits of slave labor. To ensure the success of imperial slavery, the British military fought Africans on both sides of the Atlantic Ocean, as both foreign and intestine enemies. These British fighters, trained and experienced in warfare against imperial enemies, did not know that they would soon be fighting Jamaica's internal war against the enslaved. They may not have suspected that their adversaries at Guadeloupe would soon be plotting alongside former comrades in arms like Wager, recently an able seaman in the Royal Navy. Yet the sailors aboard HMS *Harwich* and the marines on HMS *Cambridge* certainly had fresh memories of combat against African soldiers. In Senegambia and Guadeloupe, they had fought them closely in the bush and in steep mountain gullies. Now, on Jamaica, they would draw upon that experience to suppress a slave insurrection, and to keep the Jamaica garrison securely within the British empire. Just as the itineraries of slaveholders, soldiers, and slaves interwove trade, war, and empire, the Atlantic campaigns of the Seven Years' War connected the Jamaica garrison's imperial purpose to its internal war between slaveholders and the enslaved.

In early 1760, however, Jamaica's colonists felt more secure from foreign invasion than they had since the beginning of the war. And with their overwhelming power over the enslaved, the colonists convinced themselves that they were relatively safe from uprisings, too. Despite the slaves' numerical superiority, the planters enjoyed the comfort of a thoroughly militarized society, confident in their ability to meet any disturbance in the prevailing social order with massive violence. They were also consoled, perhaps paradoxically, by the diverse and fractious nature of their enslaved population. "So great a superiority one would think should render it exceeding dangerous and unsafe being amongst them," James Knight acknowledged, before explaining how the slaveholders convinced themselves otherwise. Because the Africans had been brought from various regions of the coast, where they spoke different languages and upheld different customs, the slaveholders believed most slaves could not "converse freely, nor confide in

each other." More importantly, their own rivalries were at least as immediate and pressing as their shared opposition to enslavement. "Those of different Countries have as great and Natural an Antipathy to each other, as
any two Nations in the World; so that They are under mutual apprehensions of falling into Subjection one of the other, should they shake off the
yoke of the English, which makes them easy, and have no thoughts of attempting it."[127]

Having written in detail about recent slave revolts, Knight certainly knew
better than to believe that the slaves had "no thoughts" of insurrection. He
did, however, perceive something vitally important: disputes among Africans did not end when they crossed the Atlantic Ocean. They might have
lost their former ranks in society, their social connections, and any wealth
they had held, but their prior experiences continued to shape their political
loyalties, even as strangers in a strange land. If the slave revolt of 1760 was
a war within the Seven Years' War, it was also a war within a long history
of conflicts beyond the African coast—conflicts transformed, given new
contours and meanings, and differently manifested in Jamaica. Jamaica's
internal and external wars took their shape not only from the economic
and military imperatives of the British Empire but also from West Africa's
diasporic warfare.

CHAPTER THREE

Coromantee Territory

A S WAR ON THE GOLD COAST fed the slave trade, it shaped territories and alliances that informed the patterns of slave revolt in the Americas.[1] Both for the subjects and foot soldiers of African states and for the many peoples living in the interstices of empire, West African warfare was a consequential historical experience. The seeds of insurrection surely germinated in Africa, but they sprouted in the fertile soil of American slavery's brutal violence. And they flowered in the light of imperial warfare, as Britain vied with France and Spain for supremacy in the North Atlantic and Jamaica's imperial managers struggled to maintain the security of a society dependent on the importation of wretched and hostile workers by the thousands.

British colonists could never take the obedience of their slaves for granted, especially during their wars with the Spanish and the French. Fears of foreign invasion, anxiety over the fate of commercial cargoes, food shortages, and political rancor kept the slaveholders tense and distracted. Imperial conflict provided opportunities for internal dissenters; subordinates could plot while their masters were preoccupied. Neither the routine brutality of slavery nor the threat of extraordinary violence was enough to keep people in line. Slaveholders' commands and threats always faced the possibility that a slave might refuse an order or, worse still, meet force with force. So the masters tempered their routine intimidation with concessions and small favors, while trusting that divisions among the slaves—their multitude of

African tongues, divergent religious customs, and status distinctions—would keep them from joining in common cause. Spread across an uneven and untamed landscape, these differences were believed to offer security to the slaveholders, who concentrated their power in the garrisoned towns and great houses. The colonists hoped to gain strength from the diversity of the enslaved population.

At mid-century, more than nine of every ten people in Jamaica were slaves. Between half and three-quarters of the slaves had been born in Africa, and those Africans had come from an expansive area of the continent between the Senegal and Kongo Rivers, and even as far away as southeast Africa.[2] Between 1701 and 1760, according to the best estimates, Jamaica received some 408,000 captives drawn from various regions of the African coast. But the distribution was neither random nor even. Fewer than fifteen hundred of these unfortunate people came from southeast Africa, and just over eight percent of them embarked from the region stretching from the Senegambia through the Upper Guinea Coast to Cape Appolonia. One of every five came from west central Africa, with a similar proportion leaving the continent from the Bight of Biafra. More than half of all the Africans arriving in Jamaica came from the Gold Coast and the adjacent Bight of Benin, the so-called Slave Coast. In excess of 150,000 Africans, thirty-seven percent of the total, came from the Gold Coast alone. These numbers reached a peak of twenty-two thousand in the five years preceding the outbreak of the Seven Years' War before falling back by nearly two-thirds between 1756 and 1760. Jamaica's population was diverse indeed, but migrants from the Gold Coast represented its largest fraction, larger by far than the cohort of people from England and Scotland.[3]

The breadth of these regional origins meant myriad languages, polities, and historical experiences. Yet, as they migrated, first within Africa and then across the Atlantic, the Africans found, shared, and made many commonalities. People regrouped with those who spoke similar languages, worshipped similar deities, or recognized similar forms of authority. From the designations foisted on them by the slave traders they made new categories of belonging: Angolas, Ebos, Papaws, Whidahs, and Coromantees, among others. Slaveholders imagined these peoples to be quite different in character. Often their impressions of Africans were nothing more than crudely drawn stereotypes, but even these caricatures were deeply rooted and could have far-reaching consequences.

In 1688, during his travels in Jamaica, the naturalist Sir Hans Sloane witnessed a diverse group of Africans performing at what he called a "festival." He convinced a local musician with European training and an ear for black compositions—possibly one of the "Negro musicians" playing at the event—to document some of the pieces. In Sloane's *Voyage to the Islands of Madera, Barbados, Nieves, S. Christopher's, and Jamaica,* published in 1707, he listed short notations for "Papa" and "Angola" music and a longer, more complex section of "Koromanti" music, perhaps indicating that the latter variety enjoyed the greatest prominence. Already, in the late seventeenth century, slaves from various regions of Africa were recognized for distinct styles of cultural expression. And yet they articulated these differences at a convivial gathering where they could both continue the traditions of their birthplaces and create new ones in diaspora. That they might have learned to play and enjoy each other's music suggests that neither their alliances nor their antagonisms were as predetermined by their origins as the slave-holders liked to assume.[4]

Said to be from more than twenty different "Countries or Nations," the Africans called by the British "Coromantees" garnered the most favorable commentary and inspired the most trepidation. Slave traders used the denomination to describe Africans from the Gold Coast generally, but slaveholders recognized that they were "of different Provinces or Clans, and not under the same Prince or Chief, nor do They speak the same language." According to James Knight, Jamaican slaveholders preferred to own people who came from the better-known African polities near the coast, with whom Europeans had long maintained trading relations. These Africans were familiar with regimented labor, and their accustomed diet of maize, plantains, yams, and other ground provisions could be easily supplied in Jamaica. Coromantees were "ingenious," wrote Knight, and in their youth could be "easily taught any Science or Mechanick Art." He even praised them for being "neat & cleanly," with good dental hygiene.[5]

Celebrated for physical strength, mental acuity, and disciplined manners, Coromantees appealed to planters as ideal instruments of their desire to profit from colonial settlement. The planters sometimes perceived in these particular Africans distinctive skills that would serve them well in certain specialized roles of slave society. The nautical talents of the coastal peoples could make them ideal pilots, sailors, canoemen, and fishermen. To most of those from the forest belt, the Jamaican bush was not impenetrable, although it remained dangerous. People from the mountainous areas could steward goods along Jamaica's steep and winding pathways. And the military bearing of some Coromantee men made them ideal drivers of other slaves, and even exemplars of a certain kind of mastery.

In early 1750, the Board of Trade, which at the time included William Pitt, conducted a hearing on the further liberalization of trade to Africa. While the various witnesses differed over how to achieve the greatest benefit to imperial enterprise, both sides agreed that the trade to the Gold Coast was their most valuable branch, and that Africans from the region were the most desirable of human commodities, considered to be "fitter for labor" than others and "absolutely necessary" for the success of the colonies. Traders asserted that "the planters had rather give £40 for a Gold Coast slave than £20 for a Calabar" from the Bight of Biafra. A slave-ship captain with long experience in the trade likewise maintained that Africans bought windward of the Gold Coast "do not stand so well on board, and are not so good to the planters." Slaves from the Gold Coast were so desirable that traders tried to pass off captives from other regions as Coromantees. The ship captain had himself "sold Windward slaves for Gold Coast, the planters being often deceived" by the fervency of their demand.[6]

In Jamaica, the planters' special preference for Coromantees coincided with a rampant hunger for laborers. In the fast-growing colony, planters lamented that the island was still "not one-tenth settled" in 1750.[7] Slaves were desperately needed for the brutal and killing work of clearing and cultivating the land, and slavery grew rapidly in the parishes where new lands came into tillage after an internal war with the maroons ended in 1739. The enslaved populations of outlying and formerly marginal parishes such as St. James, Hanover, St. Mary, and St. Thomas in the East increased dramatically through the middle of the century, drawing in a disproportionate share of those newly arrived from Africa.[8]

Even in more established parishes like Westmoreland, where there were already more than eleven thousand slaves in 1740, planters were eager to exploit more Africans, especially from the Gold Coast. People from that region made up nearly one-third of the two hundred fifty slaves on James Woodcock's Westmoreland plantation—the remainder included a hundred creoles and seventy from other regions, including "Ebors Calabars etc." By 1750, Woodcock had cultivated three hundred of his estate's eleven hundred acres, backed up against the mountains a short distance from Thomas Thistlewood's Egypt and Arthur Forrest's Masemure estates, and leaving great areas of hilly woodland sloping up through the untamed areas between the Westmoreland, Hanover, and St. James parishes. Testifying before the Board of Trade, Woodcock confirmed that he had heard planters "complain for want of Gold Coast slaves" and that they generally "would rather chuse a majority of Gold Coast negroes" for their plantations. Owning eighty himself, he wanted no more. He found them to be "a dangerous people," prone to rebellion.[9]

Woodcock's hesitation pointed to the double-edged nature of the slaveholders' esteem. As most well knew, the same traits they admired in Coromantees made them exceedingly threatening as enemies. "They are not only the best and most faithful of our slaves," the slaveholding Governor Co-drington of the British Leeward Islands had written in 1701, "but are really all born Heroes." He maintained this even upon hearing that fifteen Coromantees had slain Major Samuel Martin, a prominent planter and speaker of the House of Assembly in Antigua. "There is a difference between them and all other negroes beyond what 'tis possible for your Lordships to conceive," he reported to the Board of Trade. Martin must have been "guilty of some unusual act of severity, or rather some indignity towards the Corramantes," Codrington rationalized. He inferred from his own experience and from that of his father, who had held enslaved Africans for forty-five years, that Coromantees were "grateful and obedient to a kind master, but implacably revengeful when ill-treated."[10] As such, Coromantees represented both hazard and opportunity.

More than any other Africans, Coromantees had a worrisome reputation for rebellion. British commentators nearly always tempered their praise for the Coromantees' attractive qualities with warnings about their supposedly warlike disposition. "They are Fractious, and in Their Nature Deceitful, Revengefull & blood thirsty," wrote Knight. They might be favored as slaves, but masters could be ruined by failing to respect the potential danger that Coromantees presented. They "require a stricter hand being kept over Them, than those of any other Country," Knight urged, "for which reason every prudent Planter is cautious of having too many of Them in his Plantation; and therefore the common Custom is to mix other Countries with Them." Knight and others believed that Coromantees posed a singular threat: "There never was as I have heard of in this or any other Colony any Plot or conspiracy but They were at the bottom of it." He and other slaveholders had formed these views from a combination of conventional perception, historical precedent, direct experience, and tenacious prejudice.[11]

Somewhat paradoxically, this stereotyping probably encouraged slaveholders to give Coromantees special roles and favors. What little is known about the selection of plantation drivers—those most directly responsible for enforcing discipline among the work gangs—suggests that they were most often Jamaica-born creoles.[12] Yet slaveholders consistently valued Gold Coast Africans highly enough to elevate them above others in the plantation hierarchy. Arthur Forrest's Wager, for example, served as a headman on Masemure plantation after serving aboard a Royal Navy warship. So, it seems, did the future rebel leader Tacky, who labored on an estate in Jamaica's rapidly growing St. Mary's Parish, which had recently absorbed many enslaved arrivals from the Gold Coast. Given his name, which was also the term in the Ga language for a man of royal office or lineage, Tacky would appear to have been a man of political and military importance from the area near Accra, and a Coromantee when he arrived in Jamaica.[13] Perhaps the martial prowess that slaveholders perceived in Coromantee men resonated with the personal characteristics of their own mastery, which was militaristic and therefore capable of powerful assertions of will, and at the same time destructive—fractious, revengeful, and bloodthirsty. These were the kind of people who could make great empires—and destroy them, as well.

Slaveholders did not know much about the African societies and histories that made their captives who they were, but they distinguished among them nonetheless by drawing upon stories that had long circulated in print and by word of mouth. Their perceptions cohered around their view of the Gold Coast as a particularly war-torn region of the African continent. Long European interaction with this part of coast, and a prominent English presence there, gave them some faint ideas of state development, warfare, and enslavement in Africa. In America, British colonists traded stories of multiple Coromantee rebellions in the hemisphere and pondered their implications for patterns of slave recruitment, management, and repression, comparing what they knew of others' experiences with their own customary practice. They knew very little about how Coromantees identified with one another beyond the similarities in their languages, or how they organized and sought to maintain group cohesion—nor did they much care.

In recent historical analysis, the Coromantees have been described as members of a "loosely structured organization of co-nationals who socialized with and aided one another," forming what contemporaries called a "nation" in the Americas. There was no direct antecedent to this "ethnicity" on the Gold Coast, where a common tongue was not enough to supersede local divisions. The nation comprised people who shared what are today known as Akan and other regional languages, recognizably familiar religious practices, some similar political ideals and symbols, and many principles of communal incorporation. Among their countrymen, Africans would recognize similar ways of worshiping the divine, gathering in fellowship, and burying the dead. As a basis of social communion in an environment where dislocation was the common experience, the nation could also provide a forum for planning, organizing, and staging revolts.[14]

Coromantees in the Americas could sometimes be recognized by their names. Slaveholders renamed their human property at will, choosing generic tags, pet diminutives, place names, literary allusions, or classical Roman appellations. These were ordinary expressions of contempt, meant to overlay African origins with the emblems of their oppressors. Sometimes, however, slaveholders chose African names, and just as often they didn't bother to give new names at all, leaving slaves to name themselves. It was customary in Gold Coast societies to name children for the day of the week on which they were born. These day names appear frequently in the records, transcribed phonetically (and ethnocentrically) by English-speakers. Sunday through Saturday—Kwesi, Kojo, Kwabena, Kweku, Yaw, Kofi, and Kwame—were prevalent versions of the male names, corresponding to Akosua, Adwoa, Abenaa, Akua, Aba, Afua, and Amma for females. Slaveholders would change Kwesi to Quashie, Kojo to Cudjoe, and Kwaku to Quack—or, to make that even more familiar, Jack—but the sound of the names largely kept its integrity. Amongst each other, Coromantees such as Kojo and Akyeampong kept their naming traditions alive. Eventually, names from the Gold Coast became common enough that they were given by slaveholders without regard to an African's place of origin, especially in the case of highly valued men with skilled jobs or authority over other slaves. The preponderance of these names indicated the strong presence and influence of the Coromantees in Jamaican slave society.[15]

As a designation, *Coromantee* itself appeared frequently in English-language texts. In a database of runaway-slave advertisements in eighteenth-century Jamaican newspapers, the term appears in a variety of spellings—Calamante, Calamantine, Caramote, Caramantine, Cormantine, and Coromantine—until about the 1750s, by which time it was uniformly written as Coromantee. Later in the century, the listings distinguished Coromantees from Ashantees and Fantees, perhaps reflecting the expansion of Asante and the consolidation of the Fante Confederacy in the second half of the century, when these nations' political distinctions were even more pronounced. As prevalent as the Coromantees were, such changes remind us not to confuse the consolidation of the spelling with the coherence of the cultural identity.[16]

In fact, as a category of belonging, "Coromantee" was crosscut by many other axes of identification. Coromantees spoke more than one language and came from many different regions and kingdoms, from which they brought a variety of historical experiences.[17] Just as importantly, once in Jamaica, they served different roles in the slave society. No amount of cultural similarity could resolve all the difficult negotiations of multiple interests and experiences among them. Even with their compatriots, enslaved Africans made friends and foes through a politics of belonging that made the debate about what it meant to be Coromantee in Jamaica as urgent as the forging of the identity itself. In the face of continual assaults on their personal dignity, slaves distinguished themselves by their political commitments as much as by ascribed classifications. Among the Coromantees, different ideas of how to live in slave society, how to evade its worst abuses, and how to destroy it altogether shaped their rebellions even as they re-called their prior experiences in Africa. This was an inherently unstable and contingent process, which raises doubts about the extent to which the Coro-mantee ever truly become one people. Rather, out of many came many others.

This process played out across the treacherous martial geography that connected the Gold Coast to the Americas. The places slaves came from, the routes they traveled, and the places they went to all contributed to their political understanding. As they became Coromantees, enslaved Africans defined new spatial networks, attached distinctive meanings to places, and called upon their senses of locality to draw the boundaries that distinguished safe places from dangerous ones and outsiders from insiders. In the turbu-lent world of Atlantic warfare, nothing was more important than learning where and how to form loyal units, alliances, and coalitions in the face of superior power. They had won this wisdom through hard experience on the Gold Coast before coming to America, where they learned it anew and with different particulars. When enslaved Coromantees made war on their masters, they used these insights to chart courses through the fissures in colonial sovereignty.

Densely settled with populous towns and interconnected with long-established trading routes, the Gold Coast had become a major region of departure for African slaves in the last half of the seventeenth century. The English had first established their trade at Cormantyn in 1618 and began building their first fort there in 1638. Trading more actively for gold than for slaves at first, they soon came to label all the people they purchased there after their place of embarkation. The Dutch did the same after they displaced the English in 1665. Even after the English had established their administrative center at Cape Coast Castle and after Anomabo had become their busiest trading center in the eighteenth century, some version of *Cor-omantee* remained the acknowledged name for their captives from the region.[18]

The slave trade fed upon conflict. In the 1660s, even before slaves overtook gold as the region's principal export, Wilhelm Johann Müller, a Lutheran priest in the service of the Danish African Company, noted that "neighboring countries and domains in Guinea live in perpetual disunity and open war." Polities in close proximity fought to claim tribute, to settle grudges and matters of honor, and to extend their frontiers. The social elite drew soldiers from across the community; Müller described how they would "scrape together as many of their people, both freemen and bondsmen, as they can possibly provide and afford," excepting women and children, who

FIGURE 3.1. Fort Amsterdam, Cormantyn, late 17th century.

From Willem Bosman, *A New and Accurate Description of the Coast of Guinea* (London, 1705). *Courtesy of Tozzer Library, Harvard University.*

stayed at home or sought protection in other allied countries. Leading the soldiers in battle were the military captains, called *braffos* among the Fante. Already in the mid-seventeenth century these men were among the most prominent in Gold Coast polities, and their importance would only increase with the progressive militarization of African societies.[19]

These earlier intra-African conflicts, while frequent and violent according to European accounts, were often small-scale affairs. Describing the country of Fetu, which encompassed Cape Coast Castle, Müller noted how the wars usually ended in two or three days, with contending belligerents "usually content with a hard fight, especially when they notice that one of the parties in dispute is a match for the other."[20] Europeans often admired Africans' skill with weaponry, even if the observers were confused by native military strategies and tactics. Locally made hand spears, throwing spears, swords, and bows were supplemented by guns purchased from Europeans. Müller was especially impressed by how skillfully they used shields to defend against hard blows and projectiles. He watched military exercises that featured techniques of close combat, evasive maneuvers, and individual flare:

> One man displays with his shield and javelin how he will encounter the enemy in battle. Another makes all kinds of cuts and thrusts with his bare sabre: sometimes he throws the bare sabre in the air with one hand and catches it with the other; sometimes he swirls it around his head; sometimes he displays how he will decapitate the enemy. Another makes similar motions with his musket: at one moment he lays it down, to lie in wait for the approaching enemy; then he again raises himself a little, to see if the enemy has not marched off; then he creeps forward on his knees, to draw nearer to the enemy, unsuspected; then he fires his musket and acts as if he has shot the enemy.[21]

Such public drills advertised the martial prowess of individual warriors even as they honed their skills with weapons both of long-standing use and of more recent adoption, like the latest firearms imported from Europe.

Willem Bosman, the chief Dutch agent at Elmina in the late seventeenth century, was similarly impressed by Africans' dexterity with muskets and carbines during exercises. "They handle their Arms so cleverly," he wrote, "discharging them several ways, one sitting, the second creeping, or lying, &c. that 'tis really to be admired they never hurt one another." But Africans' individual skill in hand-to-hand fighting impressed Europeans more than their overall military effectiveness, accustomed as Europeans were to different kinds of regimental discipline. Bosman thought Africans on the Gold Coast were "very irregular in their Engagements, not observing the least shadow of Order." Their skirmishing tactics baffled him, and he castigated them for failing to hold firing lines in attack and defense. "In fight the Negroes don't stand upright against one another," he complained, "but run stooping and listening that the Bullets may fly over their Heads." With racist condescension, Bosman wrote that the Africans' "ridiculous Gestures, stooping, creeping and crying, make their Fight look more like Monkeys playing together than a Battle." Yet these same tactics kept Europeans at bay on the African coast and would give colonial militias and imperial armies considerable trouble in the Americas.[22]

During these mid-seventeenth-century campaigns in Africa, establishing honors and distinctions was often more urgent than acquiring territory and trade. In their great exercises before the mêlée, soldiers displayed their battle dress, weapons, and ornamentation, which signaled rank and status. Military victors displayed their trophies—often heads taken from their enemies—and recounted acts of valor in postbellum celebrations after the losers had fled the battlefield to escape death or enslavement. Rare was the widespread devastation of later wars, "where the enemy, having obtained the upper

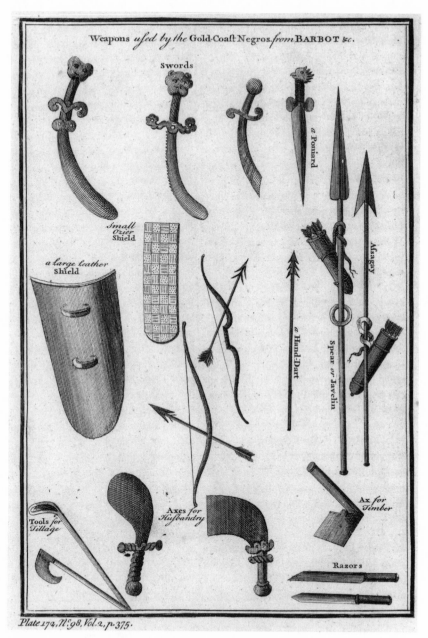

Weapons *used by the* Gold-Coast Negros. *from* BARBOT &c.

FIGURE 3.2. Gold Coast Weaponry, late 17th century.

Engraved by G. Child, from Thomas Astley and John Green, eds., *A New General Collection of Voyages and Travels,* 4 vols. (London, 1745–1747), plate 172, No. 98, vol. 2, 375. *Collection of the author.*

FIGURE 3.3. A Gold Coast Warrior, ca. 1750s. Pictured with sacred objects and adornments that conferred protection from enemies.

By Georg Wilhelm Bauernfeind, from Christian Lindholm Schmidt, *Beskrivelse over den her paa Kaabberstykket aftegnede Fri-Neger Qvou Ursovs Fetisserier og Krigs-Rustning, samt hvoraf same giøres . . .* (Copenhagen, 1761). Caption reads: "Qvou, son of Eikoe, born in the town of Ursue, at Accra on the Guinea Cost. This [engraving] illustrates the manner in which a prominent Negro is equipped when he goes into battle" [trans. Selena Axelrod Winsnes]. *Courtesy of the Kongelige Bibliotek, Copenhagen, Denmark.*

hand, practised great violence, stealing, plundering, burning the houses, particularly the corn huts which stood in the open fields, and laying waste to the whole country." These more destructive wars, which accompanied the expansion of the Atlantic trade in slaves and guns, featured states with greater ambitions and an enhanced capacity to project force across the land.[23]

From the 1650s to the 1680s, a military revolution spurred by competition among elite "big men" of the central forest region radically transformed Gold Coast warfare. Beginning in Denkyira and Akwamu, armies began to emphasize missile weapons, especially bows and arrows, over hand-to-hand fighting with javelins, clubs, and swords in their battle tactics. Increasingly, this came to mean the employment of guns as the decisive element in war. At the same time, armies swelled by mass conscription of commoners began to supplant modestly sized forces of professional soldiers. These developments magnified the scope and duration of wars. As great armies of more than ten thousand soldiers marched against each other and against smaller forces, war engulfed whole districts and provinces and could last for weeks or months.[24] Running through the Gold Coast's dense population, such wars left few noncombatants unaffected by the violence.

In the late seventeenth and eighteenth centuries, the region witnessed the transformation of major empires: Denkyira, Akwamu, Akyem, Asante, and the powerful coalition of Fante states, in addition to dozens of smaller polities, which vied with each other for dominance, influence, and autonomy.[25] The larger polities, which invested more heavily in the slave trade, mounted larger armies and fought more consequential campaigns, producing greater quantities of captives for sale. The smaller coastal states fielded armies of no more than two thousand men, but the Fante states could field twenty-five thousand and the kingdom of Akwamu an even larger force. Bosman had learned from the locals that the "Inland Potentates" such as Akyem and Asante far exceeded the coastal forces, "they being able to over-run a Country by their numerous Armies."[26]

As Europeans competed for trade, they distributed guns and powder along the coast and funneled them to the increasingly militarized African communities and battlefields in the interior.[27] "Years ago, with considerable justification, people had misgivings about trading muskets on the Guinea coast," Müller wrote in the mid-seventeenth century. "Nowadays, however, it has become a general free trade, so that one sees with amazement what quantities of old and new muskets are sold there."[28] At the turn of the century, Bosman explained how Europeans competed to supply weapons for African conflicts. "We are forced to it," he insisted, "for if we would not, they might be sufficiently stored with that Commodity by the

English, Danes, and *Brandenburgers;* and could we all agree together [not] to sell them any, the *English* and *Zeeland* Interlopers would abundantly furnish them: And since that and Gun-powder for sometime hath been the chief vendible Merchandise here, we should have found but an indifferent Trade without share in it."[29] With firearms lubricating the exchange, war and the slave trade would thrive in the decades ahead.

A rapid succession of military campaigns marked the political history of the region. In the thickly forested region that ran north from Cape Three Points, Denkyira expanded its conquests through the 1690s before the emergence of Asante at the beginning of the eighteenth century. Further up-country, as the land rose through hills toward the mountain range bordering the Afram River, Asante looked anxiously from its capital, Kumasi, toward the southeast, where Akyem, rich in gold and slaves, grew in strength between two prominent ridges of mountainous terrain. These two Akan powers fought a war in 1717 that ended in the death of Asante's founding ruler, Osei Tutu. Akyem bordered Akwamu, which straddled the forest, the mountains, and the coastal grasslands north of Accra.[30] Akwamu show-cased its remarkable power in the decades on either side of 1700, conquering Accra in a series of battles between 1677 and 1682 and driving its subjects east to Little Popo, before driving east itself in 1702 and north in 1707, dominating the trade from Accra to the Volta River, until their defeat by Akyem in 1730, which fell in turn to the ever-expanding Asante a dozen years later. Through the coastal thickets on the edge of the forest, a number of Fante states formed a coalition government in the 1730s for a common defense against Asante. As these powerful states jockeyed with each other and reduced many smaller polities to subjection, victories and defeats in their campaigns were seldom total and final. Leaders and soldiers in the losing states often regrouped, nursed their grievances, found allies among former enemies, and fought again another day.

This dynamic political climate encouraged the formation of shifting alliances, producing a turbulent social and political environment in which wars involved both European and African rivalries, multiple alliances, negotiations, and treachery.[31] There was often a mercenary incentive, but alliances were also necessary for political survival against more powerful forces. Such compacts were sealed by solemn oaths. Swearing to assist each other "with utmost Vigour to Extirpate the Enemy," the parties to an agreement would customarily ingest a potion mixed and consecrated by a spiritual authority. They believed that the brew had the power to kill false witnesses and oath-breakers, who would be "swelled by that Liquor till he bursts; or if that doth not happen, that he shall shortly dye of Languishing Sickness." While there often remained ways to slip out of the contracts or to renegotiate the terms at a later time, these oaths offered a powerful way to organize for new campaigns.[32]

Most famously, the fractious Fante states had by the 1730s created a coalition to resist the advance of Asante. In the 1740s, they forged a timely alliance with Wassa and Twifo, two formidable inland states that paid tribute to Asante but nonetheless buffered the Fante from Kumasi's expansion. Yet, in the 1750s, during a period of civil strife in Asante following the death of its king, Opoku Ware, the Fante coalition helped Asante to suppress a rebellion of several vassal polities, including Wassa, Twifo, Denkyira, and Akyem.[33] In practice, these changing allegiances facilitated temporary security for some amid continuous warfare for all, and the increased production and circulation of slaves enhanced the wealth of empires on both sides of the Atlantic Ocean.

War and conquest also stimulated important cultural transformations. Not only did smaller states come to pay tribute to the expansionist states, they also learned and adopted second and third languages and new mores and customs. These wars led to greater familiarity with the family of Akan languages throughout the region—as well as with the trade languages developed along the coast—even among speakers of Ga, Adangme, and Ewe in the areas along either side of the Volta River. The process made a common set of symbols and cultural practices widely available. Throughout the region between the mountains and the coast, people recognized and often adopted Akan names, worshipped in similar ways, employed similar practices of divination, and were conversant with each other's folktales. They acknowledged comparable emblems of state power and principles of social hierarchy, even when they fought over how these should apply in particular circumstances. If the social elite legitimated their claims to territory and power by referring to the long endurance of their blood-kinship lineages, commoners had to make their claims more immediately and opportunistically, by demonstrating facility with the cultural practices of the powerful.[34]

As Africans migrated, interacted, and incorporated each other's ways of life into their own, the region's social turbulence required considerable cultural dexterity, especially for non-Akan-speakers subject to the rule of the Akan empire-states. What they shared made them familiar to each other and enabled them to communicate in the Americas, especially when they were thrown together with Africans from different parts of the continent—but, nonetheless, these were in no way a homogenous people. In America, as in Africa, they would compete for status, resources, and power, meager as these were under conditions of slavery. Markers of affiliation and performances of belonging served both competitive and collaborative ends.[35]

Just as important as these signals of identity and affiliation were the immediate experiences of warfare, dislocation, and capture that Africans learned to cope with during the period. The military theater in Africa left an enduring impression on belligerents and noncombatants alike. Extensions in the scale and scope of regional warfare transformed conceptual geographies, reorienting approaches to space. As political danger intensified with the expansion of the slave trade, the peoples of weaker and smaller polities strove to build more defensible villages in remote areas, including inaccessible islands in rivers and lagoons, dense forests, and hilly enclaves. Moving along established trading paths that were intermittently blocked in times of conflict, or marching to war along the great roads constructed by emerging empires like Asante, or fleeing invading armies on winding footpaths and animal trails, denizens of the Gold Coast acquired a comprehensive sense of the region and a fine sense of the places within it where they could be secure from aggression or enslavement.[36]

Those thousands who fell captive moved through numerous coffles and collection points in the interior and then, if destined for sale to the Europeans, to the dank barracoons on the coast. There, they "observed the regular arrival of new prisoners in the coastal factories, the disappearance of those who died or escaped, and periodically, the departure of those who were led out by the castle slaves and never returned again."[37] The knowledge gleaned from these movements was as important a part of their experience as their ancestral customs. The history that Africans carried from the Gold Coast to the Americas had as much to do with immediate understandings of landscape and maneuver—finding spaces of egress, choosing battlegrounds, and making allies—as with becoming Coromantee. These modes of orientation were, in fact, an important aspect of what it meant to be Coromantee. In slavery, the lessons they had learned in their pasts addressed urgent circumstances as they continued to fight other Africans, other enslaved black people, and other whites, as well.

European slave ships swelled with the captives of these expansionary African wars. Exports of slaves from the Gold Coast spiked from fewer than a thousand in the 1650s to nearly thirty thousand during the period between 1661 and 1680 as the military revolution took hold, then dropped back somewhat for the rest of the century before leaping again to forty thousand in the first decade of the eighteenth century and fifty thousand in the second, as war engulfed the region. As many as seventy thousand and no fewer than forty thousand Africans were shipped away from the coast during each of the four decades between 1720 and 1760. Between 1641 and 1700, the Gold Coast exported a total of about fifty-eight thousand slaves to the Europeans; between 1701 and 1760, the number was nearly

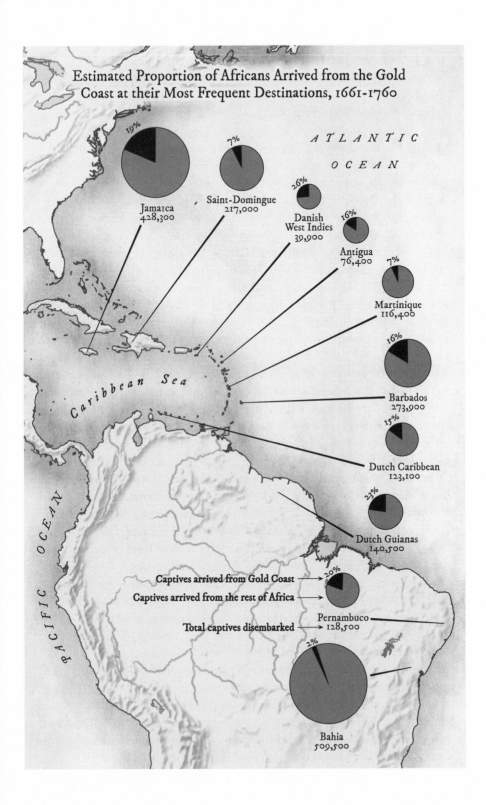

Estimated Proportion of Africans Arrived from the Gold
Coast at their Most Frequent Destinations, 1661-1760

ATLANTIC

OCEAN

19%

Jamaica
428,300

7%

Saint-Domingue
217,000

26%

Danish
West Indies
39,900

16%

Antigua
76,400

7%

Martinique
116,400

16%

Barbados
273,900

15%

Dutch Caribbean
123,100

22%

Dutch Guianas
140,500

Caribbean Sea

PACIFIC OCEAN

Captives arrived from Gold Coast →

Captives arrived from the rest of Africa →

20%

Total captives disembarked →

Pernambuco
128,500

2%

Bahia
509,500

328,000. Heavy concentrations of these captives originated in the coastal, forested, near-inland areas, as well as the eastern mountainous regions caught in the upheavals of the era.[38]

Between 1661 and 1760, slave ships transported more than three hundred and fifty thousand Africans from the Gold Coast across the Atlantic Ocean. They concentrated more than three-quarters of them in the colonies of the British, Dutch, and Danish, who maintained the most active trading companies and forts on the Gold Coast. Nearly seventeen percent went to the Dutch Guianas and Dutch Caribbean islands. The Danes imported Africans from the region in numbers well out of proportion to their share of Atlantic trade, carrying some three and a half percent of the total, and these captives formed the overwhelming majority of their small plantation societies. The French Caribbean received nine percent—most of these arriving in St. Domingue and Martinique—though the French boosted their share to a third of the total during the 1740s, when they posed their most serious challenge to British traders in the region. Nearly twelve percent arrived in Brazil, with a majority of these going to Pernambuco. But the English captured the majority, with Jamaica as their principal destination. More than fifty percent of all Africans shipped from the Gold Coast went to the British Caribbean—forty-six percent to Antigua, Barbados, and Jamaica alone—and another three percent went to mainland North America. Barred by treaty and long-standing practice from trading directly with Africa, the Spanish received fewer than two percent of captives directly from the region, although they received many more, especially at Cartagena and Porto Bello, through the inter-American trade with places like Jamaica.[39]

Jamaica took more than eighty thousand, a full twenty-seven percent of the total. During the decade immediately preceding the 1760 insurrection there, coinciding with the period of civil strife following Opoku Ware's death and Asante's war with its neighbors, more than forty percent of Africans shipped from the Gold Coast to the Americas landed in Jamaica. Many of these people, who numbered more than twenty-two thousand, had been swept up in the same campaigns and battles, knew each other, had fought alongside one another, and had been enemies or allies, or even family members. Many of the captives had been soldiers. Many more had been victimized by war. These people would discover that war was still frequently at hand in the Americas, even though the slaveholders had mostly recruited them for non-military work.[40]

Concentrated as they were in the Caribbean, Africans from the Gold Coast reckoned with analogous landscapes.[41] After growing up in tropical forests, wooded highlands, and coastal lowlands, most arrived on the volcanic tropical islands to find an ecology that looked like a condensed exag-

geration of their homelands, with familiar features jammed into a minia-
ture surrounding. Dense vegetation hugged the shorelines and bordered
man-made savannas, partitioned and overlain with row after row of crops.
Mountains rose sharply from the sea, cragged with deep forested gorges.
This was the terrain where they labored, where they sought refuge from
slavery, and where they organized revolts against new enemies.

THE Coromantees first achieved widespread notoriety among English
speakers with the publication in 1688 of Aphra Behn's *Oroonoko: or, the
Royal Slave*. The fictional story features an enslaved African prince, the last
of his royal line, from Coramantien; he is described as "very warlike and
brave, and having a continual campaign, being alwzays in hostility with
one neighboring prince or other"—a description that fit English royalty
just as well. Behn may have been in Surinam in 1663, just two years before
the Second Anglo-Dutch War (1665–1667), during which she worked as an
English spy in Antwerp. She surely celebrated when English forces sacked
scores of Dutch plantations and seized their slaves, introducing great numbers
of captives from the Gold Coast to British colonies even before the great
expansion in British transatlantic slave trading. Behn's narrative draws on
this turbulent history of wars within wars. Enslaved by treachery, Oroonoko arrives in Surinam during its brief period as an English colony, before
it was captured by the Dutch in 1667. There he meets the narrator, who
recounts the story of his tragic love, rebellion, and execution. Adapted for
the stage by Thomas Southerne in 1695 and published as the play *Oroonoko: A Tragedy* in 1696, the story remained continuously in print throughout
the eighteenth century and helped to define the image of Coromantees as
noble but bellicose people who could arouse the sentiments of readers, the-
atergoers, and perhaps slaveholders, too.[42]

The story of Oroonoko's rebellion raised awareness of the long history
of Coromantee slave revolts that had begun not long after the military
revolutions in the Akan states and the export of waves of captives to the
Americas in the mid-seventeenth century. Of course, Coromantees did not
lead all the slave revolts and plots known to colonists; wherever there was
slavery, there were slaves plotting and rebelling.[43] But observable patterns
and confirmation bias combined to convince the British that Coromantee
revolts were a special problem. Colonists, already assuming that Coromantees were rebellious, received news of each new rebellion with heightened interest. Accounts of many of these revolts circulated widely, framing
the perceptions of slave insurrection as it happened. And the descriptions
were never presented in isolation; they were attached to widely dissemi-
nated portrayals of similar events.[44] Some were exaggerated, yet they were

rarely pure fictions or wholly contained within European perceptions. Violence provoked stories of violence; war was a subject of interest because it was ubiquitous.

In 1676, English colonists throughout America read a vivid account of a rebel plot in Barbados the previous year by many "Cormantee or Gold-Cost Negros." They had chosen a king, seated him upon a stool of state, and planned to "fire the Sugar-Canes" and "Cut their Masters the Planter Throats in their respective Plantations whereunto they did belong." Rumors of two subsequent Barbados conspiracies circulated in 1683 and 1692, although these were said to involve more than just Coromantees. In Antigua, organized bands of runaway slaves, including Coromantees, threatened the plantation colony through the late seventeenth century, even before Coromantees killed a prominent planter in 1701. Africans from the Gold Coast and Popo, along with some "Spanish Indians," staged a bloody uprising in New York in 1712: numbering about thirty people, armed with guns, clubs, and cutting tools, they killed nine whites and wounded seven others before Governor Robert Hunter could raise the militia to suppress them.[45]

Readers of Captain William Snelgrave's *New Account of Some Parts of Guinea,* published in 1734, learned about how Coromantees—"stout stubborn People" who were "never to be made easy," according to Snelgrave—rose up aboard the slave ship *Henry* in 1721. Eight Africans slipped their irons, attacked the sentries, and leapt into the ocean before being recovered and recaptured by the sailors. Through a translator, the captives told Snelgrave that he was a "great Rogue to buy them, in order to carry them away from their own Country; and that they were resolved to regain their Liberty if possible." A few days later, Snelgrave discovered that they were indeed "plotting again, and preparing to mutiny." Before they had their chance, another uprising occurred aboard the *Elizabeth,* anchored near the *Henry* at Anomabo. A few recently embarked Coromantees killed the ship's cooper and tried to swim ashore. Having caught two of the rebels and discovered which of them had killed the cooper, Snelgrave gathered the commanders of the other ships nearby to stage an execution. They ordered all their captives upon deck to watch as sailors hoisted the accused killer upon the foreyard arm and ten men shot him to death with their muskets. "The body being let down upon the Deck, the Head was cut off, and thrown overboard." Two days later, loaded with the *Elizabeth's* other captives, the *Henry* sailed from Anomabo with 650 slaves for Jamaica, where the crew sold 562 survivors of the voyage.[46]

Many in Jamaica probably heard of this event by word of mouth in the 1720s. When others read about it during the 1730s, they considered it alongside a sharp downturn in the price of sugar and the fortunes of agricultural commerce. In this context, planters anxiously heeded reports of any threat to their fragile profit margins—and, in the 1730s, Africans from the Gold Coast were creating a new wave of rebellions in the Caribbean. Slave-holders followed news of the uprising that broke out on the Danish island of St. John in November 1733. Starting with an attack on the fort at Coral Bay, an army of "Aminas" from the eastern Gold Coast took and held the island for several months. While few planters would have been aware of it, the rebel Africans were the remnants of the Akwamu political-military ar-istocracy, recently defeated on the Gold Coast by Akyem. Danish offi-cials received aid from French troops stationed at Martinique, who ar-rived in late April 1734 and pursued the counter-revolt through the end of May. Local militia finally regained control of the colony for the slave-holders in late August, thereby preventing the resurrection of Akwamu in the Caribbean.[47]

Soon afterward, planters received news of a foiled conspiracy on Antigua. In 1736, Coromantees led by a man named Court, also referred to by the Ga royal title of "Tackey," formed a plot with a creole master carpenter named Tomboy, who helped to recruit other creole craftsmen and drivers into their plan to assassinate the governor and the most prominent planters and then seize the island. Accompanied by military officers and lieutenants— referred to as *braffos,* following the Gold Coast practice—as well as by *obeah* doctors who administered binding loyalty oaths, Court staged an elaborate coronation ceremony to announce his authority. But traitors be-trayed the conspiracy, and the slaveholders reacted with brutal vengeance fueled by panic. They executed Court, Tomboy, and ten other accused ring-leaders soon after discovering the design of the revolt, then widened the scope of their retaliation. By May 1737, the slaveholders had executed eighty-eight slaves—burning seventy-seven of them alive—and banished nearly fifty others from the island.[48]

Colonists who surveyed the broader world of Atlantic slavery also heard news of Coromantee uprisings beyond the British orbit, which indicated that the geography of slave unrest corresponded more to patterns of mi-gration than to the territorial boundaries of empires. Slaves shipped from the Gold Coast via Jamaica participated in revolts in Spanish New Granada, forming maroon communities near Cartagena. Portuguese and Brazilian ships imported rebels to Brazil.[49] In Surinam, the Dutch fought intermit-tently with rebel slaves and maroons, many of them from the Gold Coast or descended from Coromantees, from 1690 through the 1740s and 1750s. A peace treaty signed with Saramaka maroons in 1749 provided only a brief respite from the persistent conflict, which lasted until the maroons ultimately won their independence in 1762.[50]

Given the preponderance of revolts led by enslaved Coromantees in Jamaica and beyond, many observers have focused on their backgrounds—ethnic origins, collective ideologies, and cultural orientations and practices—to describe and explain the insurrections. The Coromantees have been described as "essentially African in character" and style, aiming for the recreation of "Akan-style autocracy" or the "resurrection" of a culturally distinct ethnic group.[51] Such descriptions capture the extent to which Coromantee revolts shared common features. Conspirators and rebels often communicated their plans in "the Coromantee language" and employed common cultural symbols and signs. They turned to obeah practitioners to administer loyalty oaths and offer spiritual consultation. They organized into companies with military captains. In battle and defeat, they showed a similar fortitude, often preferring suicide to capture and facing execution with a stoicism that impressed their enemies. Governor Codrington of Antigua wrote of this in 1701: "There never was a raskal or coward of yt. nation, intrepid to the last degree, not a man of them but will stand to be cut to pieces without a sigh or groan."[52] The emphasis on the Coromantees' African background, however, has meant that more immediate and material aspects of their warfare have been less explored.

Differing ambitions, diverging interests, and practical disagreements helped shape the course of events, even when insurgents were of the same cultural group. The making of a common group consciousness in the Americas was not a sufficient condition for political unity.[53] An ethnic group did not make a political alliance. Of course, an ethnic bond *could* facilitate cooperation, but it did not necessarily or automatically do so. Enslavement blurred some distinctions even as it created others, so that the social conditions of slavery proved as consequential as the cultural distinctions made by Africans in diaspora. Even on the depersonalizing slave ships, Europeans chose the earliest Africans boarded to guard the later acquisitions.[54] Because the Coromantees of Jamaica were a loosely connected and broadly distributed population, their political strength was latent. Group cohesion had to be created with an eye to local situations through the wrangling, persuasion, and coercion that always defines politics. Such political action could unite Coromantees and bring others into league with them, but, just as easily, it could divide them and bring their strategies to ruin. Indeed, in Jamaica, the course of political struggle was determined more by political divisions among slaves, among Africans, and even among Coromantees than by their commonalities.

Transformations on the Gold Coast had taught Africans in that region to find ways of uniting competing factions to achieve common interests and to oppose the depredations of common foes, whether Akwamu, Asante, or the empires of Europe. These coalition-building strategies relied in the Americas, as they had in Africa, on collective promises consecrated by oaths, which secured bonds of political alliance for immediate purposes. One might see these oaths as an indication of ethnic similarity among people who shared a cultural understanding of the material and supernatural enforcement of sanctions. At the same time, however, the oaths were crucial to forging bonds of alliance precisely because the coalitions were so fragile— ethnic affinity was an insufficient basis for military order. Thus, where the British had their Articles of War, a code of law read out as an incantation, the Coromantees had their solemn oaths.[55]

Insurgents could be united by beliefs in the spiritual wisdom of ritual specialists, in the invulnerability supposed to be conferred by sacred spells, and in the honor of fellow conspirators. Obeah practitioners helped the rebel bands to solidify their unions. The eighteenth-century historian Edward Long described obeah as "a sort of witchcraft of most extensive influence. . . . [T]he authority which such of their old men as had the reputation of wizards, or Obeah-men, possessed over [slaves], was sometimes very successfully employed in keeping them in subordination to their chiefs."[56] The conspirators called upon the shamans to use their charms to protect them from bullets and to administer the binding pledges.[57] Spiritual counselors were crucial to rebel politics.

Even once rebels had agreed to collaborate, they faced the challenge of implementing their plans on the field of battle, where they contended with the very material demands of particular landscapes. This was as true on oceanic slave ships, in colonial towns, and on island plantations as on the Gold Coast itself. Indeed, it may be that Africans' geographic provenance from coastal, forested, or mountainous regions was as salient as their linguistic and cultural origins. Rebels mapped political opportunity by paying sharp attention to moments and spaces that afforded the best possibilities for success. Slave-ship rebellions were most common within sight of land, when sailors were busy and distracted with trading and resupply, and where Africans could set their sights on a viable escape.[58] Rebels in cities congregated in taverns and on wharves, where comings and goings of strangers were difficult for officials to monitor. Runaway slaves in the Caribbean, with groups of newly arrived Africans strongly represented among them, headed directly to untamed stretches of bush, marsh, and mountain.[59]

Keenly attuned to their spatial situation as well as their political predicament, insurgents worked to build alliances amid the fractured sovereignty created by the colonies' physical and social geography. On a densely forested and mountainous island like Jamaica, the plantation frontier was both an asset provided to and a creation of the rebels. The frontier offered refuge from slavery, while the rebels' presence and activities in the wilds checked the expanse of slave-based agriculture. When rebels acted in concert, the plantation regime faced great danger and held back from the interior. When they were divided, the slaveholders and the British empire pressed their advantage. This dynamic was unmistakable in Jamaica during the long succession of revolts and small wars that preceded the Coromantee insurrection of 1760.

WITH increasing importations of Africans in the later decades of the seventeenth century, Jamaican colonists faced a seemingly unrelenting series of slave rebellions, culminating in a full-scale war with the maroons by the 1730s. Yet the rebels were united only in specific instances. Combining Coromantees with Africans from various regions and creoles born in slavery or among the maroons, they coalesced incompletely over time as they sketched their own political map of Jamaica's territory. Writing in the 1740s, with recent hostilities fresh in local memory, James Knight narrated the history of what historians now call the First Maroon War (the second would occur in the 1790s) as the merging of various rebel bands over several decades. Maroons continued to hold out in the windward (eastern) mountains, even as Jamaican plantation society swelled in the late 1600s with new arrivals from Africa. Runaways joined the existing camps when they could, adding slowly to their numbers, which increased more dramatically as the century drew to its close.[60]

In 1673, some two hundred people rose up in St. Ann's parish on the north side of the island. Described by Knight as "mostly Coromantines, a Fractious, Turbulent bloody minded People," they killed their master and a dozen other white men, seized all the arms and ammunition they found, and retreated to the mountains between the parishes of Clarendon and St. Elizabeth, where they offered a powerful example to slaves in the area.[61] In 1678, a rebellion on an estate near Spanish Town was less successful. But while nearly all the rebels were killed or recaptured, the gruesome tortures and executions that followed did not provide the deterrent hoped for by the planters. In 1685, on an estate in Guanaboa Vale, rebel slaves attacked the house of Major Francis Price. The colonists maintained an effective defense and had the good fortune to kill one of the rebels' "conjurors, on whom they chiefly depended." Retreating to a limestone outcrop, "an advantageous hill full of craggy rocks and stumps of trees," the rebels braced for battle with the reinforcements sent from Spanish Town. Losing half their number when the colonists stormed the hill, they split into three parties and retreated to the interior. One band, led by a Coromantee man named "Cophy," made its way north to St. Mary's Parish, where the rebels harried the isolated plantations for many months. Officials received news of Kofi's death in April 1686, but parties of regular troops and militia pursued the gang through the middle of 1687.[62]

Then, in 1690, on Sutton's mountainous estate in Clarendon Parish, the entire population of five hundred slaves rose up, set fire to the great house, and confiscated fifty muskets and an artillery piece. Loading the cannon with nails, they repulsed a militia party of fifty men, before retreating when reinforcements arrived. Colonial forces killed and captured scores in the ensuing pursuits, but hundreds remained free, including many women and children. As Knight recounted, many who escaped "also settled in the Mountains separately and under distinct Commanders, who were chosen among Themselves." One of these commanders fathered a son named Kojo—called Cudjoe by the British—who would become one of the most famous maroon leaders of the eighteenth century.[63]

Initially, according to Knight, various groups of maroons were "contented to hide Themselves in those Parts where They could subsist with out doing any Injury to the Planters or giving Them the least umbrage." But there were always necessary items that could be obtained only from the circuits of Atlantic commerce—especially textiles, arms, and ammunition. The rebels had to acquire these through nighttime raids on outlying plantations or through illicit trade. "Their success," Knight lamented, "not only animated Them, but encouraged several small Bodies of negroes to desert from the Plantations." Multiple gangs lived "some years in Their respective Retreats without any knowledge of each other, or of the Spanish Negroes." Yet they collectively presented an example that other slaves continued to emulate. Knight described another rebellion in 1718 in St. Elizabeth Parish, where a body of runaways "put Themselves under the command of a Madagascar Negroe, who was a Resolute Cunning Fellow." From their mountain settlements, they "inveigled many discontented Negroes from the Neighbouring Plantations and became considerable about the year 1720." Gradually, the maroons on the leeward (western) side of the island coalesced. Brought into contact by their pathways through the mountains, they began to fight each other over territory and tactics, to collaborate, and to incorporate. First, they combined into two groups, one under the command of the man said to be from Madagascar, the other consisting of the Coromantees who had liberated themselves from Sutton's estate. "After many disputes, and bloody Battles wherein a great number were slain on both sides," they united under Captain Kojo and began to pose an existential threat to the plantation colony.[64]

A parallel problem for the planters had developed to windward, in the imposing Blue Mountain range. There, maroons built villages and planted staple crops in the steep and secluded valleys. Although they, too, staged nighttime raids on isolated plantations, their numbers grew more slowly than those of the Leeward Maroons, with runaways joining them singly or in small groups. In time, however, they "began to grow Formidable by continual desertions and many hundred stout able Negroes being born in the Woods who were trained up to Arms." Their attacks having forced many planters to abandon frontier settlements by about 1730, these Windward Maroons had "entirely possessed or overrun" large tracts of northeastern Jamaica.[65]

Numbering in the thousands by the early eighteenth century, the Leeward and Windward Maroons established pathways through the island quite distinct from those of the colonists. They corresponded with each other over the mountains, they crept by secret passages down to the estates and traded contraband with slaves, and they descended from their elevated redoubts to the sea, where they caught fish and turtles and made salt.[66] Coalescing in distinct parts of the island, raiding estates, and interacting with the slaves within reach, they made themselves masters of rough tracts of land inaccessible to the whites. "They knew every secret avenue of the country," wrote the planter Bryan Edwards in his *History of the West Indies,* "so that they could either conceal themselves from pursuit, or shift their ravages from place to place, as circumstances required."[67] Their movements along "small foot-paths, in undiscernible windings, which could not be traced but with difficulty, except by themselves," constituted a region unknown to the planters and the colonial government, a *de facto* maroon sovereignty that subdivided the island.[68]

Maroon bands were governed by military and hereditary chains of command, with spiritual practice sustaining social integration. Rebel commanders were "by the Suffrage of the whole invested with an absolute power, which out of fear or necessity was continued to Their Heirs." Beneath the chief commanders, numerous captains were appointed, each chosen for his ability and having authority over as many people as the commander "thought proportionable to His Merit & Services." This structure offered incentive to the captains, whose responsibilities were to exercise the soldiers, instructing them "in the use of the land and small Arms, after the manner of the Negroes of the Coast of Guinea"; to plan and execute "bold Resolute and active" raids on the plantations; and to send out other men to hunt, fish, or help the women with planting.[69]

If military necessity governed maroon camps, collaboration within and across maroon groups required the kinds of coalition-building strategies that had worked in West Africa. Even though Coromantees were probably in the majority, rebel encampment communities were as polyglot as the plantations. Kojo, it was said, established English as an official language of communication to prevent the misunderstandings and quarrels that could arise given the diversity of origins. At some point, too, the maroons adopted the "Kromanti language"—derived from several Gold Coast tongues—as a unifying idiom.[70] Under the pressure of perpetual warfare, mistrust ran high, and runaways who made it to maroon encampments often served periods of probation before they earned the mountain peoples' trust.[71] The maroons' procedures for incorporation relied heavily on Kromanti religion, which ritualized the union of people from multiple lines of descent through oath-taking ceremonies, and the spiritual counsel of obeah practitioners.[72] Knight learned from a correspondent in Westmoreland Parish that the Leeward Maroons often consulted a "person whom they called Obia Man whom they greatly revered, his words carried the [force] of an Oracle with them."[73] More famously, the Windward Maroons turned to their priestess, Nanny, after whom they named their principal settlement above Stony River, and who remains a revered ancestor. These figures brought spiritual and social cohesion to people under extreme duress—and, as in West Africa, they performed the sacred services that bound different factions into a military alliance.[74]

Using Jamaica's uneven terrain to form rebel units and communities where the planters couldn't root them out, the maroons adapted their military tactics to the landscape. They established secure bases where the terrain was most forbidding to intruders but also offered rich soils that yielded corn, yams, and other edible roots.[75] The planters recognized this after capturing Nanny Town in 1732: "Having many Fastnesses and Places of Retreat when They were discovered and routed from one Settlement They retired to another, where our People could not follow not being well acquainted with the Mountainous Parts nor Capable of ascending Them, but with the greatest difficulties."[76] This facility with mountaineering suggests that Africans from regions of high elevation probably contributed disproportionately to the early development of the maroons' military maneuvers. Later, however, creole maroons had an important tactical advantage, "being from Their Infancy accustomed to steep Rocky Mountains," where "it was exceeding difficult & almost impracticable for white Persons to follow them."[77] By adapting to their surroundings, Africans and their descendants made new territories, domesticating Jamaica's wilderness in a way that was uniquely their own.

Maroons situated their camps so that they could be approached by just one or two narrow or rocky entrances, easily watched and guarded. "At the entrance into those avenues They kept a continual Watch or Centinel to prevent being surprised," Knight explained. "Upon the least appearance of danger He made the best of His way to the Town or gave a signal or alarm upon which every Man who was able to manage a lance or use Fire Arms immediately repaired to His Post under His respective Captain, which was in some ambuscade or Place that was easy to be defended."[78] As one of Jamaica's military governors complained, European troops were ill equipped to fight in this environment:

> The service here is not like that in Flanders or any part of Europe. Here the greatest difficulty is not to beat, but to see the enemy. The men are forced to march up the currents of rivers, over steep mountains and precipices without a track, through such thick woods that they are obliged to cut their way almost every step, the underwoods . . . being always exceedingly tough and bushy, twisted and entangled in a strange manner; add to this they frequently meet with torrents caused by heavy piercing rains that often fall in the woods and against which tents are no shelter. . . . In short, nothing can be done in strict conformity to the usual military preparations and according to a regular manner, bushfighting as they call it being a thing peculiar to itself.[79]

In the event that enemies successfully attacked their camps, the defenders made sure that the women and children were ready to escape rapidly to an appointed rendezvous at another settlement.[80] Outmaneuvering the colonists in this way, the maroons recaptured Nanny Town early in 1733.

Maroons used the landscape just as shrewdly on attack as on defense. They could emerge suddenly from the bush to raid estates and disappear as quickly. They surveilled troop movements from their positions on high ground, pushing rocks and boulders down upon the soldiers as they approached. They set booby traps in the murky woods. They used sound bouncing among the steep canyons to spook and confuse colonial troops, who had trouble distinguishing source from echo. When engaged directly, the maroons "constantly kept blowing Horns, Conch Shells, and other Instruments, which made a hideous and terrible Noise among the Mountains in hopes of terrifying our Parties, by making Them imagine Their Number & strength much greater than it really was," understood Knight.[81]

Psychological warfare was not the only purpose of the horns. They also helped to direct the maroons' adroit tactics with firearms. Without clear sight lines through the steep jungle, sound offered a better medium than vision for coordinating attacks.[82] Maroons had trained their hearing to be "wonderfully quick, that it enabled them to elude their most active pursuers," according to an early chronicler of their history. "They communicated with one another by means of horns; and when these could scarcely be heard by other people, they distinguished the order that the sounds conveyed."[83] These horns—*abeng,* as they were called on the Gold Coast—

helped to organize musters, tactical maneuvers, and major engagements on dense and uneven ground.[84]

A remarkable diagram of maroon infantry tactics in Surinam hints at how similar methods might have been used in Jamaica. In the 1770s, when the Dutch fought a protracted war against the Surinamese maroons, an English soldier named John Gabriel Stedman joined the Dutch counterinsurgency. From a black guide named Hannibal—and later from direct experience—Stedman learned something of what he called the "Manner of Bush-fighting by the African Negroes." The information he gathered recalls Bosman's descriptions of West African fighting. Hannibal told Stedman that maroon expeditions were divided into "small Companys of 8 or 10 Men & Commanded by one Captain With a horn," which signaled the major maneuvers of an engagement. When they chose to fight, the men in the company would separate, lie close to the ground—or, where the foliage was thick, prop their firearms on the limbs of trees—and fire "through the Green" at the flash of their adversaries' weapons. They would then shift position to reload, fire again, and move on, cutting kaleidoscopic angles through the battle space. Each shooter was accompanied by two men in support, one to take up the gun if and when the primary shooter fell, the other to carry away the body to prevent it from falling into the hands of the enemy. Given the scarcity of guns and ammunition, employing three men to each firearm also helped to make every shot count. The engagement would continue in this way until the sound of the horn signaled the retreat of one party or the other. These tactics tormented the Dutch in Surinam, much as similar methods distressed the British in Jamaica.[85]

Maroons' attacks grew increasingly daring. By the late 1720s, having defeated or frustrated numerous parties of colonists sent out against them, the maroons had sufficient strength to threaten Britain's hold on the island, at least as judged by official statements. In his June 1730 address to Jamaica's House of Assembly, Governor Robert Hunter, who had governed New York during the 1712 slave uprising, worried that the maroons had "grown to that height of insolence that your frontiers that are no longer in any sort of security, must be deserted, and then the danger must spread and come nearer if not prevented."[86] A year and a half later, despite the arrival of eight hundred regular troops from Gibraltar, his alarm had grown: "There never was a point of time which more required your attention to the safety of this island than at present; your slaves in rebellion, animated by their success, and others (as it is reported) ready to join them on the first favourable opportunity . . . all former attempts against these slaves having been either unsuccessful or to very little purpose."[87] Then, in 1733, the Windward

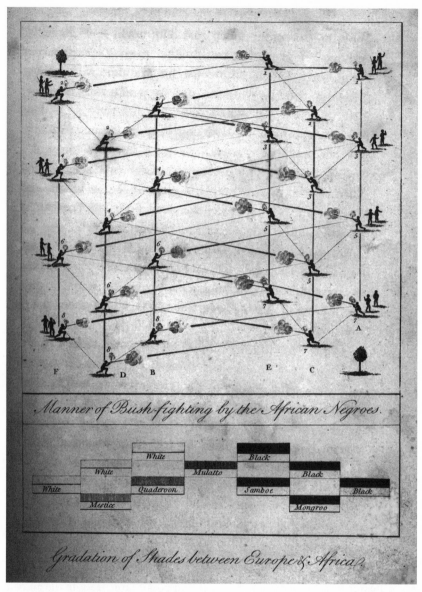

FIGURE 3.4. "Manner of Bush-fighting by the African Negroes." This illustration of a maroon firing drill in Surinam shows African infantry tactics in America employing a shifting "See Saw Manner," which continued until "by Sounding *the horn* one of the Parties gives Way by flight & the Battle is over."

From John Gabriel Stedman, *Narrative of a Five Years Expedition against the Revolted Negroes of Surinam* (London, 1790). *Courtesy of the Library Company of Philadelphia.*

Maroons defeated a "Grand Party" of one hundred soldiers and fifty sailors. Panic spread among the planters, who begged London for aid. "We are not in a Condition to defend ourselves," wrote one.[88]

Though the planters quavered on the edge of despair, the campaign against the maroons was not without some success. The government brought more troops and resources to bear, arming several parties of Indians from the Mosquito Coast of Central America and companies of slaves whom they called the Black Shots.[89] In April 1734, after a fierce and deadly battle lasting five days, the colonial forces took Nanny Town back again, set fire to the surrounding settlements, and destroyed nearby provision grounds. The colonists then improved their access to the mountains by cutting a road down to Port Antonio and continued to press their attacks.

The surviving maroons dispersed into smaller groups. Some, led by Nanny herself, resettled to the east. Another group traveled west to meet Kojo's band on the leeward side of the island, hoping to seal an alliance. Many of these established new homes in St. Elizabeth Parish, settling in and around Accompong Town. Others making up a large party stayed leeward for some time but were not permitted to settle permanently. By Knight's account, Kojo rebuffed them, "unwilling to receive another Body, who were Independent of Him, and subject only to Their own Chiefs who would not submit to Him." Kojo entertained them as guests but would not allow them to settle, so they returned to windward with their military capacity much reduced.[90]

Through the mid-1730s, British forces fought a protracted and indecisive struggle with the Leeward Maroons. The attrition of men, money, and munitions sapped the military, who anticipated war with Spain. Indeed, the colonists later learned that the maroons had been corresponding with the Spanish in Cuba, who promised to join them with ammunition and supplies "in order to reduce the Island and dispossess the English."[91] Frequent mustering of militia parties interrupted plantation production, and the maroons' raids stymied plans for the expansion of commercial agriculture. At the same time, open war depleted the maroons' soldiers and supplies, while the need for more frequent movement prevented them from cultivating their own crops. The maroons rejected a plea for peace in 1734, but by the time Edward Trelawny arrived to assume the governorship in 1738, both sides were ready for an armistice.[92]

An experienced soldier and statesman, Trelawny appointed a wealthy and well-respected Westmoreland Parish planter and militia officer named Colonel John Guthrie to lead an expedition to Kojo's town to negotiate a peace.[93] It is likely that either Trelawny or Guthrie—or both—had read the work of Santa Cruz de Marcenado, a Spanish soldier, diplomat, and military theorist whose influential *Reflexiones Militares* had been published in Spanish in eleven volumes between 1724 and 1730, and in a more widely read French translation between 1735 and 1740. In his suggestions on how to discover, prevent, and counter insurgencies, Marcenado advised clemency.[94] The Spanish had a long-standing practice of negotiating terms of peace with maroons in the Americas. Similarly, Guthrie believed that the only way to end the fighting would be to grant the maroons a "full and general pardon, on certain conditions," ratified and confirmed by an Act of the Jamaica Assembly. Trelawny accepted his proposal.

With about two hundred militia men, forty regular soldiers, and a number of volunteers from among the Westmoreland planters, Guthrie marched up into the mountains, fending off sporadic attacks. Knight recounted that some of the rebels personally knew several of the planters and "called to Them by Their Names, and with much abusive language, asked Them why They came out against Them, who never had done Them any Injury?" Drawing nearer to the town after two days of such "small Skirmishes and bitter reproaches," the colonists convinced the maroons to discuss a general truce.[95] During the great palaver between Kojo and Colonel Guthrie, the colonists hosted a reception and offered gifts, and the two sides exchanged hostages. Finally, they agreed upon a treaty.[96]

Signed March 1, 1739, the fifteen-article treaty formally ended the war with the Leeward Maroons, assured them of a "perfect state of freedom and liberty," and established an alliance between King George the Second and Captains Kojo, Accompong, Johnny, Cuffee, and Quaco. As for the Windward Maroons, who continued to fight for several more months, the colonists signed a similar agreement with their Captain Quao in July. The accords committed both groups to fight for Great Britain against its external and internal enemies, adding the maroons' military strength to the Jamaica garrison. In case of foreign invasion, the maroons were to deploy at the governor's request "in order to repel the said invaders" with "utmost force." The treaty with the Leeward Maroons obliged Captain Kojo and his successors to "use their best endeavours to take, kill, suppress, or destroy" all other rebels throughout the island. The Windward Maroons acquiesced to forming parties to fight rebels and capture runaways at the governor's request.[97] The maroons also agreed to return any future runaway slaves for a reward.

In return, the treaties ratified the maroons' mastery of the regions beyond slave society. Given the maroons' distinctive territorial claims, the agreement recognized their possession of fifteen hundred acres of land between their principal town (renamed Trelawny Town) and the Cockpit Country (so-called for its steep-sided hollows and conical hills) in the island's northwest, and also a similar area in the mountainous east. Here, they would be allowed to cultivate coffee, cocoa, ginger, tobacco, and cotton, and to keep, graze, and breed livestock. The maroons could also hunt game freely, except within three miles of a plantation. With licenses from local officials, they could bring their commodities to market, where they mingled with plantation slaves. Yet the colonists also hoped to reduce their own disadvantage in navigating the landscape of the interior. Select white men were to reside in the main maroon towns to maintain communication between the regions and to keep abreast of developments. The treaty also stipulated that the maroons "shall cut, clear, and keep open, large and convenient roads from Trelawny Town to Westmoreland and St. James's, and, if possible, to St. Elizabeth's." These roads would facilitate the movement of colonial troops, making it easier to keep the maroons in their designated places.

Almost certainly, the road-building produced unintended consequences, because plantation slaves worked on these roads, too. James Knight believed that because of the extent of the island and its topographical subdivisions, slaves had not been able to communicate across any great distance, "or if They had, it would be almost impossible They should join to Execute Their Designs." Building new roads into the interior gave slaves more familiarity with the landscape between plantations. Some of those who built these roads had probably worked on Asante's great road-building projects in the West African forest and had firsthand knowledge of how those roads facilitated military campaigns. Others soon learned that the new arteries intersected the capillary footpaths that enabled clandestine movement between the estates and the slaves' "friends in the mountains," as wary slaveholders continued to call the maroons.[98]

THE maroons had immediate opportunities to demonstrate their commitment to the new alliance—and to discover if the slaveholders would keep their own end of the bargain. Early in 1742, some enslaved Coromantees tried to escape into the forest but were caught and returned to the planters by Kojo's maroons. In exchange, Jamaican officials offered gifts: some cattle, five yards to each person of *osnaburg* (flax) cloth, and the freedom of one maroon captain's daughter-in-law, who was enslaved in the region.[99] The pact had passed an early test, yet Jamaica's slaves remained restive.

Late in 1744, with Britain again engaged in war with France, a dozen drivers on several neighboring plantations in Louidas Vale, St. John's Parish, conspired to wage a campaign against their oppressors. Led by a charismatic headman, said to be a "Favourite, a kind of Overseer, rather over the White Man of the plantation than under him," the drivers sought to use their position in the plantation hierarchy to organize the entire area's slaves for rebellion. They were betrayed by an enslaved man named Hector, who warned his mistress that she would be among the victims. She sent word to Governor Trelawny in Spanish Town, who immediately deployed a force to ambush the conspirators at their appointed meeting place. Catching them by surprise, the colonists apprehended more than a dozen slaves immediately and "continu'd to take more of them by Degrees."[100]

In the hasty and haphazard trials that followed, the colonists condemned the accused to be hanged, burned alive, or banished from the island. Of the seven executed, at least two had Gold Coast names. Among the five exiled conspirators was one named Shantee, possibly from the kingdom of the same name ruled by Opoko Ware.[101] In Trelawny's view, the "wicked and bold" conspiracy "might have been of very fatal consequence if it had not been timely discover'd."[102] The slaves who helped to suppress the plot received their due rewards from the House of Assembly: Hector won his freedom for revealing the conspiracy, and four others—three with Akan names—earned £5 each for capturing an accused conspirator named Tom and delivering him to the slaveholders for execution.[103]

Within months there was another uprising, this time at the navy yard in Port Royal. Late on a Sunday night, about twenty enslaved Coromantees and Pawpaws, tradesmen and women led by a bricklayer called "King's Cudjoe," mustered on the Palisadoes, the narrow *tombolo* that protected Kingston Harbour and tied Port Royal to the island. These thirteen men and seven women were supposed to be joined by a gang of twenty others, who were kept from the rendezvous by a deep breach in the sand bar. According to one colonist's report, the rebels first killed a black man they met on the strip of land—perhaps he had tried to stop them or threatened to raise the alarm—and then marched eastward along the New Road, hoping to make their escape. The next morning, they killed more people—a free black fisherman and four elderly women—before continuing another three miles up toward the Blue Mountains and into St. David's Parish. Passing through the twenty-eight hundred acres of John Innis's estate, they killed the overseer and several more slaves. Marching on, they came upon a house, where they killed another three slaves before burning the structure to the ground. By this time, the surrounding country was alarmed, certain that the rebels had only one design: "to kill all they met with; both Whites and Blacks, who were not willing or able to join them in their bloody Purposes." Several parties of militia set off in pursuit as the rebels ascended the mountains.[104]

The Windward Maroons caught up with the rebels first. "Our Friend Negros," as a local gentleman now called them, killed four rebel men and one woman in the engagement, and took three women as prisoners. Thirteen others escaped, making their way into the parish of St. Thomas in the East. Already, the local militia party there amounted to about a hundred men, and a bounty had been announced: £5 for every rebel killed, and £10 for each one taken alive. Over the next days and weeks, the militia killed one rebel; the other twelve were captured or killed by plantation slaves seeking rewards.[105]

These events in the 1740s signaled the irreducible importance of local political alignments. The maroons acted to secure their hard-won sovereignty.[106] Their alliance with the slaveholders limited the spatial horizon of plantation slaves, diminishing their hopes of fighting their way to freedom in the interior. Gold Coast origins and fluency with the cultural practices of the homeland were not enough to surmount the political divisions created in Jamaica. Coromantees could unite and fight the whites, and they could also fracture into smaller groups and struggle against each other. The slaveholders' demonstrated willingness to employ and reward enslaved people in the fight against the maroons created other opportunities. If it would no longer be possible to form autonomous polities in the mountains, perhaps slaves could eke out incremental material improvements within slave society.

There was another lesson to be learned. Status, responsibility, and skill within slavery could facilitate rebellion, too. The drivers in Louidas Vale and the bricklayers and blacksmiths working for the Royal Navy had used the authority granted to them by the slaveholders to fight enslavement.

Along with developments in the war with the French, these insurrections of slaves with special status and skills would have been the talk of the port when HMS *Wager* arrived at Jamaica in February 1746. The Coromantee revolt and the role of King's Cudjoe in it must have made an especially memorable impression on all the black people working around the harbor or serving the Royal Navy, including Apongo, who would muster aboard the *Wager* just weeks after it arrived.[107] Picking among rumor, gossip, and hard information, would-be rebels could learn from this attempt by King's Cudjoe that what they needed most was to build the right coalitions, find the right timing, and identify the places where a revolt might meet with greater success.

In the aftermath of the St. John plot, Governor Trelawny considered the strategic state of affairs. In late 1743, with the First Maroon War behind them and renewed war with the French ahead, Trelawny had raised a new regiment from the eight independent companies on the island, drawing them from their countryside barracks into the towns. He took direct command of the unit as its first colonel, and it was named "Edward Trelawny's Regiment of Foot." Later, in 1751, when a royal warrant reorganized the British infantry, it became the Forty-ninth Regiment of Foot, and served as the British Army's principal force in Jamaica until the Seventy-fourth Regiment arrived in the late 1750s. Having created the new regiment, Trelawny was sure that it offered more security against foreign invasion. By late 1744, however, he was already worrying, as he wrote to the Duke of Newcastle (then secretary of state), that moving the soldiers away from the plantations "may have given the Negroes the boldness to venture" a conspiracy.[108]

In light of this concern, the governor pressed for more troops. Informing Newcastle of the peculiarities of Jamaica's landscape, he stressed that the plantations were "more scatter'd & remote from each other so upon any rising the Rebellious may immediately possess themselves of a large compass of Land." With the estates so far from each other, planters could not assist their neighbors' estates without leaving their own defenseless. Trelawny thought it imperative "at all times to have some Soldiers Quartered in the Country Barracks to be ready on all emergencies for the protection of the out Settlements & such parts of the Island as cannot readily receive any assistance from the Towns." Fresh troops, distributed throughout the island, "would be a great Security & comfort to the Inhabitants, especially those in the remote Parishes, who are now under great apprehensions both of the Foreign Enemy & the rising of their own Negroes."[109] This would allow the Jamaica garrison to continue its multi-front war.

The St. John conspiracy and the naval yard insurrection also prompted Trelawny to contemplate a dramatic reform of Jamaican society. In 1746, he published an anonymous pamphlet in London, *An Essay Concerning Slavery and the Danger Jamaica is expos'd to from the Too great Number of Slaves, and the too little Care that is taken to manage Them, and a Proposal to prevent the further Importation of Negroes into that Island*. He withheld his name because he knew his ideas would be detested by Jamaica's colonists. Yet he felt compelled to publish them by the urgency of the situation, with Jamaica being "so insecure" that the colonists were "not only alarm'd by every trifling Armament of the Enemy, but under the greatest Apprehensions frequently from their own Slaves." He warned, "Something must be done, and that speedily, or this valuable Colony will be undoubtedly lost, and the British Empire in the West-Indies much curtail'd, if not totally ruin'd." Having little confidence in the willingness of Jamaica's colonists to put civic duty ahead of private desire, he hoped instead to sway the legislators in Parliament.[110]

In the form of a fictional dialogue between two archetypal figures—called simply *Planter* and *Officer*—Trelawny made a case against slavery as unjust and proposed the abolition of the slave trade. Using the Officer character as his mouthpiece, he went so far as to denounce slavery as "against the Law of God and Nature"—refuting John Locke's philosophical argument that enslavement could be justified as a right of conquest. At the same time, he recognized that emancipation was impractical for an empire grown rich off the labor of the enslaved.[111] The pamphlet framed the actions of large slaveholders, who in their zeal to import ever more Africans were like children "playing with edge tools," as inimical to public, imperial interests, especially at a time of simultaneous war with the Spanish, the French, and the Jacobite rebels in Scotland.[112] Trelawny was deeply worried about the racial composition of the colony. "By the Poll-Tax in 1740," he noted, "it appeared that the Negroes were ten times more in Number than the white Persons."[113] As a remedy, he proposed that a British Act of Parliament should put a stop to the slave trade. "When we have already more Slaves than are consistent with our Safety, let us not bring in more and more to make our Perdition sure."[114] In the absence of importations, a pro-natal policy could "keep up the present Stock" if women in childbirth received "a little Linnen, or other Necessaries," and if barren women were ceremonially whipped "on a certain Day every Year."[115] There was clearly no contradiction in his mind between distaste for slavery and his advocacy for continuing male domination.

Yet both Trelawny's abolitionist sentiments and his racial fears were subordinate to a more general concern about the number of alienated workers on Jamaica who were in positions of authority but had no stake in maintaining the existing order. "To me it is a perfect Solecism to trust a Slave with Power," declares the Officer in his dialogue.[116] It was a supreme lapse of judgment, Trelawny thought, to allow slaves to work in the skilled occupations that upheld the colonial economy. His proposal to save the colony from being "over-run, and ruined by its own Slaves" featured a racially flexible social reform: ensuring a due proportion of free people "of one Colour or another, white, black or yellow, since white Men enough cannot immediately be got," preventing slaves from entering trades or being employed in domestic service, and limiting them to "the Field or such kind of Drudgery as cannot be carried on but by them."[117] It was too dangerous to enslave bricklayers like King's Cudjoe and the blacksmiths who had joined him in revolt. Their skill and influence could too easily be turned against their masters. With the St. John conspiracy foremost in his mind, Trelawny insisted that drivers, especially, should be free men.[118]

More generally, the pamphlet argues against displacing free white workers with slaves. Jamaica's wealthier landholders preferred to employ slaves, who were supposed to be subject to their absolute control. By contrast, with European settlers in short supply and laws on the books requiring estates to employ a minimum number of whites or pay significant fines, white workers had significant bargaining power. Those whites who came, survived, and stayed could call Jamaica the "best poor man's country" in the world. They commanded high wages, moved easily between jobs, and showed little deference to their employers.[119] The adage, of course, obscured the fact that poor blacks performed most of the important work at nearly every level of the society, save the very pinnacle. On the other hand, it did highlight the way racism allowed whites of lesser talent and skill to lord over the masses of enslaved blacks.

Trelawny thought that banning slaves from skilled trades would make these jobs more attractive to whites. To illustrate this argument, he pointed to the enslaved pilots doing the crucial work of guiding ships around the local shoreline. White men felt sullied by having to compete with them and generally refused the job. As Trelawny's Officer explains, "A white Man doth not care to be put upon the same Foot—with Negroes, and serve with them under another." So, if a white man agreed to be a pilot, "he will be now nothing less than a Master Pilot," earning his living by sending out slaves to perform the work. The same was true of all the trades, "For it is Fact, and may be laid down as an infallible Maxim, that whatever you allow to be done by Slaves, you will never afterwards get White Men to do."[120] Lacking the entitlements of great wealth, the whites' very sense of self depended upon black subordination.

Trelawny had no problem with racial hierarchy. He just favored an arrangement in which black labor served the interests of the empire as well as its wealthiest subjects. He imagined that a diverse population of free men would defend the colony with more vigor. Trelawny's Officer suggests that drivers could be freed, legally bound to their estates for seven years, and then leased or granted small parcels of land. As freeholders and tenants with some property to protect, relatively privileged black men would be sown throughout the island like "hydra-teeth," ready to spring up like the skeleton warriors of Greek mythology in defense of British sovereignty.[121]

In some ways, his suggestion reflected practical experience. The utility of the Black Shots during the First Maroon War had demonstrated the value of enslaved adherents. Bound by treaty, the maroons themselves had recently demonstrated their effectiveness as military adjuncts. Trusted plantation slaves like Hector had been crucial in revealing the St. John parish plot. Worchester, a carpenter owned by a militia colonel, had been "killed in the country's service" while helping to suppress the navy yard revolt.[122] Given the demographic realities of the station, both the Jamaica Squadron and the Forty-ninth Regiment would always include many people of color. Great Britain's military was an agglomeration of peoples—white, black, and all the colors between—who were conscripted, bought off, and disciplined into a polyglot fighting force. For Trelawny, as for most Atlantic military officers, an inclusive imperial hierarchy was a necessity and a norm.

The pamphlet convinced no one to end the slave trade. In fact, it did not inspire much of a response at all, suggesting that it had limited readership and little influence in London. Jamaican plantations, with ever-increasing numbers of Africans to work them, expanded into the parishes once made insecure by the maroons. Black trade workers continued to perform skilled labor. Whites maintained themselves by commanding blacks of all ranks, including the drivers, who remained enslaved. With the maroon threat reduced, the slaveholders gained a crushing advantage in their everyday war against the enslaved, and they looked forward to decades of magnificent prosperity. "Providence always gives sufficient Warnings, we have had ours," cautioned Trelawny. "Providence has done its Part, we should do ours, in taking Warning and altering our Course." But his counsel fell on deaf ears.[123]

THROUGH the end of Trelawny's governorship in 1752, the maroons offered the settlers little trouble. The new governor, Admiral Charles Knowles, toured the island soon after his arrival and reported positively on the growth of the colony in March 1753. He noted "vast improvements," with large new tracts of the country cleared and cultivated and the number of inhabitants and sugar plantations increased. He was especially pleased with the state of St. James Parish, where the Leeward Maroons had previously curtailed white settlement. While the parish had had only six sugar works in 1740, now there were thirty-six, with more than twelve hundred white people, also growing coffee, cotton, and ginger. Knowles visited some of the maroon towns too and hosted several of their captains at the nearest plantations. These meetings, in which he renewed treaties and distributed presents, convinced him that the maroons were "extremely satisfied and I verily believe will prove of more Service to the Country than they ever were of Prejudice."[124]

Knowles was overconfident. A year later, he faced an insurrection at Crawford Town, a maroon village situated high on the Buff Bay River. An internal disturbance had already led two dozen people from Crawford Town to splinter off and form Scotts Hall in 1751.[125] Then, on February 23, 1754, Knowles learned that Crawford Town's captains had "revolted and killed Ned [Edward] Crawford," the lieutenant assigned to one of their military parties. The governor named eleven ringleaders in his report to the Board of Trade: Quaw, Adago, Mingo, Dansu, Boqua, Pompey, Badoo, Yan, George, Assutia, and Accompong. They "seized on all the Arms," burned the town, and detained the three white men posted there, along with those black people who refused to join the revolt. Acting quickly, Knowles sent a company of the Forty-ninth Regiment to guard Spanish Town in case the uprising spread, then raised the Kingston militia and ordered a company to take up a position at Buff Bay. From there, they joined with the maroons from Scotts Hall, a party from Nanny Town, and a detachment of soldiers from Port Antonio.[126]

One Lieutenant Ross, a former resident of Crawford Town, who had the respect of many there, went up the mountain with the intent to negotiate a surrender. He stayed there "expostulating with the Chiefs" for more than a day, managing to secure the release of the white and black hostages but failing to obtain a capitulation. Instead, he persuaded the rebels to come down to an estate on the coast to continue negotiations. When they still could not come to terms, the rebels left, and British forces ambushed them on their way home. "A Battle ensued," reported Knowles, "in which were taken Capt. Quaw, Adago, Mingo and Dansu, the last of whom is mortally wounded, and Boqua, Pompey and Badoo were killed and their heads brought in." Of the supposed ringleaders, only four escaped, including Accompong, who was thought to be wounded. Acting as intermediaries, the captains of other maroon towns appealed on behalf of the surviving rebels for the governor's pardon, which Knowles granted.[127] But Accompong would remain at large for some time.

In October 1755, as the island again girded for war with the French, a colonist wrote to Rose Fuller—a sugar planter and until recently Jamaica's chief justice—with positive news. "One good thing has happened to the Country, about three weeks ago, the head of that Arch Rebel Acampung was Brought in by some of the Wild Negroes." By this time, the colonists believed of Accompong that "he was projecting a general revolt of the Slaves, & was to be their King." Indeed, "he actually had on his head when he was Shot, a Crown of Gold, according to the ancient fashion." Upon seeing the head brought to Kingston, one of the slaves declared, "it was the head of the King of the Negroes."[128]

If this was true, and Accompong had in fact been planning a general revolt since the previous March, his killing was extremely fortunate for the colony. The uprising would have been timed to coincide not only with the resumption of inter-imperial hostilities but also with a grave political dispute between colonists. Governor Knowles was at odds with the House of Assembly throughout his tumultuous administration. Most seriously, in

1754, he took the side of merchants who petitioned to move the capital from Spanish Town to Kingston. The Spanish Town elite, led by Chief Justice Rose Fuller and Speaker of the Assembly Charles Price, reacted with angry street protests and petitions of their own. Spanish Town locals insulted Knowles's wife while he was away touring the island, doctors refused service to his sick child, and someone broke into his house and vandalized his possessions. Knowles then moved to Kingston, transferring the courts of law and the government archives, and pushed a handpicked House of Assembly to sanction the maneuver. More furor ensued, engulfing the political class in recriminations, accusations, and lawsuits for several months.[129]

In London, the Board of Trade decided to veto the removal laws and return the capital to Spanish Town, but the uproar continued through 1755, with factions of the assembly treating each other with increasing acrimony. In October a fracas broke out in the assembly, and Knowles arrested sixteen members of Charles Price's faction. Upon hearing the news, the Lords of Trade recognized that "the Island is in the greatest Disorder and Confusion, that Riot and Tumult have taken place, and Acts of Violence have been committed."[130] Early in 1756, they granted Knowles's request to resign, and selected Lieutenant Governor Henry Moore, a native of Jamaica, to take his place until the arrival of the next appointed governor, General George Haldane. At the public celebrations that followed in the Spanish Town square, the crowd lit two great bonfires and burned effigies of Knowles and his flagship.[131]

What slaves thought of this political crisis is unknown. Some number of them must have seen an opportunity. Accompong, evading capture while "projecting a general revolt" through most of 1755, would certainly have followed the "Disorder and Confusion" among the whites with keen interest. There is little question that he knew there was a dispute, whether or not he knew its causes and developments. The men involved were big planters and wealthy merchants, each with retinues of domestic slaves who talked to other slaves. Through the circuits of information that connected the towns to the estates and the plantations to the mountains, rumors of "Riot and Tumult" in Spanish Town and Kingston would have encouraged many of those discontented with British rule to consider the possibilities afforded by the situation.

Accompong, a fugitive from colonial authorities and at odds with other maroons, surely saw the whites' public squabbles as a sign of military weakness. His conspiracy would have exploited the island-wide network of communication established during the First Maroon War of the 1730s. As a Coromantee captain with a prominent Akan name, Accompong would have hoped to draw in his compatriots from across the island, perhaps especially from the parishes with the most new arrivals from Africa. Moving along the clandestine pathways in the mountains and the bush, he would have stolen into slave quarters to agitate and recruit. Maybe he encountered Tacky in St. Mary's Parish, or traveled as far as Westmoreland and St. Elizabeth Parishes, where Accompong Town bore his name.

It is even possible, if perhaps unlikely, that the "arch rebel" Accompong was the same man as the maroon captain Accompong, "brother" to Captain Kojo. In March 1755, the Moravian missionary Zacharias George Caries discovered Captain Accompong and six other maroons visiting the slave quarters at the Bogue estate in St. Elizabeth. Having recently arrived on the island, Caries was fascinated by the so-called "wild Negroes" and took care to describe Accompong's appearance. He noted the Captain's embroidered waistcoast and the silver chain around his neck that supported a silver medal; inscribed "on one side was King George ye 2nd's Picture and on the other his Commission with this subscription Captain Acampong." Accompong was bejeweled with earrings, and there were "on each of his Fingers 5, 6, or 7 Rings of silver," as well as iron rings on his barefooted toes. He also prominently wore gold lace around his hat—perhaps the "crown of gold" noticed when the rebel's head was brought to Kingston later that year.[132] Captain Accompong is not mentioned in documents after the 1750s and may have been the same one killed in 1755. Many of the maroons executed by Kojo for a 1742 coup attempt were from Accompong Town, which maintained a tense relationship with Trelawny Town.[133] On the other hand, there is good reason to believe that the "arch rebel" Accompong was a different man altogether. The Captain Accompong met by Zacharias Caries still wore his King George II medal, perhaps signifying his continued respect for the maroons' alliance with Great Britain, and Caries makes no mention of his being a fugitive. Still, the captain's presence in the slave quarters indicates that maroons moved fairly freely among the enslaved, giving them ample opportunity to share news from distant parts. Recent arrivals might tell of happenings in West Africa, while maroons might educate these newcomers about Jamaica's relevant history, connecting Coromantees in different regions and sowing a fertile field for recruiting insurrectionists.

From these circuits, interested Coromantees learned in 1754 that, back in Africa, a combined army from Denkyira, Twifo, Wassa, and Akyem had gone to war with Asante. So many men were in military service that few were left to harvest food crops, and famine threatened the entire region.[134] Africans captured in this war and brought to Jamaica soon found themselves in a similar situation. When the Seven Years' War came to the Caribbean in 1756, it brought shortages and starvation. In June of that year,

Brother Caries described visiting sick and weak slaves in their houses and in the fields at Bogue estate. "Most of them are in distress from want of necessaries of Life," he wrote in his diary. "At other Estates it is still much worse, for there some actually dye for want & many run away." Conditions were even worse the next month. All over, the starving were stealing food from each other's provision grounds because, according to Caries, "Many of their Masters and Overseers are so hard that they will not give their Negroes any thing, but rather let them dye for Hunger." In their desperation, at tremendous risk, slaves stole from their masters, too. Some of them, noted Caries, had "lately been hang'd" for it, and others shot.[135]

The Seven Years' War also brought a sharp decline in the numerical dominance of Jamaica's Coromantees. The conflict had depressed trade along the Gold Coast, but it picked up significantly in West Central Africa. Between 1751 and 1755, the nearly twenty-two thousand Africans shipped from the Gold Coast made up forty-five percent of the total imports, with fewer than three thousand arriving from West Central Africa. In the next five years, only eight thousand people came from the Gold Coast and more than ten thousand from West Central Africa, nearly thirty percent of those arriving through most of the war.[136]

Amid increasing numbers of newcomers who spoke Kikongo, Kimbundu, or other West Central African languages, Coromantees might have sensed a weakening of their cultural influence and diminishing opportunities to make alliances with potential co-conspirators. The facts are probably unknowable, but it is possible that they decided to try again to foment a general insurrection before their position slipped any further. Alternatively, they might have seen that the people from West Central Africa had gone through similar experiences of war in their homelands, and sought to join with them for the coming battles against the slaveholders. Since the late seventeenth century, the Coromantees had wielded broad influence on the island. Just as they could dominate the music at the festival witnessed by Sir Hans Sloane, or provide the basic vernacular for multilingual bands of runaways, they might have shaped the political objectives of a diverse population of restive slaves. Like the British military, which conscripted whites and blacks from three continents to fight for the English, various Africans might have united as Coromantees for the immediate purpose of toppling the slave regime.

As difficult as it is to determine the rebels' precise motives or to follow the planning for the rebellion that would break out in 1760, we know that whatever conspiracy was brewing drew from long-established patterns. The cultural affinity of Coromantee plotters was certainly a factor, but it was

far from the only important one. The Coromantee nation cohered culturally, and also found common ground in the practical experience of life,
labor, and struggle in Jamaica. When rising up against the slaveholders, the
rebels certainly drew upon their familiarity with warfare across multiple
terrains in Africa. Yet it was a long way from the seventeenth-century Akan
military revolution to the insurrections that rocked Caribbean plantations,
the maroon wars in the mountains, and the careful plotting of general insurgencies. These were rooted in and routed through the political geography of the Jamaican landscape.

The ways in which slaves revolted depended on their knowledge of the
local contours of Coromantee territory, which determined how they used
it to their military advantage, to maintain avenues of escape, to find temporary refuge, and to build communities outside slavery. This was not just
a matter of natural ecology; it also concerned social histories of place.
Conspirators and rebels formed potential alliances and antagonisms by
knowing who was on the estates, who controlled particular regions in the
towns, the mountains, and the bush, and what battles had defined these
spaces as safe, dangerous, or uncertain. Once they had charted the social
situation, potential slave rebels could carry on the indispensable work of
coaxing people toward the pursuit of a military and political objective. No
straightforward extension of experience in Africa, performance of Coromantee identity, or simple reaction to the fact of enslavement would ac-
complish this. Rather, cultural affinity, migratory experience, and ceaseless
social struggle combined in particular and proximate locations to determine the course of events. African warfare in diaspora drifted far from
its origins, landed firmly on new soil, and adapted effectively to its new
surroundings.

CHAPTER FOUR

Tacky's Revolt

IN MARCH 1759, the new governor, Brigadier General George Haldane, finally arrived to relieve Lieutenant Governor Henry Moore. Fresh from the conquest of Guadeloupe, Haldane proposed that the Jamaica Regiment should attack St. Domingue with the aid of five hundred maroons.[1] Nothing came of the plan, in part because Haldane soon fell gravely ill and died in November. To honor his brief service, the legislature gave his name to the fort at Port Maria, in St. Mary's Parish.

Again, Henry Moore was to govern the colony. This displeased Zachary Bayly, who had been a political opponent of Moore's during his first term as acting governor. "Good God! What a country is this," he wrote to Rose Fuller, now in England serving as a member of Parliament. "If he [Moore] is to continue long I will get out of the Island upon any terms."[2] This was hyperbole, but the slave revolt that began at Fort Haldane in April 1760 and spread across Jamaica for the next many months would soon give Bayly an entirely different and better reason to wish he could quit the island.

Fort Haldane stood upon the bluff commanding the entrance to Port Maria Harbour. It was a formidable structure, with barracks large enough to host some sixty men, but it was an unhealthy place and was largely undefended on the night of the rebel attack.[3] Looking out to sea, a single watchman guarded the main port of trade for the parish. He was the first white man killed in the uprising. Just after midnight on April 8, nearly one hundred Africans marched on the fort, overwhelming the sentinel and seizing four barrels of gunpowder, a keg of musket balls, and all the small arms, numbering about forty working weapons. To supplement their ammunition, some went down to the bay and cut weights from the fishing nets for use in the guns. From a nearby store, the Africans took a pair of pistols, some dry goods, and Madeira wine. Armed and provisioned, this lethal insurgent army prepared to make war on British slavery. Over the next several days, the rebels killed, burned, and raided across a broad swath of the parish.[4]

The sudden violence sowed alarm and confusion among Jamaica's slaveholders, and accounts of the rebels' progress and intentions conflicted. But by drawing together the various eyewitness accounts, anecdotes, and rumors, Jamaica's whites pieced together a narrative—a story in which the main characters were all Africans from the Gold Coast, but whose goals remained unclear. An anonymous "Letter from a Gentleman at St. Mary," dated April 14, 1760, circulated in colonial newspapers and formed the basis for many subsequent narratives. Probably written by Zachary Bayly, who played a key role in organizing the militia's response to the initial outbreak, it begins with a disclaimer: "I am informed you have received several erroneous and contradictory Accounts of the proceedings of the rebellious Negroes; which I am not surprized at, as the Truth is difficult to come at here on the Spot. The following is the best information I can give you."[5]

The planters figured they knew the instigators. Witnesses identified a "Koromantyn Negro of the name of Tacky, who had been a chief in Guiney," another Coromantee called Jamaica, and "three other Chieftains of their country, who were each of them to have an Estate for his good Services." These men were all described as "Gold Coast negroes newly imported" to the island.[6] Having identified the leaders as Coromantees, the slaveholders largely ignored the question of whether the followers were all from the Gold Coast, as well. Early reports even identified a ground zero for the planning and launching of the plot. Although Tacky and Jamaica had been slaves on Ballard Beckford's Frontier estate, which overlooked the harbor and lay close to the main road behind the town of Port Maria, they first assembled their forces further up the Western Port Maria River at Zachary Bayly's Trinity estate, where rebels gathered from Whitehall, Ballard's Valley, and other plantations in the heart of the parish.

While the slaveholders could identify the ringleaders and the estates where the plot had been hatched, they were baffled by the ultimate scope and setting of the unfolding insurrection. They had urgent questions about its parameters. What had caused the revolt, and why did it follow its eventual course? Was the revolt caused merely by the unhappy condition of particular plantations, or was it an extension of African warfare? Most wanted to believe that uprisings were usually isolated incidents caused by the cruelty of particular masters, but many of Jamaica's slaveholders had also undoubtedly heard about the Coromantee slaves executed for conspiring to revolt in Danish St. Croix late in 1759.[7] Was this a local episode—or part of a regional war against slaveholders? If this was a domestic affair, it could be contained with the political tools locally at hand; if not, then the island was at the mercy of capricious policymakers in London, rapacious European merchants, and, worst of all, utterly alien African warriors. Their sense of mastery was at stake. In their desperate attempts to make sense of a fast-changing and bewildering predicament, they told themselves a misshapen story that has been repeated ever since.

"Tacky's Revolt" is the standard name for the violent events that began with the attack on Fort Haldane and ended months later with the defeat of Wager and others on the far side of the island. By using Tacky's name, this customary designation makes St. Mary's Parish the primary locus of the events, collapsing what turned out to be a complex and confusing process into a symbolic moment in place and time. More than anything, the label "Tacky's Revolt" is an artifact of the fear and disorientation caused by the uprising. Colonists' accounts of the rebellion convey more than information about its content; they overflow with the terror of the times. Sources describe an ecology of fear, in which Jamaica's very landscape resonated with panic and horror. The dread of insurrection eclipsed the slaveholders' observations on the aims of the Africans, who left no record of their own. Focused by their response to the initial outbreak of hostilities, the colonists overemphasized the role of the rebellion's first leaders, Tacky foremost among them. The territory of the revolt, however, offers clues to a more nuanced account. Paying careful attention to movements in space and over time offers a new perspective on the military maneuvers of the combatants. By mapping the narratives sketched by planters onto the geography of St. Mary's Parish we can discern patterns of political intent for both the rebels and the counterinsurgents and see that Tacky's Revolt was just one episode in a much larger Coromantee war.

FOLLOWING the attack on Fort Haldane, the rebels doubled back to Trinity for more arms and reinforcements. As their numbers swelled with allies from neighboring estates, the rebels marched up the main road. Here they were guided by the geography of the parish. Thinly settled by whites but profitably devoted to sugar production, St. Mary's teemed with newly imported slaves from the Gold Coast, who worked the plantations sited all along the parish's river system. Located on the windward side of the island, St. Mary's was one of Jamaica's wettest and most densely forested districts.

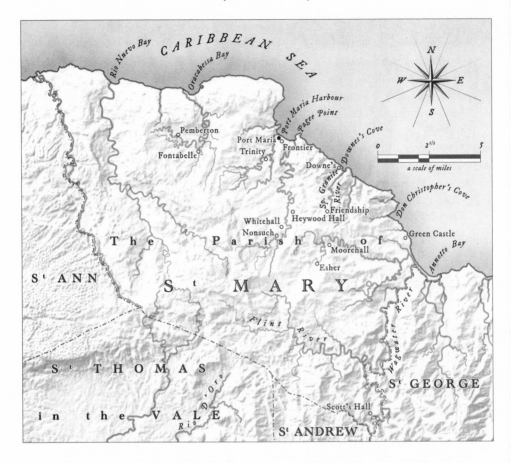

Deep ravines and gullies, carved into the landscape by some two dozen rivers and many smaller streams, subdivided the parish. The planter Edward Long described it well: "Nearly the whole of this parish is composed of hill, mountain, dale, and valley."[8] Travel off the main roads was slow and difficult, and the insurgents hoped to hit many plantations as quickly as possible, rallying their comrades to the prospect of rapid success. So the path of the insurrection ran through the commercial heart of the parish.

Early in the morning, the rebels surrounded the overseer's house at Ballard's Valley estate. Zachary Bayly had been in St. Mary's for a few weeks, touring plantations that he owned or managed for others. He had been at his own Trinity estate the day before the uprising, inspecting newly purchased Africans and distributing clothing and cane knives among them. On the night of the revolt, he had slept at John Cruikshank's Ballard's Valley, a few miles upriver from Trinity. At daybreak, some of Bayly's enslaved domestic workers woke him with startling news. The insurgents were close. A hurried consultation with Cruikshank and a few others produced an agreement to begin collecting arms and gather together at an estate nearby. Bayly then descended the hill from Cruikshank's house to see "the whole body of rebel Negroes in full march" and hear what he believed to be a "Koromantyn yell of war." He rode toward the rebels, hoping to convince them to stand down.[9] Approaching cautiously, he waved his hat in the air and called out to those from his Trinity estate: "Boys, don't you know me?" They answered with gunshots, compelling Bayly's hasty retreat.[10] Then the rebels attacked the house, killing the overseer and three other white men inside.

Writing decades later, the planter-historian Bryan Edwards would claim these white workers had been murdered in their sleep. Edwards then added that the rebels "literally drank their blood mixed with rum," a detail presented to make the attack look more barbaric, which does not appear in the earliest account.[11] Edwards included the detail to heighten the horror for his readers, but such a practice would have had a different significance for the rebels. People from the Gold Coast commonly believed that blood and alcohol were spiritually potent fluids. Power, especially military capacity and the authority of command, derived equally from the temporal and supernatural realms; war gods and spirits could be entreated for aid through libation and blood sacrifice. Victorious warriors would sometimes be given rum, enriched with drops of a fallen enemy's blood, to protect them against avenging ghosts and boost their courage. In Jamaica, the Africans probably drew upon these traditional practices to accrue spiritual force while appropriating and counteracting the power of their immediate foes, the colonists.[12]

Proceeding further upcountry toward the base of the mountains, the rebels advanced on William Beckford's Esher estate. Along the way, still hoping to prevent news of their movements from spreading quickly among the whites, they met and killed a white man who was traveling on foot. When the rebels reached Esher, fourteen or fifteen more Africans rallied to the uprising. The whites on the estate, including the overseer, a surveyor, a young Scot named Gordon, and two others, fired upon the rebels but were overwhelmed by the responding volley and barricaded themselves in the main house. Low on ammunition, they holed up in a single room and cowered in anticipation of the rebels' next move.[13]

The rebels soon broke into the house and came to the room's door, telling the whites that "if they should offer any resistance they would certainly be put to death, but if they would come out & lay down their arms their lives would be safe." The ruse worked. One of the men, a German, ventured out

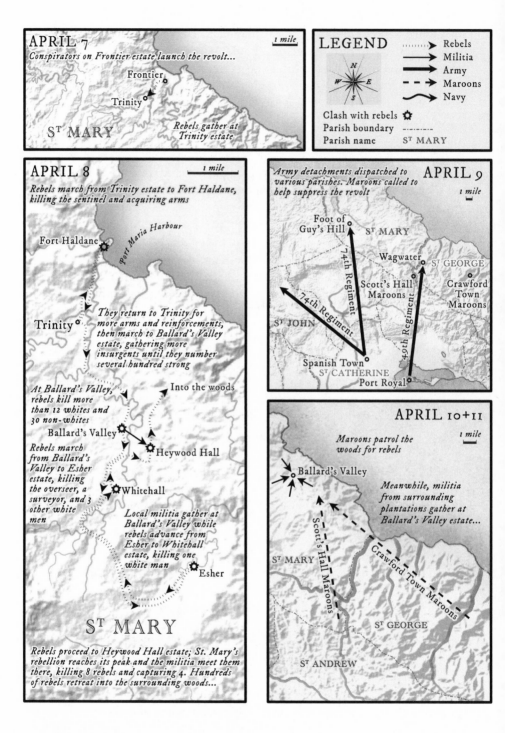

APRIL 7

Conspirators on Frontier estate launch the revolt...

Frontier

Trinity

S⊤ MARY

Rebels gather at
Trinity estate

LEGEND

1 mile

·········▷ Rebels
——————▷ Militia
——————▶ Army
– – – – ▶ Maroons
⌇⌇⌇⌇▶ Navy

Clash with rebels ✿
Parish boundary – · – · –
Parish name S⊤ MARY

APRIL 8

1 mile

Rebels march from Trinity estate to Fort Haldane,
killing the sentinel and acquiring arms

Port Maria Harbour

Fort Haldane ✿

Trinity

They return to Trinity for
more arms and reinforcements,
then march to Ballard's Valley
estate, gathering more
insurgents until they number
several hundred strong

Into the woods

At Ballard's Valley,
rebels kill more
than 12 whites and
30 non-whites

Ballard's Valley ✿

Rebels march
from Ballard's
Valley to Esher
estate, killing
the overseer, a
surveyor, and 3
other white
men

✿ Heywood Hall

✿ Whitehall

Local militia gather at
Ballard's Valley while
rebels advance from
Esher to Whitehall
estate, killing one
white man

✿ Esher

S⊤ MARY

Rebels proceed to Heywood Hall estate; St. Mary's
rebellion reaches its peak and the militia meet them
there, killing 8 rebels and capturing 4. Hundreds
of rebels retreat into the surrounding woods...

APRIL 9

Army detachments dispatched to
various parishes. Maroons called to
help suppress the revolt

1 mile

Foot of
Guy's Hill ○   S⊤ MARY

Wagwater   S⊤ GEORGE

74th Regiment   Scott's Hall
Maroons   Crawford
Town
Maroons

74th Regiment   40th Regiment

S⊤ JOHN

Spanish Town ○
S⊤ CATHERINE
Port Royal ✿

APRIL 10+11

1 mile

Maroons patrol the
woods for rebels

✿ Ballard's Valley

Meanwhile, militia
from surrounding
plantations gather at
Ballard's Valley estate...

Scott's Hall Maroons

Crawford Town Maroons

S⊤ MARY

S⊤ GEORGE

S⊤ ANDREW

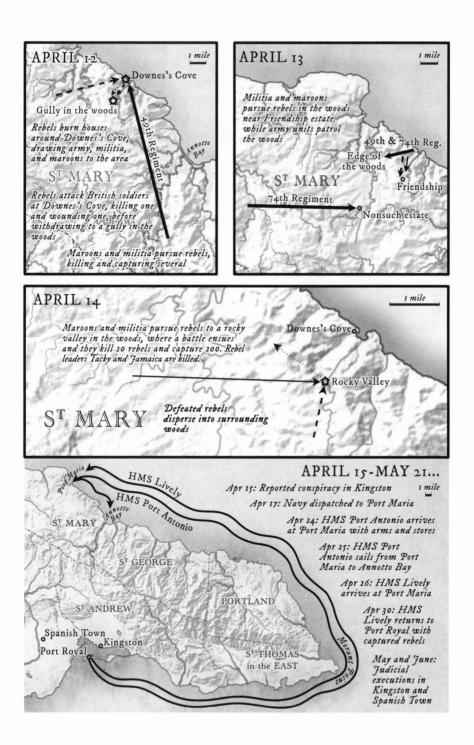

APRIL 12

1 mile

Downes's Cove

Gully in the woods

Rebels burn houses around Downes's Cove, drawing army, militia, and maroons to the area

49th Regiment

St MARY

Annotto Bay

Rebels attack British soldiers at Downes's Cove, killing one and wounding one, before withdrawing to a gully in the woods

Maroons and militia pursue rebels, killing and capturing several

APRIL 13

1 mile

Militia and maroons pursue rebels in the woods near Friendship estate while army units patrol the woods

49th & 74th Reg.

Edge of the woods

Friendship

St MARY

74th Regiment

Nonsuch estate

APRIL 14

1 mile

Maroons and militia pursue rebels to a rocky valley in the woods, where a battle ensues and they kill 20 rebels and capture 200. Rebel leaders Tacky and Jamaica are killed.

Downes's Cove

Rocky Valley

St MARY

Defeated rebels disperse into surrounding woods

APRIL 15-MAY 21...

Port Maria

HMS Lively

HMS Port Antonio

Annotto Bay

St MARY

St GEORGE

PORTLAND

St ANDREW

Spanish Town

Kingston

Port Royal

St THOMAS in the EAST

Morant Point

Apr 15: Reported conspiracy in Kingston

1 mile

Apr 17: Navy dispatched to Port Maria

Apr 24: HMS Port Antonio arrives at Port Maria with arms and stores

Apr 25: HMS Port Antonio sails from Port Maria to Annotto Bay

Apr 26: HMS Lively arrives at Port Maria

Apr 30: HMS Lively returns to Port Royal with captured rebels

May and June: Judicial executions in Kingston and Spanish Town and was immediately and quietly knocked over the head. Ignorant of the German's fate, another man followed and suffered the same treatment. Then the attackers rushed into the room, decapitating the overseer and killing the remaining men, except for Gordon, who had hidden under a bed.[14]

Contrary to the earliest printed account of the battle at Esher, which reported that Gordon had been killed along with the others, he survived, and told his version of the story to Pierre Eugène du Simitière the next year.[15] Still, it was a narrow escape. The rebels discovered Gordon and fired under the bed, wounding his knee. Then they dragged him out and fell upon him with cane knives and cutlasses, mangling him nearly beyond recognition until he was still. Finally, the rebels hauled him out of the house by his feet, his head thumping on the stone steps that led down to the piazza, where they laid him alongside the bodies of the slain. Although he was "almost senseless," he discerned that some were preparing to cut off his head, but they were restrained by others, who declared him already dead. Left that way, he lay hours "upon the Border of life & death," unconscious and draining blood until a party of white men arrived to bury the corpses. Finding Gordon barely alive, they dressed his wounds and carried him to a neighboring estate, where he entered the care of his uncle, who happened to be an eminent doctor. Two surgeons attended Gordon for an extended time, "every day fatigued with the multiplicity of bandages and dressings, necessary to be applied upon almost all parts of his body." In time, he returned to health, and Jamaican whites described his recovery as "next to miraculous."[16] Ever after, he bore great "numbers of scars upon his face & several parts of his body" that distinguished him as a celebrity among his acquaintances. Having arrived in Jamaica only seven months before the revolt, the young Scotsman found that his tribulation made him a historic figure in his time. He even gained the nickname "Coromantee Gordon" as a mark of distinction.[17]

Having taken Esher, the insurgents turned to the business of proclaiming their authority among the slaves. Slaveholders generally believed that the most important social cleavage during a slave revolt was between black and white, but distinguishing friend from foe was always more complicated. The rebels had spared the overseer of Trinity estate, Abraham Fletcher, who had a good reputation among the enslaved, allowing him to flee the plantation unmolested.[18] On the other side, they did not hesitate to slay fellow slaves who failed to join them or impeded the uprising. In the initial burst of violence, when the rebels killed more than ten whites, they also killed some thirty non-whites who opposed them.[19]

As it had during the planning stages, success in battle depended on a calculus of trust and betrayal. Once the rebellion was underway, the plotters struggled to convince those on the fence that they were in control, and that the planters had lost their power to determine the slaves' collective or individual fate.[20] This made the war a matter of personal histories of fellowship and animosity. Whatever new order the rebels would establish, it would build upon their estimation of the alliances and antagonisms of daily life. A prior grievance or an earlier kindness might determine who could be trusted and who would be killed. As in all wars, the physical contest for power conscripted elemental emotions: fear, rage, and lust.

Among the rebels' victims at Esher was the overseer's concubine. As a woman of mixed black and white descent, she was a likely target for the sexual predations of slaveholders, fair enough to test racist standards of beauty yet marked for low status by her brown skin: simultaneously attractive in whites' eyes and easy to exploit. Proximity to the master class also made her an object of suspicion among the enslaved. To many of the rebel men, who knew they could be castrated for "trespass" on a white man's "mistress," she represented a dangerous capitulation. She also offered an opportunity for this particular group of men to bond with each other through an act of collective sexual violence. They "ravished" her, according to Edward Long, and intended to put her to death. The intervention of other slaves saved her life. They testified that, by her persuasion with the overseer, she had frequently saved them from punishments. Or so they believed. Long thought that the woman had been spared "not owing really to any merit on her part" but because the "overseer had only chose to let his forgiveness appear rather to come through the importunity of another, than from the lenity of his own disposition." There was an unresolved question of agency at stake here. In her desperate situation, did she have some ability to shield other slaves from immediate dangers, as her defenders claimed? And if so, many rebels surely wondered, did this merely allow her to borrow some of the masters' power, which could be wielded selectively at her whim? Or, as Long suspected, were these capacities only illusory, subject to the ultimate dominion of the overseer? Whatever the ultimate truth of the matter, the slaves' views on the subject meant the difference between execution and clemency.[21]

From Esher, the rebellion moved back down the river valley through Whitehall estate, where they killed one white man, and on to Heywood Hall, a strategically located sugar plantation just across the river from Ballard's Valley, in the geographical and agricultural heart of the parish. The rebels set fire to the cane field and the windmill, signaling their success and attracting new recruits to the uprising. By midday, their numbers had increased to about four hundred men and women.[22] Unbeknownst to the rebels, however, the St. Mary's insurrection had already reached its peak.

The insurgents gathered together in a tree-shrouded clearing a little re-moved from the road, where they took stock of their provisions: pigs, poultry, plantains, rum, and other goods they had amassed from the morning raids. Roasting an ox over an open fire, they sought to seal their early sense of victory with bonds of fellowship and communal consumption. As the slaveholders later described it, this was the rebels' moment to "carouse"; just as likely, it was time to assess the strategy, logistics, and progress of the campaign.[23] Gathering forces in open celebration was an important mili-tary exercise. Whatever plans had been hatched in anticipation of the up-rising, this was the moment to establish the unity of the assembled rebels and to recommit to the effort. Food, drink, and song helped to generate the fellow feeling crucial to bolstering morale.

This was also a time to administer loyalty oaths to all new recruits. Obeah men and women, trained practitioners in African spiritual arts, had been instrumental in organizing the war. As they had done in previous conspira-cies, the practitioners now counseled and inspired the plotters. In addition to preparing and offering the sacramental oaths, they furnished the rebels with "a magical preparation which was to render them invulnerable," boosting their morale for battles against forces of superior arms. Edward Long credited obeah men with persuading the rebels that Tacky "could not possibly be hurt by the white men, for that he caught all the bullets fired at him in his hand, and hurled them back with destruction to his foes." Now that the rebellion had gathered strength, the rebels' obeah seemed to be working its magic well.[24]

Their initial burst of activity had been remarkably successful. The in-surgents had laid their plans without discovery, acquired firearms from the fort, and marched back into the heart of the parish to raise an army, raiding and burning the estates in their path. Fire served at least two pur-poses. First, it signaled the expansion of the insurrection to others who were looking for a signal or who were waiting for the balance to tip in the rebels' favor. Second, it struck a direct blow to the means of plantation production, the source of so much of the slaves' suffering. Arson changed sites of toil to places of triumph. The fires proclaimed as no other means of communication could that, for the moment, the rebels were in control. But to what end?

The rebels' military tactics reveal something of their ambition. Their well-planned and fast-running strikes followed the prevailing patterns of earlier Caribbean slave revolts, as well as precedents in Gold Coast warfare. Af-rican armies often pursued a policy of skirmishing in small bands, weak-ening their opponents with hit-and-run tactics. Because dense forest didn't allow for large-scale pitched battles, African combatants used roads and clearings with strategic precision, remaining in small, highly mobile columns that converged on battlefields from various routes. Moving through the Jamaican bush from plantation to plantation, the rebels capitalized on their experience with forest combat, easily evading the militia, who invariably trained in open fields and parade grounds. Jamaica's insurgents also arrived at estates ready to recruit as well as fight. Just like military leaders in eighteenth-century West Africa, rebel strategists considered whole populations capable of bearing arms as potential recruits.[25] As they sorted foes from possible friends, they declared their aims and ambitions. Of these declarations there is no direct record—only Edward Long's tendentious interpretation of the intelligence gathered by his fellow slaveholders.

Long would later contend that the rebels had aimed at controlling and operating plantations, perhaps hoping to manage overseas trade upon their own account. At first blush, Long's view seems absurd. After all, the rebels consistently set plantation buildings and cane fields ablaze. These acts of destruction seem to signify a social revolution, an intention to clear the landscape of commercial exploitation. Based on a deep knowledge of Gold Coast societies, the historian Walter Rucker has surmised that the Coromantees maintained a "commoner consciousness," articulating "distinctively subaltern worldviews."[26] These views would guide a polity made up of "independent provinces bound together by political alliances," or what Long construed as "small principalities in the African mode."[27] In this case, many of the rebels were probably in tension with leaders like Tacky, who were determined to recover the rank and privilege they had known in Africa, and who probably favored a more unified sovereignty with a hereditary elite.[28]

And yet, from the path of the insurrection it appears possible that the rebels did indeed hope to control the commercial zone. The routes traveled by the rebels through woods, over mountains, and along rivers suggest their strategic objectives. At Fort Haldane, insurgents had gathered arms and ammunition before marching up the main road to the heads of some of the parish's most important waterways, which fed Port Maria Bay and Annotto Bay, principal ports on the island's north side. The rebels had supposedly planned to attack at the west end of the parish, too, upriver from Oracabessa Bay: the night of the outbreak, planters caught a "noted runaway" from Pemberton estate, whom they hanged for trying to convince others to join the rebellion. Pemberton lay in a pivotal location, between several plantations hemmed by the mountains and Fontabelle estate, at the head of a winding stretch of river leading past Crab Lanthorn Gully and into the bay. Had this man organized a successful attack, the rebels might have gained the upper hand from one parish to the other.[29] The core conspirators had planned the revolt on Trinity, Whitehall, Frontier, and Heywood Hall estates, which were owned by some of the most important men in the colony. A strike on these properties was simultaneously an attack on the island's political elite. The battles, moreover, occurred on terrain that the rebels knew well from their labors. This is where they came to demonstrate to potential recruits that the rebellion was in full swing and gaining in force. The rendezvous near Heywood Hall was within easy striking range of some of St. Mary's biggest plantations. Fighting within the economic heart of the parish, the rebels certainly were not seeking out mountainous enclaves. When the counterattack came, they struck for the coast, breaking into small bands to traverse the area's deep woods and ravines, and conducting raids all the way down to the shoreline inlets. This pattern of warfare indicates an attempt at territorial and political control, a strategy of maneuver rather than of retreat, evasion, or escape.

Of course, we cannot fully know the rebels' intent. It is entirely possible, even likely, that they disagreed among themselves, failing to reach any consensus on the revolt's ultimate aims. Slaveholders later learned that an island-wide revolt had been timed for the Whitsun Holidays six weeks later but that the St. Mary's insurgents rose too soon, "owing to Tackeys getting Drunk."[30] Even if Tacky had indeed upset the careful planning of other leaders, dissension was probably latent from the beginning. It would have continued as they debated whether to seek defensible encampments and hideouts, continue to press the immediate attack, or try to link up with conspirators in other parishes. Later there were reportedly "such Dissentions among them, that several were killed in their own Quarrels."[31] But by that time, the colonial counterinsurgency was on the offensive, and the tide had turned against the rebellion.

In the midst of the mêlée at Esher, a slave named Yankee had defended the house and assisted the whites. When he found that they were overpowered, he escaped to the neighboring estate, Moore Hall. There he collaborated with Blackwall, another "faithful Negroe," who belonged to Jamaica's Lieutenant Governor, Henry Moore. Together, Yankee and Blackwall devised "concerted measures for alarming the neighbouring plantations, and assisting the white people."[32] Meanwhile, Zachary Bayly mustered the militia. After his initial brush with the rebels, Bayly rode hard from plantation to plantation, giving notice of the uprising and urging all able-bodied men to join him in arms immediately or to rendezvous at a defensible house near Ballard's Valley. By the time they discovered the assembly of rebels near Heywood Hall, the militia had gathered nearly one hundred and thirty "tolerably armed" black, brown, and white men.[33]

Mounted on seventy or eighty horses, they advanced upon the rebel encampment, and the insurgents took up positions in the surrounding woods. Firing at will, the rebels found that the fishing weights they were using for ammunition flew in irregular arcs and caused little damage to the militia, who held their ranks during the early volleys. Cautiously, the militia decided to move into the woods, but they determined that they did not have enough ammunition for everyone to join the fight. Instead, most of the men stood their ground in the clearing, while sending their servants and "some others well armed" in pursuit.[34] The tactic highlighted a fundamental problem with the country militia. Men of high status were overrepresented and disdained the grubbiest work of soldiering. As far as the elite colonists were concerned, the woods were no place for the well-to-do. So all the captains, majors, and colonels, who constituted the bulk of the militia, agreed that it was the commoners who should advance into the bush.

Yet the attack had been encouraging. Early accounts reported that the militia killed eight rebels and took four captives.[35] One Mulatto Billy "was said to have slain three with his own hand," recounted Edward Long, "and a brave North Briton about the same number."[36] Most importantly, the planters began to gather useful intelligence about the insurgency. After beatings and threats, one of their prisoners begged to trade information for his life. Among other things, he disclosed the crucial part played by the rebels' spiritual counselors. The colonists now knew one important source of the rebels' morale and fortitude, which they would work to break in the coming days.[37]

For now, the insurgents melted into the forest and the militia proceeded to the meeting point near Ballard's Valley. Long and Edwards, as committed apologists for the planter class, rendered their actions in heroic terms. In Long's view, the militia assault was a matter of wise and careful strategy. The "bold attack" had intimidated the rebels into retreat, but "it was not judged proper at that time to pursue them."[38] Edwards credited the tactical success to "the Whites," who attacked the rebels "with great fury, killed eight or nine of them on the spot, took several of them prisoners, and drove the rest into the woods, where they acted afterwards wholly on the defensive, and were soon exterminated."[39] But the rebels were far from vanquished; to quell the revolt, someone other than the haughty parish elite would have to fight them in the deep woods.

News of the uprising soon reached the colonial government in Spanish Town. At the first alarm in St. Mary's, Billy and Philip, two of William Beckford's trusted slaves, were ordered to mount horses and make haste for the capital. While the distance was less than forty miles, it was a steep ride up into the forested ridges along the Flint River and down again into St. Thomas in the Vale, where the messengers could finally pick up speed along the banks of the Rio D'Oro. As they crossed through the Red Hills shielding the Spanish Town Savannah, they approached the capital on the Rio Cobre, which ultimately fed into Kingston Harbour, the principal seat of British military power in the Americas. Charging along poor roads and narrow pathways, the couriers brought notice to Lieutenant Governor Henry Moore by the early afternoon, just about the time when the militia was engaging the rebels near Heywood Hall.[40]

Moore acted quickly. Spanish Town was itself a powerful military enclave, with the garrison hosting considerable units of mounted militia and regular British army troops. Situated near the middle of the island, these forces could be rapidly deployed to windward. Moore immediately dispatched a detachment of three officers and sixty private soldiers of the Seventy-fourth Regiment to march through St. Thomas in the Vale by the road leading over Archer's Ridge. From Port Royal, Moore called upon the Forty-ninth Regiment, ordering them to march to St. Mary's along a new road recently cut through St. Andrew to the head of the Wagwater River. Express letters went out to British officers stationed among the windward maroon villages at Crawford Town, Nanny Town, and Scotts Hall, commanding the officers to invoke the treaties of 1739 and 1740 and bring the maroons into the fight.[41]

The town militia, both foot and mounted, were to stand ready under arms, "in case any attempt should be made by the Negroes of other Parishes to join those already in Rebellion."[42] But tensions between free common folk and the wealthy elite undermined Moore's orders. The residents of Spanish Town were more likely to have independent trades and small businesses than those in either Kingston or the countryside. Accordingly, commoners in the towns did not have the same direct dependence on the plantations or the big merchants, and were less beholden to their betters. When called upon to defend the merchant-planter alliance, many demurred. "Many of the Private Men had the Insolence to tell their officers that they would not appear under arms," and would rather pay the ten-shilling fine mandated by the Militia Act for failure to muster.[43]

Lieutenant Governor Moore excoriated their seeming lack of civic virtue, fuming at "so unnatural a behavior in a time of Public Calamity, joined to so much Insensibility of the Danger with which the whole Country was threatened." Jamaica was a military stronghold in an empire at war, and it now required belligerence from its subjects. So, on April 9, having "recourse to the only means left of compelling them to do their Duty," Moore proclaimed martial law:

By the King, A Proclamation

Whereas a great Number of Negroes in the Parish of Saint Mary's are now in an actual State of Rebellion and have killed many White People and destroyed several Settlements in that part of the Country, We have thought fit for the service of this our Island and to prevent any attempts that may be made by the Slaves of other Parishes to join with those concerned in the present Insurrection, that for the Defence and Security of this our said Island and for the Immediate Suppression of the said Rebellion Martial Law should be put in force—

We have therefore caused this Proclamation to be Published hereby commanding and Requiring that the Articles of War be publickly read upon this Ninth day of April Instant in the Towns of Saint Jago de la Vega, Port Royal and Kingston from which Publication Martial Law is hereby enforced.[44]

Martial law was intended to mobilize the entire non-slave male population, subjecting them to the strict discipline of the Articles of War.[45] The result was the formal militarization of racial slaveholding. Disputes between large and small slaveholders or big merchants and petty traders, between Protestants, Catholics, Jews, mulattoes, and free blacks, were all to be set aside in the interests of defending slavery, which was the will of the Crown. As du Simitière explained, under martial law "all the inhabitants of the Island are put upon the same footing as a Regular army & during the time it lasts all civil procedures can have no effect, from hence it is not in anybody's power to sue or arrest another for debt which makes many a man holding a commission in the militia look big, which would not dare in a time of publick tranquility shew his face abroad [for] fear of the marshal's men. Therefore the inconveniences of that Law appear very plain & must stop in great measure most sort of Business & specially trade."[46] The courts closed, and legal business came to a halt. Especially obnoxious to the society's elite was the confusion of rank. "You'll have perhaps for your officer & of course for your Superior a man in Every respect below you which & at other times would be scarce worth your notice," du Simitière lamented. "Every body without distinction has been oblig'd to take up Arms to destroy the Common Enemy," wrote one Kingston attorney.[47] "Every man was a soldier."[48]

Now, fully embodying his role as the island's Commander in Chief, Moore directed a multi-pronged response along multiple pathways. He ordered troops of the Spanish Town militia to march and ride immediately to the western end of St. Mary's by the road leading through Bagnell's, and a detachment of the Kingston militia to follow the regular army troops of the Forty-ninth Regiment through the eastern side of the parish. From the Seventy-fourth Regiment, he sent two detachments northwest to St. John's

Parish to be stationed at the vulnerable upcountry estates in the vales of Guanaboa and Louidas. Still another unit of the Seventy-fourth marched for St. Mary's via Archer's Ridge to join the unit already dispatched to that place. From there, one unit would guard the pass out of St. Mary's while another proceeded to the pass at Bagnall's on the western end of the parish, to prevent the rebels from communicating with potential confederates in neighboring St. Ann. For added firepower, Moore sent the Captain of the Train from Spanish Town to march two cannon to Archer's Ridge. An escort of mounted troops from the capital would convey a supply of provisions, arms, and ammunition over the mountains. Moore now sent for the maroons to leeward, from Trelawny Town, Furry's Town, and Accompong's Town. And again, with the Articles of War ringing in their ears, every militia officer was ordered to be ready to march at a moment's warning.[49]

Finally, the Lieutenant Governor called upon the Royal Navy. Having sent one carriage of supplies by land, he applied to Vice Admiral Thomas Cotes for a vessel to carry stores and provisions around the coast for the "great number of People which were then Assembled in the parish of Saint Mary on Account of this unhappy event."[50] In this way, the government securely integrated the colonists on the island's north side into the vast supply chain of the imperial military. Meanwhile, to seal off the insurgents and focus the colony's energies on suppressing the insurrection, the colonial government laid an embargo on all shipping. Jamaica was under quarantine.

The next day, Moore called a meeting of the Governor's Council to explain his actions. Among the six men present was Ballard Beckford, owner of Whitehall and Frontier estates. He was surely pleased to hear of the governor's commitment to arresting the troublemakers, who had already done so much damage to Beckford's own interests in St. Mary's. Indeed the Council was unanimous in its approval, praising Moore's "most prudent Steps for the relief of that Distressed part of the Country" and lauding his efforts "for the service and General Security of the whole Island." They also accepted the necessity of martial law "to crush the Rebellion in its Infancy and prevent those fatal Consequences which must have Arisen if the Negroes of the other Parts of the Island could have had time to Join those Concerned in the present Insurrection." The Lieutenant Governor should keep the island under martial law, the Council recommended, "till all these Disorders were suppressed and Tranquility again restored to the Country."[51]

As Moore mobilized the imperial forces from Spanish Town, rebels and slaveholders traded attacks in St. Mary's. The insurgents had at first possessed the advantage of surprise and speed, but now the British began to hem them in. Steep valleys and dense forests limited the number of clear pathways through and out of the parish. As counterinsurgent troops blocked the main roads and mountain passes, they forced the rebels deeper into the tangles of bush, sharp ravines, and hidden grottos. If these tactical redoubts were ill-suited to British soldiering, they also prevented the rebellion from gathering force and advancing from estate to estate, as it had before.

The colonists also benefited from the capture and execution of a leading obeah man. They had learned from the prisoners captured near Heywood Hall how important spiritual advisors were to the rebels, and that an "old Cormantin Negro" had been named as "the chief Instigator and Oracle of the Insurgents." Such oracles wielded great influence on the Gold Coast, in some places commanding the authority to appoint war captains and guide political strategy. Whoever was serving this role in Jamaica probably helped to organize and inspire the insurrection in a similar way. The slaveholders caught him, Long wrote, "whilst he was tricked up with all his feathers, teeth, and other implements of magic." Summarily tried and sentenced to die, the shaman remained defiant, declaring, "It was not in the Power of the White People to kill him." He died by hanging, which surprised and disheartened the enslaved spectators gathered for the execution. Long guessed that this act prevented many slaves from deciding to join the rebels.[52]

The maroons joined the battle immediately. Patrols from Scott's Hall and Crawford Town went into the woods, drawing upon a century of experience in traveling, tracking, and fighting in the bush. On Thursday, April 10, a party from Crawford Town attacked a large group of rebels in the forest but were outnumbered and repelled, Captain Cudjoe's son being killed in the clash. Other parties of maroons continued to scour the woods for watchful bands of insurgents, fighting sporadic and indecisive engagements.[53] Meanwhile, the militia from surrounding plantations gathered near Ballard's Valley. On Thursday evening, a planter captain arrived with about sixty men mounted on horses. The next day, joined by several more planters and their men, the colonists patrolled the neighboring estates.[54] Women, children, the elderly, and infirm colonists from the area most immediately affected by the revolt made their way east toward Annotto Bay, congregating around Green Castle estate, where they awaited relief from the sea.

The rebels headed for the sea, too. Withdrawing northeast of Heywood Hall, they regained the initiative in the area around Downes's Cove. This region was sparsely settled, being separated from the big estates along the Port Maria River by a jagged stretch of verdant peaks and gulches bending from Pagee Point to Don Christopher's Point. Short rivers and streams rushed through the steep gullies toward the rocky coastline. Down the Spanish Granite River, a few thorny miles from Friendship estate, Downes's

Cove opened out of a forested ravine that hosted a variety of hidden caves.[55] Named "Rocky Cove" in a map of 1755, the inlet and its little beach offered a clandestine harbor for small craft, a haven for fishermen, smugglers, and fugitives. From this shore one could launch for the short distance to Cuba. If the rebels sought defensible dominion over a modest port and waterway, this place might serve. It was hard to access, provided good hiding places, and yet held the promise of communication with the world beyond Jamaica.[56]

A single rough road led from the Port Maria River down to Mr. Downes's isolated estate on the coast. By controlling that road, the rebels might maintain the cove. On Saturday morning, April 12, the rebels set fire to several houses on the property. A combined force of counterinsurgents gathered at Downes's to answer the threat. Detachments from the Forty-ninth Regiment led by Captain Rigby had arrived from Port Royal, joining Lieutenant Forsyth's militia company and the Crawford Town maroons. Also present was Captain William Hynes, a mercenary who commanded a party of well-armed slaves. Having intelligence that the rebels were close by, one group went up to Carlton Wood House, which stood atop a hill on the east side of the cove, while Forsyth and most of the Forty-ninth Regiment stayed at Downes's. The Crawford Town maroons, ushered by Charles Sweigle, joined Captain Hynes and his private slave army in going after the rebels.[57]

The rebels had secured themselves in a great cave situated within a rocky gully. Here, in this "little glade, or cockpit, so environed with rocky steeps that it was difficult to come at them," they made their main encampment. Several of the men, women, and children stayed here with their provisions and limited stores of ammunition, while others remained out on patrol. Hynes's party discovered the camp first, with the maroons close behind. For an hour, they fired on the rebels and "assaulted them with hand grenades" as they climbed a hill out of the gully, killing two men and two women. Hynes captured two more women and a child, and recovered some baggage, a keg of powder, and two guns in the raid. With only two of his men wounded, Hynes and the maroons continued in pursuit, splitting up and combing the woods up the Spanish Granite River to Friendship estate, where they decided to camp until morning.[58]

That night, Tacky led the counterattack at Downes's Cove. The strike, coming so soon after the rout of their main encampment, signaled the rebels' commitment to driving British forces from the area and suggests that the rebels intended to build their future here—or perhaps that they had no better choice. They surprised and killed the sentinel of the Forty-ninth Regiment's advanced guard and wounded two other men in the ensuing battle. But three rebels died, and Tacky himself was wounded. Having been assured by the shamans that he was invulnerable, he now lost confidence in his own leadership. According to later accounts, he "could not again be persuaded to head his Men, until they threatened to put him to Death."[59] With the rebels' oracle executed and their chief leader wounded, morale began to ebb from the insurrection.

British forces continued to constrict the geography of insurgency. Reinforcements from Spanish Town arrived with "60 Stand of Arms, and two Barrels of Powder" at Nonsuch Estate, where tributaries formed the main stem of the Port Maria River. From Friendship estate, Hynes, Sweigle, and the maroons pressed their advantage, despite the insurgents' continuing to mount a vigorous defense. At one point the rebels ambushed William Towers, Superintendent of Nanny Town, and his party of twelve maroons. Towers managed to fight his way through the trap, but he suffered grave wounds in the action. Maroons continued to scour the woods for bands of insurgents, while regular army forces lined the edge of the forest.[60]

Finally, on April 14, the maroons pursued the rebels to a rocky valley upriver from Downes's Cove. The Scott's Hall maroons attacked the main body of insurgents "with great Impetuosity," forcing them to retreat in disarray. The rebel leader Jamaica was killed, and Tacky tried to make his escape, pursued closely by Lieutenant Davy of the maroons. Davy fired at Tacky "whilst they were both running at full speed," according to Edward Long's account, and shot the rebel commander dead. Colonial forces then seized a great many prisoners and all the baggage and stores they found, along with four half-barrels of gunpowder. The maroons collected proof of death to show their part in the battle to the British, taking seventeen pairs of ears, each of which they traded for a doubloon.[61]

Having failed to secure Downes's Cove, the rebels faced defeat. The earliest reports stated that no more than a dozen rebels had escaped from the rocky valley and were being tracked down by the Trelawny Town maroons, who had arrived soon after the battle.[62] Many surrendered. Others chose suicide over reenslavement. There were reports that "many cut their Throats" or hanged themselves in the woods. Still others were killed in internal quarrels, as failure turned some of the insurgents against one another.[63] According to various accounts, about sixty people "betook themselves to a cave, at the distance of a mile or two from the scene of action, where it was thought they laid violent hands on one another, to the number of twenty-five."[64] Stories circulated that the maroons under Charles Sweigle tried to claim undue credit for these internecine conflicts. Du Simitière heard that Sweigle, "no great Conjurer in pursuing the rebels," had gone into the woods with his party and discovered "several Corpses of negroes that had shot one another in their private quarrel." With Sweigle's permission, the "maroons under his command insisted to cut the Ears of all of them in order to be intitled to the Reward." They brought the trophies directly to Lieutenant Governor Moore for compensation.[65]

Many of the recaptured rebels submitted to interrogation, hoping that perhaps the colonists would spare their lives. The prisoners revealed that the insurrection had begun to collapse even before the deaths of Tacky and Jamaica. "By the Accounts of some of those that surrendered themselves," the colonists learned that "the Rebels were in great Distress for Want of Provisions: That when any of them became lame or wounded, they were immediately killed, to prevent their giving Intelligence. That their Leader, Tacky, after his being first wounded, could not again be persuaded to head his Men, until they threatened to put him to Death: That there were such Dissentions among them, that several were killed in their own Quarrels; and that many would have quitted them, could they have done it with Safety."[66] The fugitives who remained at large after the battles for Downes's Cove had little to do but negotiate their surrender. Sending a delegation to Mr. John Gordon, a planter whom the hold-outs felt they could treat with, they offered to come in if they could leave the island instead of being put to death. One of them, a man named Kingston implicated in the murder of the overseer at Esher estate, received no clemency. He was bound to be executed, even though, in handwritten marginal notes on his *History of Jamaica,* Long later acknowledged that Kingston was innocent of the charge. What mattered now, however, was that the uprising appeared to be over.[67]

On April 17 in Spanish Town, three days after the deaths of Jamaica and Tacky, Lieutenant Governor Moore convened the Council again to declare the progress of the counterinsurgency. He boasted that his timely deployments had "cut off the Communication of the Rebells with the other parts of the Country and prevented any Assistance coming to them." More directly, he declared that imperial forces "had constantly met with success and that they had killed and taken so many of them as left no doubt of their being totally Destroyed in a few days." Moore shared with the Council the latest news from St. Mary's: the troops of horse from Kingston and Spanish Town were no longer needed and had been ordered home, while maroon parties pursued the small "Remains of the Rebells" by "scouring the Woods where many had secreted themselves." Again, the Council unanimously approved Moore's actions, proclaiming that "nothing could have contributed more to the safety of the whole Island than the vigilance he had shewn on this occasion, and his readiness in sending such a number of Troops into that quarter to prevent the Spreading of a Rebellion which seemed to threaten the whole country with Destruction."[68]

The Lieutenant Governor then turned to the question of martial law. Admitting that the state of emergency "could not fail of being productive of many inconveniences to a trading People," Moore expressed his desire to end martial law as soon as the situation justified it. For the time being, however, he wanted to maintain the detachment from the Forty-ninth Regiment in and around St. Mary's and to keep the maroons "constantly out in the woods" until further orders. Pleased to continue this vigilance against the slaves, the Council nonetheless wanted planters and merchants to get back to business and recommended the lifting of martial law and of the shipping embargo four days hence, provided the Lieutenant Governor did not hear of more "Tumults or disorders in other parts of the Island."[69]

From HMS *Marlborough,* the flagship of the Jamaica station, Vice Admiral Thomas Cotes concurred with Moore. On April 19, he wrote to London to inform the Board of Trade of the uprising, avowing that the rebels "would certainly have done a great deal more Mischief if the Lieutenant Governor Mr. Moore had not taken the most Vigorous and prudent Measures to suppress them by proclaiming Martial Law & putting the whole Island under Armes." Cotes calculated that fifteen or sixteen white men had been killed—he said nothing of faithful slaves—along with three or four maroons, and that six or seven maroons had been wounded as well as Lieutenant Bevill. But he noted that, despite these losses, Moore had "gained great applause by putting so speedy an End to a Rebellion that broke out with such Fury." While no one yet knew how many slaves had revolted, the colonists generally believed that their numbers would have increased if the rebels "had gained the least Advantage over the Troops." He assured London that the military had killed and captured between sixty and seventy rebels and that the dispersed remainder "must be either killed, taken or Starved" before long: "The Tranquillity of the Island is now restored and Martial law will end the 21st Instant."[70]

The Royal Navy was to secure the pacification. Although the Navy's land engagements were slight, its actions were still vital to suppressing the revolt. By moving troops, provisioning colonists in distress, and closing avenues of maneuver for the rebels, Britain's maritime forces projected the power of the Atlantic empire ashore. During times of crisis, these kinds of logistical maneuvers were the lifeblood of the colony. More than any other institution, the Navy articulated the British Empire's component parts. Its other great function, in this case, was to weaken the enemies by denying them opportunities to traverse territory on their own terms. That, too, was the broad function of the shipping embargo, an act of quarantine that made the Royal Navy the only avenue of mobility between the island, the region, and the wider world.

As soon as Cotes received Moore's word of the insurrection, he had ordered the *Marlborough's* long boats to Port Royal Fort to carry the company of the Forty-ninth Regiment across the harbor to Passage Fort, whence they proceeded overland to St. Mary's.[71] Directly afterward, Cotes commandeered a privately owned schooner, manning her with a lieutenant, a mate, and a midshipman, along with ten seamen, twenty marines, an armed sergeant, and a corporal from the flagship. Hauling the schooner alongside the *Marlborough,* sailors loaded the smaller vessel with provisions for the troops: "5164 lbs of Bread, 20 Barrells of Pork, 10 Do. of Beef and 31 Gallons 2 Quarts of Rum, to Carry to Natto Bay for the soldiers that was enroute after some Rebellious Negroes."[72] The warships HMS *Port Antonio* and HMS *Lively* followed the schooner around to the north side of the island with more fresh supplies of provisions and "warlike stores."[73]

These ships tightened the perimeter around the insurrection, even as they channeled the movements of the counterinsurgency. Sailors, soldiers, provisions, and munitions flowed into the theater of combat; only captured prisoners came out. The frigate HMS *Lively* came into Annotto Bay on April 22 and made contact with the colonists. Soon afterward, its captain, Frederick Maitland, sent "30 Casks of Beef 20 Cask of Bread Two Half Barrels of Powder and one of shott" on shore to Green Castle estate, where the St. Mary's colonists had made a refuge for planter families and a base of counterinsurgent operations. The *Lively* also distributed beef, bread, powder, and flints to a smaller private ship that could divide these among the troops as needed.[74] The frigate thus secured the colonists' connection to the resources of empire, while helping to keep the rebels hedged west of the bay, between the mountains and the sea. Meanwhile, the sloop HMS *Port Antonio* arrived at Port Maria Harbour, a few miles to the northwest. Its captain, John Lewis Gidion, ordered six armed men ashore to assist the guard, which was holding some two dozen rebel prisoners. On the morning of April 25, Gidion received "15 of the Rebellious Negro Men and 10 Women" aboard the ship.[75] Having little room to keep prisoners aboard the small sloop, Gidion sailed to Annotto Bay and transferred them to the *Lively* before returning to Port Maria. There, he helped to pursue the rump of the insurrection, sending twelve armed men ashore "to Assist a party that was going after the Rebellious Negroes." These men returned with another prisoner.[76]

Aboard the *Lively,* sailors took down the names of the prisoners. These names were either given by their captors, many of whom would have known the rebels as slaves from local plantations, or elicited during rough questioning—probably both. Either way, nothing guaranteed a direct correspondence between the names these men and women went by, the names heard by the sailors, and the names recorded in the ship's muster. Indeed, the names must reflect some combination of dissemblance on the part of the rebels, confusion among the colonists, and the inevitable indifference of wartime accounting. Even the number of prisoners received is in question. The captain's log for the *Port Antonio* records the delivery of twenty-five men and women, but the Lieutenant's log for the *Lively* acknowledges the receipt of just twenty-three, fourteen men and nine women.[77] Still, the names are there. Whether these were actual conspirators and combatants or simply bystanders swept up in the repression, twenty-five people are listed together in a column of "Rebell Negroes." The men were named Jenery, Port Royal, Kingston, Cudjo, the first of two Quaminos, Robin, George, Anthony, Hector, Matthew, Philip, Suckham, Mathew Fintee, Jack, and Abbe. The women were named Sarah, Sabira, Cate, Sophia, Betty, Dod, Dianna, Sentosia, Quamino, and Minah.[78]

Historians and their readers have commonly assumed that women were less militant in their resistance to slavery than men. Despite the prominence of Nanny of the maroons in accounts of Jamaican slave rebellion, women's resistance to slavery has seldom been viewed as a military phenomenon.[79] Because women often had children and domestic worlds to fight for, violent uprisings were the prerogative of men; so we have thought. Yet here women represent forty percent of the first known rebels captured during the largest insurrection of the British Caribbean in the eighteenth century. Whether they acted in supporting roles or engaged in direct combat, some of these women must certainly have been part of the core community of insurgents.

The names themselves may tell us something more about that community. Five of the names are clearly of Akan derivation: the two Quaminos, Cudjo, Mathew Fintee, and Minah. Jack was also a common translation for Quaco, which would make six identifiably Akan names among the twenty-five.[80] There is only one person listed with a surname of sorts, Mathew Fintee, probably of the Fante in West Africa. Slaveholders had clearly imposed most of the names for these people, especially in the case of place-names like Port Royal and Kingston, Christian appellations such as Sarah and Matthew, or the classical name Hector. In all likelihood, many of these men and women went by more than one name—a slave designation, a communal identity, and a nickname. So the muster of rebel prisoners connotes little of certainty, but it suggests that these people had multiple identifications and were more than just Coromantee. It also confirms that the slaveholders and the military state knew little about them.[81]

The *Lively* had sailed from Port Royal Harbour on April 18, but within two days a sail appeared on the horizon and the *Lively* gave chase. The quarry, a French schooner named *Le Friponne,* was no match for the swift 24-gun frigate and surrendered without a fight. The *Lively* took forty-four French prisoners, who were still captive in the hold when the African rebels came on board on April 26. The next day, the *Lively* ran down a French privateer and acquired several more prisoners, who shared the cramped hold with the "rebell negroes" on the way back to Port Royal Harbour, where the frigate moored alongside HMS *Marlborough* on April 30. If the rebels had previously lacked the sense that their campaign was part of a larger war, they surely knew it now. The *Marlborough's* longboat carried the French to Greenwich Prison, and the rebels were forced aboard the Squadron's flagship. From there they went to Kingston and Spanish Town for torture and trial.[82]

By the time these men and women arrived in the towns, the colonists had a growing suspicion that there was more to the uprising than the events in St. Mary's. Two weeks prior, on the evening of April 15, "a young Man was shot at, as he passed by some Negro Huts" in the Kingston Savannah. He informed the guard, who marched a party of militiamen to the slave dwellings. Several black people jumped a fence and escaped, but one was seized and his house subjected to a thorough search. There the authorities discovered a "Sword of an extraordinary Size and Weight, the Hilt covered with black Velvet, and studded with Brass nails, and under the Velvet a Parroted Feather."[83]

The man came to trial at a hastily convened slave court, with the case focused on the meaning of the sword. Made of mahogany, it measured three feet and eight inches in length, decorated along the blade with "oil paint in irregular Squares raised in relieve of different colours." The velvet-covered hilt was nine inches long, with a five-inch cross-guard of golden nails between the velvet and the blade. The blade itself spread out to encompass a large hole about five inches in diameter at the top, with a smaller square cut out in the middle of the blade. From depositions, the panel of two justices and three freeholders learned that the sword was a "token of war & of Rebellion amongst the Coromantees," signifying war when grasped by the hilt and peace when held by the round hole at the top.[84] In all likelihood, this was a makeshift sword of state modeled after the Gold Coast fashion, which was meant to signify the authority of a distinguished notable or the existence of a polity in the making. The slaves were literally taking power into their hands.[85] The accused man confessed to having made the sword and was hanged with the weapon at his feet. Kingston residents heard that this very sword had been seen at the Spring Path market, where slaves gathered in large numbers, on each of the previous three Sundays.

"And it has been observed, that the Coromantee Negroes, about Kingston, have been very audacious since the Account came of the Insurrection in St. Mary's." This was a warning to the colonists to be "circumspectly on their Guard" for signs of broader trouble.[86]

News of the St. Mary's revolt and the Kingston episode circulated throughout the island in the last two weeks of April. Word of mouth, letters, and official statements accumulated. The schooner that had brought relief supplies to St. Mary's returned to Kingston Harbour on April 18, bringing firsthand stories of the events there.[87] The next day, the newspaper ran the first widely read accounts. On the far side of the island, at Mesopotamia estate in Westmoreland Parish, the resident Moravian missionary heard the news from a fellow evangelist: "Negros have rebelled in various places on this island and have already killed various white people gruesomely." They saw "more details about this in the Newspaper." In neighboring St. Elizabeth Parish, colonists read the same confirmation of rumors that had been churning for days. One missionary there noticed how the enslaved reacted: "som with fear others with joy as thare Hearts were incline'd."[88]

Slaveholders all over the island feared the number of slaves who might react with joy, and perhaps anticipation, at news of a war against the masters. Whenever the printed news appeared, they compared it to previous accounts, recalibrated the threat, and shared their assessments with each other. Although copies of these Jamaican papers do not survive, one can see the news accounts reflected in the colonists' letters, which routinely summarize the printed stories. What they passed on to kin and colleagues overseas was often what they had read, as well as what they had heard with their own ears or seen with their own eyes. Often, the ultimate source of what they read and heard and told to others was the tortured confessions of captured Africans, beginning with the twenty-five rebels brought to Kingston at the end of April. As the white officials tortured and interrogated and executed these prisoners, they were increasingly keen to the possibility that the revolt on the north side of the island was not an isolated event. Indeed, the bloody reprisals visited upon these St. Mary's rebels soon began to reflect a growing racial panic at the thought of a general servile war.

In early May, the twenty-five captives from St. Mary's reached the end of their time in common. They had been held together for anywhere from one to three weeks, wondering about the fate of the uprising, supporting each other's morale, and considering how they might escape. Some surely calculated what information they could possibly trade for their lives. Among them were men said to be leaders of the insurrection and others who merely had some advance knowledge of the conspiracy. Several had probably been in custody since the early battle near Heywood Hall. They would have been privy to important discussions of strategy and tactics, as the rebels tried to consolidate their initial success and gauge the prospects for the progress of the insurgency. Now the authorities separated them for questioning and trial, sending eleven people to face the ordeal in Spanish Town while the others stayed in Kingston.[89] The trials were to stretch over several weeks, as the colonists executed the convicted rebels in stages, trying to learn more from the remaining prisoners by holding out terrifying examples of the punishment for noncompliance.

The colonial state condemned its enemies with an eye to public instruction, killing some immediately after trial in the towns and executing others at the places where they had supposedly "committed their Barbaries."[90] The government staged the first spectacles of suffering in the capital. A man who had not joined the uprising but had reportedly "sworn to cut his Master's and Mistress's Heads off, and to make Punch Bowls of them," was burned at the stake within hours of being delivered to the court. On Saturday, May 3, one traveler to Spanish Town witnessed the trials of four men "who were found guilty of being concerned in the Murder of the white People." Facing the crowd assembled at the savannah on the edge of town, two rebels were roasted alive and two hanged. Executioners then burned the lifeless bodies of the hanged, chopped off their heads, and fixed them to the tops of poles, *in terrorem*.[91]

The following Monday, in Kingston, the slave courts convicted the men named Fortune and Kingston and sentenced them to be gibbeted on May 10.[92] When the day came, people gathered to see the two rebels hang twenty feet high above the town savannah. Pierre Eugène du Simitière was there and later wrote a detailed description of the execution. In his native French, he knew the punishment as *Pendre au Sec*. The condemned were each enclosed in a cage made of iron hoops closely fitted to different parts of the body: "There was two of them that went across each other from the Summit of their head reaching under the feet in perpendicular direction & many others kept them together by being fasten[ed] upon it in a horizontal line at equal distances." A board under the feet allowed the bound men to stand, yet "their hands were tied across their breast with a pair of shackles." A chain ran through two hoops that met above the men's heads, fastening the cage by a hook to the gallows above. The blacksmith who made the cages locked the prisoners inside. Then they were loaded onto a cart and drawn by a single horse to a gallows erected at the parade near Halfway Tree on the edge of town. Hoisted high above the throng, the men were left to dehydrate and starve, to hang until dry.[93]

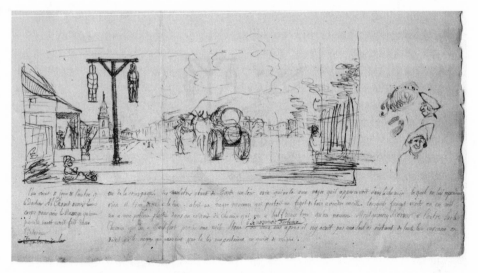

FIGURE 4.1. The Execution of Fortune and Kingston.
Sketched by Pierre Eugène du Simitière. *Courtesy of the Library Company of Philadelphia.*

"They hung a great while," witnesses noted, "in an excessive hot place" that was nevertheless cold at night.[94] A detachment of the Kingston militia, who occupied a small house next to the gallows, guarded them from rescue. One night a mulatto militiaman then on duty hailed an African man passing by with a load of wood. When the African did not answer, the militiaman shot him dead. Kingston and Fortune continued to hang, occasionally gawked at, jeered at, and regarded with solemn stares. One planter wrote disapprovingly that the Africans "diverted themselves all day long in discourse with their countrymen, who were permitted, very improperly, to surround the gibbet."[95] Fortune survived for seven days. Kingston, "who kept his speech" and treated white onlookers with "hardened insolence," lived for nine.[96] The morning before he died, Kingston's body shook with convulsions, drawing the interest of a Dr. Chovet, who wanted to "make some anatomical observations upon so strange a death" and had the bodies delivered to him for dissection. Having satisfied his medical curiosity, he sewed them up, and they were returned to the same cages as before. Authorities then hanged them from two different gallows erected on the main roads leading from opposite sides of town to signify the city's service to the British rule of law.[97]

By several accounts, the two men had displayed remarkable fortitude in their suffering. Some descriptions of the Africans' stoicism surely reflected whites' desire to view black bodies as unfeeling and the gruesome tortures as reasonable and legitimate. "I don't think this Death is so Cruel as people imagine," wrote one Kingston resident, noting that the gibbeted men "scarcely Complain'd." Speaking for the planters, Edward Long contended that the cruel and spectacular punishment was the rebels' just reward and a frank warning against further "murders and outrages," but that Fortune and Kingston "appeared to be very little affected by it themselves," behaving with "brutal insensibility."[98] Bryan Edwards' account of the executions also stressed that "they never uttered the least complaint, except only of cold in the night." They even "laughed immoderately" to his face at some private joke. When describing the death of a different man burned at the stake for having committed murder at Ballard's Valley, Edwards marveled: "His body being chained to an iron stake, the fire was applied to his feet. He uttered not a groan, and saw his legs reduced to ashes with the utmost firmness and composure; after which, one of his arms by some means getting loose, he snatched a brand from the fire that was consuming him, and flung it in the face of his executioner."[99] In all these descriptions it is tempting to see only the whites' self-justification and disavowal of their own brutality. But accounts of African courage and dignity in the face of execution appear in many languages from various parts of the Americas. Coromantees were especially noted for their stoicism, a trait befitting their martial discipline. If this African self-assurance was a conventional trope, it was also an observation.[100] Indeed, in the days ahead, people would have many more opportunities to witness similar displays of African poise during exhibitions of violence all across the island.

The most important purpose of these early interrogations and executions was to provide exemplary warnings to other would-be rebels. To break the spirit of rebellion and to prevent its spread, the slaveholder state fashioned a landscape of terror. Public authorities in Spanish Town and Kingston erected gallows adorned with mutilated black bodies at public markets and thoroughfares, along well-traveled highways, and at entrances to towns to convince potential dissenters that the government had no earthly peer in its power over life and death. Haunting the public in this way, the slaveholders sought to invoke the awe of the supernatural as a counterinsurgency tactic. For this reason, once they knew that obeah practitioners enhanced rebel morale, the state conducted special executions for condemned shamans. One witness later described how "various Experiments were made with Electrical Machines and Magic Lanthorns." These produced little practical effect, "except on one who, after receiving many severe Shocks, acknowledged his Master's Obeah exceeded his own."[101] In their competition for authority over the enslaved, the slaveholders did not hesitate to employ their own forms of wizardry.

The secondary aim of public torture was to gather information about why the revolt had started and how extensive the rebels had intended it to be. The first answers to these questions were comforting. A report from April 22, after the death of Tacky but before the St. Mary's captives came to Kingston and Spanish Town, supposed that the insurrection "was occasioned by the negroes being refused a holiday, by one of their masters on Easter-Monday."[102] Such a local and particular grievance carried no general threat. But Lieutenant Governor Moore had reason to fear a broader danger. Having ordered an end to martial law and the shipping embargo for April 21, he suddenly received word of a fresh insurrection in Westmoreland Parish and belayed the orders. By April 24, he had learned that there was no uprising, only a local disturbance on some adjacent estates, which "by the fears of the People were improv'd into an Insurrection of all the Negroes" in the parish. "Every thing is quiet there, and appears to be so in the other parts of the Island," wrote Moore. He had learned that most of the rebels in St. Mary's "have been either kill'd or taken" and that "Great numbers of suspected Negroes are now under confinement, who will be soon try'd and punish'd according to their Deserts." But Moore was nevertheless persuaded by "some discoveries which have been lately made, and from the quantity of hidden arms which have been found," that "the Insurrection began in Saint Marys was intended to be general."[103]

From soldiers and sailors returning to the towns, and from the first prisoners tortured in early May, the colonists heard confirmation that the uprising in St. Mary's was to be one of many. By May 8, the slaveholders suspected a "deep and cruel" plot by the enslaved. "Their Design was to rise at Kingston and Spanish Town, in one Night; to have set Fire to these Towns in several Places at once, and to murder every Body in them. At the same Time they were to have risen in St. Mary's and Sixteen-Mile-Walk." This simultaneous assault might have been overwhelming, but "the Negroes in St. Mary's began too soon."[104] Tacky had gotten drunk, the colonists gathered, and launched the rebellion "before the others were quite ripe."[105] Now maroons brought his decapitated head to Spanish Town to collect the bounty. Colonial authorities hoped to signal the end of the affair by sticking the leader's head upon a pole on the main highway. But the sign came down before long, "stolen, as was supposed, by some of his countrymen, who were unwilling to let it remain exposed in so ignominious a manner."[106] Slaveholders might have taken this supposed repossession as a countersign from below, an indication that they could vanquish the rebels in battle but could not make the enslaved accept their defeat.

News of more trouble came almost immediately. In the parish of St. Thomas in the East, Coromantees led by men named Akim and Pompey had been planning an uprising around Plantain Garden River, near Manchioneal. Fortunately for the planters, the conspirators included a man named Cuffee, who had at first declined a role in the plot, according to Edward

Long's account, but then, "recollecting that some advantages might be gained to himself by a thorough knowledge of their intentions, he afterwards pretended to have thought better of their proposals, and, professing his zeal to embrace them, he associated at their private cabals from time to time, till he became master of the whole secret, which he took the first opportunity to discover."[107] The British military dispatched a troop of the Kingston horse militia and a detachment of forty marines, brought around to Port Morant Harbour by the navy, to join the local militia as twenty-odd rebels escaped from several plantations into the cover of the woods. British forces gained the initiative before the rebels could marshal their own attacks, but the threat added to the colonists' sense of upheaval.[108]

Then came news of another uprising in Westmoreland—not a false alarm this time—that confirmed their deepest fears. This, we now know, was a larger Coromantee war led by Wager and others, not Tacky's revolt. Late in May, couriers rushed to Spanish Town and Kingston with urgent word of the fresh uprising: "Several Estates in Westmoreland rose in Rebellion, killed about twelve white People and committed great ravages there, and put all that part of the Country into the utmost confusion." The letters that the Lieutenant Governor received from parish residents warned him that this revolt involved no fewer than six hundred slaves. Zachary Bayly returned to Kingston, after six weeks spent suppressing the rebellion in St. Mary's, just in time to receive the news from leeward. Having just learned of the disturbance in St. Thomas in the East, relieved that the Manchioneal conspirators had done "little mischief," he now heard that "before that Insurrection is well quash'd" a much worse uprising had broken out to the west. "Frequent Alarms of Insurrections & Rebellions of Negroes keeps me constantly in action," he groaned. This seemed now to be a colony-wide eruption. From what the colonists had gathered from their prisoners, and from the evidence of the violence, they reached a dreadful conclusion about their predicament: "It is believed that the plan was laid for a general insurrection all over the Island by the Corromantee Negroes who are by much the most numerous & resolute." The war had been planned for the Whitsun Holidays, not Easter, when the St. Mary's rebels had prematurely launched their attack on Fort Haldane.[109]

Again and again, the colonists had tried to reassure themselves that the uprising's scope was narrow, that its spread could be easily contained, and that it was always almost over. Moore had heralded the revolt's suppression on April 24. At the same time, planters like John Morse could "thank God" that the rebels were mostly "kill'd & taken." The slaveholders' constant attempts at self-comfort partly explain their growing zeal to slaughter the rebellious slaves. Colonists tried to convince themselves—and their slaves—that the rebellion was not unmanageable, could not continue, and would go no further. The growing extent and durability of the insurrection dawned on them like the onset of a fever, unsettling at first, then offering definite proof of illness in the heat and sweat of a deep sickness. To cure the malady, they projected all of their forbidden fears onto the black body, which they destroyed as if it were an effigy in the course of a ritual purge. By June, a Kingston resident could note matter-of-factly, "There's scarsely a day passes but some of the Negroes are Executed."[110]

In early June, the colonial state executed Scipio, Harry, and Cuffee at Spring Path. "They were first hanged, then their Heads struck off, and fixed on Poles, and their Bodies burnt." Within days of these killings, trials showed that three more men and two women "appeared to have some Knowledge of the Conspiracy." The slave court had them "severely whipped through The Town." In mid-June, Quaco and Anthony were executed at Spring Path—Quaco burned at the stake and Anthony hanged, with his head then cut off and fixed atop a pole close to Zachary Bayly's house on the road to Greenwich prison. At about the same time, the court determined that the women Sappho, Princess, Sylvia, and Doll appeared to have had "some Knowledge of the Conspiracy." With iron halters around their necks, the women were forced to watch Quaco and Anthony suffer, die, and undergo mutilation. The women's lives were spared. They returned to jail to await transportation from the island, and were threatened with death if they ever returned to Jamaica. Meanwhile, in Spanish Town, the government hanged a man "for endeavouring to seduce several other Slaves into Rebellion."[111]

In all likelihood, these men and women who were tried in June had been among the twenty-five captives who came around the island on the *Lively*. That was almost certainly the case with Anthony, whose name appears on the *Lively's* muster. The list had probably confused Sophia for Sappho, Dod for Doll, Jenery for Harry, and Jack for Quaco, which people often shortened to Quak. Without transcripts of the prisoners' testimony, it is impossible to know what they actually told their captors about the origins and aims of the insurrection in St. Mary's Parish. Even if such testimony had survived, it would be difficult to discern the truth from the coerced fabrications meant to appease the torturers. It would be harder still to learn what vision of society these Africans had espoused when they gathered near Heywood Hall or in the gullies near Downes's Cove, when they thought they might win their war. Some new vision of an Akan polity, perhaps, or some more radical departure from West African forms of state and social order? There is no satisfactory answer to the question. We can be certain, however, that the slaves had formed their own plans for a society in the making, and that whatever they wanted of life in Jamaica, they would not find it in the planters' pageant of bloodletting and human sacrifice.

ONLY the plotters truly knew if their plans had called for a general uprising from the beginning. The colonists were guessing based on evidence garnered from torture, and historians have little more to go on than their speculations. Were the events in St. Mary's, Kingston, St. Thomas in the East, and Westmoreland part of a general insurrection?

Something important is at stake in the answer to this question. Historians sometimes view slave-conspiracy trials as evidence of panic, projections by slaveholders upon hapless victims. Another perspective casts the slaves' actions as mostly reactive responses to immediate circumstances and opportunities, rather than as the outcome of careful organizing.[112] By contrast, the first named historian to interpret Tacky's revolt, Edward Long, agreed with his fellow colonists that the rebellion had been carefully planned:

> These circumstances show the great extent of the conspiracy, the strict correspondence which had been carried on by the Coromantins in every quarter of the island, and their almost incredible secrecy in the forming of their plan of insurrection; for it appeared in evidence, that the first eruption in St. Mary's, was a matter pre-concerted, and known to all the chief men in the different districts; and the secret was probably confided to some hundreds, for several months before the blow was struck.[113]

For Long, Tacky was the "chief man" at the head of the conspiracy. But Long's account is an unreliable guide. Most importantly, he offers an erroneous chronology of events. Wanting to show an island-wide conspiracy, he depicted the events in St. Mary's Parish as simultaneous with later events in Westmoreland, extending the timeline for the St. Mary's uprising and making it appear to last well beyond the Westmoreland insurrection. At least one detail of the account makes this misrepresentation seem willful. Long states that it was Admiral Charles Holmes who dispatched the naval vessels to the north side of the island, despite the fact that Holmes did not arrive at Jamaica until May 13, weeks after Tacky was killed and the rebels had dispersed. Long surely knew this, but distorting the sequence of events in this way had the effect of making the whole affair seem that it was indeed Tacky's revolt.[114]

This theory gave the insurrection an identifiable scapegoat, whom Long could blame and belittle all at once. Acknowledging Tacky as a "young man of good stature, and well made," he called him "handsome, but rather of an effeminate than manly cast." Mocking and demonizing black sexuality was an important part of establishing racial hierarchy, and Long hastened to add that Tacky "had flattered himself with the hope of obtaining (among other fruits of victory) the lieutenant governor's lady for his concubine"— that lady being Edward Long's eldest sister. In Long's estimation, Tacky's elevation stemmed not from his leadership abilities or military experience but from his supposed resemblance to "some favourite leader of their nation in Africa." Probably Tacky had himself been a leader in Africa, but for Long this was merely a sign of Coromantees' credulity. He compared Tacky's followers to some Africans who had once encountered the bronze statue of a gladiator erected on a local plantation, which "the Coromantins no sooner beheld, than they were almost ready to fall down, and adore it."[115] With Tacky at the head of the uprising, Long had devised an intelligible narrative of the violence that conveniently discounted the strategic implications he most feared. According to him, the uprising resulted from a concerted effort, but it was doomed by Africans' intrinsic faults.[116] Yet, as he knew, from the attack on Fort Haldane to Tacky's death in the rocky valley upriver from Downes's Cove, "Tacky's Revolt" lasted only a week.

What explains Long's desire to subsume the entire rebellion within a chronology that elevates the primacy of the events in St. Mary's? Other sources, too, conspired to highlight the importance of the earliest clashes. The April 14 "Letter from a Gentleman at St. Mary's" was the first and only coherently plotted account; the ones that followed displayed the irregularity and confusion of the colonists' predicament. Dread governed their experience. By May, they were growing wild with fright as they ginned up the docket of African savagery. It is difficult to tell which stories came from captured rebels and which sprang from slaveholders' imaginations, especially when the specter of cannibalism appeared in print. Colonists read that the rebels at Ballard's Valley "cut off the Overseer's Head, put his Blood in a Calabash, mixed gunpowder with it, and [ate] their Plantains dipp'd in it, as they did by every white Man they killed: In short, their savage Barbarity can scarcely be paralleled."[117] If there had indeed been a blood sacrifice at Ballard's Valley, this report made it seem as if the rebels were taking some holy communion, with bananas instead of bread. The story made the sacrament all the more heinous by comparing the Coromantees to Catholics—Protestant Britain's foremost global adversaries—and contributed to the sense that the colony was besieged from within and without by enemies at once familiar and strange. With each successive discovery of new unrest, the slaveholders grew more fearful and bewildered. Suddenly the uprising seemed to be happening everywhere at once. The shocking reminder that power did not guarantee security drove colonists wild with fear.[118]

Over the next several weeks, lasting into July, they discovered several more conspiracies. In the commercial capital, colonial officials deepened their investigation into the circumstances surrounding the war-token mahogany sword. They learned that Kingston's Coromantees had rallied around a woman named Cubah, more likely Akua, whom they elevated "to the rank of royalty" and dubbed the "Queen of Kingston." Like other Africans, she claimed territory for herself and her followers in the knowledge that the boundaries of her dominion were drawn more by peoples' loyalties than by land surveyors. At meetings "she had sat in state under a canopy, with a sort of robe on her shoulders, and a crown upon her head," adopting the "paraphernalia of power" she might have known on the Gold Coast. Upon this intelligence, the government seized Cubah and ordered her to be transported from the island.[119] In the Vale of Louidas in St. John's Parish, Coromantees belonging to the speaker of the House of Assembly, Charles Price, "had agreed to rise, ravage the estates, and murder the white men there." Three people familiar with the plan betrayed the rebels, and the "ringleaders were taken up, and upon conviction, executed; others, who turned evidence, were transported off the island thus the whole of this bloody scheme was providentially frustrated."[120] More plots were afoot in the parishes of St. Dorothy's, Hanover, and Clarendon, where Edward Long owned his estate. Throughout this time Henry Moore kept martial law in effect, and the military remained on the march all over the island.[121]

Fear transported the slaveholders into a delirious fever dream from which they would not soon recover.[122] Possibly the experience of frightened alarm during the uprising sent some of them into a fugue state, in which linear temporality lost some of its purchase. They had lost the plot. The narrative they pieced together at the start of the rebellion represented the most linear description they could manage, until Long sat down a decade later in London to reconstruct the sequence. Partly for this reason, and partly because of events that occurred later in the 1760s, the St. Mary's revolt established an enduring narrative pattern, providing an intelligible origin and knowable characters, with the colonists' actions bending a discernible story arc from beginning to end.

The slaveholders were paranoid, and their slaves really were out to get them. Sometimes, these two facts could exist independently; the events of 1760 knotted them together. The causes of the insurrection were probably more broadly distributed and far more contingent than Long and the other slaveholders knew.[123] Even so, whether or not these revolts were the result of a single grand design, they were not disconnected from each other, nor merely opportunistic. The rebels coalesced around affiliations of language, regional identification, and military verve. If each uprising had its own inspiration, each also took careful account of local conditions, potential connections, and broader opportunities. In St. Mary's, the path of the insurgency strongly suggests a defined objective: control or destruction of the commercial zone along the rivers. Yet if what happened in St. Mary's Parish could be called Tacky's Revolt, it was only one conflict within a larger war, an unfolding uprising itself encompassed by wars within wars.

In the cascading series of events initiated by the rebels in St. Mary's, we see how African militancy derived from the entanglements of empire, trade, and war across the Atlantic. Tacky's Revolt was smaller and less significant than Long and subsequent historians have supposed only because the slave war it advanced was larger and more consequential. "A more dangerous or troublesome Affair I was never engaged in, in all my life," wrote Zachary Bayly about the St. Mary's insurrection. And still the Coromantee War was closer to its beginning than its end.[124]

CHAPTER FIVE

The Coromantee War

WAGER AND HIS COMPATRIOTS struck while the colonists were still digesting the news from St. Mary's Parish. Tacky's revolt had been largely suppressed by the end of April, but rumors of new conspiracies and reports about the tortured confessions of captured insurgents kept slaveholders on high alert. The onset of the insurrection in Westmoreland on May 25 confirmed to most colonists that the entire island was under attack from within. The shock and alarm that greeted the St. Mary's rebellion grew into the dread certainty of a general insurrection. The location of this new outbreak heightened the fear, because colonists considered Westmoreland a far more important place than St. Mary's. Acre for acre, Westmoreland Parish was one of the most profitable territories in the British Empire. Unlike St. Mary's Parish, lightly settled in the landscape's folds and creases, the broad Westmoreland plain was densely populated with sugar plantations and legions of slaves, making the parish a powerful engine of accumulation.

"The face of the country" was beautiful to planters. They praised Westmoreland's "continued succession of well-cultivated sugar-estates and rich pastures," pleased by the prospect of the wealth these represented.[1] Indeed Westmoreland was booming with growth by 1760. In the first half of the eighteenth century, its rate of settlement outpaced that of any other parish in Jamaica.[2] By the time of the revolt, about fifteen thousand slaves labored on more than sixty sugar plantations, many of them owned by the leading men of the island.[3] William Beckford, the planter who served continuously

FIGURE 5.1. The Westmoreland Plain, looking west from St. Elizabeth Parish toward the Hanover Mountains.

Painting by Joseph B. Kidd. From *Illustrations of Jamaica in a Series of Views* (London, 1838–1840). *Courtesy of Yale Center for British Art.*

in the British House of Commons from 1747 to 1770 and would serve two terms as Lord Mayor of London, owned more than seven hundred acres here. Captain Arthur Forrest of the Royal Navy owned nearly three thousand acres between his holdings in Westmoreland and neighboring St. Elizabeth.[4] Westmoreland was also home to Thomas Thistlewood, the English overseer whose rise over three decades from struggling immigrant to self-sufficient landholder depended on the abundant wealth generated by the plantation economy.

The gateway to the parish, Bluefields Bay, was among the finer harbors in the Americas. Although the district hosted a few serviceable ports, including one at the main town of Savanna la Mar, the entrance to Savanna la Mar Bay was too narrow to accommodate ships above 350 tons, including most warships. Bluefields Bay was broad and deep, allowing heavy ships to enter, exit, and ride at anchor in any tide. Just as important, sailors regarded the fresh water at Bluefield River to be "as good as any in the World." British ships bound through the Gulf of Florida generally came to Bluefields for wood and water, and the bay was a crucial rendezvous for the West India commercial convoys that gathered during wartime to await their military escorts to North America and Great Britain.[5] Given the parish's economic and strategic importance, a military defeat in Westmoreland would be a serious blow to the British Empire.

Yet, though the parish was a valuable hinge for Britain's commerce, much of the region was out of the way. As elsewhere in the Americas, this pivotal place was adjacent to rough and forbidding lands, abutting several great tracts of marsh, hill, and mountain. At the western end of the parish, a great morass stretched between Negril Harbour and South Negril Point and extended a few miles inland until it met the western reaches of the Hanover Mountains. The mountains rose high above dense woods and thickets, then dropped off sharply before rising again to divide Westmoreland from Hanover Parish, continuing north of the agricultural plain and reaching higher still in St. James and St. Elizabeth.[6] Residing in these "vast high mountains" were the leeward maroon villages of Furry's Town, Accompong Town, and Trelawny Town—the last built "by that Gang of Wild Negroes," explained local historian James Knight, "who were the first that submitted themselves in 1738, and were the means of bringing in the others."[7] With the mountains patrolled by the maroons, runaways now more often sought refuge in the swamps that interrupted the flatlands in Westmoreland and neighboring St. Elizabeth. Writing more than a decade after the insurrection, Edward Long considered Westmoreland the parish "most likely to be infested with such disturbances; for it is a part of the country where there are a great multitude of slaves, and few proprietors of estates reside; and where the neighborhood is filled with woods and thickets, that might the oftener tempt them to mutiny, by the shelter they afford."[8] This uneven landscape—variously subject to the discipline of imperial capitalism but wild and unruly, too—shaped the course of the Coromantee War.

Such juxtapositions of margin and center in Jamaica's imperial geography linked the local scale of slave revolt to the hemispheric scope of Atlantic empire. Here the economic, political, and military labor of British dominion passed through the rough-hewn trails of an uneven and violently contested terrain. Because the colonists shunned the uncultivated forests and mountains, the matrix of movement that defined the British Atlantic Empire overlapped imperfectly with the movements of the black people in its territory. Their routes through the hills, forests, and mountains made up a distinct set of itineraries that the British did not know and could not control. And this interior region was the battleground for small wars within larger wars. In this way the revolt in Westmoreland bound the inter-imperial Atlantic to the local landscape in ways that illuminate a composite political geography in the making. More directly than the revolt in St. Mary's Parish, the Coromantee War in the leeward parts of Jamaica connected the insurrection to African and European military campaigns on the far side of the Atlantic Ocean. Rebel strategy here drew upon African experiences of forest warfare and mountaineering even as British troops fought the rebellion as one battle in an integrated global conflict. In this way diasporic warfare

FIGURE 5.2. William Beckford's Estate in Westmoreland Parish.

A View in the Island of Jamaica of Roaring River Estate belonging to William Beckford Esq.r near Savannah la Marr, engraved by Thomas Vivares from a painting by George Robertson. *Courtesy of The British Library.*

defined the region, as all combatants strained to secure the affiliations and alliances that would map the territory for future generations.

MARTIAL law had just ended when Thomas Thistlewood noticed two men belonging to Captain Arthur Forrest's Masemure estate mingling among the slaves at Egypt plantation, where he served as overseer. He thought little of it at the time, adding nothing to the brief mention of the visit in his diary. A few days later, however, on the afternoon of May 25, a planter from the mountains came around with a rumor told to him by a "strange Negroe man" of a "supposed Insurection to be to-Morrow, when 8000 Negroe Men are to Muster in Certain Places ffrom hanover and th[is] parish." In his weather journal, Thistlewood recorded intermittent rain showers; there was thunder at a distance, and when the sky darkened, he saw the lightning. Late in the evening, Thistlewood heard a horn blowing in the slave quarters, and soon after midnight several white men called at his door to tell him of the uprising at Forrest's Masemure estate.[9]

Masemure's managing attorney John Smith, a female friend, the overseer, and a bookkeeper had gathered for a Whitsun Holiday supper with several

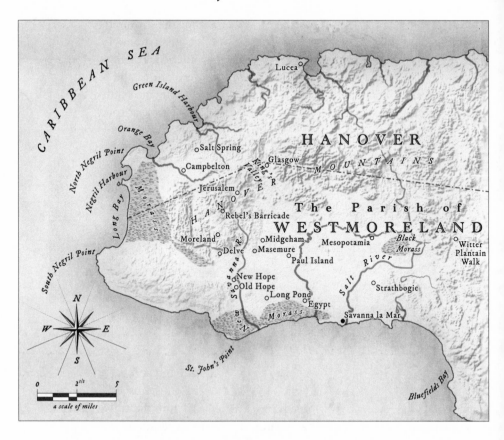

others, including Captain Hoare, commander of a merchant ship, his nephew, and Captain George Richardson. The guests remarked upon "how still and quiet everything was." Given the previous several weeks of news and rumor, the calm might have been reassuring and unsettling in equal measure. Then, without warning, someone fired a musket through the window, immediately killing John Smith. All at once, African rebels rushed into the house with cane knives to slay the whites. Captain Hoare barely survived severe knife wounds. Captain Richardson and another man made a narrow escape, "running to the Bay on Foot" to give the alarm. Several of Forrest's slaves—Nero, Congo, Molly, and Beckford—also slipped away and warned the neighborhood, while three or four hundred insurgents rose on nearby plantations and marched to Masemure.[10]

The militants followed tactical conventions, seeking to kill as many whites as they could and as quickly as possible while their force increased in number. As the rebels had in St. Mary's, the Westmoreland rebels first coalesced on large plantations where they could quickly overwhelm a few managers, overseers, and loyal slaves before raising the surrounding estates. Immediately killing the whites not only served the military aims of removing enemies from the battlefield and buying time against the reaction of the opposing forces by suppressing the alarm, it also broadcast the boldness of their determination. Attorneys and overseers, the white men closest to daily slave management, who knew the workers and their social routines, were especially important targets. Ransacking Masemure, the rebels surrounded the house of Alexander Crawford, who owned the property jointly with Arthur Forrest. There they encountered the resistance of some slaves, who refused to join the rebels and protected their master. Not wanting to lose time, the rebels crossed the New Savannah River and advanced on James Woodcock's Delve estate near the foot of the Hanover Mountains. Woodcock had previously worried about the danger of possessing too many Coromantees—he had owned at least eighty at one point—and now as many as two hundred of his slaves joined the uprising; not all were from the Gold Coast.[11] From Delve the rebels ascended to Moreland, a multiple-estate plantation complex high above the plain, where several hundred more people joined the revolt. Seizing Moreland, the rebel army occupied it as a military base. By the accounting of the colonists, nearly one hundred of them were well armed, having taken "60 Stand of Arms from Forrest's Estate & some few from the other Estates they thought proper to visit."[12] Meanwhile, insurgents rose up on some estates on the other side of the mountains, in Hanover Parish. In less than twenty-four hours, the Africans had killed eleven whites and an unnamed number of blacks who resisted them, before ensconcing themselves upon defensible high ground.[13]

From Moreland, the rebels pressed further up the mountains, where they began to build a fortified refuge. According to Edward Long, "They formed a strong breast-work across a road, flanked by a rocky hill; within this work they erected their huts, and sat down in a sort of encampment."[14] The engineers for this fort were supposed to have been some of the "French Negroes" who had been captured during the British occupation of Guadeloupe and bought by agents for Masemure. "These men were the more dangerous," said Long, "as they had been at arms" for the French "and seen something of military operations there." At the "Rebel's Barricade" the Coromantees made a stand, repulsing several parties of colonists, "owing to their advantageous situation and having arms and ammunition in plenty."[15] As rebels coalesced at the mountain stronghold, colonists feared the insurgent army to be about a thousand strong.[16]

LIKE the rebels in St. Mary's, those in Westmoreland and Hanover came to a brief pause after the first burst of fighting. Wager, also known as Apongo,

MAY 25 *1 mile* WESTMORELAND

In Westmoreland Parish, rebels rise up on Masemure estate, killing several...

Moreland

Delve

Masemure

They proceed to Delve and Moreland estates, gathering forces

LEGEND

N W E S

·······> Rebels
——> Militia
——> Army
– – –> Maroons
⌇⌇> Navy

Clash with rebels ✿
Parish boundary ---------
Parish name WESTMORELAND

MAY 26, earlier *1 mile*

HANOVER

Hundreds of rebels rise up on multiple estates throughout the region

Campbelton

Fish River WESTMORELAND

From their base at Moreland, rebels begin to gather at a mountain encampment

Moreland

Delve

Retrieve

New Hope

Old Hope

MAY 26, later HANOVER *1 mile*

Lucea

WESTMORELAND

Jerusalem

Montego Bay

Moreland

Meanwhile, British Army units march to Egypt, Moreland, and Jerusalem estates

Masemure

Militias march to Masemure and Moreland estates to engage rebels

Egypt

Salt River

Savanna La Mar

MAY 27+28 *1 mile*

HANOVER

Rebels erect a fortified encampment 1200 people strong, the highest estimate of numbers assembled

Rebel's Barricade

Moreland

...while militia and soldiers hunt rebels in the woods around Moreland estate

WESTMORELAND

MAY 29 *1 mile*

Rebel's Barricade WESTMORELAND

Jacobfield

Moreland

Rebels at barricade repulse militia attacks; militia retreat to Moreland estate

Salt River

Militia suppress uprising at Jacobfield estate

MAY 30 HANOVER

1 mile

Furry Town Maroons

Trelawny Town Maroons

ST JAMES

Accompong Town Maroons

Moreland

WESTMORELAND

Savanna La Mar

Maroons join British forces at Moreland

Army and naval reinforcements dispatched to Westmoreland and St. Elizabeth parishes by sea from Port Royal

Lacovia

ST ELIZABETH

JUNE 2

1 mile

HANOVER

Maroons surround rebel encampment; militia and army attack from Moreland estate, killing scores of rebels and overtaking the rebel base

Rebel's Barricade

Moreland

WESTMORELAND

The rebel encampment disperses...

JUNE 3-5

HANOVER

1 mile

Navy vessels are deployed from Port Royal to Westmoreland Parish, and army reinfocements arrive after suppressing the St. Mary's rebellion

Moreland

WESTMORELAND

49th Regiment

Savanna La Mar

HMS Harwich
HMS Port Royal
HMS Viper

Several Westmoreland rebels are executed at Savanna La Mar

JUNE 6-16

Glascow
Jerusalem

HANOVER

1 mile

Rebels ambush parties of soldiers around Moreland estate, and maroons capture and kill scores of rebels

Moreland

Mesopotamia

WESTMORELAND

Rebels sack Jerusalem estate and threaten Glascow estate, but are repelled. In the mountains around Mesopotamia estate, many rebels are killed and captured.

Militia search for rebels in the mountains; a body of rebels led by Simon begins a retreat from Westmoreland parish

JUNE 17 - AUGUST 3

As some rebels leave the parish, those left face the combined British forces, who attempt to drive rebels out of the mountains and force them to surrender

HANOVER

1 mile

King's Valley

Jacobfield

Crawford

Mesopotamia

Moreland

Masemure

Paul Island

WESTMORELAND

Savanna La Mar

Most still in rebellion are either killed, commit suicide in the woods, or surrender through June and July

Rebel leaders including Wager, aka Apongo, are captured and executed at Savanna La Mar was among the militants. Also present were Simon (who had fired the first killing shot at John Smith), Goliath, Fortune, and Davie, all the human property of Captain Arthur Forrest. As they gathered at the Rebel's Barricade, they considered the progress of their opening strategy. By the time the uprising engulfed Westmoreland, the colonists were convinced of the rebels' ambition to conquer the entire island. As Admiral Charles Holmes informed the Admiralty, this "fresh insurrection" was "much more formidable than the first, and the whole Island remained in great Terror and Consternation for some time, having had more Evidence than before of their Disobedience & Revolt being intended to be universal."[17] There was no urgent desire for a nuanced explanation of insurgent strategy. Yet here again, the timing and location of rebel movements reveal a clearer outline of the Africans' plan than the colonists gained from the tortured confessions of prisoners and their own panicked speculations. The colonists were correct that the Westmoreland revolt was anything but haphazard; its progress suggests the rebels' complex appraisal of and adaptation to Jamaica's political geography.

The timing of the outbreak could not have been accidental—at least not in Westmoreland. May 25 was the date set for the merchant fleet and its naval escort to depart from Bluefield's Bay for North America and Great Britain, having been rescheduled after the uprising in St. Mary's. The rebels knew that for days and weeks leading up to the expected launch, the entire attention of the parish would be moving toward the docks, focused upon staffing, loading, and provisioning the ships. No one would be looking to the mountains, and when the convoy put to sea, it would take some protection for the parish with it. Even more fortunately, this occasion would coincide with a public celebration.

Colonists ascertained that "the plan was laid for a general insurrection all over the Island by the Corromantee Negroes" and that "the time fix'd was the Witsun Hollidays."[18] In St. Mary's, they now believed, the rebels had mistaken Easter Sunday for Whitsunday and risen up too soon.[19] It would have been an understandable mistake for Africans to make, given that many of the rebels in St. Mary's were newer arrivals unfamiliar with the holiday. The Whitsun Holidays encompassed the Christian festival of Pentecost, the seventh Sunday after Easter, commemorating the descent of the Holy Spirit upon Christ's disciples. In England, White Sunday, or Whitsunday, was a feasting day followed by the weeklong holiday Whitsuntide. Traditionally, this week marked a pause in the agricultural calendar and was a vacation week for the medieval *villein,* during which time slaves were free from service on the manor and lands of their lord. The laws of

Jamaican slave society recognized the holiday, but planters differed in how much "leisure-time" they allowed their own *villeins*.[20]

Having timed the rebellion for the Whitsun Holidays, when slaves received a break from their punishing work routines, the conspirators could count on laxer restrictions on the activities and movement of slaves, both leading up to the holiday, as they prepared their celebrations, and during the festivities. The mobilization would thereby gain a bit more latitude without raising the suspicions of the planters. Thomas Thistlewood, for example, had been unconcerned when two men from Masemure came to see Jackie just three days before the uprising. Months later, having learned that "[a]t the beginning of the rebellion, a shaved head amongst the Negroes was the signal of war," he remembered that on the day of the uprising, "our Jackie, Job, Achilles, Quasheba, Rsanna etc had their heads remarkably shaved."[21] At the time, he must have assumed they were merely styling themselves for the parties.

Coordinating the uprising with the liturgical calendar had another benefit. By choosing a date that was significant across the entire island the conspirators could hope to shock and overawe the slaveholders with simultaneous attacks. For any slave familiar with the meaning of Pentecost, when the Holy Spirit filled the bodies of the disciples, there may have been special significance in the words of Acts 2:18: "Even upon my slaves, both men and women, in those days I will pour out my Spirit; and they shall prophesy." But most Africans had little knowledge of or interest in Christian theology, and would have found it easy to confuse the Pentecost with the Resurrection. Although planters came to believe that Tacky had gotten drunk and initiated his action too soon—alcohol was an important ingredient in battlefield bravery for most early modern soldiers, in any case—confusion over the holidays may instead account for why Tacky's Revolt began on Easter while the Westmoreland rebels rose up at Whitsuntide.[22]

In the event that there existed no single scheme, there was a more general mutinous disposition given shape and direction by the contours of the island. The great distance between Westmoreland and St. Mary's compounded the difficulty of transmitting and coordinating plans. News between parishes had to travel over Jamaica's high mountains or come through Kingston and Spanish Town, the two most significant nodes in the island's network of information. Although the enslaved carried on extensive communications, much detail must have been lost as they conveyed messages orally and surreptitiously through plantation stewards or runaways. This meant that, however the rebels may have hoped to connect various uprisings throughout the island, local geographies set the immediate stakes and strategies of each insurrection.

Arthur Forrest's Masemure estate, the center of the Westmoreland uprising, lay within a long stretch of plantations along the skirt of the Hanover Mountains, which loomed behind. Between these peaks and the heavily forested range of high mountains to the east, the road to Hanover Parish ran through King's Valley, a fertile glade dotted with several more estates.[23] In Hanover Parish, just behind the mountains, a rich cluster of plantations lined the rivers that ran down to Green Island Harbour and Orange Bay, at the head of the vast morass behind Negril and Long Bay, on the western end of the island. Within a day of the outbreak at Masemure, uprisings had occurred on estates all around the base of this range. Almost certainly, this indicates a strategic focus arising from a network of communication and planning that ran through the mountains.[24]

The Rebel's Barricade was perched high upon a precipice in the Hanover Mountains, presumed to be defensible from both the planters who dominated the sprawling plains in Westmoreland and Hanover and their maroon allies in the great mountains and cockpits east of King's Valley. Here, the rebels would establish a new maroon village, completing the black occupation of the leeward highlands. Women and children came in large numbers to the camp, where insurgents immediately began to build what they hoped would be an enduring alternative society. Whether or not an island-wide insurrection was in the works, this mountain redoubt would be a central township in the rebels' local territory.

There was another alternative. Later, during the suppression of the revolt, when slaveholders tortured captured rebels, it emerged that they had considered heading directly for the bay to occupy the strategic gateway to one of the most profitable districts in the empire.[25] Interpreting a rumored conversation supposedly occurring between a captured rebel and a Jewish man in the Savanna la Mar jail, Edward Long believed that the rebels had hoped to ally themselves with the Jews, drive out the whites, enslave blacks who failed to join the uprising, and continue to make sugar and rum for export. According to Long, the rebel believed the hoped-for black state could continue its commerce through the auspices of sailors, who "do not oppose us," he averred, "[as] they care not who is in possession of the country, Black or White."[26] If these stories were at all credible, then there was surely a dispute among rebel leaders between a faction that wanted to carve an independent village out of the mountains—a strategy proven viable by Kojo's maroons—and those who favored a more aggressive offense, emulating the coastal trading states of West Africa. Perhaps there was a middle ground. If the Hanover insurrection had been successful, the rebels might have secured access to Orange Bay, a capacious and deep harbor lying behind North Negril Point.[27] Unlike the maroon towns in the mountains to the east, this village might have maintained access to the sea and to external trade, a compromise, perhaps, between two different visions of black freedom in Jamaica.

MEANWHILE, the British were developing their strategy to curtail black liberty. By now, the colonists' reaction to slave insurrection followed a fairly clear pattern. First, militia units composed mostly of white men from the surrounding plantations confronted the rebels, often with poor success. At the same time, white women, children, and elderly people fled the estates for the ports, where they huddled in fear. As soon as he received word of the first uprising in St. Mary's Parish, Lieutenant Governor Henry Moore had declared martial law and mobilized the formal counterinsurgency: the army, who were much more effective than the militia at traveling long distances in fighting formation and in waging set-piece battles; the Navy, which conducted relief and resupply efforts while lending sailors and marines to engagements on land; and the maroons, who excelled at pursuing rebels through dense forest and mountains. The militia, sticking close to the plantations, continued to skirmish with the bands of rebels who survived major engagements. The countryside became a militarized free-fire zone where any suspicious "Negro" could be taken, tortured, or killed on sight. However, the coordination of these various forces was fraught with difficulty. The British faced their own problems of planning and organization, caused by the centrifugal effects of distance from central authority. Fissures in the chain of command and divergent interests among the various elements of its coalition created severe challenges to the military effort. If the British ultimately prevailed over the Coromantees, it was only with great effort and expenditure over a long stretch of time.

News of the uprising traveled fast. Already distressed by the previous weeks' events, colonists reacted with violent fright as they ran among the estates, spreading the alarm. The whites who had come to warn Thistlewood were in various states of undress, telling him he "should probably be murdered in a short time." Flying up the road to the estate of militia colonel James Barclay, Thistlewood forgot his keys and papers and had to rush back to Egypt to secure the property. From there he went down to the bay for militia duty until daylight, when he returned again to the estate. There he found John Groves, one of the white plantation hands, in a murderous frenzy. "Like a madman," Groves shot wildly at several black boys, wounding the personal servant of a prominent planter, then fled to Savanna la Mar without Thistlewood's permission.[28] Across the parish, Moravian missionaries at Mesopotamia estate quickly received the "distressing message" that "Negroes had broken out in rebellion" and "gruesomely murdered many." Within hours, the missionaries learned, "all the white people in this parish were going to rifle practice" as the slaveholders drilled for war.[29] Planters also selectively armed slaves they thought they could trust. Thistlewood's slaves largely remained loyal, as did those at Mesopotamia. Other slaveholders were not as fortunate. Colin Campbell at New Hope estate armed twelve slaves who promptly joined the rebellion. Likewise, Tom Williams at Old Hope estate armed twenty Coromantee men in whom he had the "utmost confidence," instructing them to guard his house, but as soon as they received the firearms "they assured him they would do him no harm, but that they must go and join their countrymen, and then saluting him with their hats, they every one marched off."[30]

By midday on May 26, the entire parish was in a state of chaotic mobilization. Passing through Egypt on the road to the Hanover Mountains were "vast Numbers off people, belonging to the Troop, Militia &c.," while other colonists transmitted numerous dispatches in response to "Frequent alarms."[31] British army troops began marches from as far as Lucea in Hanover and Montego Bay in St. James Parish to Jerusalem estate on the edge of King's Valley to guard the mountain pass to Hanover. More British regulars assembled along with the Westmoreland militia at Savanna la Mar and at Salt River, just east of the town, and advanced west along the main road. They passed close to Egypt, continued along the edge of the morass, then turned up toward the mountains. Sporadic engagements with the rebels yielded irregular results. Colonel Barclay's militia party captured seventeen prisoners at Masemure, while a party of loyal slaves belonging to Campbelltown estate in Hanover brought in seventeen more from Moreland. On May 27, parties from Westmoreland and Hanover captured eighteen rebels and began to hang their captives the very next day.[32] As soldiers chased after the main body of rebels, they also lashed out at anyone they found to be suspicious. "Sambo & Mitilia killed at Egypt," noted Thistlewood, with no mention of an inquiry or trial.[33]

The uprising was a tense predicament for the Moravians at Mesopotamia because they were pacifist and declined to carry arms. Brother Nicolaus Gandrup described how "a great Company of armed white people on horses passed by our house and at the big house they got off their horses and stayed until the evening around 8 o'clock, when they came again to our house and called us: they said we had to take weapons and appear at Cross-

Path in the morning." The missionaries confronted the militia with determined principle:

> "We said to the captain (named Richard) that first of all we had no weapons and second of all, we didn't think we needed them, and third of all, it was not our thing to carry arms. We were then thought to be Quakers. He said to us: that Quaker-Principles were not accepted in Jamaica, and that if we were Bishops, we had to go with him. Then we told him: we weren't Quakers but Brethren, and we had the privilege of the power of an Act of Parliament, so that we were allowed in all the English lands. Then they desired to see the Act, but we didn't have one to show. The Captain however was satisfied that Brother Gandrup promised to show him the Act the next day, and on that the Captain took his leave politely and went on his way."[34]

The brethren then prevailed upon the estate's attorney to speak to the militia captain on their behalf, and the missionaries were left to their consciences. As the parish awoke to the sound of military drums, the Moravians found themselves torn between the practice of their faith on one side and their attachment to the planters on the other: "We poor things live as ever between fear and hope," one wrote, "because we still have to legitimate ourselves in our manner of being." Still, they must have felt some relief when the attorney told them the militia "had already captured 15 rebels and had done justice on some of them already."[35]

The early battles again showed the mediocrity of the militia, who initially engaged the rebels with indifferent results. One colonist admitted, "We were a little imprudent at first I believe having sent out small parties & they not being able to stay for want of water &C which has been the occasion of our Loose.g so many more than we should have done."[36] In fact, the colonists' response was rife with confusion and indiscipline. Soldiers and sailors who passed through Egypt called on Thistlewood for food and grog, which he readily gave. "Sad work amongst the Sailors," who had gotten too drunk, Thistlewood lamented. A soldier who had fallen asleep in the bush had lost his weapons the night before. Nearby, "a party of Rebellious Negroes" had "Stopp'd a Canoe loaded with Sugar" and other goods. But militiamen, visiting planters, and Egypt's own slaves could do little but keep a strict watch day and night. With the insurrection still growing two nights after the initial outbreak, Thistlewood's diary recorded his nervous vigilance: "I lay down Some times with my Cloaths on and Slept little."[37]

He awoke early the next morning, had his way with an enslaved woman in the curing house, and was cheered a few hours later when a party of soldiers came through with twenty-one prisoners, nineteen men and two women, bound for trial and execution at the bay. As Thistlewood distributed grog to the soldiers, he learned that one of the captured men was a leader, "his hair shaved in the fform off a Cap on his head." This man was followed not only by African rebels, but by terrifying rumors, too. Supposedly, he had eaten "the heart & tongue off one off the White People Murder'd." The colonists believed he "was to have been king."[38] Despite his capture, however, the rebels continued to gather strength. Thistlewood began to wonder which of Egypt's slaves might be conniving with the rebellion. He had perceived a "strange alteration" in some of them upon hearing the news of the uprising at nearby Old Hope estate; he remembered that there had been rumblings in the fields the day before the uprising at Moreland; Lewie had been at Forrest's the night of the uprising, and Coffee and Job were acting very strange. Many, he worried, were "very ready if they durst," and he was "pretty certain they were in the Plot."[39] He maintained his watch, continued to provision the whites who called on him, and hoped the armed men passing through Egypt on their way to the mountains would soon suppress the rebels.

On May 29, in what turned out to be a major setback for the colonists, the militia made a failed attempt on the Rebel's Barricade. Led by Captain John Myries, whose family owned six hundred acres south of the morass, a large militia party charged the rebels' forward base at Moreland, killing and wounding many, and proceeded confidently up toward the African stronghold.[40] In the steep and narrow passage, however, the rebels surprised and overwhelmed them, killing four men and sending the rest flying back down the mountain. Edward Long later described the defeat with palpable dismay: "The men were badly disciplined, having been hastily collected; and falling into an ambuscade, they were struck with terror at the dismal yells, and the multitude of their assailants. The whole party was thrown into the utmost confusion, and routed, notwithstanding every endeavour of their officers; each strove to shift for himself, and whilst they ran different ways, scarcely knowing what they were about, several were butchered, others broke their limbs over precipices, and the rest with difficulty found their way back again."[41] The Africans acquired about fifty more rifles, which the colonists "very imprudently left behind when they ran."[42]

In Long's analysis, this loss stemmed from poor judgment on the part of the colonists. It was folly, he thought, "to make the first attack upon them with a handful of raw, undisciplined militia, without advancing at the same time a party in reserve, to sustain their efforts, and cover their retreat." Only "tried and well-trained men" could suppress such revolts. Failure in this first major action had potentially catastrophic strategic consequences. The rebels' victory "raised the spirits of the Coromantins in this part of the country" and encouraged many others to join the uprising. Just as the Africans aimed to strike fast and amass their forces before the planters could react, the logic of counterinsurgency depended on checking the rebels immediately. Long averred that "every other insurrection that has occurred in this island" vindicated this wisdom. "The winning the first battle from the rebellious party, usually decides the issue of the war; it disconcerts the conspirators, not as yet engaged, and who keep aloof, irresolute whether to join or not; and it intimidates all that are in arms, and most commonly plunges them into despondency: the reverse is sure to follow a defeat of the Whites on the first encounter; and nothing can add greater strength to rebellion, or tend more to raise the authority of the priests and leaders who have set it on foot." Now, the rebels were "flushed with a confidence in their superiority, and gathered reinforcements every day."[43] The colonists immediately recognized the potential fallout of the event.

As the insurrection surged, a wave of fear crested over the plain. Within a day, most people in the parish had learned of the defeat at the Rebel's Barricade. "The Negroes have no notion of Prisoners, they give no quarter," cried the planters.[44] Thistlewood was "under dreadful apprehensions" after Colonel Barclay brought news of the reversal. The overseer perceived that his slaves had "good intelligence" of the battle's outcome, "being greatly Elevated and ready to rise." Another planter warned him, "for god's Sake," to take care of himself. "Now we are in the most danger," they agreed. In the afternoon, three black youths came running from Jacobfield estate near Masemure to inform Thistlewood that some rebels, shouting and firing guns, had torn down much of the great house before escaping the militia.[45] The next evening, Thistlewood harbored a fugitive overseer from nearby Long Pond estate: "Mr: [Thomas] Reid Come and Slept on my Bed, he was Warned by one off their Negroes to go off the Estate, as one off their Coromante's was reported to Come in the Night With a Party off the rebellious Negroes to take all they Could with them, many off the Well affected Negroes lefft the Estate, lest they should be fforced to Join the Rebells."[46] At Mesopotamia, the missionaries "heard that the rebellion had burned another Plantation; and we saw the smoke rise up." White women fled for a ship anchored in the bay "in order to escape the atrocity."[47] On another estate nearby, it was said that "all of the negroes have run away and the place is supposed to be totally vacated."[48]

Desertions began to spread through the militia, and many in the parish commended property owners like Mr. Cornell, who was said "to have allowed no deserters into his house, otherwise they would have come to visit and themselves drive out others." The Moravians found themselves nearly alone, left to God's care: "None of the white people are here except us; but we are not in fear; we are cheerful and at peace; and we release ourselves all singly to our dear heavenly Father's protection and keeping." The Anglican Reverend John Venn, who arrived with a relief effort at Savanna la Mar on Saturday, May 31, described the swirling chaos: "I found the Women and Children on board the Ships, the Men gathered all in a heap at Savannah La Mar, in the utmost Confusion, all the White Men were drawn from the Windward part of the Parish."[49] At this point, it seemed, Westmoreland Parish might be lost to the Africans.

In the wake of the debacle, a new intensity gripped the counterinsurgency. "This last affair makes people put on a serious face," noted one man when the news reached Spanish Town and Kingston.[50] Already, the British military was gathering and redirecting its forces. A company of the Seventy-fourth Regiment quartered at Savanna La Mar joined the Westmoreland militia and two detachments from the maroon towns. More militia arrived from neighboring St. Elizabeth, where alarmed whites were frantically "searching all the Negro Houses [and] from whence took every Gun & whatever warlike weapon" they found.[51] Two companies of the Forty-ninth Regiment, which had been quartered at Lucea and Montego Bay, joined with the militia companies from Hanover and St. James on the other side of the Hanover Mountains.[52] To contain the rebellion, British army units deployed at Lacovia in neighboring St. Elizabeth Parish. Hearing that the "great ravages" committed by the rebels had put "all that part of the Country into the utmost confusion," Lieutenant Governor Moore again declared martial law.[53] Then he requested that Admiral Holmes immediately send a vessel around with arms and ammunition, followed by three warships carrying "such a number of Forces, as must necessarily, joyn'd to the Militia of those parts, put an end to this Insurrection very shortly."[54] Now, with the military fully mobilized to leeward, this became a war for the British Empire itself.

MORE support was arriving daily by sea. The Royal Navy played a more integral role in the Westmoreland counterinsurgency than it had in the St. Mary's revolt, deploying more quickly, bringing more men to the fight, and dispensing greater quantities of provisions. Indeed, the Navy brought the full resources of transatlantic empire to bear against the rebels, articulating the local conflict to the wider war. The superior mobility of naval forces allowed faster deployments across greater areas. Delimiting some territories and linking others, depending on where forces were positioned, these deployments helped to determine access to pathways of territorial maneuver. The Navy also coordinated the provisioning of troops and colonists, freeing them from dependence upon contested plantation lands. And because Jamaica's wealth depended on maritime commerce, which in turn relied on the wartime convoy system, the involvement of the Royal Navy ensured that the efforts of the counterinsurgency would ripple through the Atlantic world.

Admiral Charles Holmes's flagship, HMS *Cambridge,* was the nerve center of the war effort in the West Indies. From the bridge of the *Cambridge,* or the *Marlborough* before that, the Admiral at the Jamaica station directed the most powerful squadron in British America. But though the flagship boasted eighty cannon and a complement of some seven hundred men, its power was not primarily in physical force but in its logistical capacity. The flagship directed the regional distribution of soldiers, provisions, and other material stores among the fleet. No less important, it was the central conduit of responsibility and discipline for the station, allocating assignments and hosting courts martial. The flagship also played a crucial role in the system of reporting and accounting that allowed for some consistency in regional planning and operations. Thus, in June of 1760, HMS *Cambridge* led the British war against the slave rebels, with Port Royal Harbour as its imperial headquarters.

Admiral Holmes had arrived at the harbor on May 13, after landing troops at Guadeloupe and escorting a convoy of seventeen merchant ships from Europe safely to the station.[55] Announcing his entrance, the *Cambridge* fired a fifteen-gun salute to Admiral Cotes, which he returned from the *Marlborough*. For the next week, Cotes briefed Holmes on the situation in Jamaica and prepared him to take command of the squadron when Cotes left the harbor on May 22, a day after the lifting of martial law.[56] Days later, as soon as Holmes received the aid request from Lieutenant Governor Moore, the Admiral dispatched a ship with arms and ammunition to Westmoreland for the use of the militia. Then he ordered two sloops, HMS *Port Royal* and HMS *Viper,* to sail to Westmoreland with soldiers and supplies.[57] On Monday, June 2, sailors transferred provisions from the *Cambridge* to the *Viper.* Then on Tuesday morning, Holmes "had an Express from the Lt. Governour that the Rebellious Negroes were got together to amount of twelve Hundred"—the panicked message that had been sent after the debacle at Rebel's Barricade.[58]

Without delay, Holmes sent a longboat to Fort Charles to pick up nearly sixty men from the Forty-ninth Regiment of Foot, and filled another boat with fifty-eight marines from the *Cambridge*.[59] More than half of the marines had seen combat at Guadeloupe.[60] All the soldiers went aboard the 50-gun HMS *Harwich,* which sailed on June 4 for the brief trip to Westmoreland Parish.[61] By directing the landing of as many sailors as the ship captains could spare to accompany the soldiers, Holmes figured he had added four hundred fighting men to the leeward combat zone, fully supplied with provisions, powder, and ammunition. He had even more human resources at his disposal in men who could be pressed from commercial vessels. As one merchant explained to a colleague: "The Number of North America Flags of Truce Vessels that have lately been brought into this Port by our Men of Warr added to the Force's the Country have been obliged to Employ against the Rebellious Negroes."[62] Over the next few days, Holmes sent out press gangs to buttress his crew and had the Articles of War read aloud to renew their commitment.[63] Finally, Holmes ordered his officers "to give the best Accommodation on board of the ships to all the Ladies and the Wounded who might stand in need of their Protection & Succor."[64] To the "gentlemen of the Parish" he sent a note of assurance, telling them that if they thought it necessary, he would "pick the Choice Men out of the Whole fleet, bring them down [by the] Cambridge, and head his men himself, to keep them in order and under Command." Thistlewood thought this pledge was "very pretty indeed" and noted that it gave "great satisfaction" to local planters.[65]

Another detachment of twenty-five men went by sea to St. Elizabeth, where the slaveholders were "very apprehensive that the Slaves of several Estates in that parish had an intention of Rising and joining those in the Neighboring Parish of Westmoreland." After the chaos and confusion of the past week, Holmes believed these reinforcements had "mastered the Government & People to their Spirits."[66] The colonists did not need to fear that the Royal Navy would fail to guarantee the plantation system. On June 8, "Arrive'd here a Guinea man wth Slaves," noted the *Cambridge's* First Lieutenant without further comment.[67] These were just some among the nearly one thousand enslaved Africans who arrived in slave ships that year to a colony at war with them.[68]

The previous week, British reinforcements had been gathering at Moreland estate to plan a coordinated assault on the rebel encampment for June 2. HMS *Port Royal,* the lightest and swiftest of the squadron's sloops, was the first naval vessel to arrive at Westmoreland, coming into Bluefields Bay on May 31. Hearing that the colonists were massing for a second assault on the Rebel's Barricade, the ship sailed west to St. John's Point, near the road up to the mountains, and landed about eighty men, armed with bread and musket shot, on Sunday, June 1. Under heavy rain, the soldiers and sailors made their way up to Moreland for the next day's attack.[69]

Early in the clear and breezy morning, the regular army led a vanguard up the mountain, with the militia in the rear, while the maroons took up positions in the woods to guard against potential ambush. From behind their fortifications, the entrenched rebels kept up a steady fire, wounding a few but killing none of the attackers. The soldiers held their fire until they reached the battlement, then poured in a tremendous volley of shots, killing many rebels and sending others running for still higher ground. The troops invaded the camp and began plundering provisions from the rebels' huts. The slaveholders marveled at what the rebels had carried away from the estates. Along with more than seventy hogsheads of gunpowder, there were fine mahogany chests full of clothes, ruffled shirts, laced hats, shoes, stockings, and cravats—much more than what they needed for bare sustenance.[70] As the British contemplated this new African village, the rebels fired down on them, just missing several officers. Kojo's maroons then spread out and came up through the forest on the opposite slope to attack the rebel flank. This action was decisive; the encampment was overrun. British forces drove untold numbers of men, women, and children over a steep precipice, where they fell to their death in the canyon below. Scores, perhaps hundreds, of other Africans were shot and killed or taken captive.[71]

Slaveholders cheered when the news spread down to the plain. A man wounded in the attack called on Thistlewood in the evening to boast of the "smart" engagement, "their provisions and town took, also most of their powder."[72] The colonists pressed their victory with bloody-minded fury, driving the rebels "with precipitation and loss from their Lodgements."[73] One party reported capturing as many as thirty or forty prisoners, "which they executed as fast as they took them."[74] A merchant from Lucea, who took part in the attack, boasted that British forces had killed the Africans "with great Slaughter & the Prisoners they took, they hanged up without ceremony or Judge or Jury." He believed that no more than four hundred rebels had survived the battle.[75]

The colonists now expected to crush the rebellion quickly and hoped that the massacre would "leave a Terrour on the Minds of all the other Negros for the future."[76] But the uprising was far from finished. Driven from the Rebel's Barricade, the insurgents prepared for a long guerrilla campaign in the wooded mountains. There, the colonists continued to hunt them with three thousand stand of arms supplied from Kingston and some thousand men gathered from all over island.[77]

The flow of forces increased over the next several days. Having received fifty bags of bread, along with "beef, pork, peas, butter, and rum, etc" from the stores of HMS *Cambridge,* HMS *Viper* landed the provisions and a party each of soldiers and marines at Savanna la Mar on Wednesday and Thursday, June 4 and 5.[78] On Wednesday, a company of the Forty-ninth Regiment led by Lieutenant Hugh Forsyth arrived after "having quelled the rebellion" at St. Mary's. They stopped at Thistlewood's Egypt estate for grog in the evening, then marched toward the mountains, with a slave named Abraham as a guide. Not far up the road, some rebels shot at them from the woods, and Forsyth's unit opened fire in return, but without apparent result.[79] On the same day, the *Port Royal* also sent another two thousand pounds of bread ashore for the soldiers. On June 5, the *Port Royal's* sailors returned aboard, flushed with their recent victory over the rebels.[80] If they had met Lieutenant Forsyth's company on the road to the bay, they might have been warned by the news from St. Mary's that no single pitched battle would end the insurrection.

Accompanied by a smaller merchant vessel, the heavy warship HMS *Harwich* moored in Bluefields Bay by the watering place on June 4. Early the next morning, Captain Marsh sent all the soldiers on board the merchantman for transport to Savanna la Mar.[81] Most of the *Harwich's* sailors and marines had a fresh memory of fighting West Africans. It had been a scant two years since their failed attempt on the French fort at Allbreda on the Gambia River, when nearly two hundred sailors and marines had been repelled by native forces.[82] The *Harwich's* marines now combined with those from the *Cambridge,* more than thirty of whom had fought black soldiers at Guadeloupe. The Royal Marines, newly reorganized for the Seven Years' War, had gained many of their first combat experiences fighting Africans, both enslaved and free.[83] If the Coromantees drew on their wartime experience in Africa, so too did the soldiers and sailors of the *Harwich*. On each of the next several days, the *Harwich* sent its longboat to the town filled with bags of bread for the troops, who again went into the bush to make war against black people, this time in Jamaica by mere dint of circumstances. Surely, as they exchanged stories with men who had taken part in the attack on the Rebel's Barricade, they shared their own lessons from their defeat on the Gambia, or their victory in Guadeloupe, and hoped for success in Jamaica.

For a month, the *Harwich* stayed alongside the *Viper* at Bluefields, supporting the land campaign and watching over the assembly of the merchant convoy for North America and Great Britain.[84] The convoy had been much-delayed. After the initial shipping embargo in April, the convoy had been scheduled to depart Jamaica on May 25. But, as Admiral Cotes explained to his superiors in London, the insurrection had "put so entire a stop to Business for more than a month, that it was impossible for the Convoy to get ready to sail" by that time. Through the Governor's Council, Jamaica's merchants and planters had appealed to Admiral Holmes, who succeeded Cotes on the station, to put off sailing until June 10. Now, however, the colony needed the Navy's full strength, and Lieutenant Governor Moore prevailed upon Holmes to reschedule a first departure for June 22 from Port Royal, with a subsequent one from Bluefields Bay.[85] All during that time, as merchant ships gathered in the bay, sailors were pressed into service against the Africans, while immediate news of the revolt continued to spread and people pondered its consequences for the fortunes of the colonial enterprise. This was a truly transatlantic affair.

It was at the same time a resolutely local conflict. The rebels would not be defeated by a superior plan or organization alone, but by the mundane grubby work of tracking, fighting, and killing throughout the island's hills and jungles. In early June, after the victory over so many Africans at Rebel's Barricade, Holmes could confidently say, "We are in daily Expectation of having the whole reduced to Obedience." Weeks later, however, he had learned the fleeting wisdom rediscovered again and again by imperial warlords throughout history: "Experience has since proved that is much easier to Vanquish & Rout them in the Field, or in a Collective Body Entrenched, than to Grab them out of the Woods." Accordingly, his presence was "absolutely necessary" in Port Royal to help direct the counterinsurgency. He could not depart Jamaica aboard the *Cambridge* as scheduled in late June, "as long as there was reason for Apprehending fresh Innovations in other parts of the Island." Holmes therefore decided to transfer his command to HMS *Edinburgh*. The *Cambridge* should no longer wait for him but instead proceed on its cruise with several other warships. At 4A.M. on June 22, the *Cambridge* "Struck Adm Holmes Flagg which was hoisted on Board ye Edinburgh," and Britain's chief commander in the Caribbean theater remained in Jamaica to fight the Coromantee War, fully aware that "the Insurrection would be a Work of time."[86]

W AR swept across western Jamaica throughout the month of June. Soldiers, sailors, militia, and maroons pursued search-and-destroy missions through the forests and mountains while reacting to sporadic attacks on specific estates. They followed a scorched-earth policy, trying to make the environment inhospitable to the rebels, even as they continued a campaign of public terror to impress the slaves. Yet the counterinsurgency was a vexed and fractious enterprise. Like the Africans, the British contended with their own problems of diasporic warfare. The slaveholders' coalition was complex, encompassing many different groups whose interests were sometimes contradictory. Martial allegiances over distance and time had to be made and enforced through military practice and the discipline of fear. Disputes among the colonists thereby allowed some maneuvering room for the insurrection, which continued to survive the persistent effort to suppress it.

Rebels reacted to the British counterattack by dispersing and coalescing in the classic manner of guerilla insurgency. If the insurgents never withstood more than one volley of fire before running into the woods, as colonists complained, it was because the Africans were following tried and tested tactics.[87] During the long campaign of skirmishes through the summer months, the rebels harassed plantations that bordered mountain retreats, ravines, and forests, where small bands could use the landscape to their advantage. They raided smaller estates for recruits and supplies when larger attacks proved impossible. Rebels gathered and dispersed depending on their contingent estimation of the balance of power, opportunities for association, and military favorability in any particular territory. Alternating between force and persuasion, coercion and consent, they continued to try to convince slaves that they had more to lose by remaining enslaved than by rising up. In this way, under the right circumstances, any plantation the rebels visited could become a node of the rebellion.

Command of the British ground campaign fell to Brigadier General Norwood Witter, Esquire, who organized the efforts of the militia, and Lieutenant Colonel Robert Spragge of the Forty-ninth Regiment of Foot. A native of the island and the son of a soldier, Witter was in the upper echelon of great planters. Previously a member of the Governor's Council, he owned more than sixty-five hundred acres of land in the parishes of Westmoreland, St. James, and St. Elizabeth.[88] Spragge was a career soldier, also descended from a family with a tradition of military service. Born in the walled city of Chester, England, in 1715, Spragge had been Captain of Charles Fort in Port Royal as early as 1751, and earned his promotion from Major to Lieutenant Colonel in 1753.[89] Though he, too, owned a considerable estate (Chester, named for his birthplace) on the Martha Brae River in St. James, he wasn't nearly as wealthy as Witter.[90] At forty-five years old, Spragge was a respected senior officer but not a local aristocrat.

Both men arrived in Westmoreland after the battles at Rebel's Barricade. With his troops already gone to leeward aboard the *Harwich* the previous day, Spragge boarded HMS *Renown* with two other "Land Officers" on June 5. The three went ashore at Bluefields the next day, took command of the troops, and headed for the encampment at Moreland estate.[91] When Spragge arrived in the mountains, he learned that following the overthrow of the rebel camp, only the maroons seemed to be making progress against the insurgents. Captains Furry and Quashy had killed more than a dozen and captured nearly sixty, whom they brought to Moreland on June 6. The previous day, rebels had shot and killed Daniel Lawder, a militia man who had fallen behind his party and gotten lost in the bush.[92]

Indeed, the rebels seemed to be on the offensive again. On June 7, they ambushed a party of Hanover militia, severely wounding a white man.[93] At the same time, the colonists heard, the slaves had collectively refused to work at Salt Spring estate, not far from Fish River and Campbelton, where uprisings had coincided with the outbreak at Masemure. The next day, it was said, "the Rebellious Negroes took Jerusalem" estate on a mountain above King's Valley, which cradled the narrow pass between Hanover and Westmoreland.[94] After the loss of their stores of powder and ammunition at the Rebel's Barricade, the rebels were desperate for armaments. By one account, "their Ammunition being almost expended," they were "already obligd to make slugs of Dollars & pieces of 8 to fire." The whites had evacuated Jerusalem, and the rebels found no arms and ammunition among the enslaved there, who refused to join the rebellion. The insurgents pulled down the dwelling house, presumably to keep colonists from reoccupying the area, then crossed the valley to Glasgow estate.[95] In all likelihood they hoped to control the pass to Hanover, at least long enough to allow their forces to join together from the two parishes. The Africans ransacked one house, but Glasgow was a hard target. Situated on rising ground, another house held a battery for defense manned by a number of white employees and sailors, who combined with loyal slaves to repel the attackers from the plantation.[96] Near Glasgow, Captain Furry's maroons ambushed the rebels on their way east, killing several, but most slipped away.[97]

Concerned with "how wrongly all the operations of the Militia were conducted," prominent Westmoreland planters pleaded with Norwood Witter to take command of their operations. "He could not but see in how bad a Condition we were" and accordingly accepted the duty, said one of the petitioners. About June 11, Witter went to meet with Spragge to "consult about the best method to distress the Rebells."[98] They agreed that they should make their base at Moreland, sending out various parties to kill and capture rebels whenever they had intelligence of their whereabouts. By this time, the weather was turbulent with gales and squalls. Heavy rain and thunder continued through the next several weeks, turning the camp at Moreland into a "most wretched hovel."[99] Nevertheless, from here, for the next two months and more, the combined British forces combed the parish for insurgents.

According to an official report, the various parties of counterinsurgents killed nearly one hundred and captured about two hundred black people in June. But the confusion of war made precise accounting impossible. Scores died in the woods of their wounds, as colonists drove countless numbers over steep precipices, and disease claimed others. Many wasted away in muddy caves. Without stored provisions, the rebels had to survive off the land. So the British destroyed food crops. By the end of the month, one colonist reported, "there is now about 200 out, but in a most starved condition, without any thing to subsist upon, as the people have cut down their plantain trees, which is the only food Negroes have in this country."[100] Another claimed that provisions were "so scarce among them that we have found them roast our whites as they kill them."[101] Whether this was true or false, the rebels killed only three or four white men in June, and these were not enough to feed an army.

Having sworn oaths to fight or die, many rebels now considered mass suicide. "They are not only daily dropping off for want of sustenance," went one report, "but the prospect of the miseries their brethren suffer induces many to put an end to themselves."[102] They did not spare the youths, who were to have been the future of the new village. Rather than see them return to plantation slavery, the rebels saw a "great number of Children destroyed in the Woods."[103] On their daily excursions against the insurgents, the colonists happened upon dozens of black men, women, and children hanging from trees, their bodies twisting in the driving rain.[104] By the end of June, one colonist could claim that slaveholders had "taken and destroyed near 700 Negroes."[105] From Thistlewood's estate near the coast, he could smell "the dead Negroes in the Woods," which reminded him of stinking oil.[106] Many insurgents gave up the rebellion and crept back to their plantations, feigning innocence and claiming loyalty to their masters.

Of those captured, some were killed on the spot by vengeful slaveholders, some were executed on their owners' estates, and others were bound over to Savanna la Mar for torture, trial, and sentencing. "Our party has taken and kill'd about two hundred, what they bring in a Live We Burn & some we hang in Gebbits," announced a planter in mid-June.[107] Captors often brought their prisoners through Egypt estate on their way to town, and Thistlewood witnessed many executions on his frequent errands to the bay. Following custom, he would hear and exchange news of the insurrection gleaned from and about the condemned. One rebel was burned alive "by degrees with a Slow fire made at a distance from him," but "Never flinched, moved a Foot, nor groan'd or Cried oh." This man had apparently continued to plot right up until his execution, promising one white guard that he would give him all his coins and make him the overseer of Midgeham estate near Masemure in exchange for letting him escape. On June 19, Thistlewood went to Savanna la Mar to report to the military about the possible involvement of Egypt's slaves in the insurrection. While in town, he saw Captain Forrest's Goliath gibbetted alive. He had been accused of having "Cutt off Mr: Rutherfford's thigh & pulled out his Eyes whilst Alive," during the first failed attack on the Rebel's Barricade.[108]

Such stories of rebel insensitivity and cruelty served a useful social function. Not only did the colonists hope to learn who had been involved in the insurrection and what they had done, they also wanted to distinguish their own brutality from the violence of the Africans. The more they narrated black violence—directed toward whites, most shockingly, but also toward other blacks—the easier it was to suppress the revolt without concern for black lives. Yet the counterinsurgents were not in perfect agreement about how much brutality was needed to end the rebellion. Reflected in the military's accounts of "Rebels Taken and Kill'd" was a tension between immediate security concerns and the financial interests of the planters. Despite being based on regular reports from Norwood Witter, the accounts were "not to be look'd upon as particularly exact and just," explained Lieutenant Governor Moore, "for notwithstanding every Means have been used proper & Warrants issued to oblige the several Estates to make due returns of what People they had out, and what Number had returned, they most of them have neglected to do it properly with a View of concealing their Absentees."[109] In other words, some planters wanted to protect themselves from the loss of their human property more than they wanted blood.

The friction between these impulses showed through in the contradictory tactics of Norwood Witter and Robert Spragge. Thistlewood was most impressed by the actions of the Forty-ninth Regiment. "Col: Spragg's off with the heads of the Rebell's who fall into his hands immediately," approved the overseer: "He Says he is Sent to destroy the Rebells, & destroy them he will to the utmost off his power," though apparently Spragge made some exceptions for women and children.[110] Not all slaveholders felt the same way. Once the rebels were driven from their base in the Hanover Mountains, Witter encouraged them to go back to the plantations. He gave tickets to those who surrendered, granting them a reprieve if they returned immediately to their masters. To many slaveholders, this was unconscionably lenient. Suspicious of Witter's intentions, Thistlewood complained bitterly when he learned that the Brigadier General had given tickets to Captain Forrest's Fortune, "a principal offender," and several others who had come back of their own accord to estates that had been caught up in the rebellion. "Policy, or Something else?" he wondered.[111]

Thistlewood was not wrong to suspect the workings of private interest. Witter may have even acknowledged as much when he dined with Thistlewood and other planters in mid-August.[112] In fact, many owners of rebel slaves had approached Witter to plead for their property. "There was a General inclination in the Rebells to come in," the slaveowners said, "provided their lives and limbs might be spared; as to any other punishment they were to lay at the Mercy of the Lieutenant Governor." Although "many of the Rebell Negroes had returned to their Masters," said one defender of the policy, "their Masters were afraid to produce them lest they should be put to Death." After consulting with the most influential planters, those people he considered to be "of the best Sense," Witter began to issue the tickets, then applied to Lieutenant Governor Moore for permission to pursue the strategy. Convicted murderers were to be excepted from the pardon, but it was agreed that "they should not be put to death by Torture," if condemned. Of course, rebels who had killed white persons should receive no mercy of any kind.[113] As soon as Moore approved the policy, authorities laid hold of those men suspected of murder.[114] Thistlewood applauded when John Cope Jr. and several other troopers seized some Africans "unawares" and marched them past Egypt to the fort at Savanna la Mar.[115] There they remained for as long as six months, awaiting their fate.

Many slaveholders hoped with Thistlewood that these rebels would all be executed.[116] In late October, the House of Assembly formally asked Moore to order "that the several negroes or other slaves in the rebellion to leeward, who have been tried, and condemned to die, may respectively be executed, agreeably to their several sentences, except such who have received promises of life, for serving the public, by killing or forcing home other rebels; and that you will be pleased to give orders, to bring to trial all those who have or may be charged with committing murder, or bearing arms in the rebellions in the parishes of St. Mary and Westmoreland, who have surrendered, and have not been tried, that they may be punished according to their several offenses."[117] Thistlewood's neighbor Colonel Barclay came to Spanish Town to make a special plea for the execution of Fortune and Pluto, who were deemed to be ringleaders.[118] Mr. Stone, another Westmoreland planter, applied to the Lieutenant Governor to have fifteen men put to death. To allay the concerns of the slaves' owners, the Assembly reaffirmed on November 19 that they would receive up to £40 in compensation for any rebel put to death by the government.[119]

Assemblymen called a special session to investigate Witter's conduct, but he had Moore's full support.[120] At least fifteen of the rebels—named Blackberry, Peter, Primus, Davy, Bristol, Leicester, Prince, Jonathan, Robin, Adjaquao, Isaac, Tackey, Quamina alias Gubbee, Jack, and Boatswain—received an official pardon from the Lieutenant Governor, who ordered that they be transported from the island instead of killed.[121] The Assembly resolved that Witter's "treating with the rebels, while they were in rebellion, and under arms, was an impolitic measure, but that it appears to the house he did it with good intentions."[122] A contrary view held that Witter's policy was a "humane and politic" measure, which provoked the surrender of more than 250 insurgents. By granting these terms to the rebels, testified John Venn in the hearing on the subject, "not only the Lives of these Wretches were saved and Tortures prevented, but those of many White People and others who would have been kill'd or died of fatigue in the pursuit of them."[123] This was unconvincing to Thistlewood, who imagined that Witter was responsible for a "total relaxation" of civil and military government.[124]

Thistlewood identified more with Robert Spragge. Like Thistlewood, Spragge was an Englishman, not a creole like Witter, who belonged to one of Westmoreland's most prominent families. And though Spragge was a formidable property owner, he was closer in status to common white folk than to Witter and his fellow great planters. There also may have been a salient difference in their sentiments toward black people. Like most Jamaican patriarchs, Witter had several mixed-race relatives. Unlike most whites, however, he recognized them as his kin. A year after the insurrection, when the Jamaica Assembly passed an act to prevent black people from inheriting significant property from whites, Witter was one of the few dissenting voices.[125] Racial animus could just as easily spring from Englishmen without social roots in the island as from native whites, with their long tradition of negotiated racial hierarchy. But the conflict over the tickets and pardons indicated more than conflicting approaches to suppressing the rebels or the difference between two sorts of military men; it highlights the fragile complexity of the counterinsurgent coalition.

Witter and Spragge supervised a great variety of public and private forces. The accounts of their June operations list militia parties from Westmoreland and Hanover Parishes, as well as private parties from several different plantations, armed slaves, and maroons, alongside the soldiers and sailors of the imperial military.[126] Military cohesion was anything but automatic. These groups often had divergent interests, conditioned by class, race, politics, and the sheer will to survive in a deadly predicament. When Thistlewood worried that the great planters would sacrifice public security in order to get back to business, he acknowledged that the priorities of these great men did not always align with those of more common slaveholders. Indeed, there were divergent priorities all around.

Racial belonging was another potential fissure in the slaveholder alliance. The colonists were nearly as dependent on black people for domestic security as for plantation production.[127] Almost always, it was slaves who reported conspiracies to the slaveholders before they discovered them on their own. And slaves were active in the fighting as members of gangs led by planters or as individual assistants. Jemmy, a slave belonging to John Smith, the slain attorney at Masemure, guided the soldiers to the rebel positions, shooting one insurgent himself.[128] A party of the "King's Negroes" was active in the counterinsurgency. Even the Forty-ninth Regiment, raised largely in Jamaica, combined blacks, whites, and those in between. Although the maroons' fragile and hard won independence was at stake in any shift of the balance of power, they were semi-autonomous actors, obligated by treaty but owing little to the colonists. None of these black peoples' loyalty could be taken for granted.

FIGURE 5.3. Black grenadier in the 49th Regiment of Foot, 1751.

Painting of a grenadier, with fifer and drummer, by David Morier (1705–1770). *Courtesy of Royal Collection Trust/© Her Majesty Queen Elizabeth II 2018.*

Nor were all whites equally eager to fight on the military's terms. The Moravians' pacifism earned scorn from local militia leaders. In St. Elizabeth Parish, more than a dozen men with weapons arrested one missionary, Carl Schultz, "putting him between 6 men with rapiers," as they escorted him to the captain of their company at Barton Isles estate. After a sharp interrogation, the militia captain demanded that Schultz "stay there and become a soldier." Schultz replied that "he was not in the state of mind for swordplay" and informed the captain that an Act of Parliament had exempted his brethren from all military service. The captain mocked these words, telling Schultz that "if he didn't want to fence he could stay around there and help them with their prayers," but he ultimately released Schultz to his mission. The militia continued to mistrust the Moravians, repeatedly demanding they prove their allegiance to the slaveholders.[129]

Military discipline was a problem for regular soldiers, too. They chafed at the overweening authority of their commanders, and they often preferred to attend to their private interest. Much of this interest involved their basic survival. When plantation managers didn't offer provisions willingly, common soldiers survived by seizing food for themselves. On the north side of the island in September, Lieutenant Hollingberry and two parties of soldiers occupied Iter Boreale and Gibraltar estates in St. George Parish. The overseer of Iter Boreale came in from the field to find the soldiers overrunning the great house, having forced open the doors. Hollingberry told him that "if he did not give the soldiers proper necessaries, he would break open any house, and take them." To prevent more damage, the overseer "was obliged to give them rum, beef, plantains, &c." Soldiers similarly "broke open the stores" at Gibraltar, a plantation under Zachary Bayly's management.[130] With martial law in force, the property owners had little recourse but to appeal for relief to the House of Assembly in Spanish Town.

Propertied officers prioritized the defense of their own assets. Lieutenant Jeremiah Gardner of the Forty-ninth Regiment suffered two courts martial during his time in the service. In 1759, at a trial presided over by Robert Spragge, Gardner stood accused of beating a man to whom he owed a debt of twenty shillings. That man had left for England by the time of the trial, and the court acquitted Gardner of "having behaved unlike an officer and a Gentleman."[131] Then, during the slave revolt, Gardner left his unit without permission. When Spragge went to join his detachment in Westmoreland, he left a few officers, including Gardner, on duty at Port Royal. Gardner absconded to his own plantation in St. Elizabeth Parish, probably in order to defend his property from the threat of insurrection. He claimed to have permission from Lieutenant Governor Moore, but he failed to notify his commanding officer, despite, Spragge said, having "secreted himself in the next Parish" from where his unit was engaged in combat. Months after the insurrection, Gardner still had not returned to his duty, and now Spragge had had enough, declaring that for the six or seven years he had known him, Gardner had taken "every Step to evade doing his Duty as an Officer." Finding him guilty, the army cashiered Gardner for "absenting himself from his Regiment and Duty without leave, and not behaving himself as an Officer."[132]

Even in the famously disciplined Royal Navy, some sailors' defiance reflected their alienation from the mission, as well as the knowledge that it was endangering their lives. Drunkenness, disobedience, and desertion were regular features of naval life. But these problems were exacerbated in port, where the command of men operated without the aid of the ocean's natural threats. Insubordination increased when a naval ship made landfall, especially when the sailors disliked the duties at hand. Suppressing the slaves' insurrection was distasteful and hazardous work, which grew more dangerous as the task wore on.[133] As soon as HMS *Port Royal* had arrived in Bluefields Bay in early June, its captain punished two seamen for "Drunkeness & Mutinous expressions." A day later he punished two men for "Mutiny on Shore."[134] Two weeks into the Westmoreland operations, marine private deserted the *Harwich*.[135]

Torrents of rain fell through most of June. The coastal roads, "deep and dirty" at the best of times, became "scarcely passable."[136] Sewage flowed freely through Savanna la Mar, tainting water and food supplies. Mosquitoes bred briskly in the barrels, buckets, and pots dispersed throughout the plantations, in the water casks of portside ships, and in the muddy ruts and shallow pools that spread over the land. Soon "there was an almost universal sickness throughout the Parish."[137] On July 2, the *Viper's* marines returned to the ship, almost certainly bringing an epidemic aboard. Two days later, two men, including the marine Richard Hutchinson, received three dozen lashes each at the gangway for "Neglect of Duty & Disobeying Command." Not long after that an able seaman "departed this life." The officers punished another man for "Mutiny & Drunkenness" on July 8, and another sailor died on the 9th. When Richard Hutchinson died on July 13, the crew washed the ship with vinegar in an attempt to stem the contagion. Another marine died the next day; the crew again disinfected the ship, and then carried pots of smoldering wood and pitch between the decks, thinking they could fumigate the infection from the timbers of the hull.[138] If the Navy was ignorant of modern epidemiology, common sailors surely blamed the illness on this inauspicious war.

As the campaign dragged on, it became difficult to continue to raise the militia. One captain complained that he could not, with his "utmost endeavours, get one third of the Men fit for service" from the estates in his jurisdiction.[139] It was more than morbidity that made recruiting difficult, it was also a general fatigue with martial law. Between the "Death of such a great number of Negroes & the Detention of the Fleet and the almost total stop to business," planters and merchants were desperate to retreat to their own affairs and to repair their private losses.[140] The Lieutenant Governor grumbled to the Board of Trade that he could not lift martial law in August, as he had planned, because "the Obstinacy and Infatuation of the People in that part of the Country were so great, that notwithstanding many of them had suffer'd extreamly, and the danger was still near them, there was no possibility of getting them to do their Duty, and the moment the Power ceased which compell'd them to appear under Arms, they laid them down." He must continue military rule, he said, "till the Rebellion is cut up by the roots."[141]

The roots of the conflict ran deep into the slave quarters, and there terror was the sharpest weapon in the British armory. To keep the enslaved from joining the rebellion, the counterinsurgency continued to stage gruesome executions, to harass and threaten any black person seen to be out of place, and to make great shows of collective belligerence as militiamen rode from estate to estate. Fear and anxiety might be the best explanation for the refusal of more slaves to participate in the insurrection.

Slaves certainly had more than white people to fear, as they worried, in addition, about the loss of their own provisions, gardens, and small possessions.[142] Meager as they were, they held great value to the enslaved, and the havoc of warfare threatened their preservation. With farming in disarray and the British destroying staple crops, famine menaced Westmoreland Parish. In early July, an enslaved Moravian convert at Mesopotamia told the brethren about "the great Hunger-emergency among the negroes." They asked the estate's attorney "why some of them had to starve and if he wouldn't help them," but this only made the attorney wary of the petitioners. A week later, he had twenty of them secured in the stockade "because they had complained about their hunger etc. and the Attorney was afraid that if they went out at night, they would steal."[143] The enslaved were caught between tyranny and scarcity.

Yet slaves were as likely to blame their immediate condition on the rebellion as on the planters. Common oppression did not resolve political differences among the enslaved, and the rebels in their desperation could be as ruthless as the slaveholders. Some slaves caught a rebel at Mesopotamia even as he was "busy making his killing knife sharp," and they secured him beneath the floorboards of a house until the local militia captain came for him. A hasty trial convicted the rebel of having murdered two black children just days before and promptly sentenced him to be burned alive. The Moravians recognized that these slaves had "now legitimated themselves in the neighborhood," earning the provisional trust of the slaveholders.[144] The missionaries themselves felt vindicated when they heard that many slaves under their teaching said that, since they had heard the Gospel, "they'd sooner be cut in pieces than have any part with the Rebel Murderers."[145] The violence of the slaves' language was hardly metaphorical; terror and counter-terror stalked every political calculation.

Fear was effectively the glue that fastened together the entire counterinsurgent coalition. Superiors directed threats of persecution, punishment, and death outward toward the rebels and also inward at subordinates. Dread was a great disciplinary tool, keeping soldiers in line, tamping down mutinous sailors, and bucking up shirking militiamen. Stories of African atrocities bound the colonial forces even more tightly than threats from their leaders. Every time the rebels killed a slave, and especially when they harmed a white person, the anecdotes flew from ear to ear. Even as these accounts licensed the excesses of the counterinsurgency, they held it together with anxiety about what might happen if the war effort failed. As much as they might have chafed at martial law, the colonists coveted the presence of British troops. As much as planters disdained the Moravians' pacifism, they valued their partnership as white men. Surrounded by black slaves, even a great planter would open his house to a lowly missionary, as when Caleb Dickinson, "being something in fear," pressed a Moravian to "abide Over-night."[146] Like Dickinson, the other counterinsurgents—Thomas Thistlewood and Norwood Witter, Charles Holmes and Richard Hutchinson, the militia captain we know only as Richard and Brother Nicolaus Gandrup, even Kojo and faithful Jemmy—all feared a Coromantee colony more than they hated the war.

THE end of June brought good news for the slaveholders. After multiple delays, the first convoy finally sailed on June 22, with 112 merchant ships under the escort of HMS *Dreadnought*.[147] More auspiciously, colonists thwarted a "formidable" new conspiracy in St. James Parish when a slave named Will informed on a plot "to rise and joyn those already in Rebellion." Slaveholders captured more than sixty men, most of whom were executed in short order, "some burnt, others hanged, others gibbeted alive"—though many others escaped and managed to unite with runaways from neighboring Hanover and other rebels in the mountains.[148] Nevertheless, the strategy employed by Witter and Spragge was making progress in Westmoreland. Counterinsurgents steadily pushed most of the rebels from the area around Moreland, then drove them from the Hanover Mountains.

Dispersed bands of rebels moved east along the base of the mountains, trying to stay between the maroons and the planters. Their passage was difficult in the heavy rains, but the slaveholders' pursuit was no easier. From Mesopotamia estate, midway through the parish near the mountains and the Black Morass, Moravian missionaries noted the rebels' eastward track. Rebels were active in that area from the third week of the uprising. Some openly threatened a white man nearby, telling him "they wanted to visit him in the evening." He immediately sent his wife to seek refuge at Mesopotamia "with her children, negroes and best household goods," and then set off with the militia. By mid-June, armed colonists were passing frequently through Mesopotamia on the way to the mountains, or on their way to the Bay with prisoners. The missionaries heard that after one encounter, the rebels lost their rifles and fled, retreating to "the highest mountain to arm themselves as well as they can with stones." All of Mesopotamia's whites went in pursuit, with the slaves carrying provisions. At the end of the month, Mesopotamia's overseer, Daniel Macfarlane, weary from the fighting, told

FIGURE 5.4. The Mountains near Mesopotamia Estate.

View of Fort William Estate, Westmoreland, 1778, engraved by Thomas Vivares from a painting by George Robertson. *Courtesy of The British Library.*

the brethren that parties "had taken rebels captive every day," noting that the rebels' feet were "wretchedly cut up and ripped."[149] It didn't seem possible for them to hold out much longer.

Then, in early July, the slaveholders captured Wager. He had remained at the western end of the parish, having been injured some time before. The rebels had spread out, raiding estates sporadically as they tried to evade parties of counterinsurgents. In late June, the rebels appeared again near Moreland, killing a white man formerly employed by the late Mr. Rutherford. Another group of rebels had congregated near Jacobfield estate, low in the mountains, not far north of Masemure. A party of militia set off after them, closely followed by an officer and twelve seamen from HMS *Harwich,* who returned to the ship a few days later, "the Negroes being dispersed." Thistlewood was warned that other rebels had been driven from the mountains and come across the plain, only two miles from Egypt; they were rumored to be at nearby Paul Island on the night of June 30. Militiamen captured Masemure's Davie in a watch hut and carried him past Egypt to town.[150] It is unclear why these rebels had returned so close to the coast. Perhaps, having heard that the fleet had sailed at last, some had finally agreed to follow Wager's course, heading to the bay for a desperate assault on Savanna la Mar. Or maybe they had come down to capitulate, as the colonists believed when they reported that "80 of the Rebels have voluntarily surrendered themselves; and, in order to obtain their Pardon, brought in Prisoners Wager, their Chief Coromantee Commander, and 3 others of their Seducers, the Ringleaders."[151] Either way, the leaders were taken long after their hopes for the rebellion had dimmed.

On July 3, Thistlewood witnessed "Wager or Apongo, took, and Carried by prizoner, this Evening: he was the King off the Rebells: but despised off late since wounded." The Westmoreland colonists were again confident of victory, certain that the remaining rebels, "a few desperate Villains excepted," were "soon to come in, being quite tired out with Fatigue, Famine, and Dissention among themselves." They estimated that these amounted to no more than seventy people. Having recovered its marines, the *Harwich* weighed anchor and worked its way back up to Port Royal. In Spanish Town, Henry Moore soon received "Advice that great numbers of Slaves daily surrendered in Westmoreland and that a Party had brought in Wager the Chief of the Insurgents & who had been the principal Person on Capt. Forrest's Estate." Within a few days, Thistlewood "had only 2 Negroes Watch, as formerly," returning to his regular routine.[152]

The British had similar success elsewhere on the island. During the week of Wager's capture in Westmoreland, authorities executed nineteen rebels in St. Thomas in the East. A party of maroons killed Pompey, a leader of the uprising on Plantain Garden River, and brought his head to Morant Bay. Another of the revolt's commanders, Akim, hanged himself before he could be captured. Various deployments throughout the island kept things passably quiet, despite indications of conspiracy in the parishes of St. John's and St. Dorothy's, where suspected plotters were quickly rounded up and executed or banished from Jamaica.[153] The island wore the "appearance of Tranquility," reported Admiral Holmes in late July. Nevertheless, the colony's security demanded continued vigilance: martial law remained in force, with the second convoy to Britain delayed to September 1, despite the dissatisfaction of many Kingston merchants. The "true temper of the slaves will not be known with Certainty" until some time after the government lifted martial law, said Holmes, and it was not yet time to lay it aside.[154]

Back at Savanna la Mar, jeering slaveholders crowded around the prisoners, demanding to know the rebels' plans and who among their own slaves might have been in league with the insurrectionists. They learned little from Davie, who hung in the gibbet for a week but kept his spirit until he died. He even maintained his sense of humor, proclaiming his amusement at seeing a quarrel between two white men and laughing "heartily" when a monkey leaped upon a pail of water carried on the head of a black woman.

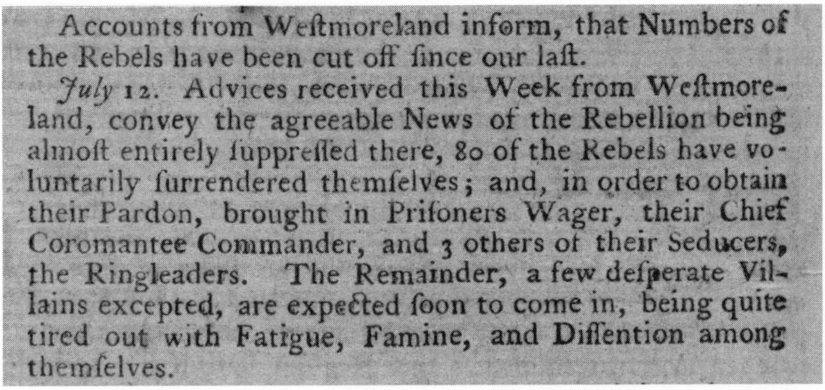

Accounts from Weſtmoreland inform, that Numbers of the Rebels have been cut off ſince our laſt.

July 12. Advices received this Week from Weſtmoreland, convey the agreeable News of the Rebellion being almoſt entirely ſuppreſſed there, 80 of the Rebels have voluntarily ſurrendered themſelves; and, in order to obtain their Pardon, brought in Priſoners Wager, their Chief Coromantee Commander, and 3 others of their Seducers, the Ringleaders. The Remainder, a few deſperate Villains excepted, are expected ſoon to come in, being quite tired out with Fatigue, Famine, and Diſſention among themſelves.

FIGURE 5.5. News of Wager's July capture reported in the *Pennsylvania Gazette*, 4 September 1760.

That monkey was a "damn'ed Rogue," he chuckled.[155] Wager divulged more in his last days. The colonists learned that he had quarreled with his wife on the day of the uprising, and in her anger she threatened to betray the plot. He confessed that the rebels had intended to time the attack for the sailing of the convoy, but then launched the insurrection immediately for fear of being discovered. In any case, with the departure originally scheduled for May 25, a minor delay would not have cost the conspirators the opportunity of the Whitsun Holiday. Wager also admitted that he had advised taking the rebellion directly to the bay, "but the others were afraid too much." When the slaveholders finished their interrogations, Wager received his sentence: he would hang in chains for three days, then be taken down and burned alive. Thistlewood went to see him hanging in town on July 29 to ask if he knew any of Egypt's slaves. "He said he knew Lewie & Wished him good bye." On August 3, Thistlewood noted that "Apongo died before his 3 days expired," suspended before the pitiless crowd.[156] But this was still not the end of the insurrection. Various bands of rebels continued to cluster in the woods and hills, evading the colonists' patrols.

AMONG the holdouts, a man named Simon, sometimes called Damon, assumed principal leadership—as least as far as the colonists knew. They believed it was Simon who had shot and killed Masemure's attorney, John Smith, in the initial outbreak. In Africa, the colonists gleaned, Simon had been a captain for his king. He had reunited in Jamaica with Agyei, a hunter for the same ruler, who joined Simon as a rebel chieftain. People said that Simon frequently reprimanded Agyei for his "immoderate love of women," suggesting that Simon continued to hold a superior rank in the rebel hierarchy, as he might have in Africa. At the beginning of August, Thistle-wood heard that Agyei had been shot but also that the remaining rebels were publicizing their war aim: they would "kill all the Negroes they Can," and as soon as the rains stopped they would set fire to as many plantations as possible, attempting to force the whites to "give them free like Cudjoe's Negroes."[157] The declaration spread quickly among the leeward planters, as Simon "sent word that if he live till the Dry weather comes in not one mill shall work the next Crop for He will burn all."[158] The rebels meant to keep the Jamaican economy at a standstill until they won their autonomy.

Simon's gang was a light and mobile force. By planters' estimates, it consisted of about fifty men and women with maybe a dozen rifles. They remained elusive in Westmoreland's mountains through August, "not to be found tho partys [were] Continually after them." Several companies of soldiers quartered in various stations along the base of the mountains and selected estates "to prevent their robbing and getting more ammunition." Aiming their tactics at recruiting and rearming, the rebels continued to find sympathy in parts of the parish. At Savanna la Mar, slaveholders seized three coffins full of rifles, pistols, and cutlasses in the process of being smuggled "under the pretence of burying dead Negroes," and other planters thought they spotted members of the rebel band in various places. But in September, the largest share of the remaining rebels made a decisive move toward the east.[159]

Simon's march was a difficult maneuver between the mountain-dwelling maroons and the planters' forces in the plains and valleys, all the way across Westmoreland, into St. Elizabeth, and ultimately into the parish of Clarendon. Thistlewood heard on September 21 that the rebels had gone to "high windward," skirting the border between the Westmoreland and St. James parishes.[160] Their trajectory took them through a plantain walk owned by Norwood Witter. Provided all the plants had not been destroyed in the easternmost part of Westmoreland, the rebels would provision themselves just before the passage to the next parish. St. Elizabeth offered plenty of places to hide. It encompassed part of the cockpit county, where steep-sided hollows and sinkholes, conical hills, and sharp ridges had offered strategic advantages to the maroons from the late seventeenth century through the 1730s. The Y.S. and Black rivers, Jamaica's largest, originated in the high gulches and traced marshy courses toward the sea, giving the rebels places to hide in the great lowland swamps near vulnerable estates.

In late September, the Moravians registered the move, hearing from overseer Macfarlane the "distressing news" that "the rebelling negroes had begun again to murder people gruesomely and that they were not far from here on their way to St. Elizabeth."[161] The Moravians had missions at five

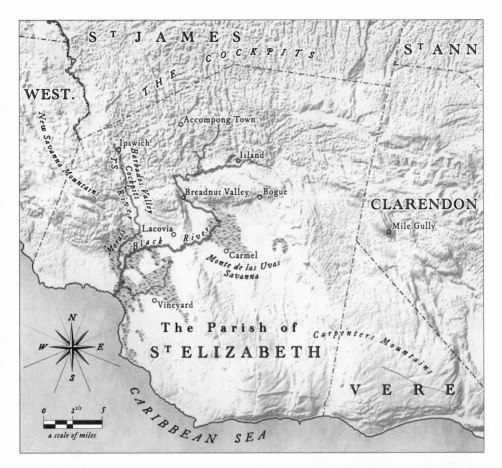

estates in the parish, including the Carmel and Bogue estates, on either side of a large morass just east of the Black River. At Bogue, the first week of October, Brother Joseph Powell observed that many were "in great fear & all in Arms on the fresh Accounts of the Rebels being mov'd up to this Parrish."[162] Simon had occupied the Barbadoes Valley Cockpits along the Y.S. River. Near the river head, the Ipswich sugar estate stood largely isolated. The rebels attacked and burned the plantation on October 21, destroying "all except the Boiling house, which having a Brick or Stone foundation, they Could only burn the door."[163] In quick succession they attacked an estate near the head of the Black River, some five miles from the Moravian mission at Island estate, and "completely and utterly ruined" another plantation.[164] But the rebels also suffered a setback in the area. Soon after their attack on these plantations, parties setting out from Island "killed some of the rebels, cut their heads off and stuck them on poles. They captured one

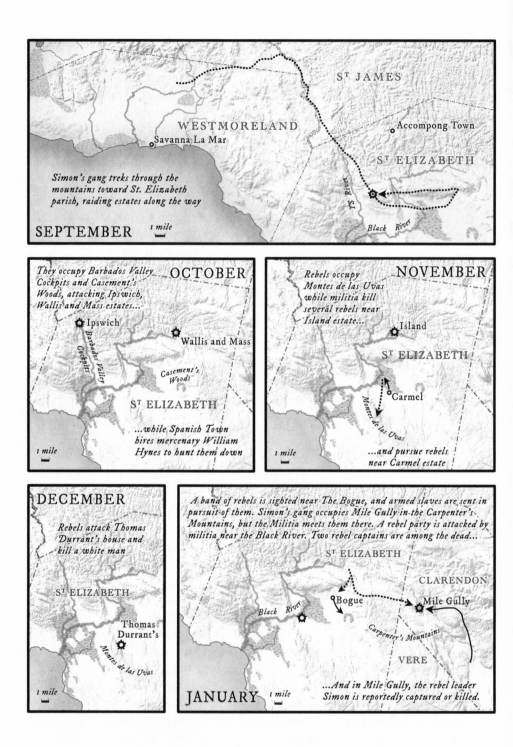

of them alive and then hung him the next day."[165] The Moravians lamented that the company sent against the rebels also killed several innocent slaves, but this was, after all, a common occurrence in counterinsurgency warfare, in which lines between combatants and noncombatants were vanishingly thin.[166] At Mesopotamia, the Moravians worried about their brethren in the neighboring parish, having heard news of "murders and burning." However, there was still enough rebel activity in the area to hold the attention of Westmoreland residents. Brother Gandrup even bought a pistol, despite his oath against military service.[167]

WILLIAM Hynes, who had met with impressive success against the rebels in St. Mary's by using parties of armed slaves, was very familiar with the new theater of battle. His family owned several estates at the east end of Westmoreland, on the St. Elizabeth Parish border, beneath the New Savanna Mountains on the road to Palmeto Point.[168] He proposed to the Jamaica Assembly that he be paid to raise a company of "100 shot among free mulattoes and negroes," financed and armed by the state to pursue the remaining rebels. He wanted a bounty of "twenty pounds for every negro killed, taken, or drove in," to be divided by his men however they should agree. For the "satisfaction of the public," all rebels killed by Hynes's party would have their heads cut off and brought to the nearest settlement.[169] In October, the Assembly approved Hynes's scheme, in addition to another for raising seven companies of black and white rangers from the existing militias, more than three hundred men armed and ready to "take to the woods in pursuit of the rebels, upon the first notice of their being near them."[170] With these policies in execution, HMS *Port Royal* sailed again for Savanna la Mar, where sailors sent twenty casks of bread ashore for Hynes's party in mid-November, returning to Port Royal Harbour with eighty regular soldiers, who were standing down from their own operations against the slaves.[171]

The campaign was not without tension. When twenty black and brown rangers, along with some black porters, arrived at Egypt, Thistlewood complained that they got drunk, went out to the slave quarters, and tried to fraternize with the women. In his diary the overseer cast himself as the women's protector—ironic, given his unrelenting sexual predations—even as he disparaged the black troops: "I was obliged to get out off Bed, take my pistolls and go to quiet them, which Soon affected, but they fought affter, one against another till almost Midnight."[172] The overseer at Bogue issued a stern warning to the rangers who came to quarter there in late November. He decreed that "disturbing the Negroes in their houses" would be punished with a severe whipping and time in the stockade.[173] As far as overseers were concerned, if black troops were a necessary expedient during the crisis, they still represented a threat to social order, best contained by treating them as much as possible like slaves.

Hit-and-run skirmishes continued in St. Elizabeth through the end of the year. In early November, the rebels occupied the swamp overlapping Carmel estate and shot several slaves sent in to get them. They stayed briefly in a cliffside cave on the fringes of the Carmel territory but moved on before the slaveholders organized a pursuit.[174] Soldiers quartered at various estates in the area, reacting regularly to sightings of rebels or actual attacks.[175] On Christmas Eve, the missionaries at Carmel learned that the rebels were just a few miles south on the Monte de las Uvas savanna, where they burned down a house and shot a white man. A neighbor warned the brethren to be on their guard because the rebels had made a camp in the bush nearby.[176] In all likelihood the rebels were moving east again, into the unpopulated highlands of Clarendon Parish, the Carpenter's Mountains, and Mile Gully, where Simon would finally meet his end.

Early in 1761, colonists began to hear rumors of Simon's capture. "A Report that Simon is took Alive, up to Windward," Thistlewood noted in his diary for January 24, 1761. "Heard today that Simeon the Captain of the rebels was taken captive, and lots of people rejoiced," recorded the Moravian missionary at Mesopotamia two days later.[177] On the 28th there was a report that two rebel captains had been shot and killed near Black River.[178] Conflicting accounts of Simon's activities or his capture appeared well into the summer. He was supposed to be back at Moreland estate in early June, and then Thistlewood heard that he had been captured on June 18, 1761.[179] Perhaps Simon's name had become legendary among the enslaved population, synonymous with insurrection, like Spartacus among Europeans.

In 1774, Edward Long published an account that described Simon's death at a climatic battle, for which he did not give a date. "Damon, one of the Westmoreland chiefs, with a small gang, having posted himself at a place called Mile Gully in Clarendon, a voluntary party, under command of Mr. Scot and Mr. Grieg, with three or four more, went in quest of them. They had a long way to march in the night, through the woods, and across a difficult country; but, having provided themselves with a trusty guide, they came up to the haunt about midnight, attacked the rebels without loss of time, killed the chief, and one of his men, wounded another, and took two prisoners."[180] This may have been the end of Simon, and the effective end of the uprising that began at Masemure on May 25—or at Fort Haldane on April 7—of the previous year. Scattered bands of rebels stayed in the mountains, and sporadic violence continued, even resulting in the death of a white Westmoreland colonist in mid-October 1761. Nevertheless, the rebels' territorial ambitions had dwindled out.

THINKING about those ambitions, and about Simon's arduous route from Masemure to Mile Gully, highlights several open questions about the social geography of the Coromantee insurgency. Along his trek, Simon demonstrated a remarkable ability to navigate Jamaica's physical and social terrain, suggesting both an acute local knowledge and probably a prior experience of mountaineering warfare. Three features of Simon's march render a clearer picture of the insurrection.

First, the exceptional hiking skills of Simon's gang probably originated in African experience. If so, Simon, Agyei, and perhaps others were unlikely to be from the coastal Fante states but probably came instead from the upland polities north and east of the Gold Coast. This territorial division in West Africa manifested itself again in America. Speculating further, one might surmise that it was Simon and Agyei who resisted Apongo's bold plan to take Savanna la Mar and maintain Jamaica as a maritime state. Maybe Simon, who killed Masemure's attorney, had outranked Wager all along. Either way, it is clear that only part of Simon's authority to command derived from his Gold Coast origins. More important was his ability to outmaneuver his enemies. If common language and cultural practice provided an opportunity for affiliation with other Coromantees, only demonstrated achievement could command allegiance over time. Even the slaveholders recognized Simon's abilities, impressed by all he had managed with a limited number of followers: "By the mischief done by the few desperadoes under Simon we might Judge what might have been done by a much greater number," said one planter.[181] Simon's leadership, which extended to the celebrity of his name, derived not from ethnicity but from his followers' direct estimations of his talent for adapting to circumstances, his ability to negotiate his surroundings, and his brief material success. Likewise, the Coromantee War was more than an expression of African heritage; it was the outcome of black military intellect in Jamaica.

Second, the trajectory of the gang's movement hints at their knowledge of the political landscape. Was it only coincidence that the march passed through a plantain farm owned by Norwood Witter?[182] Or did the insurgents suspect that the Brigadier General, so attached to his business interests, was unlikely to destroy his crops as so many other colonists had? As the rebels passed into St. Elizabeth, perhaps they also hoped to inspire an uprising among Arthur Forrest's other slaves in that parish, where he owned a great sugar estate at Breadnut Valley, on the Black River between Ipswich and Island estates, and another property at Vineyard, near the river's mouth.[183] To some degree, connections among Akan-speaking Africans overlapped with patterns of estate ownership. From the necessary interchange between Forrest's plantations, many of Masemure's workers would have known Africans in St. Elizabeth. Plotters would have had numerous opportunities to build coalitions and coordinate their activities. It is easy to imagine a possible conspiracy, though an uprising among Forrest's slaves in the parish never did come to pass.

Finally, the trek suggests that the maroons disagreed among themselves about whether or not to support the insurrection. Simon's route into St. Elizabeth took his gang dangerously close to Accompong Town, a huge risk—unless the maroons there had signaled their acquiescence. Indeed, the absence of Accompong maroons among the leeward counterinsurgency forces is remarkable. Kojo and Captain Furry were active in suppressing the rebels. Their parties were often more effective than those of the regular army, and certainly more so than the forces of the colonial militia. Possibly, Kojo had prepared for the insurrection in advance. In June, Thistlewood remarked that "Col: Cudjoe Wrote to Col: Barclay & the gentlemen off this Parish a good While ago to warn then of this that has happened."[184] Perhaps Kojo had heard rumblings among the enslaved as they traveled from plantation to plantation or to markets in preparation for Whitsunday festivities. Or perhaps he even knew maroons involved in the plot.

Recall that a maroon named Accompong had been accused in 1755 of plotting a "general revolt of the Slaves & was to be their King." One of the Crawford Town insurgents, he had remained at large for more than a year before some other maroons killed him and brought his head to Spanish Town in October 1755.[185] If the colonists were correct that Accompong had been fomenting an island-wide insurrection, then he had surely visited fellow maroons as well as slaves. Possibly, on one of his visits to his countrymen in Accompong Town, he might have persuaded the maroons there of the justice of his cause, or at least convinced them that they should remain neutral and await the outcome of the war.

Or maybe the rebels simply paid the maroons off. In October 1761, three slaves on Retrieve estate caught a man coming down from the mountains to buy gunpowder and supplies. It turned out the man was a "Treasurer of the Rebells," carrying seventy doubloons in deposits, two of which he offered the slaves in a failed attempt to buy his release. The value of the coins was £323, "a fine prize" captured by the colonists.[186] During the previous year's turmoil, with whites abandoning their estates and runaways grabbing whatever they could carry off to the mountains, the insurgency must have been much richer. Paying their way from place to place, and keenly observing political contingencies, the rebels would have found room to maneuver in the space between different groups of maroons, between the maroons and the whites, and between various factions of the counterinsurgency.

The geography of the Coromantee War illuminates the contours and fissures of martial belonging across space. Whatever bonds of language, religion, and common practice united the African militants, their strategic and tactical actions over the landscape braided, tested, and frayed these connections. Likewise, the conglomerate forces of the Royal Navy, the British army, and slaveholder militias faced the challenge of diasporic warfare no less than the maroons, who weighed similar considerations of loyalty, discipline, and coalition-building across territories. Fear of enemies was a strong adhesive within militant camps, but the demarcation of adversaries had to be determined by internal coercion, as well. If the Coromantee insurgents wanted to form their own maroon society, they could not be sure which of the existing maroon communities might ally with them, and which might side with the colonists. If slaveholders were certain of their enmity for African rebels, they did not always agree about how to combat them, and how far to distinguish seditious from loyal slaves. Slaves without links to Coromantee social networks feared their dominance, but they had much to lose if they picked the wrong side. Proximate events shaped these predicaments, even as they emerged from longer histories of association in a variety of spaces.

The war's course flowed through relations of dispersion and attraction that wound their way across a landscape of empires, confederations, and coalitions, linking Africa and Europe to Jamaica's jagged terrain. There we can glimpse Tacky's Revolt, the Westmoreland uprising, and Simon's March as peaks of an archipelago, running from the tectonic shifts of Gold Coast state-making through the volcanic struggles of sugar-plantation society. This is the image that emerges when Africa and America are viewed as part of the same history. The African roots of slave revolt show only the starting point of a journey, not its routes and pathways through the geography of warfare. Nor does the genealogy of African militancy show us all of its consequences. After all, the story of the Coromantee War did not end with the pacification of 1761. The insurrection's economic, political, and cultural reverberations spread wide across the Atlantic and stretched long into the future.

CHAPTER SIX

Routes of Reverberation

NOT LONG AFTER Arthur Forrest returned to Jamaica in early 1761, he called on Thomas Thistlewood at Egypt estate. Together with a small group that included John Cope Jr., son of the former chief agent of Cape Coast Castle, Forrest learned of the calamity that had befallen the planters.[1] He would have known the broad outlines of the story, but now he surely heard lurid details about the killings of whites on his own estate and on others nearby. Even while the danger continued—two rebels had just been captured and brought to town—he could commiserate over the cost of torched buildings, lost crops, and wasted slaves summarily executed or massacred in the fray.[2] Perhaps he shared a personal lament for the loss of some favorites, including Wager.

When Admiral Holmes died on November 21, Forrest assumed command of the naval station as commodore and commander-in-chief, hoisting his pennant above the *Cambridge* flagship—prematurely, as it turned out. He was relieved of that duty in April 1762, just before the Jamaica Squadron was to participate in the conquest of Cuba. Recalled by the Admiralty, he made an ignominious return as a passenger in a merchant ship to London, where he was scolded for promoting himself, conduct that had been deemed "most irregular and unjustifiable."[3] Certainly, people must have wondered if the financial losses Forrest had suffered in Jamaica had motivated him to commit this breach of protocol.[4] In any event, for

Captain Forrest, the humiliation closed both the imperial and the intestine fronts of the Seven Years' War.

Forrest had been a formidable force against Britain's European enemies and a fierce defender of its most prized colony. He had grown rich from the fruits of war, slavery, and commerce, and yet the edifice of his power could be shaken by his lowliest subjects. His experience as both a celebrated warrior and a beleaguered proprietor highlights the predicament of an eighteenth-century British empire committed to expansion and slavery. Its external success created internal crises, generating unintended consequences across an interconnected theater of events. The slave insurrection of 1760–1761 had been one of most arduous and complex episodes of the Seven Years' War. The Coromantee War was at once an extension of the African conflicts that fed the slave trade, a race war among black slaves and white slaveholders, an imperial conquest, and an internal struggle between black people for control of territory and the establishment of a political legacy. The economic, political, and cultural consequences of this war within wars reverberated out from Jamaica to other colonies, across the ocean to Great Britain, and back again to the island, where the revolt reshaped public life and lodged deeply in collective memory.

But explanations for the turmoil of violent expropriation tended to identify some simple cause that could account for everything. The lack of a sufficient troop presence, the liberties of movement allowed to slaves and free people of color, and the presence of a dangerous category of persons were all held to blame at various times. Property owners and colonial officials totaled their losses and introduced what they hoped would be appropriate reforms. They responded to the news of death and suffering with empathy, revulsion, or indifference, according to their predispositions. Woven into racist tropes and abolitionist sympathies, the Coromantee revolts came to signify general problems, either in the management of colonial slavery or in the danger posed by black people. In this way, events in Jamaica reverberated throughout the Atlantic basin and carried the war far beyond its island theater.

Even before the insurrection had been completely suppressed, hundreds of suspected rebels who were condemned to transportation carried the news of the conflict beyond Jamaica. Torn again from whatever intimacies, friendships, and social circles they had managed to create, these exiles would have to start over elsewhere. Wherever they found themselves, their knowledge of the war against enslavement arrived with them. Indeed, the nature of their transportation, aboard merchant ships convoyed by the Royal Navy, ensured that these deportees traveled together as prisoners of war, just as many of them had emigrated from West Africa.

Many of these exiles left the island with the merchant ships that had been delayed by the insurrection. Tacky's revolt in St. Mary's had "very much retarded Business and kept the sugars from being in that readiness which might otherwise have been expected," compelling the planters to request the detention, explained Rear Admiral Charles Holmes.[5] The subsequent uprisings caused further delays, putting "so entire a stop to Business for more than a month, that it was impossible for the Convoy to get ready to sail."[6] A first fleet of 112 vessels, originally intended to sail in mid-May, did not depart Port Royal until late June.[7] A second convoy from Bluefields Bay would be held up by the Westmoreland insurrection until September.

With the plantations in disarray and the Navy needed on hand to suppress the revolt, merchant ships laden with trade goods languished in the harbors. Among those goods were the condemned passengers, sentenced at hasty trials in Kingston, Spanish Town, and Savanna la Mar. When the convoy of fifty-five ships finally sailed from Bluefields under the escort of HMS *Edinburgh,* one of them, the *Norfolk,* listed only "Negroes" for its cargo.[8] These were probably convicts, but their ultimate destination is uncertain. Owned by Thomas Harper of Jamaica, the ship plied the slave trade between the island colony and Virginia. At about the 29th latitude and within sight of Florida, the *Norfolk,* along with nine other ships bound for the southern colonies of North America, parted with the convoy and continued northward, arriving at the port of Hampton on October 26.[9] To the customs officials the ship's master declared rum, molasses, sugar, coffee, ten bags of ginger, and two bags of pimento, but no slaves.[10]

News of the revolt had run ahead of the *Norfolk,* and colonial officials were wary of importing convicted rebels. Like most North American jurisdictions, Virginia placed prohibitive duties on importations of "seasoned" captives from other colonies for just this reason.[11] By October, the bad tidings from Jamaica were widespread. Three ships from the earlier convoy had arrived on July 14, carrying among them twenty-seven sailors with firsthand accounts of the rebellion and bloody reprisals.[12] Another ship with eight men aboard had arrived from Jamaica on August 29 with updates.[13] With Virginia slaveholders fearing contagion from the Caribbean, it is entirely likely that the *Norfolk* sold its cargo of dangerous exiles surreptitiously before declaring its arrival. Perhaps the "negroes" disembarked in Georgia or South Carolina, which had accepted at least nine captives from Jamaica in late August, if they were not smuggled to the French.[14]

Anxious slaveholders in other colonies were right to worry, for Jamaica's masters were eager to transfer troublesome people elsewhere. This desire to remove intractable slaves was not limited to transporting convicted rebels. In July 1760, for example, the Kingston merchant Robert Graham consigned an enslaved washerwoman named Mary for sale on the Mosquito Shore of British Honduras (known today as Belize), called one of the "most dangerous Stations in all the West Indies" by its superintendent.[15] Because British Honduras was conveniently close and under Jamaica's jurisdiction, it was generally easier to relocate the disobedient there than in North America. Indeed, many of the hundreds of black people transported for involvement in the rebellion went to British Honduras to cut logwood, for use in making brilliant textile dyes that were in high demand. This, however, was unlikely to be Mary's work. Graham had used Mary for sexual gratification, which he strongly hinted at in lauding her "other Qualifications which the purchaser will be soon able to discover." But Mary was "endow'd with such a surprising facility of Speech" that the merchant "found it impossible to put up with it any Longer." In the context of a raging rebellion, a vocal and sharp-witted slave woman in the house was an intimate danger. "Notwithstanding we are dayly burning & Hanging & Gibetting the prisoners that are taken," Graham knew that he and his fellow slaveholders would not "soon able to recover our former tranquility." Just as Mary might talk her libidinous master into trading special favors for her acquiescence, she could also relay detailed news of the insurrection to the household staff and, if she did not do it herself, convince someone else to cut her rapist's throat as he slept.[16]

In at least one alarming case, a rebel woman returned from exile in the midst of the revolt. In early December 1760, members of the Jamaica House of Assembly learned that the Coromantee woman dubbed the "Queen of Kingston" had returned to Jamaica from Spanish Cuba, another regular destination for exiles. Somehow, she had convinced a ship captain to land her in the parish of Hanover at Cousines's Cove, just over the mountains from the site of Rebel's Barricade. This location might easily have been a coincidence, simply an out-of-the way inlet beyond the surveillance of the state. It is also entirely possible that she knew of her fellow Coromantees' designs to occupy the hills between Hanover and Westmoreland—without knowing that their effort had collapsed—and that she hoped to rejoin the battle. In any event, she eluded capture for several weeks before being taken and conveyed back to Kingston to face a likely death sentence. The Assembly acted quickly to address the threat posed by her example, passing an act "to Prevent Any Captain, Master, or Supercargo of Any Vessel

Bringing back Slaves Transported off the Island." They were determined to make a safe space for slavery at home by pushing the danger abroad.[17]

Whatever Akua, the "Queen of Kingston," Mary, or the deportees aboard the *Norfolk,* told other slaves about the insurrection, they brought news of black struggle and white vulnerability, of the fractures in the slave-holding regime as well as its brutality. They represented the possibility of revolt as both an inspiration and a warning. More practically, what they had learned in Jamaica could be taught to others, ensuring that the re-verberations of the Coromantee War extended beyond its original participants.

THIS lesson was not lost on slaveholder governments or imperial admin-istrators. Yet the security concerns raised by such exiles paled in compar-ison to the challenge posed by the restive enslaved population that remained on the island. This was an urgent concern even for Jamaica's stakeholders in Great Britain, where they held emergency meetings to consider the fate of the island. In October, a handbill in Somerset County, England, an-nounced that "All Planters and Merchants interested in the Island of Jamaica are desired to meet on Thursday the 16 Ins.t at 6 o'Clock in the Evening at the Kings Arms in Cornhill, to consider what steps are neces-sary to be taken for the Security and Preservation of that Island, at this time in great Distress and imminent Danger from the frequent Insurrections of the Negroes."[18] At this meeting, members of the West India interest resolved to request additional troops for the Jamaica garrison, hoping to bring the numbers to two thousand regular soldiers. "Without such a force," they said, "we apprehend the Island is not sufficiently protected ag.st those in-testine broyles they have lately most sadly experienced."[19] The Jamaica Assembly would soon vote to erect barracks to receive and accommodate the additional troops, along with procuring large sums for strengthening the island's internal fortifications, stores for the forts, and a new powder magazine at Spanish Town. Convinced that the island remained not only vulnerable to external attack but also "in constant danger of devastation and destruction from within," Jamaica's colonists would continue to lobby for and welcome the presence of imperial troops for the foreseeable future.[20]

The Royal Navy balked at some of the colonists' requests. Having noted the effectiveness of sailors and marines in helping to suppress the insurrec-tion, a group of several merchants and planters in Jamaica implored the Navy to reestablish a permanent station at Port Antonio, with at least one ship cruising the east and north side of the island at all times to deter po-tential rebels. Admiral Holmes demurred, maintaining that "the brisk and impetuous attacks of Seamen should be confined to their own Element," except in extreme cases. Even then, he thought, the colonists could best enhance their security by "making proper Dispositions of the Regular Troops" and building up the island's fortifications.[21] Colonists approved the building of barracks in every parish "to secure the Tranquility of the Country," but they acted even more immediately to regulate the enslaved population.[22]

On December 18, 1760, having carefully considered the findings derived from reports, rumors, and tortured confessions about the plotting and progress of the revolt, the Assembly passed a reform of the laws governing slaves and slaveholding.[23] The colonial government sought to prevent slaves from acquiring arms and ammunition, since many trusted slaves had turned their guns on their masters and many poorly guarded stockpiles in planters' houses had "disposed slaves to Execute their bloody Intentions." It would be a capital offense for slaves to possess "any Gun Blunderbuss Pistol Gun Powder Bayonet Sword Cuttlass Lance or any other Military Offensive Weapon" in the absence of direct supervision by a white man. The new law also criminalized the practice of obeah, noting that obeah men and women had been crucial to rebel organizing and morale by offering the promise of supernatural protection. Any "Negro or other Slave" convicted of practicing obeah or witchcraft "in Order to delude and impose on the minds of others" was to be punished with death or exile. Restricting arms and ideas served the larger purpose of securing the space to hold slaves with less risk.

Above all, the new legislation continued the attempt to control Jamaica's territory by limiting, regulating, and surveilling the movement of black people. To "Remedy the Evils" arising from unauthorized gatherings, movements, and communication, the law aimed to prevent slaves from traveling without permission slips from their masters. These tickets needed to state exactly when and from what place a "Negro Mulatto or Indian Slave" had set out, where they were going, and at what time they should return. The law demanded that slaveholders prevent slaves from gathering to play their "Drums Goards Boards Barrels or any other Instrument of Noise," which might broadcast their collective strength and summon others. If they came upon such assemblies, slaveholders were required to hail immediately the nearest magistrate or militia officer, who would deploy a force to disperse them. Constables were to attend Sunday markets and be alert for suspicious activity. The legislators worried over the role that the Easter and Whitsuntide holidays had played in the timing of the revolt, but they could not simply abolish the agricultural calendar. Instead, they stipulated that no two successive holidays would be allowed, limiting the number of days available for clandestine organizing. Together these measures were designed to keep slaves in their place, but they required vigorous enforcement, and that was the responsibility of free people.

The legislation signified the draconian oppression of the enslaved, to be sure, but most of the punishments were actually directed at the free. Slaves were already routinely subject to physical violation, both legal and extra-legal; whites needed no further sanction to brutalize slaves with impunity. Rather, the new reforms sought to discipline the supervisory habits of slaveholders in order to bring their private behavior in line with the public needs of a slave society. The law allowed capricious cruelty but sought to restrict fickleness in matters of public security. Whether they were masters, owners, employers, or overseers, slaveholders were to pay forty shillings for every instance of a slave being permitted to travel from their estate without a ticket. An overseer leaving his estate on a Sunday, when the en-slaved gathered for social activities, would forfeit £5, and slaveholders would pay £50 for granting unsanctioned holidays. The fine for allowing slaves to carry any "military offensive weapon" was £100. Estate owners and managers would be fined £100 and overseers and bookkeepers could be imprisoned for up to six months for allowing slaves to assemble together to beat drums or blow horns. In all these cases, the plantocracy agreed in theory (enforcement of the law was another matter) that their own pre-rogatives should be curtailed for the sake of common security. As ever, warfare required the sacrifice of liberty.

Such sacrifice was not to be borne equally, of course. The most stringent restrictions applied to free black and brown people. Slaveholders worried that many slaves had been traveling about under the pretense of being free. The solution was to limit the mobility of all non-white people. Updating regulations first established in the 1720s and 1730s, the law called on the officials of each parish in the island to make a census of "Negroes Mulat-toes or Indians of free Condition" and to summon them all to the next parish vestry meeting to give an account of how they had obtained their freedom. Having been officially registered, they would receive certificates of freedom subject to annual renewal. Anyone failing to obtain an official certificate or neglecting to renew their document every year risked six months' imprisonment. All free non-whites were required to continuously wear "Badges of Freedom"—a blue cross upon their right shoulder.[24] Un-qualified freedom was coterminous with whiteness; all non-whites were politically suspect, and whites maintained a social and legal obligation to police, harass, and contain all black and brown people.

Just as they hoped to control the physical movement of non-whites, the slaveholders sought to regulate the social ascension of black and brown people. Some of them were descendants of property owners who recognized

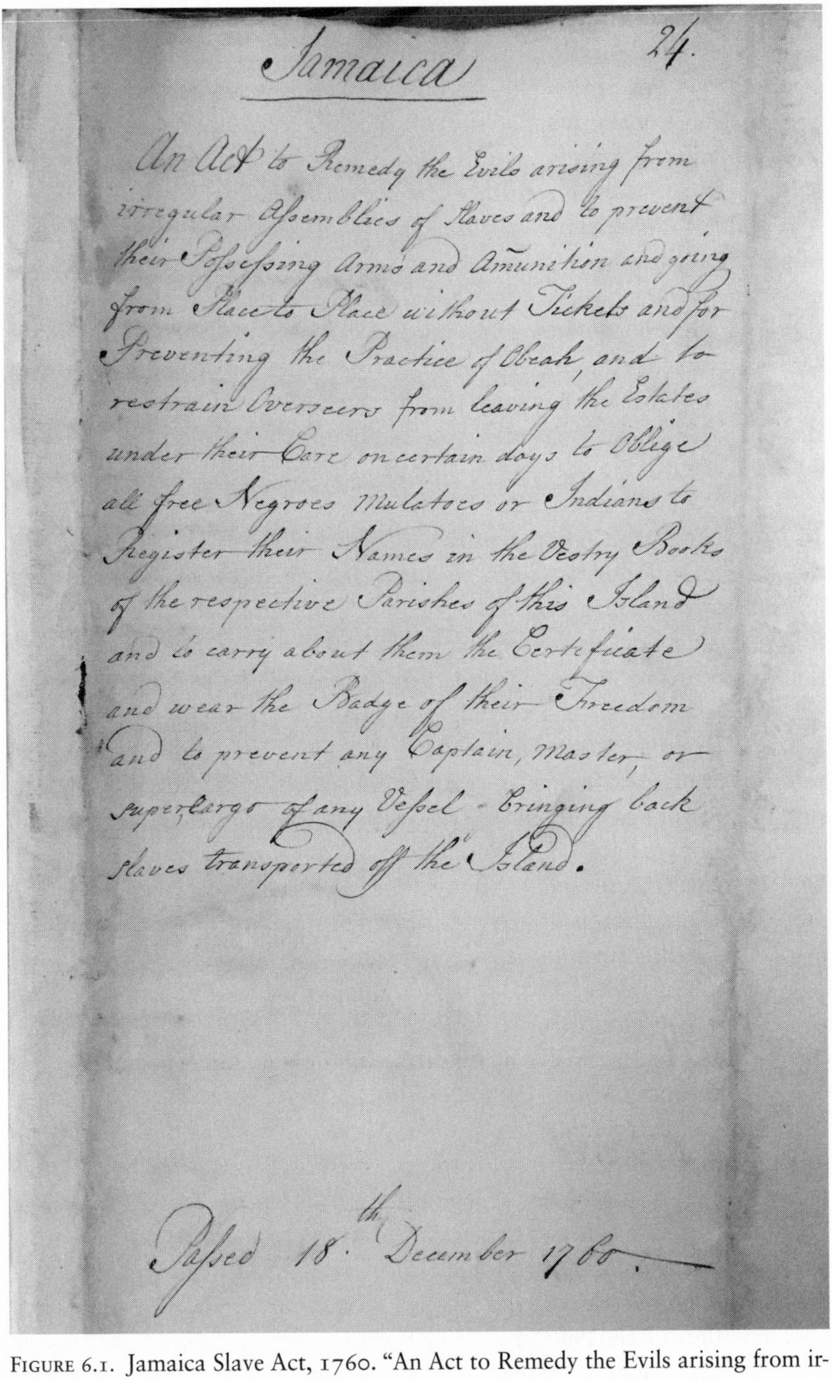

Jamaica 24.

An Act to Remedy the Evils arising from irregular Assemblies of Slaves and to prevent their Possessing Arms and Amunition and going from Place to Place without Tickets and for Preventing the Practice of Obeah, and to restrain Overseers from leaving the Estates under their Care on certain days to Oblige all free Negroes Mulatoes or Indians to Register their Names in the Vestry Books of the respective Parishes of this Island and to carry about them the Certificate and wear the Badge of their Freedom and to prevent any Captain, Master, or supercargo of any Vessel bringing back slaves transported off the Island.

Passed 18th December 1760.

FIGURE 6.1. Jamaica Slave Act, 1760. "An Act to Remedy the Evils arising from irregular Assemblies of Slaves," Jamaica, 1760.

Source: TNA, CO 139/21, 24. *Courtesy of the UK National Archives.*

a filial responsibility, but most whites mistrusted those free people of color with assets and social connections. In 1761, the Assembly moved to restrict the growth of this population by preventing anyone less than four generations removed from a "negro" ancestor from acquiring the "rights and privileges of whites," and by imposing a limit on bequests of property to slaveholders' mixed-race children born out of "lawful wedlock." Norwood Witter—who recognized the existence of nonwhites in his familial line—dissented vigorously, but his was a minority opinion. These aspects of the law represented a repudiation of former governor Trelawny's vision of an empire incorporating loyal subjects of all colors, albeit at sharply different ranks. The colony had just been saved by a multiracial coalition, but Jamaica's planter elite determined that white solidarity was the key to their security. Race was to supersede all other axes of difference and belonging.[25]

HAVING done their best to harden the legal regime, white property-holders turned to calculating the financial cost of the rebellion. The year's turmoil had disrupted production, delayed shipping, and caused markets to languish. Early in the revolt, merchants worried only about a temporary pause in debt payments by planters, who generally refused "making any payments till they see how matters are," as one Kingston trader reported in June. While he feared that the "credit of the country may be hurted by the frequent rebellions that have happen'd within these few months," he was optimistic that the "present troubles will be the means of securing the future peace of the country as people will be more watchfull of their slaves, & take care to keep them fully employed."[26] By October, however, with business still arrested and with competing colonies fulfilling Jamaica's role in the supply chain, the market was dull for everything but the finest sugars.[27]

In Great Britain, merchants cared less about the island's overall economy than about their own fortunes. Because profits from the West Indies justified the extension of large amounts of credit to planters, merchants monitored shipping schedules closely, not only for the delivery of agricultural products but also for the remittances on planters' debts. The timing of these arrivals was vital to the merchants' cash flow and their ability to keep capital circulating through the most promising investment opportunities. They grandly entertained the Royal Navy captains who had brought in the wartime convoys, as much to offer the right incentives as to express their gratitude.[28]

Slave rebellion created bottlenecks. Throughout 1760, one agent struggled to collect on the debts owed to a Scottish investor. "I did flatter myself with the hopes of being able to have made you a handsome remittance by this fleet," he wrote in August, "but such has been the Situation of this country with Marshall Law, Insurrection of Slaves & c, that business has been very little attended to for some months past." When he tried to collect thousands of pounds on the investor's behalf, the planters "always pleaded the times in excuse for not paying, knowing very well that during Marshall law I could take no steps to compel them." In the case of large estate owners, however, the agent felt it wise not to press so hard as to taint the relationship. "There is no pushing a Gentleman of Honour to Distress on such one occasion who has a Large Estate & can pay in another season." Jamaica would recover, the merchants knew, and those who could afford to cover temporary losses would profit again with the suppression of the enslaved.[29]

Simon's gang was still harrying estates in St. Elizabeth Parish when the Jamaica Assembly met near the end of 1760 to hear claims on public expenses. They appropriated more than £10,000 to pay for supporting and supplying war parties, and more to compensate owners for slaves killed in service against the rebels.[30] Edward Long would later estimate total losses of at least £100,000 sterling "in ruined buildings, cane-pieces, cattle, slaves, and disbursements," and a similar additional amount for the cost of erecting new barracks and fortifications across the island.[31]

To recoup some of the public costs, the Assembly passed new poll taxes and commercial duties, and doubled the deficiency taxes paid by proprietors with too few white men on their estates. The rate hike allowed special exemptions for resident owners, so that the increase fell more heavily on absentees. The ravages of the slave war had left many island residents resentful of those proprietors in Great Britain who, Long later wrote, "had left their slaves in want of a due controul, and the personal influence of a master, and their estates to be defended by the personal services and hardships of other men, while they themselves were reposing in ease and affluence, beyond the reach of danger."[32] Colonists had little patience for criticism of local decisions by absentees, who, not incidentally, were often creditors: "Whatever those gentlemen may think of themselves, we do not by any means allow them to be competent judges of the expediency of laws that have passed the legislature."[33] Resident slaveholders had endured nearly a year of panic, for which they sought some compensation from the wealthier members of their class.

The colonial government also committed to a more regressive tax on "vellum, parchment, and paper, ascertained by stamps," something that imperial reformers would attempt a few years later for all of America. The Jamaica Stamp Act of 1760 was meant explicitly to address the costs of the revolt. In practice, it was largely a tax on lawsuits—because of the large amounts of paper involved—which were a prevalent feature of Jamaican business life. The duty continued in force until December 1763, when it was repealed as too great a burden for all but the wealthiest colonists. As a model for the more contentious 1765 Stamp Act that would rile the colonists in North America, the 1760 tax in Jamaica was an early local instance of a far larger reform effort stimulated by the Seven Years' War.[34]

As imperial policymakers celebrated military victories in North America, Africa, and the Caribbean, they contemplated the threat to one of their most vital colonies. On November 7, two weeks after the death of King George II, the Board of Trade considered official accounts of the insurrection. They read the April 19 letter from Lieutenant Governor Moore and the minutes of the Council of Jamaica from April 10 and 17 about Tacky's revolt in St. Mary's Parish. Then they read Moore's June 9 "Account of a second & third Insurrection of Negroes," his July 24 letter, and the Council minutes detailing the continuing crisis and "Steps taken for the Security of the Island." Finally, Moore's letter of August 20 assured them that he was "under no Apprehensions of further Danger from the rebellious Negroes." While the emergency had passed, the rebellion still raised the question of how an expanding empire might contain its internal antagonists.[35]

In this liminal moment for imperial management, a new policy would take shape. British statesmen had worried over the governance of America for more than a decade, since the conclusion of the previous war with France and Spain in 1748. The colonies' demographic, economic, and strategic value had increased dramatically in the first half of the eighteenth century, and the complexity of administering them had grown in tandem. The Lords of Trade had been attempting to strengthen metropolitan control over the colonies since at least 1752, when the Board gained exclusive authority over the appointment and supervision of colonial governors, councilors, attorneys-general, and secretaries. The Board's efforts to assert its authority had largely failed, except in the important case of Jamaica, when it had vetoed the Assembly's attempt to move the capital from Spanish Town to Kingston and censured the colonial legislators in 1757 for making extravagant constitutional claims.[36] By this action, members of parliament meant to set a precedent, made urgent by the behavior of North American colonists during the Seven Years' War. In the midst of the conflict, colonial assemblies flouted the authority of governors, elected officials allowed flagrant violations of the Navigation Acts against trading with the enemy, and colonists often failed to supply enough local troops and resources to the war effort. As the historian Jack P. Greene explains, this coincided with a "dramatic shift from an essentially permissive to a fundamentally restrictive philosophy of colonial administration" in London, amplifying the "widespread conviction that the colonies had too many privileges and that those privileges ought to be reduced."[37] News of the slave war in Britain's most profitable colony strengthened the policymakers' resolve.

Jamaica had been restive and independent too, but the insurrection reminded its slaveholders of the benefits of empire. They soon conveyed their gratitude—along with a request for more troops—to the new king, George the Third, and the Lords of Trade. If not for his majesty's forces, the colonial government thanked the king, "the lives and properties of your loyal subjects would, in all likelihood, have become a prey to their slaves."[38] Slaveholders in Jamaica might have resented the influence of absentees and metropolitan intervention, as well as the imposition of new taxes. However, unlike so many in North America, they had been recently threatened by slave revolt and remained duly subject to imperial command, even passing a stamp act to help finance their own security.[39] They largely acquiesced even to those imperial reforms they did not favor. After the Seven Years' War, with Jamaica having served as a model for the assertion of imperial control, imperial policymakers proffered a raft of new legislation for their North American colonies. Yet unlike colonial Jamaica's submission, the reactions to these policies was the well-known backlash that would ultimately split the British Empire in 1776.[40]

THE optimism of Jamaica's proprietors was vindicated. In the immediate aftermath of the Seven Years' War, the colony's prosperity grew, and with it the slave trade and plantation agriculture. Productivity surged. *Per capita* product in Jamaica grew from an estimated £8 in 1750 to £13.2 in 1770, when it was just £10 in England and Wales. The affluence of propertied Jamaicans continued to increase, with the average value of inventoried estates being more than thirty percent higher in the period from 1750–1784 than it had been during the second quarter of the eighteenth century. Jamaica remained the most profitable part of the British empire.[41]

The slaveholders were thriving as never before when Arthur Forrest returned to the island in 1769, this time legitimately appointed as commodore and commander-in-chief of the station. His service to Great Britain was recognized the next year with a promotion to the rank of admiral and an elevation to the peerage as Lord Viscount Forrest, but he died in 1770 before the news could reach him. If, at the end of his life, he could take pride in his naval career, he could also be pleased with the progress of slavery.[42] Over the next two decades, Jamaica would import almost 190,000 African captives, more than a third of them from the Gold Coast.[43]

Meanwhile, the slave war in Jamaica continued to unfold. The rebellion of 1760–1761 had been suppressed, but people continued to rise up, with the Coromantees still leading the way. In September 1760, Jamaican colonists had burned a man named Cardiff at the stake. John Cope Jr. witnessed the execution. Cardiff told Cope and the other spectators that "Multitudes off Negroes had took swear that if they fail'd of success in this rebellion, to rise again the Same day" two years hence, and advised the whites "to be upon their guard."[44] A few weeks later, the recollection and recirculation of an old proverb reminded anxious slaveholders that the suppression of an insurrection was not the same thing as peace: "One thousand Seven hundred and Sixty Three, Jamaica no More an Island shall be." "Not for the Whites," Thomas Thistlewood annotated in his diary.[45]

In April 1763, Governor William Henry Lyttelton had to abort a tour of Jamaica's northern parishes when he received accounts that "two Plantations in the Parishes of Westmoreland and Hanover had been attack'd and three or four White persons slain by parties of Negroes which are the remains of those that were in Rebellion during the administration of Lieutenant Governor Moore."[46] The parish militias and the maroons put down this uprising quickly, but a short time later, in December 1764, there was another scare when residents of Spanish Town detected a "horrid Conspiracy for massacring all the white Inhabitants and taking Possession of their Estates." Slaves had reportedly amassed a large magazine of arms outside the town, but they were discovered before they were to have "begun their operations," scheduled for Christmas Day.[47]

The threat of war reverberated through less dramatic episodes as well. In October 1765, several planters in St. Elizabeth worried over a nonviolent but very revealing affair. At Appleton estate at the base of the Nassau Mountains, on the route of Simon's earlier trek through western Jamaica, a group of Coromantees replaced an unpopular overseer with one more to their liking. According to Charles Hiern, the estate's manager, Appleton's workers had enjoyed the indulgence of an overseer named John Thomason, who distributed "Salt Beef, Butter, Sope, Candles, Rum, Sugar &c. among his Female & other Favourites with unbounded liberality." Hiern removed Thomason, replacing him with a tight-fisted man named Roger Denis. Denis turned a "fine Mistress out of the House to work in the Field & punished & degraded a Driver," whom he accused of thievery. Unwilling to accept the change of circumstance, "to regain their former Overseer & by that means their state of Luxury & indulgence," twenty Coromantees either took it upon themselves or were elected to see that Denis was sent off. They marched many miles around the mountains to Elim estate to lodge a complaint with Hiern and then, not finding him there, returned to Appleton, where Hiern had arrived in the meantime. What happened next illustrates the Coromantees' negotiating power. Hiern thought their "complaint of se-

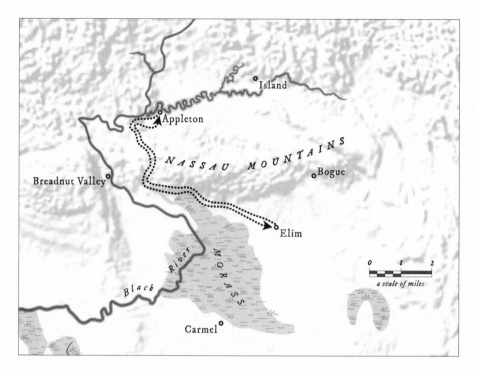

verity exercised over them" was baseless, yet he "removed Denis rather than be troubled with their murmurings & discontentments."[48]

That Coromantees lodged this successful protest is significant, to be sure, but it is no more important than the location of their activity. They traversed an area that had been in the path of Simon's marauding and that bordered mountains where the rebels had gathered and planned. Even if none of these people had joined the insurrection, they must have known a great deal about its strategies and tactics. They could be certain that Hiern would respect both their reputation and their ability to ruin his plantations if they so chose. The rebels had already implanted the seeds of war in the Nassau Mountains, and they could sprout quickly under the right conditions.

Hostilities shot up again in St. Mary's Parish in late November, when another revolt showed that Coromantees would continue to stir the politics of slavery for a long time to come, in Jamaica and beyond. It was about 2 A.M., with the moon waxing toward full, when Zachary Bayly awoke to learn that the works at Whitehall estate were on fire, that slaves were in "actual rebellion," and that Matthew Byndloss, with whom Bayly had dined the previous day, had been killed. Just as he had in 1760, Bayly mustered the white people on his estates at Nonsuch and Unity and raised the alarm throughout the neighborhood.[49]

On the road to Whitehall, his party learned that the rebels had gone on to Ballard's Valley, but the whites elected to keep their course. They found Byndloss dead on Whitehall's great house floor and learned that his sister had escaped into the cane fields with the help of a servant. Another man, the overseer at Llanrumney estate, having heard a shell blow and seen the glow from the blaze, had ridden toward Whitehall and encountered the rebels, who shot and decapitated him—Bayly's party came across his headless body in the morning on their way to Ballard's Valley.[50] At Ballard's Valley, well-armed with weapons seized at Whitehall, the rebels sang their war songs. Bayly described the chorus as a "hideous howling," and it terrified the whites, who regrouped at the overseer's house. The rebels attempted to burn it down, but one of their leaders was killed in the attack. Repulsed, the insurgents set fire to the trash houses, stuffed with the combustible kindling of dried cane fibers, then marched back toward Whitehall and from there into the woods, pursued by several parties of militia. In the bush, the colonists killed several rebels and found that several more had committed suicide.[51]

Bayly and others, with fresh memories of Tacky's Revolt, began an immediate investigation, taking account of the slaves at neighboring estates and leading a series of interrogations that would cement white impressions of the immediate and previous insurrections, of the Coromantees and their essential character, and of the prospects for the future of slavery.[52]

Tortured confessions again laid the basis for the slaveholders' interpretation of events. Gathered together at Whitehall, the slaveholders argued over the continuing urgency of the threat. Many, including Bayly, assumed that this insurrection was "only a drunken sally of a few negroes," and that "matters were again put to rights." Others doubted the "probability of a few new negroes going such lengths, without the assistance and knowledge of the old negroes in the parish; of those negroes in the very estates and neighbourhood, who had been so deeply engaged, a few years before, in rebellion and murder."[53] Bayly, the senior magistrate of the parish, interrogated a man named Cambridge just a few days after the uprising. His testimony was inconsistent and Bayly continued to doubt that there was "any deep laid plot."[54] But Cambridge kept talking and other slaveholders were less skeptical. He told his inquisitors that three weeks before the fire at Whitehall, about two dozen Africans from neighboring estates had "made bargain" at a play or festival. He gave their names. Many of them had sworn an allegiance to rise up under the leadership of Abruco, known to the slaveholders as Blackwall, "an old Coromantee," the head sugar-boiler on Whitehall.[55] Blackwall had been tried during Tacky's Revolt in 1760 and released for lack of evidence.[56] Now he was condemned to burn alive, while several of the others were hanged or bound for transportation.[57]

Roundups, interrogations, trials, and punishments went on for the next two weeks, as those who had been named impeached others in turn.[58] The planters soon came to believe that the "conspiracy was general among the Coromantee negroes," with a plan to rise at Christmas, not only at White-hall and Ballard's Valley, but also at many other estates, including Trinity, Frontier, and Esher, where Tacky's Revolt had begun.[59] A young Coromantee named Cuffee, one of the most eager informants, told his owner what the slaveholders surely feared the most: that the colonists faced yet another plot to deliver the parish to the Coromantees—and this time, perhaps, even the maroons would side with the enslaved.[60]

This event coincided with a potent scare in Westmoreland Parish when it was discovered that slaves had conspired to rebel on several of the same estates where the insurrection had begun in 1760. An enslaved blacksmith had even "made several pointed Irons to fix on the ends of Lances for one of Capt. Forrest's negroes." In the course of repeated alarms occasioned by workers at Forrest's Masemure estate, the parish magistrate "used every pre-caution necessary to strike Terrour into the minds of Slaves," keeping the militia under arms and marching "with their Drums beating through every part" of the parish.[61] The island stayed on high alert—albeit not with mar-tial law—through the end of the year, but there were no further outbreaks.

A few months later, the Assembly appointed a committee of five slave-holders, which included Edward Long and Bayly's nephew Bryan Edwards, to inquire and report upon the "rise and progress, and the means used to suppress, the late insurrection of slaves, in the parish of St. Mary."[62] Their findings removed any doubt that they had faced a direct aftershock of Tacky's Revolt. As one of their witnesses confirmed, "the first cause and spring of the late actual and intended insurrections of the Coromantee ne-groes, in the parish of St. Mary, was by the influence and persuasion of the negroes on the different estates, that had been concerned in the rebellion in that parish in the year 1760."[63] Reading the report to the Assembly in August, Committee Chair Long drove the point home: "Most of the Coro-mantees in that parish were privy to the design, and engaged in its support," he said. Despite the fact that many had been apprehended and dealt with, and this rebellion crushed, "yet there is very just reason for apprehending, that the flame has only been smothered, and that the Coromantees, who religiously adhere to the oath which is taken upon entering into these bloody associations, will, in all likelihood, embrace the first favourable occasion to renew their attempts."[64] As a cautionary measure, the committee pro-posed an additional tax "on all Fantee, Akim, and Ashantee slaves, and on all other slaves commonly called Coromantees" imported and sold on the island. To Long's chagrin, his fellow planters declined to pass it.[65]

Long decried the complacency of those who had failed to take the evidence of a conspiracy seriously enough. Many had been too eager to execute the ringleaders and return to the normal course of business without a disruptive investigation, a course which would have left the larger conspiracy undiscovered. Presumably, this latter group included Bayly, from whom the committee report included no testimony. Long went so far as to accuse Governor Lyttelton of "neglect of his duty" for failing to dispatch companies of regular soldiers or to have a warship sent around to aid the parishioners, as Moore had done in 1760.[66] The dispute over the nature and extent of the events had persisted; Long sought to close the argument.

Evidence of the threat that Coromantees posed seemed to be everywhere. There was news of a massive revolt in Dutch Berbice in 1763, which implicated Gold Coast Africans.[67] In 1764, Dr. James Grainger's widely read georgic poem *The Sugar Cane* warned readers, "Buy not a Coromantee . . . They, born to freedom in their native land, Chuse death before dishonourable bonds: Or, fir'd with vengeance, at the midnight hour, Sudden they seize thine unsuspecting watch, And thine own poniard bury in they breast."[68] Not long before the St. Mary's outbreak, a gang of rebels transported from Jamaica to British Honduras had killed and robbed their master, escaped into the woods, and cut off traffic on the colony's main river route. They slew as many as sixteen colonists while they remained free.[69] Just two months after the Jamaica committee submitted its report in mid-1766, there was another revolt in Westmoreland Parish by more than thirty Coromantees, said to have arrived together in the same ship two years earlier. They escaped as a group on the night of October 5, killing everyone in their way, before rallying at Cross Path, where they blew a call to arms on a horn crafted from tree bark. More than twenty colonists died before the parish raised the alarm, with cannon firing twice every quarter-hour at Savanna la Mar. The militia hunted the rebels for the next several weeks.[70] In early November, they were still burning Africans alive.[71]

Long later cited this last revolt as the "first fruits" of the opposition to his proposed duties on imported Gold Coast captives. It was suicidal madness, he thought, to ignore the danger they posed.[72] His lobbying against the Coromantees intensified in his 1774 *History of Jamaica*, in which he fashioned an influential and enduring racist response to antislavery threats from above and below.

LONG rose to the position of Speaker of the Jamaica Assembly in 1768, but he was in poor health and retired to England the next year. Back in

FIGURE 6.2. Edward Long. Engraving by William Sharp, after W. Denton, published 1789.

© *National Portrait Gallery, London.*

London, the imperial metropolis, he established himself as an authoritative advocate for the West Indian planter class. His reputation as an author emerged in the wake of the Somerset case in 1772, when the Court of King's Bench ruled that slavery had not been established by the common law in England and Wales and therefore slaveholders could not remove slaves from England against their will. Slaveowners rightly saw the decision as an erosion of their unfettered property rights in human beings and were prescient in viewing the decision as an opening salvo against the institution of slavery itself.[73]

Long immediately counterattacked. He rushed to print his *Candid reflections upon the judgement lately awarded by the Court of King's Bench in*

Westminster-Hall on what is commonly called the Negroe-cause, which blasted the decision as incompatible with the "spirit of English commerce." By having "every Negroe renegade protected against his master's claim," he charged, the advocates for the liberty of runaways would cause England's "hurt and disgrace, and the discouragement of its colonies, where a property in their service is unavoidably necessary." He accused these advocates of having "no other design than to vilify the planters, and turn a worthless rabble of their clients loose in this kingdom." According to Long, this "knot of blacks" in England was a "dissolute, idle, profligate crew," who would threaten the identity of the country if they were allowed to increase.[74]

Fear of displacement underlay his argument, the product of masculine anxiety as much as any confidence in white superiority. "The lower class of women in England, are remarkably fond of the blacks," he worried, "for reasons too brutal to mention; they would connect themselves with horses and asses, if the laws permitted them." In Long's poisonous cocktail of class prejudice, misogyny, and xenophobia, black people were simultaneously subhuman and superhuman, comparable to animals but capable of dominating white men in sexual competition. As a result, within a few generations, he declared, "English blood will become so contaminated" as to debase the entire nation. He denounced the black presence in England as a "venomous and dangerous ulcer, that threatens to disperse its malignancy far and wide, until every family catches infection from it."[75] In other words, he warned his readers that in time they would be swamped.

The virulence of Long's language grew directly out of his previous decade's experience with slave war. Already hard at work on his three-volume *History of Jamaica* when he dashed off his *Candid Reflections,* Long intended to rebut the widespread allegation that slave rebellions resulted from the mistreatment and mismanagement of slaves. Instead, he argued that slave revolt was a criminal trait of the Coromantee people. "Always the foremost in plotting, and heading mutinies," he said, they were uniform in character: "the most unruly, insolent, stubborn, and disaffected set of labourers, that can possibly be introduced upon our plantations."[76] No amount of mild treatment could relieve their "ingratitude" and "implacable anger." Long's fearful hatred of Coromantees fed his loathing for Africans in general. Collectively, in his view, they were "brutish, ignorant, idle, crafty, treacherous, bloody, thievish, mistrustful, and superstitious people, even in those states where we might expect to find them more polished, humane, docile, and industrious."[77] Knowing what he did about the fractious divisions among the enslaved, Long did not collapse all distinctions between black people, as so many racist writers did. He didn't have that luxury: recognizing a range of differences was critical to the survival of the master class, who employed Africans, island-born blacks, and mixed-raced people "to restrain one another within the bounds of their allotted condition." Like Trelawny before him, Long suggested the cultivation of the native-born slave population to limit the need for the transatlantic slave trade.[78]

And yet, through a chain of association linking various unwelcome traits, blackness in general came to signify the general potential for danger that Long attributed most specifically to Coromantees.[79] In the end, regardless of their differences, Long surmised that black people must actually constitute a different species of humankind. For this view, Long has been called an early proponent of scientific racism, which gained currency in the eighteenth century as writers sought to classify and rank the world's peoples.[80] More immediately, however, Long's racism was as much a specific reaction to black political agency as it was a general theory of human difference. Even his abhorrence of the tiny and generally impoverished black population living in England projected his experience of the fragility of white mastery in the West Indies, where slaveholders had recently been frustrated, at times even humiliated, in their attempts to pacify the enslaved. Racism was his ideological defense against Jamaica's intestine dangers coming home to Great Britain. Although slavery was "unavoidably necessary" for the increase of English commerce, the African presence was an unqualified evil.

In the manuscript notes for *History of Jamaica,* Long contemplated genocide. The very existence of Africans so "deforms the beauty of this globe," Long blurted, that they "deserve to be exterminated from the . . . Earth."[81] This was and remains the ultimate logic of settler colonialism: "exterminate all the brutes!" as Joseph Conrad's character Kurtz later put it so memorably.[82] One of the more enduring myths in the corpus of racial fantasy is that white people are underdogs, besieged by hyper-masculine and ultra-violent blacks. Slave revolt engendered this trope. In his reaction to Jamaica's slave war in the 1760s, Long become one the most erudite and prominent purveyors of racial panic, nurturing a virulent strain of nationalist discourse that would infect the political imagination of whites down to the present day.[83]

If the Jamaican insurrections helped to shape imperial policy toward the colonies and inspired a racist reaction, they also offered a rationale for the reform of colonial slavery. Fearing further rebellion, concerned Britons put forth pragmatic plans for enhancing the security of the colonies by limiting their dependence on the slave trade and ameliorating the condition of the enslaved. Ironically, perhaps perversely, Edward Long's work had a significant impact on a budding antislavery discourse.

In arguing that the principal threat to colonial slavery were African—and especially Coromantee—insurgents, Long promoted the idea that a native-born slave population would be more tractable. Having seen that creoles often betrayed African plots and fought bravely against rebels, Long came to believe that creolization was the only salvation. If planters could avoid working their slaves to death, attach them to estates rather than continuing to scatter them by sale, establish better conditions for child-rearing, and encourage the progress of Christianity, then slaveholders might be more secure in their possessions. They could also save money on the ever-rising prices of imported laborers from Africa. Raising up native-born slave populations would facilitate what reformers constantly referred to as the "improvement" of the plantations and would lead to a kinder and gentler—and less menacing—slavery. Through the beginning of the nineteenth century, people who campaigned against the slave trade would invoke Long's text to argue that ending the traffic would enhance the internal security of the British Empire. In this way, Jamaica's turbulence indirectly helped to nurture the emerging antislavery movement.[84]

Fear of Africans had indeed inspired the first efforts to restrict the slave trade. Responding to the 1712 Coromantee uprising in New York City, the Pennsylvania assembly imposed a prohibitive £20 duty on slave importations, citing "divers plots and insurrections . . . not only in the islands but on the mainland of America" as the reason for their action.[85] After a revolt near South Carolina's Stono River in 1739, the colony enacted a ten-year moratorium on the importation of Africans, but planters soon found they could not do without them.[86] Amid news of Jamaica's troubles in the 1760s, other colonies tried again. Virginia's slaveholders were divided between large-scale planters who hoped to increase the financial value of their slaves by limiting the supply and those of lesser means who wanted to acquire laborers at the lowest possible price. But by the late 1760s, they could agree on the dangers of slave insurrection. Legislators there attempted to levy increased duties on imported slaves in 1767, 1769, and 1772. As Virginia's governor explained to British officials, colonists had "just cause to apprehend the most dangerous Consequence" of importing Africans and should find means "not only of preventing their increase, but, also of lessening their number." He believed that "the interest of the Country would Manifestly require the total expulsion of them." Influenced more by merchant interests than by colonial concerns, London disallowed all three of these Virginia duty acts.[87]

Restrictions on the slave trade were more successful in Pennsylvania. In 1761, with news of Jamaica's slave war appearing regularly in the *Pennsylvania Gazette,* that colony's assembly noted the "mischievous Consequences attending the Practice of Importing Slaves into this Province." With their security at stake, many hoped to prohibit the trade entirely. In 1761 the colony passed a law to increase the import duties on slaves and extend its enforcement in perpetuity. In 1773 Pennsylvania doubled the impost, and finally, in 1780, the colony passed an Act for the Gradual Abolition of Slavery. As much as these laws might have expressed increasing opposition to the practice of slaveholding, they were aimed at discouraging the arrival of potentially insurgent Africans.[88]

If most people feared the presence of Africans, many others empathized with their plight. In the abolition movement's early beginnings, African rebels often drew sympathetic responses, especially from people in places that held fewer numbers of slaves than the Caribbean. Many British and North American readers were more horrified by the brutality of their British co-nationals than by the violence of the rebels.[89] Accounts of the executions circulated more widely with the growing popularity of sentimental literature and Christian martyrology, which helped the British to imagine their nation as a moral community founded in persecution, death, and religious virtue. For some, this imagined community extended to include the enslaved, however briefly, and African rebels came to be seen as victims sacrificed to the cruel tyranny of slaveholders.[90]

One pamphlet that circulated during the 1760 revolt, J. Philmore's *Two Dialogues on the Man Trade,* argued that, given the terrors of enslavement, nature's "higher law" authorized even the killing of slaveholders:

> All the black men now on our plantations who are by unjust force deprived of their liberty, and held in slavery, as they have none upon earth to appeal to, may lawfully repel that force with force, and to recover their liberty, destroy their oppressors: and not only so, but it is the duty of others, white as well as black, to assist those miserable creatures, if they can, in their attempts to deliver themselves out of slavery, and to rescue them out of the hands of their cruel tyrants.[91]

Few others were willing to go this far, at least in print. But the pamphlet influenced Anthony Benezet, the Pennsylvania Quaker who laid the intellectual foundations for slave-trade abolition in the British Empire. Although he avoided the topic of slave revolts, he frequently invoked "higher law" doctrine against the trade in human beings. Among his fellow Quakers, a fervent opposition to war induced them to see the violence stimulated by slave-trading as an unconscionable evil. Their belief that the slave trade was a constant source of war was an orthodox line of reasoning through the early nineteenth century.[92]

Even some who could not condone slave revolt could condemn slaveholder tyranny. In 1764, a Boston writer asserted that West Indian planters were "used to an arbitrary and cruel government over slaves," having for so long "tasted the *Sweets* of oppressing their fellow creatures."[93] That sentiment reverberated strongly in James Otis's *Rights of the British Colonies*

Asserted and Proved, published the same year. His defense of the rights of American settlers from the intimidation of imperial administration declared that "Colonists are by the law of nature free born, as indeed all men are, white or black."[94] In England, people mocked American colonists' pretensions to being oppressed by invoking their brutality toward their slaves. Antislavery rhetoric featured prominently in a 1768 London parliamentary campaign against the Jamaican slaveholder William Beckford, a proponent of colonial prerogatives, who had earlier received an open letter from the anti-slave-trade activist Granville Sharp—the leading "Negroe advocate" on the Somerset case—imploring Beckford not to the seek the return of a runaway slave.[95] In the early years of the American Revolution, the literary celebrity Samuel Johnson famously raised a toast to the next slave rebellion in the West Indies at an Oxford dinner party. Upon the death of a Jamaica gentleman, Johnson had once remarked, "He will not, whither he is now gone, find much difference, I believe, either in the climate or the company."[96] By the end of the century, stories of revolts against slaveholders and the gruesome executions of slave rebels had helped to promote an emerging antislavery consensus.

The slaveholder Bryan Edwards was not part of that consensus, but he had more sentimental pretensions than most of his fellow planters. He had arrived in Jamaica just in time for the insurrections of the 1760s and was Long's colleague on the committee to investigate the St. Mary's insurrection in 1765. An aspiring writer, Edwards followed the literary conventions of the time, which encouraged empathetic identification with suffering martyrs as emblems of the dying Christ. One of his first published poems, "Stanzas, Occasioned by the Death of Alico, an African Slave, condemned for Rebellion in Jamaica, a.k.a. 1760," eulogized the rebel Abruco, aka Blackwall, as a representative of the struggle for liberty. The date in the title recalled Tacky's Revolt even as the similarity between the names of the ringleader of the 1765 revolt and Edwards' muse suggests that the poem directly referred to the latter rebellion—a conflation that made the piece stand for the entire interval. "Firm and unmov'd am I," the poem exclaims, assuming the voice of the African on the stake. "In freedom's cause I bar'd my breast—In freedom's cause I die." The rebel welcomes deaths and promises everlasting insurrection: "I reach the joyful hour / But know, pale tyrant, 'tis not thine Eternal war to wage / The death thou giv'st shall but combine / To mock thy baffled rage."[97] In his 1773 "Ode, on Seeing a Negro Funeral," Edwards celebrates the African afterlife "On Koromantin's palmy soil," where "heroic deeds and martial toil shall fill each glorious day."[98]

By the 1780s, as the abolitionist movement gained momentum in England, activists cited Edwards' encomium to Abruco to rebuke slaveholders, and

FIGURE 6.3. Bryan Edwards.

Engraving by Thomas Holloway after Lemuel Francis Abbot, published 1800. © *National Portrait Gallery, London.*

Edwards renounced his youthful enthusiasm.[99] He was an ardent defender of slavery, but he nevertheless retained some sympathy for the Coroman-tees. His *History of the West Indies,* first published in 1793, described Coromantee character far more favorably than Long's *History of Jamaica,* although Edwards' portrait was no less exaggerated. He drew on all the old stereotypes, prevalent from Behn's *Oroonoko* through the 1760s. "In their wars they are bloody and cruel beyond any nation that ever existed," he waxed in describing their "ferocious" disposition and "savage manners." Having directly observed public executions, he marveled at the stoicism of the condemned, who met death "in its most horrible shape, with fortitude or indifference." Like most writers, he attributed this quality to the Coromantees' "national manners, wars and superstitions, which are all, in the highest degree, savage and sanguinary." But unlike Long, Edwards thought that these traits reflected redeemable virtues. "Hardiness of frame, and vigour of mind," "courage," and an "elevation of the soul" made them heroic. "I am persuaded," he avowed, "that they possess qualities which are capable of, and well deserve, cultivation and improvement." He could even lament that "their spirits should ever be broken down by the yoke of slavery." It was no wonder, he said, that Coromantees had launched the insurrection of 1760 "to regain the freedom of which they have been deprived." They might be savages, but they were noble ones at their best.[100]

There are several explanations for the differences between Long's and Edwards' portrayals. Long had gathered most of his information from the tortured confessions of suspected rebels and travelers' accounts of traders in Africa. Writing decades after the 1760s, Edwards conducted interviews with slaves under less immediate pressure. More directly, his description of the Coromantees and his narrative of events in the 1760s continued an argument with Long over the 1765 revolt and the nature of the threat it posed. Edwards' text was partly an attempt to vindicate Zachary Bayly against the charge that he had failed to recognize the extent of the Coromantee menace.

Edwards had been impoverished as a teenage boy by his father's death and was sent to live with Bayly, his mother's brother. When Bayly died in 1769, he bequeathed to Edwards the house where Edwards later penned his history, along with several sugar estates and hundreds of slaves. Edwards wrote Bayly's memorial inscription in the parish church where he was interred, extolling his patron as "wise without the assistance of recorded wisdom, And eloquent beyond the precepts of scholastick rhetorick." The great slaveholder had "acquired Wealth with Honour, And seemed to possess it only to be liberal." In 1766, the young Edwards had surely smarted when Long charged his beloved uncle with dithering in the face of danger.[101]

The dispute with Long extended through their differing depictions of the Coromantees and their divergent accounts of the 1760 slave insurrection. Long credited his brother-in-law Henry Moore, whom Long served as private secretary, with decisive action in that revolt's suppression, and contrasted it with the "neglect of duty" displayed by Lyttelton, who acted under Bayly's advice in 1765. Edwards' narrative instead praised the actions of Bayly, "to whose wisdom, activity, and courage on this occasion, it was owing that the revolt was not as general and destructive as that which now rages in St. Domingo (1791)."[102]

The reference to Santo Domingo highlights a vital distinction: Edwards wrote his narrative of the Jamaican insurrections during the Haitian Revolution. He had traveled to neighboring St. Domingue not long after the massive August 1791 slave uprising on the north plain of the colony, and he would go on to write the first published English-language account of the events. His rendering of the "horrors of Santo Domingo" influenced subsequent narratives through the early twentieth century.[103] In 1774, Long had identified Coromantees as the source of greatest danger. Astonishingly in retrospect, he looked to St. Domingue as an example of a secure society where the slaves were maintained in "peaceable subjection."[104] For Long, the events of the 1760s represented the possibility of his greatest fears; Edwards saw those fears realized in the French colony next door, where the Coromantee presence was not decisive. He glimpsed, in witnessing that rebellion, the fact that slavery itself was the danger, that it was sustained by slaveholder terror, and that it might well end in counterterrorism by the enslaved.[105]

Edwards' *History of the British West Indies* went through several revisions and editions from 1793 to 1819, remaining among the most widely read and influential accounts of the British Caribbean for generations. Together, Long and Edwards established a canonical history of the 1760s insurrections in Jamaica. Despite their differences, they agreed that understanding the Coromantees was the key to understanding the politics of slavery. They were partly correct: their stereotypes of the Coromantees do illuminate both the history of slave revolt and a history of racist reaction. These caricatures were never transparent reflections of Gold Coast Africans' actual existence in America, but neither were they untethered to the political history of the enslaved. Indeed, slave rebels inspired key aspects of Long's and Edwards's writings, thereby shaping the history of knowledge about racial slavery and the geography of antislavery struggle.

Through Long and Edwards, the Coromantee wars were woven into both racist tropes and abolitionist sympathies. Long's demonization and Edwards's martyrology were two sides of the same coin. Both the fear and the admiration of the Coromantees originated in the same idea, namely, that some intrinsic cultural essence defined Africans from the Gold Coast, and that this essence might distinguish something fundamental about black people in general. Indeed, Edwards thought the Coromantee "may be said to constitute the genuine and original unmixed negro, both in person and character."[106] Noted for martial masculinity, haughty pride, and relentless daring, the Coromantees in the eighteenth century defined a type that has thrilled and frightened whites—and parodied and beckoned to black men— ever since.

Long and Edwards also agreed on another issue, which points away from essential traits of Gold Coast behavior and toward the history and memory of landscape and the pathways of slaves' politics. They concurred on the geographical epicenter of the 1760s revolts: St. Mary's Parish. Continuing a debate over the interpretation of the 1765 uprising, Long and Edwards both narrated the entire period around the main events in that parish, relegating the other regions of the island, like Forrest's and Apongo's Westmoreland, to the subplot. Today, as a result, we know the Coromantee War as Tacky's Revolt. Tacky became a symbol of Coromantee character and the principal icon of the war. Bayly's, Long's, and Edwards' stories made the first and most lasting impressions on public memory, which grounded an ethnic stereotype in St. Mary's Parish.[107]

By the time of the Haitian Revolution, the Coromantees no longer posed the same threat. Edwards and Long would not have been cognizant of the reasons for this, which had less to do with ethnic character than with African history, specifically changes in political conditions on the Gold Coast. By the mid-1760s, Asante had established its rule throughout the southern forest region, checked only by Oyo to the east and the Fante Confederation along the coast. Asante now directed its conquests to the north, into polities without the same experience of military revolution and war that had marked the history of the coast. As the region settled into a tense standoff, and especially after Asante's conquest of Dagomba in the 1770s, war captives came increasingly from among peoples who did not speak the Akan languages shared by the Coromantees. These newer arrivals also had less training in the arts of war and the evasion of expansionist powers. As their numbers grew after 1765, traders often sold them as Coromantees anyway, to planters who continued to esteem the label. But they were not the same people.[108]

The Coromantee ethnicity had been the product of various historical struggles: of Africans along the Gold Coast, of slave merchants and planters adding value to their sales and purchases, of enslaved people forging new collectives against the threat of social annihilation, and of slaveholders trying to come to grips with reactions to their tyranny. In this sense, the ethnicity was a mythic reality—actual historical experiences transmuted into the stuff of legend. The famed military prowess of the Coromantees was not an essential cultural trait, but the histories of Africa and America did indeed combine to render it an observable phenomenon.[109] One of Bryan Edwards' elderly informants recalled the reign of Opoku Ware, who had done so much to expand the kingdom of Asante in the second quarter of the eighteenth century, confirming that "wars are very frequent; that all able men are compelled to bear arms."[110] By the time of their conversation in the late eighteenth century, this man remembered the Gold Coast as it had been, but what Edwards heard was a description of how Coromantees always were and would continue to be.

Slave-traders kept advertising and planters kept buying Coromantees in Jamaica in the wake of the insurrections of the 1760s. Incorporated into the West India Regiments created in 1792, Africans from the Gold Coast drew upon the Coromantee reputation to enhance their position in the British military.[111] English writers published novels featuring noble Africans from the Gold Coast, such as *The Koromantyn Slaves, or West Indian Sketches* in 1823.[112] To this day, the most sacred ancestral rituals of the Jamaican maroons draw upon Kromanti power, expressed in dance and ritual speech.[113] The name was significant long after the conditions that had brought it into being had changed precisely because the Coromantees had wielded so much influence for so long.

Reports of Jamaica's Coromantee wars of the 1760s traveled with the exiles transported from the island, who carried vital knowledge to new locales. Their physical presence in British Honduras, South Carolina, Virginia, Cuba, and the rest of Spanish America was a political and military presence too. How these vectors of rebellion spread the news, how they organized their co-nationals in other regions, and what this implied for other slave regimes is unknown, but even these questions remind us that the enslaved had a history that diverged from that of their captors. Slaveholders were well aware of this and sought to close down avenues of autonomy wherever they could.

The campaigns had cost Jamaica's colonists and investors dearly, compelling them to make consequential policy changes that reformed the workings of the British empire. If Tacky, Apongo, and Simon did not prefigure the imminent insurrection in Britain's North American colonies in 1776, their revolt at the commercial and strategic heart of Anglo-America did firm up the resolve of metropolitan policymakers, for whom the Seven Years' War generally proved the need for a more centralized and more extractive colonial policy—a policy that helped to provoke the American Revolution. Just as important, the rebellion prompted Parliament to consider ameliorating the conditions of slavery in the West Indies in the last decades of the eighteenth century—a process that began to chip away at the prerogatives of the plantocracy—which in turn initiated a cascading series of metropolitan interventions in the administration of colonial slavery, leading eventually to the abolition of the slave trade and the emancipation of the enslaved.

The insurrections resounded culturally in the meaning, narration, and memory of the events. Among whites, the wars' ambivalent representation derived from the slaveholders' dependence upon slaves they feared, and from their need to know and master a source of crisis. Slave war—campaigns to enslave, revolts against slavery, and fights to maintain it—was at the root of an anti-blackness that suffused both proslavery and antislavery discourse. The Coromantees signified a threatening presence, and this alarming archetype attached itself to black resistance in general. The violence of slaving or the suppression of slave revolt shocked many Britons who disliked what the violence of slavery said about them, even though slaveholding historians convinced many people that it was the Africans who were intrinsically dangerous. The emerging movement against the slave trade was thus shadowed by a desire to limit the threat posed by African migration. This meant that a fight against slavery would not always be a fight for black people, as an entrenched ethnic stereotype merged with and was eventually supplanted by a more general racial fear.

Even when the Coromantees had faded from the scene, the forces that generated the slave war had no definitive ending. As a category of belonging, "Coromantee" was an artifact of the seventeenth and eighteenth centuries, and the salience of the identification dissipated over the nineteenth century. The term was only a particular outgrowth of deeper processes of empire, war, dislocation, slavery, and political conflict that had given birth to it and that would go on well past the eighteenth century. The Coromantee War had ended, but the slave war continued.

Epilogue: The Age of Slave War

That until the basic human rights
Are equally guaranteed to all
Without regard to race
Dis a war

—BOB MARLEY, "WAR"

IN 1776, Great Britain's most important American colony was on the verge of insurrection. Colonists perceived that the government in Britain was conspiring against the rights of imperial subjects. They feared a plot against the English liberties they had long enjoyed. At their dinner tables they heatedly discussed the merits of open sedition. In arguments about the injustice of the British army's occupation of the Massachusetts Bay colony, one could hear "the Obligation of a subject to his Lord spurned at—the Blood spilt by Rebells extoll'd as precious drops of Record." Those disaffected with imperial governance dwelled upon the "Topic of American rebellion," flattering the rebels "with strains of Virtuous Heroism." As these Jamaican colonists debated liberty, their slaves saw an opportunity.[1]

The island was again at a critical juncture, with the British entry into yet another imperial war. Colonists traded exaggerated accounts of a French and Spanish military buildup in the Caribbean and calculated that there were thirty slaves to every white person, "ready to join the Attempts of any Enemy, in a General Massacre." On July 3, a regiment of troops left Hanover Parish for a rendezvous at Port Royal, scheduled to depart the island for England and North America by the end of the month.[2] Throughout the parish, slaves gathered frequently in houses, grounds, and open fields to hold "very serious conversations," which stopped suddenly upon the approach of anyone they did not trust. They were strategizing, in all likelihood. "Now or never, they thought, was the time to make themselves Masters of this Country." The moment seemed ripe for a successful uprising, but this American revolution was not to be. As so often happened with slave rebellions, the plot was betrayed and the conspiracy unraveled.[3]

This time, however, after focusing for so long on the threat posed by Africans, the slaveholders were surprised to learn that the design had been conceived by a combination of Coromantees, Eboes from the Bight of Biafra, and native-born creoles—with the creoles doing the organizing. The planters had trusted their security partly to divisions between Africans and creoles, "in whose Fidelity we had always most firmly relied," affirmed Jamaica's governor.[4] In this conspiracy, though, "even the Creole Negroes, who were the savers of their Masters & Mistresses in the Rebellion of 1760 were now engaged against them," as another observer wrote. The plot implicated domestic servants, too, and planters now feared that "the most dangerous enemies were in their houses with them."[5] The conspirators had formed a confederation, they learned, with the Coromantees, Eboes, and creoles each choosing a "head man or king." Although the Coromantees formed only a fraction of the rebel forces, slaves continued their war against the master class.

The insurrection scare of 1776 has been seen to mark a shift from an African to a creole style of rebellion. Following the historian Eugene Genovese, the Coromantee wars of the 1760s were viewed as the culmination of a passing phase of enslaved political activity, marking a transition from a "backward-looking" African politics, which aimed to recreate African states, to more universalist bids for "social revolution and the freedom of all," which reached their fullest expression with the uprising in St. Domingue. From this perspective, Africans revolted as often as they did either simply because they were Africans, whose experience on the continent compelled their actions, or because by the late eighteenth century the circulation of enlightenment ideals and a putatively modern political consciousness inspired novel types of insurrection. Certainly the confederacy of Coromantees, Eboes, and creoles that plotted the 1776 uprising exposed as fantasy the belief that only enslaved Africans posed a threat to slavery—and there would be many more creole revolts in the future. Yet contemporary chroniclers and subsequent historians have generally overlooked the way that Jamaica's landscape channeled slave revolt across generations. The emphasis on the changing nature of rebel participants obscures an important continuity—the reproduction of local political memory that shaped the geography of black militancy over time.[6]

ACROSS the Age of Revolution, black people in Jamaica drew inspiration from the history of their political landscape to help them navigate the turbulence of the Atlantic world. In 1760, there had already been reports of insurrectionary activity in Hanover Parish, where, in 1776, the slaveholders' inquiry found that the conspirators might have reached forty estates, holding some eighty-five hundred slaves in all, more than half the number in the parish, and were connected by a network of communication that extended through an "uninterrupted line or Chain" for twenty-five miles.[7] The plotters assigned responsibility for disseminating the plans into St. James and Westmoreland Parishes, especially the mountainous region around Glasgow estate, the scene of several battles in 1760.[8] In the mountains, according to one testimony, the Trelawny Town maroons contemplated joining the uprising. To the maroons' frustration, the slaveholders were increasingly using their own rangers to recapture runaways, depriving the maroons of vital revenue. One of their officers let it be known that when the "Estate negroes" were ready, the "Cudjoe negroes would take them up into the Country and that when the white People came after them into the woods, Cudjoe's negroes and the Estate's negroes were to come out, attack the weakest places first burn all the cane-pieces of all the Estates."[9] Whether this was an actual plan or only a fond hope of the enslaved, it represented a careful consideration of the coalition that would be needed to overcome the defeats of the 1760s, indicating that the avenue to a broader movement would widen some of the same pathways marked by the earlier Coromantee wars.

Fifteen years later, St. Domingue—the most profitable European colony in the world—erupted in a rebellion that would last more than decade and culminate in the creation of Haiti, the second independent postcolonial nation-state in the Americas, and the first to abolish slavery. Rather than being different in kind, the Coromantee revolt of 1760–1761, as the largest slave uprising in the Caribbean before the Haitian Revolution, may have shaped that revolution's early beginnings. The French colony's appetite for enslaved labor was insatiable, and St. Domingue's planters imported many of Jamaica's outcasts in the decades leading up to the 1790s. Among others, the man named Boukman, an oracle and instigator of the August 1791 uprising that launched the revolution, was said to have come from Jamaica. The connection hints at the possibility that insurgents in St. Domingue might have been influenced by the previous campaigns of their neighbors: their stories of slave war, tactics, and territorial ambitions. French writers, for their part, had certainly regarded Jamaica's history as a bad omen, warning presciently that "vengeance and carnage" might soon visit their own colonies.[10]

At the same time, in Jamaica, another series of disturbances traveled locally established tracks. British competitors might have thrilled to the destruction of their French enemies, but they knew from long experience that they were vulnerable to the same fate. Obsessively afraid of contagion, slaveholders followed news and rumor with acute attention, scanning their slaves for signs of sedition. A stray complaint or the slightest impertinent gesture might initiate a string of feverish interrogations from white authorities, who urgently assigned commissions to gather intelligence on black political activity.[11]

The "Committee of Secrecy and Safety" in St. James Parish discovered that everyone, including the maroons in their mountain redoubts, was fully aware of the St. Domingue insurrection. Rumors suggested that the "Negroes at Hispaniola were now free and enjoyed the rights of white men, and that the King of England wished the Slaves of this Island to be on the same footing but that their owners were against it."[12] This meant that Jamaica's slaves might have to follow the example of their neighbors. An enslaved Coromantee man named Duncan was forthright in his explanation: "To be sure Massa, when one country fight against another country every body stand for him own." A clerk clarified the aphorism in his transcription: "When two countries or People are at war with each other every man must fight for or stand in the defense of that which is his own."[13] This general wisdom defined a political principle, while the struggle to determine the parameters of "one's own" in slavery drew people's attention back to familiar territory.

In formulating their own plans for liberation in Jamaica, the enslaved interpreted broader events in the context of local history. "Saint Domingo had risen, killed the Boccaras [the whites] and taken the country," people relayed, but they projected domestic history onto this news: "they [the rebels] had begun in Saint Mary's killed overseers and Book keepers and burnt several Estates . . . they were next to rise in Westmoreland."[14] This was no mere anachronism. The enslaved reordered the timeline, and folded and layered the map according to their way of seeing the relevance of events.[15] The uprising in St. Domingue repeated and intensified what had happened in St. Mary's and Westmoreland, only now with a more hopeful outcome. If the same kind of revolt was happening in the neighboring colony, this interpretation suggested, it must also be happening in Jamaica, the same kind of place.

Among the first threats investigated by the committee was a report that slaves on some traditionally troublesome estates in Westmoreland—including Masemure, Delve, and Paul's Island—were "applying to the Negroes of Moreland to join against the Whites." Moreland estate's driver divulged to his overseer that two men had offered an extra price for cutlasses in preparation for an uprising, but the men offered an alibi that saved them from prosecution, saying that "if negroes rose in Rebellion they might come and plunder their provision grounds and they wanted good weapons to defend their grounds."[16] Whether this was the truth or a clever ruse, it illustrated how a knowledge of local history could inform a revolutionary political outlook.

And still, in this age of revolution, black people sought fissures in the landscape of imperial power where they might live as they pleased. One man named Brutus, condemned to life in the public workhouse for some crime or another, escaped and made a new town with other escapees in the wooded hills above Brampton Bryan estate, owned by Bryan Edwards. The fugitive often visited the slave quarters there and was "well known to all the negroes in the neighborhood." Slaveholders learned that "Captain Brutus" and his party of runaways planned an uprising to coincide with Britain's renewed war against the Spanish and French. The plotters sought out fellow conspirators at a great ball on Brampton Bryan, a festival so large that there were many "different rings for dancing on account of the large number of Negroes assembled on the occasion." At least one person at the gathering protested that the uprising could not succeed "while the whites were possessed of the communication with the Sea," but Brutus held out the hope of permanent escape from slavery. He told them that there were "plenty of Negroes, Mulattoes and Quadroons" in his town, and that the location was unassailable by the slaveholders: "It was situated on the top of a high mountain surrounded with cliffs and the only path to it was very difficult, narrow and winding, and that on the other side they could let themselves down by Ropes; and that it was in such part of the woods as no white person could ever find it out or get to it and that there were so many Negroes there that if all the white people in the country were to get there they could do no good."[17] No uprising occurred, but the rumored affair revealed an astute mapping of political territory. Even without an island-wide revolution, there might be yet another autonomous enclave.

Autonomy in slave society was always precarious, as events in Trelawny Town soon showed. Maroons interacted with the plantations constantly, socializing and trading with slaves, catching runaways for slaveholders, and sometimes stealing necessities when they could get them no other way. In 1795, a slave driver flogged two Trelawny Town men for stealing pigs. When several maroons went to complain to British authorities, they were imprisoned on suspicion of instigating a revolt. War ensued. The Accompong Town maroons, who had withheld support to the slaveholders during the Westmoreland revolt in 1760–1761, now sided with the British against Trelawny Town. The conflict quickly reached a bloody stalemate, which the British broke by importing bloodhounds from Cuba to search out the maroons' hideouts. The belligerents signed a new peace, but Jamaica's governor saw an opportunity to rid the colony of an old problem. Against the wishes of the Major General who had signed the armistice, the governor ordered the deportation of the entire population of the town to Nova Scotia. After suffering a few miserable years in Canada, most of them migrated to Sierra Leone, the new British colony in West Africa. A people who had been removed from Africa to America by diasporic warfare were thus in diaspora once again, now in the land of their ancestral origin.[18]

The Second Maroon War of 1795–1796 showed that no territorial settlement with the slaveholders was secure, yet African rebels had implanted a perennial political history. Events on the plantations continued to demonstrate that the slaves' subjugation could never be taken for granted, as the planter Simon Taylor learned in St. Mary's Parish. "I believe we are on the eve of a rebellion breaking out," Taylor wrote in 1807, as Britons debated the end of the transatlantic slave trade. Several newly arrived Africans on Taylor's plantation had attempted to stab their driver. When Taylor interrogated them, he made a startling discovery. There had been "some improper Communication" between his own slaves and those on Frontier estate, where Tacky's and Abruco's revolts had begun. Taylor, whose own overseer had been killed by rebels in 1765, recalled that the slaves on Frontier had "always been the foremost in all Insurrections from the year 1760, 1765, & 1767." What was most alarming, though, was that the enslaved were teaching the story of the 1760s to new arrivals. "All new negroes know of the insurrection of 40 years ago," he marveled. "If something were not going on, for what reason would they tell these New Negroes who have not been four months in the island of what happened before any of the negroes sent there were born?"[19] Why, Taylor wondered, were these newcomers learning Africans' history in Jamaica?

Whatever was happening was not only the result of these captives being African—from the Gold Coast or wherever else. Long and the others who thought slavery could be secured by limiting African imports were wrong; the largest slave insurrection in Jamaican slave society would be the Baptist War of 1831, and it would be led by native-born converts to Christianity. Nor could the events in St. Mary's be explained only by the mere fact of enslavement, which may have been the root cause of all uprisings but could never explain the timing or progress of any single one. And while revolutionary ferment and the circulation of abolitionist ideas might have provided an opening, it was the recollection of the Coromantee wars that offered immediate inspiration. An oppositional political history taught and learned on Jamaican plantations—a radical pedagogy of the enslaved— shaped the slaves' goals, strategies, and tactics as they rehearsed bygone battles and considered future possibilities. Ultimately, this continuous tradition draws our attention away from the ethnic origins of African insurgents and toward the geography of their collective imagination.

WHO could exert their will in a particular place? What landmarks and pathways distinguished safety from danger? Where could one find justice and live with dignity? For Africans and their descendants, as for others in the polyglot populations of colonial society, spatial schemas were the product of violent struggles to address these elemental questions. Warfare remapped and redefined territories as colonists, captives, and sojourners in the Atlantic world charted an atlas of terrors: fears of conquest and capture, of difference and unfamiliarity, of exploitation and loss, of displacement and obliteration. Arising from battlefields sown with ambition, dread, and blood, empire and diaspora set a process of place-making in motion.

In eighteenth-century West Africa, especially on the militarized Gold Coast, warring states mapped their dominion over subject peoples, contesting for trade routes that stretched from deep in the interior to the coast, where Europeans harvested the fruits of war in captives bound for America. Vulnerable people learned to evade attacks and incursions by carving out spaces in the interstices of expansionist power, and to defend enclaves with small bands of committed fighters. They continued their struggles on Atlantic slave ships and in American slave societies. Against the commercial and sexual predations of merchants, planters, and petty managers, the enslaved sought spaces of communion and succor. Insurgents carved out areas of autonomy within territory patrolled by the combined armed forces of empire. Runaways and rebels used uneven terrain to their advantage; woods, mountains, hills, swamps, rivers, and oceans defined the contours of rebellion and prescribed the options for counterinsurgency, as black militancy engendered the political meaning of the environment.

Slaves who spent their lives in rows of crops and clustered cabins knew plantations to be soul-crushing machines but also centers of social life, where one might find fellowship or potential collaborators among the majority of people simply trying to survive. The bush and the mountains presented enduring natural dangers, which, if surmounted, might be turned against enemies in pursuit. A port was more than a commercial station or a node of naval power; it was a conduit to the wider world of information, exile, or, in rare cases, permanent escape. These general associations might obtain throughout the world of Atlantic slavery, but they had specific historical connotations in a place like Jamaica, a colony created by a European empire, staffed by veterans and refugees from Old World wars, garrisoned for battle with both external and internal enemies, and continuously simmering with insurrectionary violence.

Jamaica's Coromantee wars of the 1760s represented a watershed in the course of Atlantic history. Regional political maps had been drawn by the wars that opened new territories for cultivation, stimulated the slave trade, and enhanced state power—but the slave rebellions etched another record of historical movement. They channeled people into new solidarities and gave meaning to categories of belonging, partitioned friends from foes and bystanders, and redirected the priorities of governing authorities. Since Jamaica was the commercial and military hub of the British overseas empire, its most profitable settlement and most powerful American stronghold, what happened there was bound to reverberate widely. Yet the legacy of the 1760s is ambiguous. At the close of the Seven Years' War, Great Britain kept its prized colony, although the insurrection of 1760–1761 had helped to stimulate a reform effort that provoked a much greater challenge on the North American continent. If the Jamaican revolts in some ways anticipated the Haitian Revolution, offering a beacon of hope to the enslaved, they also left maroons, free black people, and Africans divided. The Coromantees augmented their reputation as formidable fighters, helping to cast doubts on the wisdom of continuing the transatlantic slave trade, while at the same time strengthening the association between blackness and social danger. Even in the United States, as late as the mid-nineteenth century, anxious slaveholders would refer to potential troublemakers as "Tackeys among us."[20]

Perhaps the ambiguous nature of these legacies helps to explain why they register so faintly in the imagination today. The Coromantee wars that shaped the era don't fit neatly into the prevailing narrative of the rise and progress of liberal freedom. They are obscured by the much greater consequences of the American and Haitian revolutions, which seem to speak more directly to the western history of liberty. As far as we know, the Coromantees did not draw upon the Enlightenment ideas that animated British and French revolutionaries, and nor did they create an internationally recognized state. For this reason, even the better documented participants in Jamaica's slave wars remain unfamiliar. Lieutenant Governor Henry Moore, who suppressed the revolt of 1760–1761, became governor of New York, where he managed the Stamp Act crisis and the colony's fraught relations with Native Americans.[21] But he died before the revolution reached its head and is a marginal figure in the historiography of the era. Neither Tacky nor Wager became a ruler of Jamaica, as Toussaint Louverture and Dessalines came to rule Haiti. Even in Jamaica, where Tacky is nearly a national hero, Wager and Simon are largely unknown.

The relative obscurity of the Coromantee wars in the historiography of early America and the Atlantic world is also due to the reluctance to acknowledge slave revolt as an act of war. Few things terrify the wealthy and powerful more than the prospect of defeat by the poor and weak, which would signify dishonor and a world turned upside-down. Dominant peoples and nation states develop elaborate conventions for legitimating violence, maintaining their honor in victory and defeat, and deeming violence to be a normal if unfortunate feature of political struggle. But vis-à-vis those they dominate by daily habit, there is no limit to the lengths to which the powerful will go to maintain supremacy. They will commit atrocities and massacres, to be sure, but they will disavow them, too. They will refuse to admit that their combatants are legitimate enemies, and they will denigrate the past and present struggles of less powerful peoples. Edward Long and Bryan Edwards were willing to recognize the threat posed by black people, but were unwilling to concede that they were genuine political actors. Because slaveholders wrote the first draft of history, subsequent historiography has strained to escape from their point of view.

Yet from the margins, the Coromantee wars encourage a fresh perspective on the period's political landscape and a different understanding of the politics of the enslaved. In the study of slavery, the problem of emancipation has been nearly synonymous with the problem of freedom, which has in turn been integral to the post-revolutionary era in Atlantic history. The nineteenth century, when the process of emancipation convulsed states from Haiti to Brazil, has come to be seen as a discrete epoch, which threw freedom into sharp relief as an animating force of historical change. While that era's emancipations certainly represented a world historical transformation, such epochal thinking generally tempts us, as the historian Frederick Cooper warns, to "assume a coherence that complex interactions rarely produce" instead of "assessing change in whatever dimensions it occurs and analyzing the significance and limitations of conjunctures when multidimensional change became possible."[22] Emancipation, as the master sign of freedom, binds the ultimate aims and strategies of centuries of antislavery struggle to the nineteenth century, when those efforts reached their apotheosis.

Throughout the Atlantic world, the hopeful years immediately following emancipation were followed in most cases by the reassertion of dominance by former slaveholders. The social antagonisms established in slavery governed the tensions that shaped very tenuous liberties. Legacies of slavery persisted through the nineteenth and twentieth centuries' reign of white power, with continuing manifestations in the present. Struggles against white power were continuous, too, during and after slavery. Slaves and their descendants revolted not merely against the power of slaveholders and their successors but *for* a host of historically specific aims that included freedom, but transcended it in ways we have yet to discern with clarity. They undoubtedly wanted liberation from the slaveholders, but rarely as liberal subjects—that is, autonomous and self-determined individuals. Instead, they fought for the space to develop their own notions of belonging, status, and fairness beyond the masters' reach.[23]

Narrated as discrete events, all of the slave insurrections of the 1760s in Jamaica are stories of heroism and defeat. Most of the rebels were killed, exiled, or forced back into slavery. The memory of their deeds inspired future generations, but they, too, would be fighting slaveholders against the longest odds. In their courage and ingenuity, however, these insurgents charted the landscape of force and its limitations that the maps of the powerful never meant to show. These countermappings reveal a geography of hope and possibility, fugitive territories carved out through political struggle that were difficult to maintain, paradoxical in their alliances, and, in most cases, yet to be won.

THE slaves' enemies diagrammed this history differently, in images of black violence that traversed Atlantic empires. Throughout the region, people fixated on reports and renditions of slave rebellions, wondering what they might mean for the future of colonial enterprises. One can see their fears visualized in engravings such as *Soulèvement des Nègres à la Jamaïque, en 1759*, published in François-Anne David's *Histoire d'Angleterre* during the Haitian Revolution. In the depiction, black insurgents have burst into a dining hall and are killing the men while the women flee. In the foreground, a muscular black man lifts a cutlass high in the air, ready to deliver a killing blow to a white man who begs for mercy. Just behind and to the right of him, a rebel is in the act of thrusting a blade through the neck of another white man. To the left, obscured by a dining table, lies a dead man. We can only see his feet, but a black killer looms over him, too. The background is teeming with slaves brandishing swords and spears.

The image almost certainly refers to the Jamaican slave uprisings of 1760–1761, in particular the May 25 attack at Masemure estate. That the image gets the date wrong—there was no major disturbance in Jamaica in 1759—is irrelevant to its significance. *Soulèvement des Nègres* refers not so much to a specific event as to a general fear of black revolt, which made distinct occasions interchangeable in the white political imagination. The engraving conveyed something broadly shared in the Atlantic world, wherever people were interested in the maintenance of slavery and whenever black violence seemed to threaten white power. The image spoke simultaneously to its immediate present and to its viewers' ancient terror of "servile war."

The Servile Wars were three major slave uprisings that convulsed the late Roman Republic between 135 and 71 BCE, the third led by Spartacus,

FIGURE 7.1. *Soulèvement des Nègres à la Jamaïque, en 1759.*

Engraved by François-Anne David and published in *Histoire d'Angleterre* (Paris, 1800), vol. 3, following p. 36. *Courtesy of The John Carter Brown Library.*

the legendary gladiator and military leader.[24] Narrated across generations and centuries, these classic revolts remained a looming warning to the master class that violence could always come from below. As a cautionary tale about the perils of slaveholding, they conveyed a visceral horror of inverted hierarchy, of violently contorted intimacy, of orderly spaces of peace and comfort turned into battlegrounds, and of brilliant and dependable soldiers like Spartacus or Wager turning their weapons on their commanders. In the eighteenth century, the specter of servile war was a reminder that within the lawful competition between nation states and empires there was another war, simmering in every territory that Europeans depended upon for their fortunes, their power, and their sense of pride on the world stage. The threat posed by slave revolution represented not only a disturbance to property and order but also the horrifying vision of a carefully calibrated and hard-won way of life collapsed in a heap behind the dinner table.

Slaveholders organized their societies to make themselves invulnerable: their persons were to be beyond violation. In the Americas, this required that white people be held in perpetual awe. Bryan Edwards knew that terror was the fundamental rule in governing slave societies, acknowledging, in accordance with the French philosopher Montesquieu, that "in countries where slavery is established, the leading principle on which the government is supported is fear: or a sense of that absolute coercive necessity which, leaving no choice of action, supersedes all questions of right."[25] This might as well have been a writ and declaration of war without end.

By custom, we treat war as an interruption in the normal course of human affairs. War is an anomaly in the regular order, a disturbance, a break, an aberration. War is also seen as a displacement of violence from one place to another, with formal military forces pursuing the conquest of territory. We commonly assume that lines of battle between warring states constitute the most important theaters of military engagement, and that peace treaties can mark a war's definitive end, before another one begins with new causes and different fronts. By contrast, when war becomes a way of life, as in the abundant violence of slave war, there is no border and no final result. Slave war is pervasive and unending, the natural consequence of slavery itself. Servile wars did not arise from the peculiar properties of the people involved—the English or the creoles or the Coromantees, as writers like Edward Long and Bryan Edwards claimed—but as products of the larger processes that had produced their antagonisms.

The state of war that enabled Atlantic empires to flourish seemed to be limitless, yet it did follow a discernible course, winding its way through the arteries that connected Europe, Africa, and America. The violence of state-making, territorial acquisition, and strategic competition flowed into the quotidian brutality that typified the social relations of slavery, where the projection of will and the exercise of power were at their most naked and absolute. Skittering aggression joined faraway lands to the most intimate spaces.

The people who endured this aggression shifted from place to place, forging new identities and testing uncertain loyalties. One could say this of the British, forged in civil war and combat against their European rivals, or of the Coromantees, molded by the slave trade and a tradition of insurrection, as well as any number of other peoples emerging from the same crucible. In 1760 in Jamaica, these adversaries launched a war that had its beginnings elsewhere, in other times, and did not end in peace. This slave war was part of a vast transatlantic phenomenon, comprising the epic journeys of its combatants, their predecessors in struggle, and those they inspired. But it is hard to see where the story concluded. All of slave war's essential features—rapacious exploitation, racial subjugation, and the proliferation of wars within wars—would continue.

The dispersed and downtrodden could not win these wars against empires and their adherents. Even the mighty Haitians, emerging victorious and independent after more than a decade of blood and fire, were hardly able to enjoy their sovereignty, instead suffering invasions, local disruptions, and international insults up to this very day.[26] But military victory isn't the only object of struggle. The abolitionist Frederick Douglass once wrote, "A man without force is without the essential dignity of humanity."[27] As a survivor of American slavery and the U.S. Civil War, Douglass knew that slave rebellion was war and that, however degrading war itself might be, enslaved men and women fought for dignity as much as for territory. In the absence of conquest, they claimed spaces where they could defend their self-respect and made places where their bodies could enjoy just treatment.[28]

IN 1792, some Jamaican whites riding along a muddy road drove an enslaved man called Montezuma out of their way, splattering him with gobs of muck. It was a casual affront of the kind slaveholders offered to slaves many times a day, but Montezuma would not have it. He had been a "man of rank in his own Country" and he held property in Jamaica, even though he was a slave. Whatever he had been named at birth and however many monikers he had acquired since, whites complained that Montezuma was "remarkable for a lofty spirit." Sullied and angry, he warned his abusers: "You turn Negroe out of the Path now but soon Negroe will turn you out." A committee investigating sedition took note, worried that this outburst announced an imminent uprising. Perhaps it did, although members of the committee found no evidence of a coordinated plot.[29] Instead they rediscovered the never-ending campaign to follow one's course unmolested by enemies. Eventually, Montezuma might have said, everyone would learn: As long as enslaved Africans and their descendants continued to fight, they would never be defeated.

Notes

Abbreviations

Add. MS.	Additional Manuscripts
ADM	Admiralty Series
BL	The British Library, London, United Kingdom
BA	Bristol Archives, Bristol, United Kingdom
BT	Board of Trade Series
C	Chancery Series
CO	Colonial Office Series
JAJ	*Journals of the Assembly of Jamaica* (St. Jago de la Vega and Kingston, 1663–1826)
ICS	Institute for Commonwealth Studies, London, United Kingdom
NMM	National Maritime Museum, Greenwich, London, United Kingdom
NLS	National Library of Scotland
NRS	National Records of Scotland, Edinburgh, United Kingdom
SAS-RF	Fuller Family Papers, East Sussex Record Office, Lewes, United Kingdom
SRO	Somerset Record Office, Taunton, United Kingdom
TNA	The National Archives, Kew, London, United Kingdom
T	Treasury Series
UA	Unitätsarchiv, Herrnhut, Germany
WMQ	*William and Mary Quarterly*

Prologue: The Path to Rebel's Barricade

1. Thomas Thistlewood Diary, December 4, 1760, Thomas Thistlewood Papers, James Marshall and Marie-Louise Osborn Collection, Beinecke Rare Book and Manuscript Library, Yale University. I am grateful to Trevor Burnard for

generously providing a copy of his transcriptions for the years 1760 and 1761. For the biography of Thistlewood see Trevor Burnard, *Mastery, Tyranny and Desire: Thomas Thistlewood and His Slaves in the Anglo-Jamaican World* (Chapel Hill: University of North Carolina Press, 2004).

2. For eighteenth-century histories of the war and its aftermath see John Swinton et al., *The Modern Part of an Universal History, from the Earliest Account of Time Compiled from Original Writers*, 65 vols. (London: S. Richardson [etc.], 1764), 41: 455–458; Edward Long, *History of Jamaica*, 3 vols. (London: T. Lowndes, 1774), 2: 447–472, 462; Bryan Edwards, *The History, Civil and Commercial, of the British Colonies in the West Indies: In Two Volumes* (London: John Stockdale, 1793), 2: 75–79. More recent accounts include Vincent Brown, *Slave Revolt in Jamaica, 1760–1761: A Cartographic Narrative*, http://revolt .axismaps.com; Trevor Burnard and John Garrigus, *The Plantation Machine: Atlantic Capitalism in French Saint-Domingue and British Jamaica* (Philadelphia: University of Pennsylvania Press, 2016), 122–136; Maria Allessandra Bollettino, "Slavery, War, and Britain's Atlantic Empire: Black Soldiers, Sailors, and Rebels in the Seven Years' War" (PhD diss., University of Texas, Austin, 2009), 191–256; Vincent Brown, *The Reaper's Garden: Death and Power in the World of Atlantic Slavery* (Cambridge, MA: Harvard University Press, 2008), 129–156; Verene A. Shepherd, "'Groundings' with Tacky (Takyi) on History, Heritage and Activism," in *I Want to Disturb My Neighbour: Lectures on Slavery, Emancipation and Postcolonial Jamaica* (Kingston: Ian Randle, 2007), 73–80; Burnard, *Mastery, Tyranny, and Desire*, 170–174; Richard Hart, *Slaves Who Abolished Slavery: Blacks in Rebellion* (Kingston: University of the West Indies Press, 2002 [1985]), 130–156; Michael Craton, *Testing the Chains: Resistance to Slavery in the British West Indies* (Ithaca: Cornell University Press, 2009 [1982]), 125–139; C. Roy Reynolds, "Tacky and the Great Slave Revolt of 1760," *Jamaica Journal* 6 (June 1972): 5–8; and Monica Schuler, "Ethnic Slave Rebellions in the Caribbean and the Guianas," *Journal of Social History* 3, no. 4 (1970): 374–385.

3. Michael Craton, *Testing the Chains*; Randy J. Sparks, *Africans in the Old South: Mapping Exceptional Lives across the Atlantic World* (Cambridge, MA: Harvard University Press, 2016); and Sparks, *The Two Princes of Calabar: An Eighteenth-Century Odyssey* (Cambridge, MA: Harvard University Press, 2004).

4. For a model of this approach see Engseng Ho, "Empire through Diasporic Eyes: A View from the Other Boat," *Comparative Studies in Society and History 46*, no. 2 (2004): 210–246.

5. My approach draws inspiration from Paul E. Lovejoy's injunction "to examine the condition of enslaved Africans in the Americas as their past experiences in Africa affected those conditions." See Paul E. Lovejoy, "Biography as Source Material: Towards a Biographical Archive of Enslaved Africans," in Robin Law, ed., *Source Material for Studying the Slave Trade and the African Diaspora: Papers from a Conference of Commonwealth Studies, University of Stirling, April 1996* (Stirling, UK: University of Stirling, 1997), 119–140. Also see Lisa Lindsay, *Atlantic Bonds: A Nineteenth-Century Odyssey from America to Africa* (Chapel Hill: University of North Carolina Press, 2017); Nathan Irvin Huggins, *Black Odyssey: The African-American Ordeal in Slavery* (New York: Pantheon, 1990 [1977]).

6. See especially J. Lorand Matory, "The 'New World' Surrounds an Ocean: On the Live Dialogues between African and African American Cultures," in Kevin Yelvington, ed., *Afro-Atlantic Dialogues* (Santa Fe, NM: School for Advanced Research Press, 2006), 151–192; and Joseph C. Miller, "Retention, Reinvention, and Remembering: Restoring Identities Through Enslavement in Africa and Under Slavery in Brazil," in Jose C. Curto and Paul E. Lovejoy, eds. *Enslaving Connections: Changing Cultures of Africa and Brazil during the Era of Slavery* (Amherst, NY: Humanity, 2004), 81–121.

7. A sample of such revolts and conspiracies would include the following: Barbados in 1675, 1683, 1686, and 1692; New York in 1712; Cartagena de Indias through the seventeenth and eighteenth centuries; St. John in 1733–1734; Antigua in 1701 and 1736; Surinam in 1690 and during the 1740s and 1750s, 1762, and the 1770s; and Jamaica in 1673, 1685, the 1690s and 1730s, 1742, and the 1760s.

8. John Thornton, *Warfare in Atlantic Africa, 1500–1800* (London: UCL Press, 1999), 127–147, quotation on 140; John Thornton, *Africa and Africans in the Making of the Atlantic World, 1400–1800,* Second edition (Cambridge, UK: Cambridge University Press, 1998).

9. Olaudah Equiano, *The Interesting Narrative and Other Writings,* ed. Vincent Carretta (New York: Penguin, 1995 [1789]), 111–112, 171–172.

10. John Locke, *Second Treatise of Government,* edited with an introduction by C. B. Macpherson (Indianapolis: Hackett, 1980 [1690]), 17; Mary Nyquist, *Arbitrary Rule: Slavery, Tyranny, and the Power of Life and Death* (Chicago: University of Chicago Press, 2013), 326–361.

11. David Armitage, "John Locke, Carolina, and the *Two Treatises of Government,*" *Political Theory* 32, no. 5 (2004): 602–627. Defenders of slavery would frequently draw upon Locke's ideas when the institution came under attack a century later, protesting that Africans captured in war had no alternative to slavery but death.

12. Anon., *The Truest and Largest Account of the Late Earthquake in Jamaica, June the 7th, 1692, written by a reverend divine there to his friend in London* (London: Tho. Parkhurst, 1693), 11–12.

13. Equiano, *Interesting Narrative and Other Writings,* 111–112, 171–172. See also Ira Berlin, *Many Thousands Gone,* 100, where he describes the contest of master and slave as a "never-ending war in which the terrain changed frequently but the combatants remained the same," and Thavolia Glymph, *Out of the House of Bondage: The Transformation of the Plantation Household* (New York: Cambridge University Press, 2008), 97–136, where she describes slavery in the domestic household as "the war within."

14. Ada Ferrer, *Freedom's Mirror: Cuba and Haiti in the Age of Revolution* (New York: Cambridge University Press, 2014), 234.

15. This reexamination would encourage historians to explore not only how black people came to serve in formal military units, but how enslaved Africans' dispersal, recombination, and adaptation shaped the nature of transatlantic warfare itself. See especially Manuel Barcia, *West African Warfare in Bahia and Cuba: Soldier Slaves in the Atlantic World, 1807–1844* (Oxford: Oxford University Press, 2014); and Barcia, *Seeds of Insurrection: Domination and Resistance on*

Western Cuban Plantations, 1808–1848 (Baton Rouge: LSU Press, 2008). Also see Peter M. Voelz, *Slave and Soldier: The Military Impact of Blacks in the Colonial Empire* (New York: Routledge, 1993); Ben Vinson III, *Bearing Arms for His Majesty: The Free-Colored Militia in Colonial Mexico* (Stanford: Stanford University Press, 2001); Christopher Leslie Brown and Philip D. Morgan, eds., *Arming Slaves: From Classical Times to the Modern Age* (New Haven: Yale University Press, 2006; Ben Vinson, III, and Stewart R. King, eds., *Journal of Colonialism and Colonial History,* special issue entitled, "The New African Diasporic Military History in Latin America" 5, no. 2 (2004).

16. As David Barry Gaspar has argued, examining a slave conspiracy is a way of analyzing the workings of a larger society, its concerns, ambitions, inner dynamics. In a similar way, slave war highlights the interconnected dynamics across the space of empire. David Barry Gaspar, *Bondmen and Rebels: A Study of Master-Slave Relations in Antigua* (Baltimore, MD: Johns Hopkins University Press, 1985). Also see Gregory Childs, "Conspiracies, Seditions, Rebellions: Concepts and Categories the Study of Slave Resistance," in Keisha N. Blain, Christopher Cameron, and Ashley Farmer, eds., *New Perspectives on the Black Intellectual Tradition* (Evanston, IL: Northwestern University Press, 2018), 217–231; John Harpham, "'Tumult and Silence' in the Study of the American Slave Revolts," *Slavery & Abolition* 36, no. 2 (2015): 257–274.

17. See especially David Kilcullen, *The Accidental Guerilla: Fighting Small Wars in the Midst of a Big One* (Oxford: Oxford University Press, 2009); Robert Taber, *The War of the Flea: The Classic Study of Guerilla Warfare* (Washington, DC: Potomac Books, 2002 [1965]); William S. Lind, Keith Nightengale, Captain John F. Schmitt, Joseph W. Sutton, and Gary I. Wilson, "The Changing Face of War: Into the Fourth Generation," *Marine Corps Gazette* (1989): 22–26; United States, Dept. of the Army, *The U.S. Army / Marine Corps Counterinsurgency Field Manual* (Chicago: University of Chicago Press, 2007).

18. For a similar perspective see Verene A. Shepherd, *I Want to Disturb My Neighbour: Lectures on Slavery, Emancipation and Postcolonial Jamaica* (Kingston: Ian Randle, 2007), chap. 6; and Barcia, *West African Warfare.*

19. Peter Linebaugh and Marcus Rediker, *The Many-Headed Hydra: Sailors, Slaves, Commoners and the Hidden History of the Revolutionary Atlantic* (Boston: Beacon Press, 2000); Katherine McKittrick, *Demonic Grounds: Black Women and the Cartographies of Struggle* (Minneapolis: University of Minnesota Press, 2006), ix–xxxi; Lara Putnam, "To Study the Fragments/Whole: Microhistory and the Atlantic World," *Journal of Social History* 39, no. 3 (Spring 2006): 615–630; Sarah Knott, "Narrating the Age of Revolution," *WMQ* 73, no. 1 (2016): 3–36.

20. D. W. Meinig, *The Shaping of America: A Geographical Perspective on 500 Years of History, Volume 1: Atlantic America, 1492–1800* (New Haven: Yale University Press, 1986), 64–76.

21. Antionette Burton and Tony Ballantyne, eds., *World Histories from Below: Disruption and Dissent, 1750 to the Present* (London: Bloomsbury, 2016).

22. Nikhil Pal Singh, *Race and America's Long War* (Oakland: University of California Press, 2017), 74–97; Edward B. Rugemer, *Slave Law and the Politics of*

Resistance in the Early Atlantic World (Cambridge, MA: Harvard University Press, 2018).

23. On the prevalence of conspiracy fears and their distinction from actual rebellions, see Jason Sharples, "Discovering Slave Conspiracies: New Fears of Rebellion and Old Paradigms of Plotting in Seventeenth-Century Barbados," *American Historical Review* 120, no. 3 (2015): 811–843; and Jason Sharples, "The Flames of Insurrection: Fearing Slave Conspiracy in Early America, 1670–1780" (PhD diss., Princeton University, 2010).

24. Ruth Wilson Gilmore, "Fatal Couplings of Power and Difference: Notes on Racism and Geography," *Professional Geographer* 54, no. 1 (2002): 15–24.

25. George Lipsitz, *How Racism Takes Place* (Philadelphia: Temple University Press, 2011), 53–54.

26. W. E. B. Du Bois, *The World and Africa: An Inquiry into the Part Which Africa Has Played in World History* (New York: Viking Press, 1947), 22; Karl Marx, *Capital, Volume I: The Process of Production of Capital* (New York: International Publishers, 1967 [1867]), 915.

27. W. E. B. Du Bois, *The Suppression of the African Slave-Trade to the United States of America, 1638–1870* (New York: Longmans, Green and Co., 1896); C. L. R. James, *Black Jacobins: Toussaint L'Ouverture and the San Domingo Revolution* (New York: Vintage, 1989 [1938]); Eric Williams, *Capitalism and Slavery* (Chapel Hill: University of North Carolina Press, 1994 [1944]); Walter Rodney, *How Europe Underdeveloped Africa* (London: Bogle-L'Ouverture, 1972); Walter Rodney, *A History of the Upper Guinea Coast, 1545 to 1800* (New York: Oxford University Press, 1970); Cedric Robinson, *Black Marxism: The Making of the Black Radical Tradition* (Chapel Hill: University of North Carolina Press, 2000 [1983]).

28. The historian Sven Beckert has aptly characterized this relationship with the term "war capitalism." Sven Beckert, *The Empire of Cotton* (New York: Knopf, 2014), xv–xvi, 29–82; Joseph C. Miller, *The Problem of Slavery as History: A Global Approach* (New Haven: Yale University Press, 2012); W. E. B. Du Bois, "The African Roots of War," *The Atlantic* 115, no. 5 (1915): 707–714.

29. Monica Schuler, "Akan Slave Rebellions in the British Caribbean," *Savacou* 1, no. 1 (1970), reprinted in Hilary Beckles and Verene Shepherd, eds., *Caribbean Slave Society and Economy* (New York: New Press, 1991), 373–386, quotation on 373.

30. Colin A. Palmer, "Defining and Studying the Modern African Diaspora," *Journal of Negro History* 85, no. 1/2 (2000): 27–32; Kristen Mann, "Shifting Paradigms in the Study of the African Diaspora and of Atlantic History and Culture," *Slavery and Abolition* 22, no. 1 (2001): 3–21; Michael Gomez, *Exchanging Our Country Marks: The Transformation of African Identities in the Colonial and Antebellum South* (Chapel Hill: University of North Carolina Press, 1998); Michael Gomez, *Reversing Sail: A History of the African Diaspora* (New York: Cambridge University Press, 2005); Ana Lucia Araujo, Mariana P. Candido, and Paul E. Lovejoy, eds., *Crossing Memories: Slavery and African Diaspora* (Trenton, NJ: Africa World Press, 2011); John K. Thornton, *A Cultural History of the Atlantic World, 1250–1820* (New York: Cambridge

University Press, 2012); Walter C. Rucker, *Gold Coast Diasporas: Identity, Culture, and Power* (Bloomington: Indiana University Press, 2015); Ray A. Kea, *A Cultural and Social History of Ghana from the Seventeenth to the Nineteenth Century: The Gold Coast in the Age of Trans-Atlantic Slave Trade,* 2 Vols. (Lewiston, NY: Edwin Mellen, 2012).

31. James Sidbury and Jorge Cañizares-Esguerra, "Mapping Ethnogenesis in the Early Modern Atlantic," *WMQ* 68, no. 2 (2011): 181–208.

32. Stephanie M. H. Camp, *Closer to Freedom: Enslaved Women and Everyday Resistance in the Plantation South* (Chapel Hill: University of North Carolina Press, 2004).

33. Glymph, *Out of the House of Bondage,* 33–37. Also see Katherine McKittrick, *Demonic Grounds: Black Women and the Cartographies of Struggle* (Minneapolis: University of Minnesota Press, 2006), xix; Aisha Finch, *Rethinking Slave Rebellion in Cuba: La Escalera and the Insurgencies of 1841–1844* (Chapel Hill: University of North Carolina Press, 2015); and Yuko Miki, "Fleeing into Slavery: The Insurgent Geographies of Brazilian Quilombolas (Maroons), 1880–1881," *The Americas* 68, no. 4 (2012): 495–528.

34. Richard Pares, *War and Trade in the West Indies, 1739–1763* (London: Routledge, 1963 [1936]); Daniel Baugh, *The Global Seven Years War, 1754–1763* (New York: Routledge, 2014), 377–420.

35. Fred Anderson, *Crucible of War: The Seven Years' War and the Fate of Empire in British North America, 1754–1766* (New York: Alfred A. Knopf, 2000).

36. Stephen Brumwell, *Redcoats: The British Soldier and War in the Americas, 1755–1763* (New York: Cambridge University Press, 2002), 197.

37. Wayne E. Lee, *Barbarians and Brothers: Anglo-American Warfare, 1500–1865* (New York: Oxford University Press, 2011); Wayne E. Lee, "Early American Ways of War: A New Reconnaissance, 1600–1815," *Historical Journal* 44, no. 1 (2001): 269–289; and John Grenier, *The First Way of War: American War Making on the Frontier* (New York: Cambridge University Press, 2005). But for an important corrective see Alan Taylor, *The Internal Enemy: Slavery and War in Virginia, 1772–1832* (New York: W. W. Norton, 2013).

38. Marshal Smelser, *The Campaign for the Sugar Islands, 1759: A Study of Amphibious Warfare* (Chapel Hill: University of North Carolina Press, 1955); Anderson, *Crucible of War,* 308, 312–316.

39. N. A. M. Rodger, *The Command of the Ocean: A Naval History of Britain, 1649–1815* (New York: W. W. Norton, 2004); Jeremy Black, *Combined Operations: A Global History of Amphibious and Airborne Warfare* (Lanham, MD: Rowman & Littlefield, 2018), 39–62; and Jeremy Black, *Warfare in the Eighteenth Century* (1999). But see J. W. Fortescue, *A History of the British Army,* 19 Volumes (London: Macmillan, 1899), 2: 39–40, 300, 372; and more recently, Bollettino, "Slavery, War, and Britain's Atlantic Empire"; and Burnard and Garrigus, *The Plantation Machine,* 82–136. There is a more extensive literature on military efforts during the Haitian Revolution, especially during the British occupation of the colony from 1793–1798. See especially David Patrick Geggus, *Slavery, War, and Revolution: The British Occupation of Saint*

Domingue, 1793–1798 (Oxford: Clarendon Press, 1982); Michael Duffy, *Soldiers, Sugar, and Seapower: The British Expeditions to the West Indies and the War against Revolutionary France* (New York: Oxford University Press, 1987).

40. Vincent Brown, "Mapping a Slave Revolt: Visualizing Spatial History through the Archives of Slavery," *Social Text* 33, no. 4 (2015): 134–141; Jeremy Black, *Insurgency and Counterinsurgency: A Global History* (Lanham, MD: Rowman & Littlefield, 2016), 57–86; Jeremy Black, *Maps of War: Mapping Conflict through the Centuries* (New York: Conway, 2016); Beatrice Heuser, "Introduction: Exploring the Jungle of Terminology," *Small Wars and Insurgencies, Special Issue: The Origins of Small Wars from Special Operations to Ideological Insurgencies* 25, no. 4 (2014); Stan Goff, *Hideous Dream: A Soldier's Memoir of the U.S. Invasion of Haiti* (New York: Soft Skull Press, 2000). For recent examinations of the intersection of race, slavery, and imperial soldiering, see Peter Way, "Militarizing the Atlantic World: Army Discipline, Coerced Labor, and Britain's Commercial Empire," in Michael A. McDonnell, *Rethinking the Age of Revolution* (London: Routledge, 2017); and Shalini Puri and Lara Putnam, eds., *Caribbean Military Encounters: A Multidisciplinary Anthology from the Humanities* (New York: Palgrave Macmillan, 2017).

41. Michel-Rolph Trouillot, *Silencing the Past: Power and the Production of History* (Boston: Beacon Press, 1995), 26.

42. Ann Laura Stoler, *Along the Archival Grain: Epistemic Anxieties and Colonial Common Sense* (Princeton, NJ: Princeton University Press, 2010); Marisa J. Fuentes, *Dispossessed Lives: Enslaved Women, Violence, and the Archive* (Philadelphia: University of Pennsylvania Press, 2016); Natalie Zemon Davis, *Fiction in the Archives: Pardon Tales and their Tellers in Sixteenth-Century France* (Stanford: Stanford University Press, 1987); James Sidbury, "Plausible Stories and Varnished Truths," *WMQ* 59, no. 1 (2002): 179–184.

43. Kenneth Morgan, "Materials on the History of Jamaica in the Edward Long Papers," Wakefield, West Yorkshire, 2006, https://microform.digital/map /guides/R50027.pdf; Trevor Burnard, *Planters, Merchants, and Slaves,* 162–166; Elsa V. Goveia, *A Study on the Historiography of the British West Indies to the Nineteenth Century* (Washington, DC: Howard University Press, 1956), 33–96; Devin Leigh, "The Origins of a Source: Edward Long, Coromantee Slave Revolts, and *The History of Jamaica,*" *Slavery and Abolition* 40, no. 2 (2019): 295–320; Catherine Hall, "Whose Memories? Edward Long and the Work of Re-Remembering," in *Britain's History and Memory of Transatlantic Slavery,* ed. Katie Donington, Ryan Hanley, and Jessica Moody (Liverpool: Liverpool University Press, 2016), 129–148; Samuel Conrad Scott, "The Enlightenment of Bryan Edwards: Slavery, Fear, and Historical Writing in the Eighteenth-Century Atlantic" (BA Thesis, Harvard University, 2008).

44. Thistlewood Diary, December 4, 1760; Burnard, *Mastery, Tyranny, and Desire,* 103, 151, 170–174; Douglas Hall, *In Miserable Slavery: Thomas Thistlewood in Jamaica, 1750–86* (Kingston: University of the West Indies Press, 1986), 92–114; Heather Vermuelen, "Queer Kin-Aesthetics: Thomas Thistlewood and the Plantation Grotesque" (PhD diss, Yale University, 2017).

1. War's Empire

1. See especially John K. Thornton, *A Cultural History of the Atlantic World, 1250–1820* (Cambridge, UK: Cambridge University Press, 2012).

2. Lisa A. Lindsay and John Wood Sweet, eds., *Biography and the Black Atlantic* (Philadelphia: University of Pennsylvania Press, 2013), 1–16.

3. Lisa Lowe, *The Intimacies of Four Continents* (Durham, NC: Duke University Press, 2015), 21. Also see Miles Ogborn, *Global Lives: Britain and the World, 1550–1800* (New York: Cambridge University Press, 2008); James H. Sweet, *Domingos Álvares, African Healing, and the Intellectual History of the Atlantic World* (Chapel Hill: University of North Carolina Press, 2011); Henry B. Lovejoy, *Prieto: Yorùbá Kingship in Colonial Cuba during the Age of Revolutions* (Chapel Hill: University of North Carolina Press, 2018); and Roquinaldo Ferreira, *Cross-Cultural Exchange in the Atlantic World: Angola and Brazil during the Era of the Slave Trade* (New York: Cambridge University Press, 2012) for excellent illustrations of what Ferreira calls "microhistories of the ordinary" that draw together transatlantic events and patterns.

4. Vincent Brown, "The Eighteenth Century: Growth, Crisis, and Revolution," in Joseph C. Miller, ed., Vincent Brown, Jorge Cañizares-Esguerra, Laurent Dubois, Karen Kupperman, assoc. eds., *The Princeton Companion to Atlantic History* (Princeton: Princeton University Press, 2015), 36–45.

5. Walter Rodney, *How Europe Underdeveloped Africa* (Washington, DC: Bogle L'Ouverture, 1982 [1972]), 95. As historian Robin Blackburn observes, the Atlantic system "harnessed coercion to production." Robin Blackburn, *The Making of New World Slavery: From the Baroque to the Modern, 1492–1800* (London: Verso, 2010), 10.

6. Marcus Rediker, *The Slave Ship: A Human History* (New York: Viking, 2007), 291–301. See also Sowande Mustakeem, *Slavery at Sea: Terror, Sex, and Sickness in the Middle Passage* (Champaign-Urbana: University of Illinois Press, 2016), chap. 4.

7. Jane Burbank and Frederick Cooper, *Empires in World History: Power and the Politics of Difference* (Princeton: Princeton University Press, 2010), 178.

8. Paul E. Lovejoy, *Transformations in Slavery: A History of Slavery in Africa*, Third Edition (New York: Cambridge University Press, 2012), 66, 77–87, 95–99.

9. Rosa Luxemburg, "Militarism as a Province of Accumulation," in *The Accumulation of Capital*, ed. W. Stark (London: Routledge, 1951 [1913]), chap. 32. Eric R. Wolf, *Europe and the People Without History* (Berkeley: University of California Press, 2010 [1982]), 195–231.

10. Simon P. Newman, *A New World of Labor: The Development of Plantation Slavery in the British Atlantic* (Philadelphia: University of Pennsylvania Press, 2013), 54–107. Also see Hilary McD. Beckles, "A 'Riotous and Unruly Lot': Irish Indentured Servants and Freemen in the English West Indies, 1644–1713," *WMQ* 47, no. 4 (1990): 503–522; and Beckles, *White Servitude and Black Slavery in Barbados* (Knoxville: University of Tennessee Press, 1989).

11. John Brewer, *The Sinews of Power: War, Money, and the English State, 1688–1783* (New York: Knopf, 1988).

12. William A. Pettigrew, *Freedom's Debt: The Royal African Company and the Politics of the Atlantic Slave Trade, 1672–1752* (Chapel Hill: University of North Carolina Press, 2013).

13. N. A. M. Rodger, "The West Indies in Eighteenth-Century British Naval Strategy," in Paul Butel and Barnard Lavelle, eds., *L'Espace Caraibe: theatre et enjeu des luttes imperials, XVIe–XIXe siecle* (Bordeaux: Maison de Pays Iberiques, 1996), 38–60.

14. Richard J. Reid, *Warfare in African History* (Cambridge, UK: Cambridge University Press, 2012), 79; Rebecca Shumway, *The Fante and the Transatlantic Slave Trade* (Rochester: University of Rochester Press, 2011), 100–101.

15. Akosua Adoma Perbi, *A History of Indigenous Slavery in Ghana from the 15th to the 19th Century* (Accra: Sub-Saharan Publishers, 2004), 28–68, quotations on 28, 29.

16. Willem Bosman, *A New and Accurate Description of the Coast of Guinea: Divided into the Gold, Slave, and Ivory Coasts* (London J. Knapton [etc.], 1705), 183.

17. See also Randy J. Sparks, *Where the Negroes Are Masters: An African Port in the Era of the Slave Trade* (Cambridge, MA: Harvard University Press, 2014), 122–161.

18. David Eltis and Lawrence C. Jennings, "Trade Between Western Africa and the Atlantic World in the Pre-Colonial Era," *American Historical Review* 93, no. 4 (1988): 936–959.

19. Shumway, *The Fante*, 62; Albert Van Dantzig, *Forts and Castles of Ghana* (Accra: Sub-Saharan Publishers, 1980); Andrew Apter, "History in the Dungeon: Atlantic Slavery and the Spirit of Capitalism in Cape Coast Castle, Ghana," *American Historical Review* 122, no. 1 (2017): 23–54.

20. For a judicious estimation of the importance of the slave trade in the calculations of rulers on the Gold Coast and the Bight of Benin, see Thornton, *Warfare in Atlantic Africa, 1500–1800* (London: UCL Press, 1999), 131–135.

21. W. A. Richards, "The Import of Firearms into West Africa in the Eighteenth Century," *Journal of African History* 21, no. 1 (1980): 43–59.

22. Reid, *Warfare in African History,* 80–82.

23. Robin Law, "The Politics of Commercial Transition: Factional Conflict in Dahomey in the Context of the Ending of the Transatlantic Slave Trade," *Journal of African History* 38, no. 2 (1997): 213–233, esp. 215; Robin Law, *Ouidah: The Social History of a West African Slaving 'Port,' 1727–1892* (Athens, OH: Ohio University Press, 2004).

24. Perbi, *A History of Indigenous Slavery in Ghana*, 25–26; Ray A. Kea, *Settlements, Trade, and Polities in the Seventeenth-Century Gold Coast* (Baltimore: Johns Hopkins University Press, 1982).

25. Lovejoy, *Transformations in Slavery,* 80–81; Sean Stillwell, *Slavery and Slaving in African History* (New York: Cambridge University Press, 2014), 149–151; Ludewig Ferdinand Rømer, *A Reliable Account of the Coast of Guinea (1760),*

trans. Selena Axelrod Winsnes (New York: British Academy, 2000), quotation on 201.

26. Richard Pares, *War and Trade in the West Indies, 1739–1763* (London: Routledge, 1963), 517–533.

27. Michael Duffy, "The Establishment of the Western Squadron as the Linchpin of British Naval Strategy," in Michael Duffy, ed. *Parameters of British Naval Power, 1650–1850* (Exeter, UK: University of Exeter Press, 1992), 60–81; Rodger, "The West Indies in Eighteenth-Century British Naval Strategy."

28. Historian Eric Williams justifiably calls the Caribbean the "hub of the British empire." Eric Williams, *Capitalism and Slavery* (Chapel Hill: University of North Carolina Press, 1994 [1944]), 52; J. R. Ward, "The British West Indies, 1748–1815," in P. J. Marshall, ed., *The Oxford History of the British Empire, Volume II: The Eighteenth Century* (Oxford, UK: Oxford University Press, 2001), 415–439.

29. Richard B. Sheridan, *Sugar and Slavery: An Economic History of the British West Indies, 1623–1775* (Kingston: Canoe Press, 2012 [1974]), 489.

30. Brewer, *The Sinews of Power*, 175–189.

31. Lords Commissioners of His Majesty's Treasury, *Journal of the Commissioners for Trade and Plantations from January 1749–1750 to December 1753* (London: His Majesty's Stationery Office, 1932), 7.

32. David Richardson, "The British Empire and the Atlantic Slave Trade, 1660–1807," in P. J. Marshall, ed., *The Oxford History of the British Empire, Volume II: The Eighteenth Century* (Oxford, UK: Oxford University Press, 2001), 462; Ward, "The British West Indies, 1748–1815," 433.

33. Peter Linebaugh and Marcus Rediker, *The Many-Headed Hydra: Sailors, Slaves, Commoners and the Hidden History of the Revolutionary Atlantic* (Boston: Beacon Press, 2000).

34. On rival geographies see Stephanie M. H. Camp, *Closer to Freedom: Enslaved Women and Everyday Resistance in the Plantation South* (Chapel Hill: University of North Carolina Press, 2004).

35. Timothy Ingold, *The Perception of the Environment: Essays on Livelihood, Dwelling and Skill* (London: Routledge, 2000), 219–242.

36. Lauren Benton, *A Search for Sovereignty: Law and Geography in European Empires, 1400–1900* (Cambridge, UK: Cambridge University Press, 2009), 2–3; Frederick Copper, "States, Empires, and the Political Imagination," in *Colonialism in Question: Theory, Knowledge, History* (Berkeley: University of California Press, 2005), 153–203. Also see J. B. Harley, *The New Nature of Maps: Essays in the History of Cartography* (Baltimore: Johns Hopkins Press, 2002); and Harley, *Maps and the Columbian Encounter: An Interpretive Guide* (Milwaukee: University of Wisconsin Press, 1990); Denis Wood, *Rethinking the Power of Maps* (New York: Guilford Press, 2010).

37. Philip Wright, *Monumental Inscriptions of Jamaica* (London: Society of Genealogists, 1966), 190; List of Mariners belonging to the Royal African Company's *Snow the Phenix*, for Cape Coast cleared at Gravesend September 25, 1736, TNA, T70/1439, 138; *Voyages: The Transatlantic Slave Trade Database:*

http://www.slavevoyages.org; Tinker, Esson, and Cope to RAC, January 10, 1737, TNA, T70/1193, 58.

38. J. K. Fynn, *Asante and its Neighbours, 1700–1807* (London: Longman, 1971), 57–83; Sparks, *Where the Negroes Are Masters*, 17, 21–22.

39. John Cope, John Castres & Charles Bladwell to RAC, February 6, 1741, TNA, T70/4, 125–126.

40. Cape Coast Castle Journals, October 12, 1741, TNA, T70/415, fol. 18; Cape Coast Castle Journals, November/December 1740, TNA, T70/413, fol. 46.

41. Tinker Esson, Cope to RAC, January 10, 1737, TNA, T70/1193, 58.

42. RAC to Tinker, Esson, and Cope, May 19, 1737, TNA, T70/54, fols. 99–100; Williams Fort Accounts, 1736, TNA, T70/1452, 189, 231–232.

43. Law, *Ouidah,* 57; RAC to Charles Whitaker, August 1, 1734, TNA, T70/54, fol. 80; RAC to Tinker and Cope, November 24, 1737, TNA, T70/54, fols. 106–107; RAC to Charles Whitaker, August 18, 1737, TNA, T70/48, 16; William's Fort Rents and Dashes, January 1 to April 22, 1735, TNA, T70/1452, 69–70.

44. Lords Commissioners of His Majesty's Treasury, *Journal of the Commissioners for Trade and Plantations*, 21.

45. An Act of Council Made at Cape Coast Castle, November 1, 1737, TNA, T70/4, 105; John Cope to RAC, February 22, 1737, TNA, T70/4.

46. James Hope to RAC, February 13, 1737, TNA, T70/4, 104; RAC to Tinker and Cope, November 24, 1737, TNA, T70/54, fol. 103; Cape Coast Castle Journals, January 1737, TNA, T70/407, 44; Cape Coast Castle Journals, January 1737, TNA, T70/406, fols. 7, 49; Instructions for Africa Agents, November 23, 1737, TNA, T70/67; RAC to Tinker and Cope, November 24, 1737, TNA, T70/54, fols. 102–104.

47. John Cope to RAC, December 6, 1738, TNA, T70/4, 95–96; Cape Coast Castle Journals, Presents and Dashees, December 1737, TNA, T70/407, 92; January 1738, TNA, T70/408, June 1738, fols. 10, 80; Cape Coast Castle Journals, Presents and Dashees, February 1737/8, TNA, T70/408, 23. On Kurentsi, see Sparks, *Where the Negroes Are Masters,* 35–67.

48. RAC to James Hope, William Lea, and John Cope, November 28, 1738, TNA, T70/54, fol. 112.

49. RAC to William Lea, November 15, 1739, TNA, T70/54; Cape Coast Journals, October 1739, TNA, T70/411, fol. 34.

50. Hope to RAC, December 20, 1738, TNA, T70/4, fols. 100–101; RAC to James Hope, William Lea, and John Cope, November 28, 1738, TNA, T70/54, fol. 111. For background on Mrs. Phipps, see Sparks, *Where the Negroes Are Masters,* 84–85. For familial relations between European slave traders and locals on the Gold Coast, see Pernille Ipsen, *Daughters of the Trade: Atlantic Slavers and Interracial Marriage on the Gold Coast* (Philadelphia: University of Pennsylvania Press, 2015).

51. Cape Coast Castle Journals, May 1738, TNA, T70/408, fol. 75; Cape Coast Castle Journals, July and August 1738, TNA, T70/409, fol. 9; Hope to RAC, December 20, 1738, TNA, T70/4, fols. 99–100; Governor Boris, et al., to the Directors of the Dutch West India and Guinea Company, November 28, 1738, X.23, in Ole Justesen, *Danish Sources of the History of Ghana, 1657–1754,* trans.

James Manley, vol. 2 (Copenhagen: Kgl. Danske Videnskabernes Selskab, 2005), 550; RAC to Lea, Cope, and Hope, August 2, 1739, TNA, T70/4, 107; Cope, Tynewell, and Drybutter to RAC, November 30, 1739, TNA, T70/4, 109.

52. RAC to Cope, April 3, 1740, TNA, T70/54, fol. 124; Cope to Spence, September 16, 1741, TNA, T70/4, 126; Cape Coast Castle Journals, May and June 1742, TNA, T70/416, fol. 48; RAC to Lea, Hope, and Cope, October 4, 1739, T70/54, fol. 117; *Voyages: The Transatlantic Slave Trade Database:* http://www.slavevoyages.org.

53. Thistlewood diary, December 4, 1760.

54. Wylie Sypher, *Guinea's Captive Kings: British Anti-Slavery Literature of the XVIIIth Century* (Chapel Hill, NC: University of North Carolina Press, 1942), 9; Barry Weller, "The Royal Slave and the Prestige of Origins," *Kenyon Review* 14, no. 3 (1992): 65–78; Laura Brown, *Fables of Modernity: Literature and Culture in the English Eighteenth Century* (Ithaca: Cornell University Press, 2001), chap. 5; Srinivas Aravamudan, *Tropicopolitans: Colonialism and Agency, 1688–1804* (Durham, NC: Duke University Press, 1999), 250–252. For a fuller exploration of the relation between these tales and African history, see especially Randy J. Sparks, *Two Princes of Calabar: An Eighteenth-Century Atlantic Odyssey* (Cambridge, MA: Harvard University Press, 2009).

55. *The Gentlemen's Magazine* 19 (February 1749): 89–90; Wylie Sypher, "The African Prince in London," *Journal of the History of Ideas* 1, no. 1 (1941): 237–247.

56. Walter C. Rucker, *Gold Coast Diasporas: Identity, Culture, and Power* (Bloomington: Indiana University Press, 2015), 172–173.

57. On the value of applying critical speculation to sources about enslaved individuals see especially Marisa J. Fuentes, *Dispossessed Lives: Enslaved Women, Violence, and the Archive* (Philadelphia: University of Pennsylvania Press, 2016) and Saidiya Hartman, "Venus in Two Acts," *Small Axe* 12, no. 2 (June 2008): 1–14.

58. Douglas Hall, *In Miserable Slavery: Thomas Thistlewood in Jamaica, 1750–86* (Kingston: University of the West Indies Press, 1999 [1989]), 106; Trevor Burnard, *Mastery, Tyranny, and Desire* (Chapel Hill: University of North Carolina Press, 2004), 176, 297–298n; Audra A. Diptee, *From Africa to Jamaica: The Making of an Atlantic Slave Society, 1775–1807* (Gainesville: University Press of Florida, 2010), 15–16.

59. Robin Law, *The Slave Coast of West Africa: The Impact of the Slave Trade on an African Society, 1550–1750* (Oxford: Oxford University Press, 1991), 316–317; Albert Van Dantzig, *The Dutch and the Guinea Coast, 1674–1742: A Collection of Documents from the General State Archive at the Hague* (Accra: Sub-Saharan Publishers, 1978), no. 390: Diary of D-G Des Bordes's Journey to Accra, and no. 393, Declaration of the Soldier Johan Joost Steirmark, Elmina, 322, 326–332; Fynn, *Asante and its Neighbours*, 73; Justesen, *Danish Sources*, X.13: Boris to Directors of the Danish West India and Guinea Company, July 12, 1737, X.14: Recommendation and Resolution of the *Sekret* Council re a Lodge at Keta, August 17 and 26, 1737, and X.15: Boris

to Directors of the Danish West India and Guinea Company, September 30, 1737, 528–532.

60. Law, *The Slave Coast,* 315–324; Law, *Ouidah,* 59–66, quotation on 63; Robert Norris, *Memoirs of the Reign of Bossa Ahádee, King of Dahomey an Inland Country of Guiney* (London: W. Lowndes, 1789), 55–56; Thornton, *Warfare in Atlantic Africa,* 83–84; Hall, *In Miserable Slavery,* 106; *Voyages: Trans-Atlantic Slave Trade Database.*

61. Cape Coast Castle, Presents and Dashees, Nov/Dec, 1740, TNA, T70/413, fol. 47–48.

62. Bosman, *A New and Accurate Description of the Coast of Guinea,* 22–23.

63. "A Map of the Gold Coast from Isini to Alampi by M. D'Anville, April 1729," in *New General Collection of Voyages and Travels* (London: Thomas Astley, 1745–1747), vol. 2, plate 60, between 564 and 565; Robin Law, "The Komenda Wars, 1694–1700: A Revised Narrative," *History in Africa* 34 (2007): 134–168.

64. Commenda, Charges on Palavers, Jan/Feb. 1745, TNA, T70/421, fol. 91; Commenda, Presents & Dashees, May/June 1745, TNA, T70/421, fol. 117.

65. HMS *Wager* Musters, 1746–1747, TNA, ADM 36/4459, fols. 72, 101.

66. Paul E. Lovejoy, "The African Background of Venture Smith," in James Brewer Stewart, ed., *Venture Smith and the Business of Freedom* (Amherst: University of Massachusetts Press, 2010), 35–55; Van Dantzig, *The Dutch,* no. 389: Minutes of Elmina Council, May 27, 1737, 320; Fynn, *Asante and Its Neighbors,* 73; James Sanders, "The Expansion of the Fante and the Emergence of Asante in the Eighteenth Century," *Journal of African History* 20, no. 3 (1979): 349–364.

67. Cape Coast Castle Journals, Present and Dashees, September/October 1738, TNA, T70/409, fol. 26.

68. Cape Coast Castle Journals, May 1739, TNA, T70/410, fol. 53; Cape Coast Castle Journals, July 1739, TNA, T70/411, fol. 6; Cape Coast Castle Journals, March 23, 1741, TNA, T70/414, fol. 22.

69. Cape Coast Castle Journals, March 1740, TNA, T70/412, fol. 32.

70. Cape Coast Castle Journals, June 1740, TNA, T70/412, fol. 70; Cape Coast Castle Journals, July and August 1740, TNA, T70/413, fol. 7, 19.

71. Van Dantzig, *The Dutch,* no. 413: Chief Merchant Barovius to Assembly of X, April 30, 1740, 347; Cape Coast Castle Journals, Sundry Accounts to John Cope, November/December 1740, TNA, T70/413, fol. 50.

72. Van Dantzig, *The Dutch,* no. 400: Des Bordes to Assembly of X, September 17, 1738, 337.

73. Van Dantzig, *The Dutch,* no. 409: Raams, Chama, to Assembly of X, November 3, 1739, 343.

74. Van Dantzig, *The Dutch,* no. 409, 343–344; Justesen, *Danish Sources,* X.27: Boris to Danish West India and Guinea Company, September 10, 1739, 553.

75. Van Dantzig, *The Dutch,* no. 407: Johan Hessing, Pastor at Elmina, to Ass. Of X, September 18, 1739, 343; Van Dantzig, *The Dutch,* no. 409, 343–344; Van Dantzig, *The Dutch,* no. 411: WIC 122: "Contracts with Natives," September 2, 1739, 345–346.

76. Van Dantzig, *The Dutch,* no. 416: D. Hobroek, Annomaboe, to Barovious, April 24, 1740, 351.

77. Van Dantzig, *The Dutch,* no. 414: Journal containing the most remarkable incidents occurring within this Government between 16th March and 15th April, extracted by J. Elzevier, 349–350.

78. Van Dantzig, *The Dutch,* no. 412: Commies Schaik to Assembly of X, April 29, 1740, 346.

79. Van Dantzig, *The Dutch,* no. 414, 349–350.

80. Governor Boris, Christiansborg, to the Directors of the Dutch West India and Guinea Company, February 15, 1740, X.31, in Ole Justesen, *Danish Sources of the History of Ghana, 1657–1754,* trans. James Manley, 2 (Copenhagen: Historisk-Filosofiske Skrifter, 2005), 562.

81. Van Dantzig, *The Dutch,* no. 414, 349; Van Dantzig, *The Dutch,* no. 413, 348–349.

82. Van Dantzig, The Dutch, no. 413, 348; Ludwig Ferdinand Romer quoted in Shumway, *The Fante and the Transatlantic Slave Trade,* 75; Justesen, *Danish Sources,* X.31: Boris to Directors of the Danish West India and Guinea Company, February 15, 1740, 561.

83. Van Dantzig, *The Dutch,* no. 413, 348; Cape Coast Castle Journals, August 1740, TNA, T70/413, fol. 32; Cape Coast Castle Journals, March 23, 1741, TNA, T70/414, fol. 22; Cape Coast Castle Journals, May/June 1741, TNA, T70/414, fol. 35; Cape Coast Castle Journals, October 12, 1741, TNA, T70/415, fol. 18. On relations between Kurentsi and the English in the 1750s, see Shumway, *The Fante and the Transatlantic Slave Trade,* 75–81, and Sparks, *Where the Negroes Are Masters,* 35–67. Also see Ty Reese, "'Eating' Luxury: Fante Middlemen, British Goods, and Changing Dependencies on the Gold Coast, 1750–1821," *WMQ* 66, no. 4 (October 2009): 851–872.

84. Fynn, *Asante and its Neighbours,* 64–66.

85. Van Dantzig, *The Dutch,* no. 418: "Informations about the Troubles between the English Negroes of Sacconde and the Antase," August 12, 1740, 352.

86. Van Dantzig, *The Dutch,* no. 407, 344; Van Dantzig, *The Dutch,* no. 410: Verschueren to Assembly of X, November 24, 1739, 345.

87. Van Dantzig, *The Dutch,* no. 418, 352.

88. Van Dantzig, *The Dutch,* no. 413, 347.

89. Van Dantzig, *The Dutch,* no. 418, 351–352.

90. Cape Coast Castle Journals, Cape Coast Castle Presents and Dashes, August 1740, TNA, T70/413, fol. 19; Cape Coast Castle Journals, Dixcove Presents and Dashes, September/October 1740, November/December 1740, Succondee Presents and Dashes and Charges on Palavers, September/October 1740, Cape Coast Castle Presents and Dashes, November/December 1740, TNA, T70/414, fols. 34, 36, 47–48, 51; Cape Coast Castle Journals, Charges on Palavers, January/February 1742, TNA, T70/417, fol. 105.

91. For especially sensitive discussions of the special challenges of historical biography for enslaved individuals, see James H. Sweet, "Mistaken Identities? Olaudah Equiano, Domingos Álvares, and the Methodological Challenges of Studying the African Diaspora," *American Historical Review* 114, no. 2

(April 2009): 279–306; and Annette Gordon-Reed, "Writing Early American Lives as Biography," *WMQ* 71, no. 4 (October 2014): 491–516.

2. The Jamaica Garrison

1. Deborah A. Thomas, *Exceptional Violence: Embodied Citizenship in Transnational Jamaica* (Durham, NC: Duke University Press, 2011), 87–124; Rachel Woodward, "Military Landscapes: Agendas and Approaches for Future Research," *Progress in Human Geography* 38, no. 1 (2014): 40–61.

2. Carl Bridenbaugh and Roberta Bridenbaugh, *No Peace Beyond the Line: The British in the Caribbean, 1624–1690* (New York: Oxford University Press, 1972); Eliga H. Gould, "Zones of Law, Zones of Violence: The Legal Geography of the British Atlantic, circa 1772," *WMQ* 60, no. 3 (2003): 471–510.

3. Stephen Saunders Webb, "Army and Empire: English Garrison Government in Britain and America, 1569–1763," *WMQ*, 3rd Series 34, no. 1 (1977): 1–31, quotations on 6, 24.

4. Trevor Burnard, *Planters, Merchants, and Slaves: Plantation Societies in British America, 1650–1820* (Chicago: University of Chicago Press, 2015), 78.

5. Jennifer L. Morgan, *Laboring Women: Reproduction and Gender in New World Slavery* (Philadelphia: University of Pennsylvania Press, 2004); Aisha K. Finch, *Rethinking Slave Rebellion in Cuba: La Escalera and the Insurgencies of 1841–1844* (Chapel Hill: University of North Carolina Press, 2015); Marisa J. Fuentes, *Dispossessed Lives: Enslaved Women, Violence, and the Archive* (Philadelphia: University of Pennsylvania Press, 2016); Stan Goff, *Borderline: Reflections on War, Sex, and Church* (Eugene, OR: Cascade, 2015), 71–76, 86–91.

6. James Knight, "Natural, Moral, and Political History of Jamaica and the Territories thereon depending; From the Earliest account of time to the Year 1742," 3 vols., parts 5–7, unpublished manuscript, British Library, C. E. Long Papers, Add. ms. 12,420, 3: fols. 27, 26. On Knight's background, see Jack P. Greene, *Settler Jamaica in the 1750s: A Social Portrait* (Charlottesville: University of Virginia Press, 2016), 4.

7. Richard S. Dunn, *Sugar and Slaves: The Rise of the Planter Class in the English West Indies, 1624–1713* (Chapel Hill: University of North Carolina Press, 2000 [1972]), 181; Michael Pawson and David Buisseret, *Port Royal, Jamaica* (Kingston: University of the West Indies Press, 2000). Also see Mark G. Hannah, *Pirate Nests and the Rise of the British Empire, 1570–1740* (Chapel Hill: University of North Carolina Press, 2017).

8. Dunn, *Sugar and Slaves*, 154, 170.

9. Dunn, *Sugar and Slaves*, 156.

10. John White et al. to Board of Trade, June 20, 1692, TNA, CO 137/2, 192; John Bourden et al. to Board of Trade, August 26, 1692, TNA, CO 137/2, 206.

11. Burnard, *Planters, Merchants, and Slaves*, 69–70, 78. Also see Burnard, "'The Country Continues Sickly': White Mortality in Jamaica, 1655–1780," *Social History of Medicine* 12, no. 1 (1999): 45–72.

12. "Abstract of Beeston's letter to the Committee," March 23, 1694, TNA, CO 137/3, 15–19.

13. Dunn, *Sugar and Slaves,* 163.

14. Council and Assembly of Jamaica Appeal, including William Beeston's report, October 29, 1694, TNA, CO 137/1, quotation on 195.

15. Knight, "Natural, Moral, and Political History of Jamaica," fols. 9, 21.

16. John Bourden et al. to Board of Trade; Dunn, *Sugar and Slaves,* 170; Burnard, *Planters, Merchants, and Slaves,* 68–69.

17. Burnard, *Planters, Merchants, and Slaves,* 76.

18. John Bourden et al. to Board of Trade.

19. Burnard, *Planters, Merchants, and Slaves,* 63–64.

20. Mavis Campbell, *The Maroons of Jamaica, 1655–1796: A History of Resistance, Collaboration, and Betrayal* (Trenton, NJ: Bergin & Garvey, 1988), 14–87; Dunn, *Sugar and Slaves,* 259–262; Burnard, *Planters, Merchants, and Slaves,* 65–66; David Buisseret, ed. *Jamaica in 1687: The Taylor Manuscripts at the National Library of Jamaica* (Kingston: University of the West Indies Press, 2009), 274–279; Knight, "Natural, Moral, and Political History of Jamaica," fols. 92–95.

21. James A. Delle, *The Colonial Caribbean: Landscapes of Power in the Plantation System* (Cambridge, UK: Cambridge University Press, 2014), 39–45.

22. Stephen J. Hornsby, *British Atlantic, American Frontier: Spaces of Power in Early Modern British America* (Lebanon, NH: University Press of New England, 2005), 192.

23. Knight, "Natural, Moral, and Political History of Jamaica," fol. 29.

24. Delle, *The Colonial Caribbean,* 108; James A. Delle, "Power and Landscape: Spatial Dynamics in Early Nineteenth-Century Jamaica," in Maria O'Donovan, ed., *The Dynamics of Power* (Carbondale, IL: Center for Archaelogical Investigations, Southern Illinois University, 2002), 341–361, esp. 342, 351.

25. Knight, "Natural, Moral, and Political History of Jamaica," fol. 77.

26. Burnard, *Planters, Merchants, and Slaves,* 92–97.

27. Patrick Browne, *The Civil and Natural History of Jamaica in Three Parts* (London: Browne, 1756), 9. For a detailed analysis of the Jamaican economic life in the mid-eighteenth century, see Greene, *Settler Jamaica in the 1750s* and B. W. Higman, *Plantation Jamaica, 1750–1850: Capital and Control in a Colonial Economy* (Kingston: University of the West Indies Press, 2008).

28. Browne, *Civil and Natural History of Jamaica,* 24.

29. Burnard, *Planters, Merchants, and Slaves,* 180–202.

30. *Voyages: The Transatlantic Slave Database,* http://www.slavevoyages.org/assessment/estimates. On trade between Jamaica and the Spanish Mainland, see especially Adrian Finucane, *The Temptations of Trade: Britain, Spain, and the Struggle for Empire* (Philadelphia: University of Pennsylvania Press, 2016).

31. Burnard, *Planters, Merchants, and Slaves,* 205–206. Trevor Burnard, "Kingston, Jamaica: Crucible of Modernity," in *The Black Urban Atlantic in the Age of the Slave Trade* (Philadelphia: University of Pennsylvania Press, 2013), 122–144.

32. Higman, *Plantation Jamaica,* 5.

33. Perry Gauci, *William Beckford: First Prime Minister of the London Empire* (New Haven, CT: Yale University Press, 2013), 32–33; Burnard, *Planters, Merchants, and Slaves,* 158, 160.

34. Burnard, *Planters, Merchants, and Slaves,* 160, 174, 190–191.
35. Gauci, *William Beckford,* 5, 11, 48, 51–106.
36. On Zachary Bayly's wealth, see Burnard, *Planters, Merchants, and Slaves,* 95, 158, 160, 201. On the role of "transatlantic brokers," see Gauci, *William Beckford,* 16; and Burnard, *Planters, Merchants, and Slaves,* 118.
37. Burnard, *Planters, Merchants, and Slaves,* 18; Higman, *Plantation Jamaica,* quotation on 4.
38. Vincent Brown, "Eating the Dead: Consumption and Regeneration in the History of Sugar," *Food and Foodways: History and Culture of Human Nourishment* 16, no. 2 (2008): 117–126; Richard S. Dunn, *A Tale of Two Plantations: Life and Labor in Jamaica and Virginia* (Cambridge, MA: Harvard University Press, 2014), 34–35.
39. Burnard, *Planters, Merchants, and Slaves,* 55–58; Dunn, *Tale of Two Plantations,* 141–145; Philip D. Morgan, "Task and Gang Systems: The Organization of Labor on New World Plantations," in Stephen Innes, ed. *Work and Labor in Early America* (Chapel Hill: University of North Carolina Press, 1988), 189–220.
40. Keith Mason, "The Absentee Planter and the Key Slave: Privilege, Patriarchalism, and Exploitation in the Early Eighteenth-Century Caribbean," *WMQ* 3rd Series 70, no. 1 (2013): 79–102; Randy M. Browne, *Surviving Slavery in the British Caribbean* (Philadelphia: University of Pennsylvania Press, 2017), 72–101.
41. Dunn, *Tale of Two Plantations,* 141–144, 431–432.
42. Richard S. Dunn. "Sugar Production and Slave Women in Jamaica," in Ira Berlin and Philip D. Morgan, eds., *Cultivation and Culture: Labor and the Shaping of Slave Life in the Americas* (Charlottesville: University of Virginia Press, 1993), 49–72; Dunn, *Tale of Two Plantations,* 141, 178, 431; Burnard, *Planters, Merchants, and Slaves,* 59. Also see Justin Roberts, "The 'Better Sort' and the 'Poorer Sort': Wealth Inequalities, Family Formation, and the Economy of Energy on British Caribbean Sugar Plantations, 1750–1800," *Slavery & Abolition* 35, no. 3 (2014), 458–473.
43. Burnard, *Planters, Merchants, and Slaves,* 6, 78–97.
44. Knight, "Natural, Moral, and Political History of Jamaica," fols. 77–78, 82.
45. Charles Leslie, *A New and Exact Account of Jamaica* (Edinburgh: R. Fleming, 1740), 41–42.
46. Edward Rugemer, "The Development of Mastery and Race in the Comprehensive Slave Codes of the Greater Caribbean during the Seventeenth Century," *WMQ* 70, no. 3 (2013): 429–458; Diana Paton, "Punishment, Crime, and the Bodies of Slaves in Eighteenth-Century Jamaica," *Journal of Social History* 34, no. 4 (2001): 923–954; Vincent Brown, "Spiritual Terror and Sacred Authority: Supernatural Power in Jamaican Slave Society," in Edward E. Baptist and Stephanie Camp, eds., *New Studies in the History of American Slavery* (Athens, GA: University of Georgia Press, 2006), 179–210; John Collins, "Military Law" in Joseph C. Miller, ed., *The Princeton Companion to Atlantic History* (Princeton: Princeton University Press, 2015), 285–287.
47. G. Duquesne to Newman, May 15, 1728, *Fulham Papers,* Vol. XVII, Lambeth Palace Library.

48. Philip D. Morgan, "Slaves and Livestock in Eighteenth-Century Jamaica: Vineyard Pen, 1750–1751," *WMQ* 52, no. 1 (1995): 47–76; Philip D. Morgan, "Three Planters and Their Slaves: Perspectives on Slavery in Virginia, South Carolina, and Jamaica, 1750–1790," in Winthrop D. Jordan and Sheila L. Skemp, eds., *Race and Family in the Colonial South* (Jackson, MS: University Press of Mississippi, 1987), 37–80; Burnard, *Planters, Merchants, and Slaves,* 58–61; Dunn, *Tale of Two Plantations,* 146–152. For biographical treatments, see Douglas Hall, *In Miserable Slavery: Thomas Thistlewood in Jamaica, 1750–1786* (Kingston: University of the West Indies Press, 1989); and Trevor Burnard, *Mastery, Tyranny, and Desire: Thomas Thistlewood and His Slaves in the Anglo-Jamaican World* (Chapel Hill: University of North Carolina Press, 2004).

49. Thistlewood as cited in Trevor Burnard, "'Impatient of Subordination' and 'Liable to Sudden Transports of Anger': White Masculinity and Homosocial Relations with Black Men in Eighteenth-Century Jamaica," in *New Men: Manliness in Early America,* ed. Thomas A. Foster (New York: New York University Press, 2011), 134–152, at 140.

50. Burnard, "'Impatient of Subordination,'"; Diana Paton, "Gender, Language, Violence, and Slavery: Insult in Jamaica, 1800–1838," *Gender and History* 18, no. 2 (2006): 246–265. Also see Kenneth Morgan, "Slave Women and Reproduction in Jamaica, c. 1776–1834," *History* 91, no. 302 (2006): 231–253; and Natalie A. Zacek, "'Banes of Society' and 'Gentlemen of Strong Natural Parts': Attacking and Defending West Indian Creole Masculinity," in *New Men: Manliness in Early America,* ed. Thomas A. Foster (New York: New York University Press, 2011), 116–133.

51. Burnard, *Mastery, Tyranny, and Desire,* 119.

52. Burnard, *Mastery, Tyranny, and Desire,* 144.

53. Knight, "Natural, Moral, and Political History of Jamaica," fol. 78.

54. Knight, "Natural, Moral, and Political History of Jamaica," fols. 78–79; Robert Hunter to the Council of Trade and Plantations, July 4, 1730, in *Calendar of State Papers,* vol. 37, no. 311 (London: His Majesty's Stationery Office, 1939); Burnard, *Mastery, Tyranny, and Desire,* 144–145. For comparison, see Sally E. Hadden, *Slave Patrols: Law and Violence in Virginia and the Carolinas* (Cambridge, MA: Harvard University Press, 2003).

55. Pierre Eugène du Simitière, "Remarks on Extracts from Works about Uprisings of Negroes against Whites in Jamaica," Library Company of Philadelphia, Pierre Eugène du Simitière Collection, Box 4, Folders 20a–21, 177–189, quotations on 183.

56. Du Simitière, "Remarks," 182.

57. Du Simitière, "Remarks," quotation on 182.

58. Du Simitière, "Remarks," quotation on 182.

59. Du Simitière, "Remarks," quotation on 183; Census of St Jago de la Vega [Spanish Town] undertaken by Charles White, gent, in July and August 1754, East Suffix Record Office, SAS-RF 2017; Mordechai Arbell, *The Portuguese Jews of Jamaica* (Kingston: University of the West Indies Press, 2000); Daniel Livesay, *Children of Uncertain Fortune: Mixed-Race Jamaicans in Britain and*

the Atlantic Family, 1733–1833 (Chapel Hill: University of North Carolina Press, 2018), chap. 1.

60. Du Simitière, "Remarks," 181–182.

61. Richard S. Dunn, *Moravian Missionaries at Work in a Jamaican Slave Community, 1754–1835* (Minneapolis: University of Minnesota Press, 1994); Dunn, *Two Plantations,* 224–270; Great Britain, Moravian Church, Parliament, House of Commons, Committee to Whom the Petition of the Deputies of the Moravian Church was Referred, "An Act for Encouraging the People Known by the Name of *Unitas Fratrum* or *United Brethren,* to settle in His Majesty's Colonies in America," in *Acta Fratrum Unitatis in Anglia* (London: Thomas Baskett, 1749), 635–638; Katharine Gerbner, "'They Call Me Obea': German Moravian Missionaries and Afro-Caribbean Religion in Jamaica, 1754–1760," *Atlantic Studies* 12, no. 2 (2015): 160–178.

62. Katharine Gerbner, *Christian Slavery: Conversion and Race in the Protestant Atlantic World* (Philadelphia: University of Pennsylvania Press, 2018).

63. Browne, *Civil and Natural History of Jamaica,* 9.

64. Kenneth Morgan, "Robert Dinwiddie's Reports on the British American Colonies," *WMQ* 65, no. 2 (2008): 318, 340; Stephen Brumwell, *Redcoats: The British Soldier and War in the Americas, 1755–1763* (Cambridge, UK: Cambridge University Press, 2002); 55, 196–197; J. W. Fortesque, *A History of the British Army,* 13 vols. (London: Macmillan, 1899–1930), 2: 39–40, 300, 372.

65. Sarah Kinkel, "The King's Pirates? Naval Enforcement of Imperial Authority, 1740–76," *WMQ* 71, no. 1 (2014): 3–34, esp. 6n6; Knight, "Natural, Moral, and Political History of Jamaica," fol. 77.

66. Richard Pares, *War and Trade in the West Indies, 1739–1763* (London: Routledge, 1963 [1936]), 264–265.

67. Knight, "Natural, Moral, and Political History of Jamaica," fols. 15–16; Daniel Baugh, *British Naval Administration in the Age of Walpole* (Princeton: Princeton University Press, 1965), 347–352.

68. Pares, *War and Trade,* 266, 268; Present Disposal of His Majesty's Ships and Vessels, 1760, TNA, ADM 8/35.

69. Baugh, *British Naval Administration,* 216–217; Pares, *War and Trade,* 268, 273–274; J. R. McNeill, *Mosquito Empires: Ecology and War in the Greater Caribbean, 1620–1914* (New York: Cambridge University Press, 2010), 32–40.

70. Britt Zerbe, *The Birth of the Royal Marines, 1664–1802* (Suffolk, UK: Boydell Press, 2013).

71. Thomas More Molyneux, *Conjunct Expeditions: or Expeditions that Have Been Carried on Jointly by the Fleet and Army with a Commentary on a Littoral War,* 2 vols. (London: R. and J. Dodsley, 1759), 2: 5–7; Richard Harding, "Sailors and Gentlemen of Parade: Some Professional and Technical Problems Concerning the Conduct of Combined Operations in the Eighteenth Century," *Historical Journal* 32, no. 1 (1989): 35–55.

72. On the career of Thomas Cotes, see James Stanier Clarke and John McArthur, *Naval Chronicle: Containing a General Biographical History of the Royal Navy of the United Kingdom,* vol. 25, January–June, 1811 (Cambridge, UK: Cambridge University Press, 2010), 442–443.

73. Molyneux, *Conjunct Expeditions,* 2: 201.

74. Sarah Kinkel, "Disorder, Discipline, and Naval Reform in Mid-Eighteenth-Century Britain," *English Historical Review* 128, no. 535 (2013): 1451–1482; "An Act for Amending, Explaining and Reducing into One Act of Parliament, the Laws Relating to the Government of his Majesty's Ships, Vessels and Forces by Sea," in Nicholas A. M. Rodger, *Articles of War: The Statutes which Governed Our Fighting Navies, 1661, 1749, and 1886* (Hampshire, UK: Kenneth Mason, 1982), 7–11, 21–34. Also see John M. Collins, *Martial Law and English Laws, c. 1500–c. 1700* (Cambridge, UK: Cambridge University Press, 2016).

75. Rodger, *Articles of War,* quotations on 22, 29, 28.

76. Rodger, *Articles of War,* 9–10.

77. Rodger, *Articles of War,* 9–10, 21–24, quotations on 26, 24, 28; Nicholas A. M. Rodger, *The Wooden World: An Anatomy of the Georgian Navy* (London: Naval Institute Press, 1986), 221–222; Marcus Rediker, *Between the Devil and the Deep Blue Sea: Merchant Seamen, Pirates, and the Anglo-American Maritime World, 1700–1750* (Cambridge, UK: Cambridge University Press, 1989); Kinkel, "The King's Pirates?" Rodger contends that the weight of the Articles of War was "a great deal less than the Admiralty desired," but Sarah Kinkel is more convincing in her assessment that, in conjunction with other reforms, the Articles of War helped to create a "new culture of service within the Navy, based on discipline and hierarchy, in which the greatest glory was given to those who fulfilled their orders reliably and without regard to personal cost." Also see Kinkel, *Disciplining the Empire: Politics, Governance, and the Rise of the British Navy* (Cambridge, MA: Harvard University Press, 2018), chap. 3.

78. J. K. Laughton, rev. Ruddock Mackay, "Forrest, Arthur (d. 1770)," *Oxford Dictionary of National Biography,* online edition (January 2008); Nicholas A. M. Rodger, *The Command of the Ocean: A Naval History of Britain, 1649–1815* (New York: Norton, 2004), 384.

79. Richard Harding, *Amphibious Warfare in the Eighteenth Century: The British Expedition to the West Indies, 1740–1742* (London: Boydell Press, 1991), 131; McNeil, *Mosquito Empires,* 149–155.

80. McNeil, *Mosquito Empires,* 155–164; Clarke and McArthur, eds., *The Naval Chronicle* 25: 441–443. For the most comprehensive examination of the Cartagena campaign, see Richard Harding, *Amphibious Warfare in the Eighteenth Century.* On the Baradero battery in particular, see 96.

81. Clarke and McArthur, eds., *The Naval Chronicle* 25: 443.

82. Thomas Thistlewood diary, December 20, 1760.

83. HMS *Wager* Ticket Book Commencing March 9, 1744 / June 5–8, 1748, NMM, ADM / L / W / 3.

84. Trelawny to Lords of Admiralty, December 21, 1743, TNA, ADM 1 / 3917. Also see Justin Pope, "Dangerous Spirit of Liberty: Slave Rebellion, Conspiracy, and the First Great Awakening, 1729–1746" (PhD diss., George Washington University, 2014), 185, 206; Nicholas Rogers, "Archipelagic Encounters: War, Race, and Labor in American-Caribbean Waters," in *The Global Eighteenth Century,* Felicity Nussbaum, ed. (Baltimore: Johns Hopkins University Press, 2003), 211–238.

85. HMS *Wager* Captain's Journal, April 9, 1746, TNA, ADM 51/1082; HMS *Wager* Captain's Journal, April 22–27, 1746, TNA, ADM 51/1082.

86. Baugh, *British Naval Administration*, 216–217, 347–352, 364.

87. Laughton, "Forrest, Arthur (*d.* 1770)."

88. HMS *Wager* Captain's Journal, April 27 to May 14, 1746, September 8, 1746, TNA, ADM 51/1082.

89. HMS *Wager* Captain's Journal, June 6, 1747, TNA, ADM 51/1082.

90. HMS *Wager* Musters, 1746–1747, TNA, ADM 36/4459, fols. 72, 101.

91. Charles R. Foy, "The Royal Navy's Employment of Black Mariners and Maritime Workers, 1754–1783," *The International Journal of Maritime History* 28, no. 1 (2016): 6–35; HMS *Wager* Ticket Book; and personal communication with Charles R. Foy, August 4, 2015.

92. Admiral Arthur Forrest: Profile and Legacies Summary, UCL, Legacies of British Slave Ownership: https://www.ucl.ac.uk/lbs/person/view/2146643075; Laughton, "Forest, Arthur (*d.* 1770)"; *Memoirs of William Hickey*, vol. 1: 1749–1775, ed. Alfred Spencer (London: Hurst & Blackett, 1913), 261; Lists of Landholders, and Quantity of Land Occupied in Jamaica, about the year 1750, British Library, C. E. Long Papers, Add. ms. 12,436, fols. 43, 45; Rodger, *Wooden World*, 159, 319; Charles R. Foy, "Eighteenth-Century Prize Negroes: From Britain to America," *Slavery and Abolition* 31, no. 3 (2010): 379–393; Sarah Markham, *John Loveday of Caversham, 1711–1789: The Life and Tours of an Eighteenth-Century Onlooker* (Salisbury, UK: M. Russell, 1984), 379, 415; Rodger, *The Command of the Ocean*, 384.

93. HMS *Rye* Musters, March 10, 1756, TNA, ADM 36/6438.

94. Thomas Thistlewood diary, December 20, 1760.

95. Justesen, *Danish Sources*, X.27: Boris to Danish West India and Guinea Company, September 10, 1739, 553.

96. Vincent Brown, "Social Death and Political Life in the Study of Slavery," *American Historical Review* 114, no. 5 (December 2009): 1231–1249.

97. Daniel Baugh, *The Global Seven Years War, 1754–1763: Britain and France in a Great Power Contest* (Harlow: Pearson Education, 2011), 377; Frank McClynn, *1759: The Year Britain Became Master of the World* (New York: Atlantic Monthly Press, 2004), 90–99; Richard Harding, "The War in the West Indies," in Mark H. Danley and Patrick J. Speelman, eds., *The Seven Years' War: Global Views* (Boston: Brill, 2012), 303–306.

98. Pares, *War and Trade*, 268; John Lee to Rose Fuller, Spanish Town, December 21, 1756, SAS-RF 21/90.

99. Quotation from Rose Herring May to Rose Fuller, September 10, 1758, SAS-RF 21/uncatalogued.

100. *Slave Voyages: Transatlantic Slave Trade - Estimates:* http://www.slavevoyages.org/estimates/jeUhREVj, accessed December 13, 2018.

101. Pares, *War and Trade*, 257–258.

102. Zachary Bayly to Rose Fuller, Greenwich Park, Jamaica, September 9, 1758, East Sussex Record Office, Fuller Papers, SAS-RF 21/uncatalogued.

103. John Entick, *The General History of the Late War: Containing Its Rise, Progress, and Event, in Europe, Asia, Africa, and America*, 5 volumes (London: Edward and Charles Dilly, 1763–1764), 3: 64; James F. Searing, "The Seven

Years' War in West Africa: The End of Company Rule and the Emergence of the Habitants," in Mark H. Danley and Patrick J. Speelman, eds., *The Seven Years' War: Global Views* (Boston: Brill, 2012), 263–291, quotation 264; Marshall Smelser, *The Campaign for the Sugar Islands, 1759: A Study of Amphibious Warfare* (Chapel Hill: University of North Carolina Press, 1955), 73; Pares, *War and Trade,* 217; Frank McClynn, *1759,* 92. Also see Julian S. Corbett, *England in the Seven Years' War: A Study in Combined Strategy,* vols. 1–2 (London: Longmans, 1918).

104. William Beckford to William Pitt, November 6, 1756, and William Beckford to William Pitt, September 11, 1758, *Correspondence of William Pitt,* William Stanhope Taylor and John Henry Pringle, eds. (London: John Murray, 1838), vol. 1: 185–186, 352–354; Gauci, *William Beckford,* 93–95.

105. Harding, "The War in the West Indies," 306; Baugh, *The Global Seven Years War,* 377; McClynn, *1759,* 99–104.

106. Laughton, "Forrest, Arthur (d. 1770)"; Sarah Markham, *John Loveday of Caversham,* 379; HMS *Augusta* Musters, 1757–1758, ADM 36/4782, fol. 76.

107. Rodger, *Command of the Ocean,* 272.

108. William H. G. Kingston, *How Britannia Came to Rule the Waves, Updated to 1900* (London: Gall and Inglis, 1875), 189.

109. Clarke and McArthur, eds., *Naval Chronicle* 25: 445–447; Pares, *War and Trade,* 280–281; Notice from Kingston, Jamaica, January 5, 1758, *Gentlemen's Magazine* 27 (1758): 259; Forrest to ADM, January 10, 1758, TNA, ADM 1/1785.

110. HMS *Rye* Musters, 1755–1757, TNA, ADM 36/6438, fols. 150, 177; HMS *Augusta* Musters, 1757–1758, TNA, ADM 36/4782, fols. 76, 106, 360.

111. *Memoirs of William Hickey,* 263; Sarah Markham, *John Loveday of Caversham,* 415; Laughton, "Forrest, Arthur (d. 1770)." The *Centaur* had been captured at the Battle of Lagos by Admiral Edward Boscawen commanding the *Namur,* with Olaudah Equiano carrying powder to the cannon. Equiano, *The Interesting Narrative,* 82–84.

112. Tobias Smollett, *The History of England, from the Revolution to the Death of George II,* 4 vols. (Philadelphia: Robert Campbell, 1810), 4: 8–9; Entick, *General History of the Late War,* 63–66; John Lindsay, *A Voyage to the Coast of Africa, in 1758: Containing a Succinct Account of the Expedition To, and the Taking of the Island of Goree, by a Squadron Commanded by the Honourable Augustus Keppel* (London: S. Paterson, 1759).

113. Zerbe, *The Birth of the Royal Marines,* 186–188.

114. As quoted in Zerbe, *The Birth of the Royal Marines,* 186; Marsh to ADM, April 7, 1759, TNA, ADM 1/2111.

115. Marsh to ADM, May 7, 1758 in Zerbe, *Birth of the Royal Marines,* 186; Entick, *General History of the Late War,* 64–65; William Toone, *The Chronological Historian, or a Record of Public Events,* 2 vols., Vol. 2 (1826), 93; Searing, "The Seven Years' War in West Africa," 280–281.

116. Quotations from HMS *Harwich* Master's Log, May 21–27, 1758, TNA, ADM 52/892; Zerbe, *Birth of the Royal Marines,* 187.

117. HMS *Harwich* Master's Log, May 30 to June 9, 1758, TNA, ADM 52/892.

118. HMS *Harwich* Master's Log, June 25 to July 30, 1758, TNA, ADM 52/892; William Marsh to ADM, March 21, 1759 and April 7, 1759, TNA, ADM 1/2111.

119. HMS *Harwich* Master's Log, November 11 to December 2, 1758, TNA, ADM 52/892; William Marsh to ADM, April 7, 1759, TNA, ADM1/2111.

120. McClynn, *1759*.

121. Maria Allessandra Bollettino, "Slavery, War, and Britain's Atlantic Empire: Black Soldiers, Sailors, and Rebels in the Seven Years' War" (PhD diss., University of Texas, Austin, 2009), 102–103, quotation on 103; Smelser, *Campaign for the Sugar Islands, 1759*, 77, 175.

122. Richard Gardiner, *An Account of the Expedition to the West Indies, against Martinico, with the Reduction of Guadelupe, And the other Leeward Islands; subject to the French King, 1759* (London: G. Steidel, 1762), 30; Pares, *War and Trade*, 245–246; Smelser, *Campaign for the Sugar Islands*, 22–23, 92–93.

123. Gardiner, *Account of the Expedition*, 28–37; Fred Anderson, *Crucible of War: The Seven Years' War and the Fate of the British Empire in North America, 1754–1766* (New York: Vintage, 2001), 312–316.

124. A List of Governour Haldane and His Retinue Borne for Victuals Only, HMS *Renown* Musters, May 16, 1758 to February 3, 1761, TNA, ADM 36/6516, fol. 242; Smelser, *Campaign for the Sugar Islands*, 119; Gardiner, *Account of the Expedition*, 42.

125. Smelser, *Campaign for the Sugar Islands*, 89, 140.

126. Marines, HMS *Cambridge* Musters, December 1, 1759 to August 31, 1760, TNA, ADM 36/5260, fols. 243–250.

127. Knight, "Natural, Moral, and Political History of Jamaica," fol. 77. Here and elsewhere Knight echoed Leslie, *New and Exact Account of Jamaica*, 327.

3. Coromantee Territory

1. John Thornton, *A Cultural History of the Atlantic World* (Cambridge, UK: Cambridge University Press, 2012), 160.

2. Trevor Burnard, *Planters, Merchants, and Slaves* (Chicago: University of Chicago Press, 2015), 170.

3. Burnard, *Planters, Merchants, and Slaves*, 168–169. *Voyages: The Transatlantic Slave Trade Database*: http://www.slavevoyages.org/estimates/oMP9bLon.

4. Hans Sloane, *A voyage to the islands Madera, Barbados, Nieves, S. Christophers and Jamaica with the natural history of the herbs and trees, four-footed beasts, fishes, birds, insects, reptiles, &c. of the last of those islands; to which is prefix'd, an introduction, wherein is an account of the inhabitants, air, waters, diseases, trade, &c. of that place, with some relations concerning the neighbouring continent, and islands of America. Illustrated with figures of the things described, which have not been heretofore engraved. In large copper-plates as big as the life*, 2 Volumes (London: Sloane, 1707), 1: l–li; Laurent Dubois, David Garner, and Mary Cary Lingold, *Musical Passage: A Voyage to 1688 Jamaica*: http://www.musicalpassage.org/#read; Richard

Cullen Rath, "African Music in Seventeenth-Century Jamaica: Cultural Transit and Transition," *WMQ* 50, no. 4 (1993): 700–726.

5. James Knight, "The Natural, Moral, and Political History of Jamaica and the Territories Thereon Depending," C. E. Long Papers, British Library, Add. ms. 12420, fols. 78–79, 89. For similar opinions also see "Some Remarks on the Trade from Africa to Barbados by Mr. John Ashley," Papers relating to African Affairs, c. 1725, Huntington Library, Stowe-Brydges Papers, Box 9, 44–45.

6. *Journal of the Commissioners of Trade and Plantations Preserved in the Public Record Office, from January 1749–1750 to December 1753,* Volume 58 (London: His Majesty's Stationery Office, 1932): 4–35, quotations on 6, 13, 7, 9. On the debate over the liberalization and regulation of the slave trade, see William Pettigrew, *Freedom's Debt: The Royal African Company and the Politics of the Atlantic Slave Trade, 1672–1752* (Chapel Hill: University of North Carolina Press, 2013), chaps. 5–6.

7. *Journal of the Commissioners of Trade and Plantations,* 58: 35.

8. Burnard, *Planters, Merchants, and Slaves,* 166; Jack P. Greene, *Settler Jamaica in the 1750s: A Social Portrait* (Charlottesville: University of Virginia Press, 2016), 34.

9. Richard S. Dunn, *A Tale of Two Plantations: Slave Life and Labor in Jamaica and Virginia* (Cambridge, MA: Harvard University Press, 2014), 62; A List of Landholders in Jamaica together with the Quantity of Acres of Land each one Possesses, & the Quantity Supposed to be Occupied & Planted, BL, Add. ms. 12,436; *Journal of the Commissioners of Trade and Plantations,* 58: 20–21.

10. "Governor Codrington to the Council of Trade and Plantations, December 30, 1701," in *Calendar of State Papers, Colonial Series,* vol. 19, no. 1132, 720–722.

11. Knight, "Natural, Moral, and Political History of Jamaica," fol. 79. See also G. Duquesne to Newman, May 15, 1728, Fulham Papers, Volume XVII: Bermuda and Jamaica, 1661–1739, Lambeth Palace Library, fol. 252.

12. Dunn, *Tale of Two Plantations,* 141, 178–180, 324–328.

13. Edward Long, *History of Jamaica,* II: 447; Walter C. Rucker, *Gold Coast Diasporas: Identity, Culture, and Power* (Bloomington: Indiana University Press, 2015), 173.

14. John Thornton, "War, the State, and Religious Norms in 'Coromantee' Thought: The Ideology of an African-American Nation," in Robert Blair St. George, ed., *Possible Pasts: Becoming Colonial in Early America* (Ithaca: Cornell University Press, 2000), 181–200, quotations on 183; John Thornton, "The Coromantees: An African Cultural Group in Colonial North America and the Caribbean," *Journal of Caribbean History* 32, nos. 1 & 2 (1998): 161–178. See also Rucker, *Gold Coast Diasporas*; Rucker, "'Only Draw in Your Countrymen:' Akan Culture and Community in Colonial New York City," *Afro-Americans in New York Life and History* 34 (2010): 76–118; Rucker, *The River Flows On: Black Resistance, Culture, and Identity Formation in Early America* (Baton Rouge: Louisiana State University Press, 2006), 17–58; Kwasi Konadu, *The Akan Diaspora in the Americas* (New York: Oxford University Press,

2010); Jessica A. Krug, "Social Dismemberment, Social (Re)membering: Obeah Idioms, Kromanti Identities, and the Transatlantic Politics of Memory, c. 1675–Present," *Slavery & Abolition* 35, no. 4 (2014): 537–558; Michael A. Gomez, *Exchanging Our Country Marks: The Transformation of African Identities in the Colonial and Antebellum South* (Chapel Hill: University of North Carolina Press, 1998), 88–113; Robert P. Stewart, "Akan Ethnicity in Jamaica: A Re-examination of Jamaica's Slave Imports from the Gold Coast, 1655–1807," *The Maryland Historian* (Fall 2003): 69–107; Douglas B. Chambers, "Ethnicity in the Diaspora: The Slave Trade and the Creation of African 'Nations' in the Americas," *Slavery and Abolition* 22, no. 3 (2001): 25–39; Robert Hanserd, *Identity, Spirit, and Freedom in the Atlantic World: The Gold Coast and the African Diaspora* (New York: Routledge, 2019); Amy Marie Johnson, "Expectations of Slavery: African Captives, White Planters, and Slave Rebelliousness in Early Colonial Jamaica," PhD diss., Duke University, 2007.

15. Rucker, *Gold Coast Diasporas,* 83–84; David DeCamp, "African Day-Names in Jamaica," *Language* 43 (1967): 139–149; Jerome S. Handler and JoAnn Jacoby, "Slave Names and Naming in Barbados, 1650–1830," *WMQ* 53, no. 4 (1996): 685–728; Trevor Burnard, "Slave Naming Patterns: Onomastics and the Taxonomy of Race in Eighteenth-century Jamaica," *Journal of Interdisciplinary History* 31, no. 3 (2001): 325–346; Margaret Williamson, "Africa or Old Rome? Jamaican Slave Naming Revisited," *Slavery and Abolition* 38, no. 1 (2017): 117–134.

16. Douglas B. Chambers, ed., *Runaway Slave Advertisements in Jamaica (I): Eighteenth Century* (February 2013): http://ufdcimages.uflib.ufl.edu/AA/00/02/11 /44/00001/JamaicaRunawaySlaves-18thCentury.pdf.

17. Knight, "Natural, Moral, and Political History of Jamaica," fol. 79.

18. E. Kofi Agorsah, "Spiritual Vibrations of Historic Kormantse and the Search for African Diaspora Identity and Freedom," in Akinwumi Ogundiran and Paula Sanders, eds., *Materialities of Ritual in the Black Atlantic* (Bloomington: Indiana University Press, 2014), 87–107.

19. "Müller's Description of the Fetu Country, 1662–1669," in Adam Jones, ed., *German Sources for West African History, 1599–1669* (Weisbaden: Steiner, 1983), quotations on 191, 192, 198; Robin Law, ed., *The English in West Africa, 1691–1699: The Local Correspondence of the Royal Africa Company of England, 1681–1699,* part 3 (Oxford: Oxford University Press, 2007), xiii.; Ray A. Kea, *Settlements, Trade, and Polities in the Seventeenth-Century Gold Coast* (Baltimore: Johns Hopkins University Press, 1982).

20. "Müller's Description of the Fetu Country," 198.

21. "Müller's Description of the Fetu Country," 197.

22. Willem Bosman, *A New and Accurate Description of the Coast of Guinea: Divided into the Gold, Slave, and Ivory Coasts* (London: J. Knapton [etc.], 1705), 181–184, quotations on 184, 182; also see John Thornton, *Warfare in Atlantic Africa, 1500–1800* (New York: Routledge, 1999), 55–74. On such exercises in other parts of Atlantic Africa, see especially T. J. Desh Obi, *Fighting for*

Honor: *The History of African Martial Art Traditions in the Atlantic World* (Columbia, SC: University of South Carolina Press, 2008), 17–76.

23. "Müller's Description of the Fetu Country," 196, quotation on 198.

24. Kea, *Settlements, Trade, and Polities,* 164.

25. Kea, *Settlements, Trade, and Polities;* Paul E. Lovejoy, *Transformations in Slavery: A History of Slavery in Africa,* Second ed. (Cambridge, UK: Cambridge University Press, 2000 [1983]), 57–58, 80–85; Stephanie E. Smallwood, *Saltwater Slavery: A Middle Passage from Africa to American Diaspora* (Cambridge, MA: Harvard University Press, 2007), 9–32; Kofi Affrifah, *The Akyem Factor in Ghana's History, 1700–1875* (Accra: Ghana Universities Press, 2000); K. Y. Daaku, *Trade and Politics on the Gold Coast, 1600–1720: A Study of the African Reaction to European Trade* (Oxford: Oxford University Press, 1970); J. K. Fynn, *Asante and Its Neighbours, 1700–1807* (London: Longman, 1971).

26. Bosman, *A New and Accurate Description of the Coast of Guinea,* 181.

27. Law, *English in West Africa,* part 3, xiii; Law, "The Kommenda Wars, 1694–1700: A Revised Narrative," *History in Africa* 34 (2007): 133–168; David Henige, "John Kabes of Komenda: An Early African Entrepreneur and State Builder," *Journal of African History* 18, no. 1 (1977): 1–19.

28. "Müller's Description of the Fetu Country," 193.

29. Bosman, *A New and Accurate Description of the Coast of Guinea,* 184.

30. K.Y. Daaku and Albert Van Dantzig, "Map of the Regions of the Gold Coast in Guinea," *Ghana Notes and Queries* 9 (1966), 14–15; Map of the Gold Coast from Assini to Alampi, 1729, in John Green, *A New General Collection of Voyages and Travels,* vol. 2 (London: Thomas Astley, 1745), plate 60, between 564 and 565; Map of the Gold Coast, TNA, Co West Africa 1744; Kea, *Settlements, Trade, and Polities,* 3.

31. Thornton, *Warfare in Atlantic Africa,* 56.

32. Bosman, *A New and Accurate Description of the Coast of Guinea,* 191, quotations on 149; Rucker, *Gold Coast Diasporas,* 90–91.

33. Rebecca Shumway, *The Fante and the Transatlantic Slave Trade* (Rochester, NY: University of Rochester Press, 2011), 89; J. K. Fynn, *Asante and Its Neighbours,* 87–88, 92–93; Thornton, *Warfare in Atlantic Africa,* 68; James Sanders, "The Expansion of the Fante and the Emergence of Asante in the Eighteenth Century," *Journal of African History* 20, no. 3 (1979): 349–364.

34. Rucker, *Gold Coast Diasporas,* 69–93.

35. Rucker, *Gold Coast Diasporas,* 75; Smallwood, *Saltwater Slavery,* 111–115.

36. Kea, *Settlements, Trade, and Polities,* 31–32; and Kea, "'I Am Here to Plunder on the General Road': Bandits and Banditry in the Pre-Nineteenth Century Gold Coast," in Donald Crummey, ed., *Banditry, Rebellion, and Social Protest in Africa* (London: J. Currey, 1986), 109–132.

37. Smallwood, *Saltwater Slavery,* 36, 54, quotation on 94.

38. *Voyages: The Transatlantic Slave Trade Database:* http://www.slavevoyages.org/voyages/FfK8grvk. See also Rucker, *Gold Coast Diasporas,* 97–100.

39. *Voyages: The Transatlantic Slave Trade Database:* http://www.slavevoyages.org/voyages/QmnEgJqI. Also see Rucker, *Gold Coast Diasporas,* 97–100; David

Eltis, *The Rise of African Slavery in the Americas* (Cambridge, UK: Cambridge University Press, 2000), 245–246.

40. *Voyages: The Transatlantic Slave Trade Database:* http://www.slavevoyages.org /estimates/P1xByeUh.

41. For comparison, see Manuel Barcia, *African Warfare in Bahia and Cuba: Soldier Slaves in the Atlantic World, 1807–1844* (Oxford: Oxford University Press, 2014), chap. 2.

42. Joanna Lipking, "The New World of Slavery—An Introduction," in Aphra Behn, *Oroonoko*, edited by Joanna Lipking (New York: Norton, 1997), 75–90; Thomas Southerne, *Oroonoko, a Tragedy* (London: T. Johnson, 1695); Janet Todd, *Aphra Behn: A Secret Life* (New Brunswick, NJ: Rutgers University Press, 1997); Wim Klooster, *The Dutch Moment: War, Trade, and Settlement in the Seventeenth-Century Atlantic World* (Ithaca: Cornell University Press, 2016), 104–106; Ramesh Mallipeddi, "Spectacle, Spectatorship, and Sympathy in Aphra Behn's Oroonoko," *Eighteenth-Century Studies* 5, no. 4 (2012): 475–496.

43. People from the Senegambia region had a reputation for rebelliousness as well. The great rebel *quilombos* of Brazil, like Palmares in Pernambuco, hosted a mix of peoples. Africans from Angola were responsible for the 1739 Stono Revolt in South Carolina and the slaves accused of setting a series of fires in New York in 1741 came from several places, including the Gold Coast. Thornton, *Warfare in Atlantic Africa*, 140–142; David Richardson, "Shipboard Revolts, African Authority and the Atlantic Slave Trade," *WMQ* 58, no. 1 (2001): 69–92, esp. 76–77, 86, 89. Jane Landers, "Leadership and Authority in Maroon Settlements in Spanish America and Brazil," in *Africa and the Americas: Interconnections during the Slave Trade,* ed. José C. Curto and Reneé Soulodre-La France (Trenton, NJ: Africa World Press, 2005), 173–184; John K. Thornton, "African Dimensions of the Stono Rebellion," *American Historical Review* 96, no. 4 (1991): 1101–1113; Jill Lepore, *New York Burning: Liberty, Slavery, and Conspiracy in Eighteenth-Century Manhattan* (New York: Knopf, 2005); Jessica A. Krug, *Fugitive Modernities: Kisama and the Politics of Freedom* (Durham, NC: Duke University Press, 2018), 146–163.

44. Jason T. Sharples, "Discovering Slave Conspiracies: New Fears of Rebellion and Old Paradigms of Plotting in Seventeenth-Century Barbados," *American Historical Review* 120, no. 3 (2015): 811–843, and Sharples, "The Flames of Insurrection: Fearing Slave Conspiracy in Early America, 1670–1780" (PhD diss., Princeton University, 2010).

45. *Great Newes from the Barbadoes, or, a True and Faithful Account of the Grand Conspiracy of the Negroes against the English and the Happy Discovery of the Same with the Number of Those That Were Burned Alive, Beheaded, and Otherwise Executed for Their Horrid Crimes: With a Short Description of That Plantation* (London: L. Curtis, 1676); Craton, *Testing the Chains: Resistance to Slavery in the British West Indies* (Ithaca, NY: Cornell University Press, 1982), 105–114; David Berry Gaspar, *Bondmen and Rebels: A Study of Master-Slave Relations in Antigua* (Baltimore, MD: John Hopkins University Press, 1985), 173–183; E. B. O'Callaghan, ed., *Documents Relative to the*

Colonial History of the State of New York (Albany: Weed, Parsons, 1858), V: 341; John Sharpe, "The Negro Plot of 1712," *The New York Genealogical and Biographical Record* 21 (1890): 162–163; Rucker, "Only Draw in Your Countrymen," 94–97.

46. William Snelgrave, *A new account of some parts of Guinea, I. The history of the late conquest of Whidaw by the king of Dahomey. II The manner how the negroes become slaves III. A relation of the author's being taken by pirates* (London: P. Knapton, 1734), 168–185, quotations on 170, 178, 185; Voyage 76398, *Henry* (1722), *Voyages: The Transatlantic Slave Trade Database*: http://www.slavevoyages.org/voyage/76398/variables.

47. David Barry Gaspar, "A Dangerous Spirit of Liberty: Slave Rebellion in the West Indies in the 1730s," in Laurent Dubois and Julius S. Scott, eds., *Origins of the Black Atlantic* (New York: Routledge, 2010), 11–25; Pierre J. Pannet, *Report on the Execrable Conspiracy Carried Out by the Amina Negroes on the Danish Island of St. Jan in America, 1733*, trans. & ed. Aimery P. Caron and Arnold R. Highfield (Christansted: Antilles Press, 1984), 1–23; Ray A. Kea, "'When I die, I shall return to my own land': An 'Amina' Slave Rebellion in the Danish West Indies, 1733–1734," in John Hunwick and Nancy Lawler, eds., *The Cloth of Many Colored Silks: Papers on History and Society Ghanaian and Islamic in Honour of Ivor Wilks* (Evanston, Ill: Northwestern University Press, 1996), 159–193; Sandra E. Greene, "From Whence They Came: A Note on the Influence of West African Ethnic and Gender Relations on the Organizational Character of the 1733 St. John Slave Rebellion," in George F. Tyson and Arnold R. Highfield, eds. *The Danish West Indian Slave Trade: Virgin Islands Perspectives* (St. Croix: Virgin Islands Humanities Council, 1994), 47–67; Rucker, *Gold Coast Diasporas,* 147–150. On the provenance of the "Aminas," see Gwendolyn Midlo Hall, "African Ethnicities and the Meanings of 'Mina'" in Paul E. Lovejoy and David R. Trotman, eds., *Trans-Atlantic Dimensions of Ethnicity in the African Diaspora* (London: Bloomsbury, 2003), 65–81; and Robin Law, "Ethnicities of Enslaved Africans in the Diaspora: On the Meanings of 'Mina' (Again)," *History in Africa* 32 (2005): 247–267.

48. Gaspar, *Bondmen and Rebels*; Thornton, "The Coromantees," 170–172; Rucker, *Gold Coast Diaspporas,* 108–111; Justin Pope, "Dangerous Spirit of Liberty: Slave Rebellion, Conspiracy, and the First Great Awakening, 1729–1746" (PhD diss., The George Washington University, 2014); James F. Dator, "Search for a New Land: Imperial Power and Afro-Creole Resistance in the British Leeward Islands, 1624–1745" (PhD diss., University of Michigan, 2011), 311–353; Jason T. Sharples, "Hearing Whispers, Casting Shadows: Jailhouse Conversation and the Production of Knowledge during the Antigua Slave Conspiracy of 1736," in Michele Lise Tarter and Richard Bell, eds., *Buried Lives: Incarcerated in Early America* (Athens, GA: University of Georgia Press, 2012), 35–59.

49. On the slave trade from Jamaica to Cartagena, see especially Colin A. Palmer, *Human Cargoes: The British Slave Trade to Spanish America, 1700–1739* (Urbana: University of Illinois Press, 1981); Jane Landers, "*Cimarrón* Ethnicity and Cultural Adaptation in the Spanish Domains of the Circum-Caribbean,

1503–1763," in *Identity in the Shadow of Slavery*, ed. Paul E. Lovejoy (London: Continuum, 2000), 30–54; Landers, "Leadership and Authority in Maroon Settlements in Spanish America and Brazil," 173–184.

50. Richard Price, *To Slay the Hydra: Dutch Colonial Perspectives on the Saramaka Wars* (Ann Arbor, MI: Karoma, 1983); Wim S. M. Hoogenbergen, "Marronage and Slave Rebellions in Suriname," in Wolfgang Binder, ed., *Slavery in the Americas* (Würzburg, Germany: Konigshausen & Neumann, 1993), 165–195.

51. Quotations in Craton, *Testing the Chains*, 99–100, and Rucker, *Gold Coast Diasporas*, 13–17. Also see Konadu, *Akan Diaspora in the Americas*.

52. "Governor Codrington to the Council of Trade and Plantations, December 30, 1701," in *Calendar of State Papers, Colonial Series*, vol. 19, no. 1132, 720.

53. Here my emphasis differs from the important recent analysis of historian Walter Rucker in *Gold Coast Diasporas*, esp. 107, 114, 122–123.

54. Stephanie E. Smallwood, "African Guardians, European Slave Ships, and the Changing Dynamics of Power in the Early Modern Atlantic," *WMQ* 64.4 (October 2007): 679–716.

55. Here I am following the suggestion by Jessica Krug that oath-taking strategies anchored a political logic of community building. See Krug, "Social Dismemberment, Social (Re)membering."

56. Edward Long quoted in *The Proceedings of the Governor and Assembly of Jamaica, in regard to the Maroon Negroes . . .* (London: J. Stockdale, 1796), xxvii; Robert Hanserd, "Okomfo Anokye Formed a Tree to Hide from the Akwamu: Priestly Power, Freedom, and Enslavement in the Afro-Atlantic," *Atlantic Studies* (March 2015): 1–23.

57. On oath-taking among Africans and their descendants in Jamaica, see Charles Leslie, *A New and Exact Account of Jamaica* (Edinburgh: R. Fleming, 1740), 324; Edward Long, *History of Jamaica*, 2: 422–423; Kenneth Bilby, "Swearing by the Past, Swearing to the Future: Sacred Oaths, Alliances, and Treaties among the Guianese and Jamaican Maroons," *Ethnohistory* 44:4 (Fall 1997): 655–689; Rucker, *Gold Coast Diasporas*, 90–92, 180–185; Krug, "Social Dismemberment, Social (Re)membering;" and Michael Mullin, *Africa in America: Slave Acculturation and Resistance in the American South and the British Caribbean, 1736–1831* (Urbana: University of Illinois Press, 1992), 62–75. For comparison with British practice, see Miles Ogborn, "The Power of Speech: Orality, Oaths, and Evidence in the British Atlantic World, 1650–1800," *Transactions of the Institute of British Geographers* 36: 1 (2011): 109–125.

58. David Eltis, David Richardson, et. al., *Atlas of the Transatlantic Slave Trade* (New Haven: Yale University Press, 2010), Map 132, 190.

59. Mullin, *Africa in America*, 289–291.

60. Knight, "Natural, Moral, and Political History of Jamaica," fols. 89–91. Also see Bev Carey, *The Maroon Story: The Authentic and Original History of the Maroons in the History of Jamaica, 1490–1880* (Gordon Town, Jamaica: Agouti Press, 1997) and Helen McKee, "From Violence to Alliance: Maroons and White Settlers in Jamaica, 1739–1795," *Slavery and Abolition* 39, no. 1 (2018): 27–52.

61. Knight, "Natural, Moral, and Political History of Jamaica," fol. 91.

62. David Buisseret, ed., *Jamaica in 1687: The Taylor Manuscript at the National Library of Jamaica* (Kingston: University of the West Indies Press, 2008), 274–279; Craton, *Testing the Chains*, 76.

63. Knight, "Natural, Moral, and Political History of Jamaica," fol. 91.

64. Knight, "Natural, Moral, and Political History of Jamaica," fols. 91, 93.

65. Knight, "Natural, Moral, and Political History of Jamaica," fol. 92.

66. Knight, "Natural, Moral, and Political History of Jamaica," fol. 92.

67. As quoted in Orlando Patterson, "Slavery and Slave Revolts: A Sociohistorical Analysis of the First Maroon War, 1665–1740," in Richard Price, ed. *Maroon Societies: Rebel Slave Communities in the Americas* (Baltimore: Johns Hopkins University Press, 1979), 234.

68. Robert C. Dallas, *The History of the Maroons from their Origin to the Establishment of Their Chief Tribe at Sierra Leone,* 2 Volumes (London: Longman and Rees, 1803), 1: 83; Kenneth M. Bilby, *True-Born Maroons* (Gainesville, FL: Florida University Press, 2005), 99.

69. Knight, "Natural, Moral, and Political History of Jamaica," fol. 93. See also Werner Zips, *Black Rebels: African Caribbean Freedom Fighters in Jamaica* (Kingston: University of the West Indies Press, 1999) and Zips, "Obscured by Colonial Stories: An Alternative Historical Outline of Akan-Related Chieftaincy in Jamaican Maroon Societies," in E. Adriaan B. van Rouverory van Nieuwaal and Rijk Van Dijk, eds., *African Chieftaincy in a New Socio-Political Landscape* (Hamburg: Lit Verlag, 1999), 207–239.

70. Mervyn Alleyne, *Roots of Jamaican Culture* (London: Pluto, 1989 [1988]), 120–130.

71. Knight, "Natural, Moral, and Political History of Jamaica," fols. 93–94.

72. Bilby, *True-Born Maroons*, 79–87.

73. I. Lewis to James Knight, Westmoreland, 20 Dec 1743, BL Add. ms. 12431, fol. 99. I am grateful to Diana Paton for bringing this reference to my attention.

74. Craton, *Testing the Chains*, 81–82; Barbara Kopytoff, "The Development of Jamaican Maroon Ethnicity," *Caribbean Quarterly* 22, nos. 2–3 (1976): 33–50; Philip Thicknesse, *Memoirs and Anecdotes of Philip Thicknesse Late Lieutenant Governor, Land Guard Fort, and Unfortunately Father to George Touchet, Baron Audley* (Dublin: William Jones, 1788), 120–121; Bilby, *True-Born Maroons*, 99, 182–213.

75. Kofi Agorsah, "Archaeology of Maroon Settlements in Jamaica," in Agorsah, ed., *Maroon Heritage: Archaeological, Ethnographic, and Historical Perspectives* (Barbados: Canoe, 1994), 163–187.

76. Knight, "Natural, Moral, and Political History of Jamaica," fol. 89–90.

77. Knight, "Natural, Moral, and Political History of Jamaica," fol. 92.

78. Knight, "Natural, Moral, and Political History of Jamaica," fol. 94.

79. Edward Trelawny as quoted in Barbara Klamon Kopytoff, "Guerilla Warfare in Eighteenth Century Jamaica," *Expedition* 19, no. 2 (1977): 23.

80. Knight, "Natural, Moral, and Political History of Jamaica," fol. 94.

81. Knight, "Natural, Moral, and Political History of Jamaica," fol. 94.

82. Kopytoff, "Guerilla Warfare," 24; Rucker, *Gold Coast Diasporas*, 155.

83. Dallas, *The History of the Maroons*, 1, 89.

84. Rucker, *Gold Coast Diasporas,* 155.

85. John Gabriel Stedman, *Narrative of a Five Years Expedition against the Revolted Negroes of Surinam. Transcribed for the First Time from the Original 1790 Manuscript,* Richard Price and Sally Price, eds. (Baltimore: Johns Hopkins University Press, 2010 [1988]), 397–398.

86. As quoted in Patterson, "Slavery and Slave Revolts," 263.

87. Craton, *Testing the Chains,* 83; As quoted in Patterson, "Slavery and Slave Revolts," 265.

88. Pope, "Dangerous Spirit of Liberty," 152–153; As quoted in Kopytoff, "Guerilla Warfare," 21.

89. Pope, "Dangerous Spirit of Liberty," 152–153, 156–157.

90. Craton, *Testing the Chains,* 85; Knight, "Natural, Moral, and Political History of Jamaica," fols. 94–95.

91. Knight, "Natural, Moral, and Political History of Jamaica," fol. 107.

92. George Metcalf, *Royal Government and Political Conflict in Jamaica, 1729–1783* (London: Longmans, 1965), 61–62; Craton, *Testing the Chains,* 87; Patterson, "Slavery and Slave Revolts," 267–268; Bilby, *True-Born Maroons,* 261–273.

93. Kenneth Morgan, "Trelawny, Edward (*bap.* 1699, *d.* 1754), colonial governor," *Oxford Dictionary of National Biography* (online edn., 2008): http://www.oxforddnb.com/index/101027686/Edward-Trelawny.

94. Beatrice Heuser, *The Strategy Makers: Thoughts on War and Society from Machiavelli to Clausewitz* (Santa Barbara, CA: Praeger, 2010), chap. 7. I am grateful to David Krueger for bringing this reference to my attention.

95. Knight, "Natural, Moral, and Political History of Jamaica," fol. 96.

96. Craton, *Testing the Chains,* 88–92; Zips, *Black Rebels,* chap. 4; Bilby, *True-Born Maroons,* chap. 8.

97. Dallas, *History of the Maroons,* 1, 58–65, 75–77; Barbara Kopytoff, "Colonial Treaty as Sacred Charter of the Jamaican Maroons," *Ethnohistory* 26, No. 1 (Winter 1979): 45–64; Kathleen Wilson, "The Performance of Freedom: Maroons and the Colonial Order in Eighteenth-Century Jamaica and the Atlantic Sound," *WMQ* 66, no. 1 (2009): 45–86; and Wilson, "Rethinking the Colonial State: Family, Gender, and Governmentality in Eighteenth-Century British Frontiers," *American Historical Review* 116, no. 5 (2011); Craton, *Testing the Chains,* 91.

98. Knight, "Natural, Moral, and Political History of Jamaica," fol. 77.

99. *Journals of the Assembly of Jamaica,* Vol. 3 (May 1, 1742), 594; Krug, "Social Dismemberment, Social (Re)membering," 546–547.

100. *Boston Evening Post,* April 1, 1745; *Pennsylvania Gazette,* April 12, 1745; Trelawny to Newcastle, December 20, 1744, TNA, CO 137/57, 106; Pope, "Dangerous Spirit of Liberty," 160–162.

101. *JAJ,* Vol. 4 (April 23, 1746), 27.

102. Anonymous, *An Essay Concerning Slavery and the Danger Jamaica is expos'd to from the Too great Number of Slaves, and the too little Care that is taken to manage Them, and a Proposal to prevent the further Importation of Negroes into that Island* (London: C. Corbett, 1746), 46.

103. *JAJ*, Vol. 3 (December 20, 1744), 673, 671.

104. Anonymous, *An Essay Concerning Slavery*, 21, 46; "Extract of a Private Letter from a gentleman in Jamaica, dated in St David's Parish, Nov. 18 1745," *American Weekly Mercury*, January 21, 1746; Map of the County of Surrey, 1763, TNA, CO700-JAMAICA 19.

105. "Extract of a Private Letter."

106. Zips, *Black Rebels*, 242.

107. Lieutenant's logbook for HMS *Wager*, February 26, 1746, NMM, ADM/L/W/3.

108. J. W. Fortesque, *A History of the British Army* (London: Macmillan, 1899), 2: 39–40, 300, 372; Edward Trelawny to Duke of Newcastle, December 20, 1744, TNA, CO 137/57, 106.

109. Trelawny to Newcastle, December 20, 1744, TNA, CO 137/57, 106–107.

110. Anonymous, *An Essay Concerning Slavery*, i–ii. For attribution to Trelawny, see Peter C. Hogg, *The African Slave Trade and its Suppression: A Classified and Annotated Bibliography of Books Pamphlets and Periodical Articles* (London: Frank Cass & Co., 1973), 140.

111. Anonymous, *An Essay Concerning Slavery*, iii, 10–15.

112. Anonymous, *An Essay Concerning Slavery*, vi.

113. Anonymous, *An Essay Concerning Slavery*, 18.

114. Anonymous, *An Essay Concerning Slavery*, v–vi.

115. Anonymous, *An Essay Concerning Slavery*, 35.

116. Anonymous, *An Essay Concerning Slavery*, 45.

117. Anonymous, *An Essay Concerning Slavery*, 18, iii.

118. Anonymous, *An Essay Concerning Slavery*, 45–46.

119. Trevor Burnard, *Mastery, Tyranny, and Desire: Thomas Thistlewood and His Slaves in the Anglo-Jamaican World* (Chapel Hill: University of North Carolina Press, 2004), 37–68.

120. Anonymous, *An Essay Concerning Slavery*, 44.

121. Anonymous, *An Essay Concerning Slavery*, 55.

122. *Journals of the Jamaica House of Assembly*, Vol. 4 (April 11, 1746), 15.

123. James Robertson, "An Essay Concerning Slavery: A Mid-Eighteenth Century Analysis from Jamaica," *Slavery and Abolition* 33, no. 1 (2012): 65–85; Trevor Burnard, "Slavery and the Causes of the American Revolution in Plantation British America," in Andrew Shankman, ed., *The World of the Revolutionary American Republic: Land, Labor, and the Conflict for a Continent* (Abingdon: Routledge, 2014), 54–76, esp. 58–59; Anonymous, *An Essay Concerning Slavery*, v.

124. Charles Knowles to Board of Trade, March 26, 1753, TNA, CO 137/25, 312–313.

125. Campbell, *Maroons of Jamaica*, 166.

126. Knowles to Board of Trade, March 12, 1754, TNA, CO137/27, 146–147; Campbell, *Maroons of Jamaica*, 169; Metcalf, *Royal Government and Political Society*, 115.

127. Knowles to Board of Trade, March 12, 1754, TNA, CO137/27, 146–147. Also see *The Gentlemen's Magazine*, Vol. 24 (June 1754), 290.

128. Mark Hall to Rose Fuller, October 21, 1755, SAS-RF 21/35.

129. Metcalf, *Royal Government and Political Conflict,* 121–136; James Robertson, *Gone is the Ancient Glory: Spanish Town, Jamaica, 1534–2000* (Kingston: University of the West Indies Press, 2005), 89–93; Jack P. Greene, "'Of Liberty and the Colonies': A Case Study of Constitutional Conflict in the Mid-Eighteenth-Century British American Empire," in *Creating the British Atlantic: Essays on Transplantation, Adaptation, and Continuity* (Charlottesville: University of Virginia Press, 2013), 140–207.

130. Metcalf, *Royal Government and Political Conflict,* 134.

131. Robertson, *Gone is the Ancient Glory,* 93.

132. Diary of Brother Zacharias George Caries's Voyage to Jamaica, March 27, 1755, Moravian Church Archive and Library, London.

133. Campbell, *Maroons of Jamaica,* 251–252.

134. Thornton, *Warfare in Atlantic Africa,* 68.

135. Caries Diary, June 21 and July 9, 1756.

136. *Voyages: The Transatlantic Slave Trade Database:* http://www.slavevoyages.org/estimates/Vo8qdQk4.

4. Tacky's Revolt

1. Metcalf, *Royal Government and Political Society,* 148; Haldane to Board of Trade, June 2, 1759, TNA, CO 137/30.

2. Zachary Bayly to Rose Fuller, Kingston, July 23, 1759, Fuller Papers, SAS-RF Folder 21-Uncatalogued.

3. Edward Long, *The History of Jamaica: Reflections on its Settlements, Inhabitants, Climate, Products, Commerce, Laws, and Government,* 3 Vols. (London: T. Lowndes, 1774), 2: 75–76.

4. "Extract of a Letter from a Gentleman at St. Mary, April 14, 1760," *The Pennsylvania Gazette,* June 5, 1760; Long, *History of Jamaica,* 2: 448; *The Modern Part of an Universal History, from the Earliest Account of Time Compiled from Original Writers,* 65 vols. (London: T. Osborne [etc.], 1764), 41: 455.

5. "Letter from a Gentleman at St. Mary." This letter is probably excerpted from one that Zachary Bayly wrote to his brother Nathaniel in London. An associate wrote that Bayly "Escaped & has wrote a very long Letter to his Brother giving a full History of this St. Marys affair." Francis Treble to Caleb Dickinson, June 2, 1760, Somerset Record Office, Caleb Dickinson Letters DD\DN/218.

6. Bryan Edwards, *The History, Civil and Commercial, of the British West Indies,* 5th ed., 5 vols. (London: G. and W.B. Whittaker, 1819 [1793]), vol. 2, 75–76; "Letter from a Gentleman at St. Mary."

7. Waldemar Westergaard, "Account of the Negro Rebellion on St. Croix, Danish West Indies, 1759," *Journal of Negro History* 11, no. 1 (1926): 50–61.

8. Long, *History of Jamaica,* 2: 74.

9. Quotations in Edwards, *History of the West Indies,* 2: 76–77; Also see Long *History of Jamaica,* 2: 448; Francis Treble to Caleb Dickinson, Kingston, June 2, 1760, SRO, Caleb Dickinson Letters DD\DN/218.

10. Pierre Eugène du Simitière, "Remarks on Extracts from Works about Uprisings of Negroes against Whites in Jamaica," Library Company of Philadelphia, Pierre Eugène du Simitière Collection, Box 4, Folders 20a–21, 178.

11. Edwards, *History of the West Indies,* 2: 78.

12. Emmanuel Akyeampong, *Drink, Power, and Cultural Change: A Social History of Alcohol in Ghana, c. 1800 to Recent Times* (Portsmouth, NH: Heinemann, 1996), 5, 10–14, 22–23, 28; Hugo Huber, *The Krobo: Traditional Social and Religious Life of a West African People* (St. Augustin, Germany: Anthropos Institute, 1963), 268; Michael Mullin, *Africa in America: Slave Acculturation and Resistance in the American South and the British Caribbean, 1736–1831* (Urbana: University of Illinois Press, 1992), 67–68.

13. Long, *History of Jamaica,* 2: 448–449; du Simitière, "Remarks on Uprisings of Negroes," 179–180.

14. Du Simitière, "Remarks on Uprisings of Negroes," 179.

15. Du Simitière, "Remarks on Uprisings of Negroes," 179–180. One news item printed in August 1760 differs from the account presented here, which I have drawn primarily from Eugène du Simitière, who relied on Gordon's memory of the attack. See "Notice from Jamaica," May 8, *Cork Evening Post,* August 11, 1760.

16. Long, *History of Jamaica,* 2: quotation on 449.

17. Du Simitière, "Remarks on Uprisings of Negroes," 180; It is likely that Edward Long confused Gordon with his uncle the doctor, described in Long, *History of Jamaica,* 2: 449.

18. Edwards, *History of the West Indies,* 2: 75–76.

19. Edwards, *History of the West Indies,* 2: 78.

20. Eugene Genovese, *From Rebellion to Revolution: Afro-American Slave Revolts and the Making of the Modern World* (Baton Rouge: Louisiana State University Press, 1979), 11.

21. Sheila Lambert, ed., *House of Commons Sessional Papers of the Eighteenth Century,* 147 vols. (Wilmington, DE: Scholarly Resources, 1975), 82: 56; Long, *History of Jamaica,* 2: quotation on 449. On wartime rape as a method of creating cohesion within small groups, see Dara Kay Cohen, *Rape During Civil War* (Ithaca: Cornell University Press, 2016).

22. "Letter from a Gentleman at St. Mary"; Long, *History of Jamaica,* 2: 449.

23. "Letter from a Gentleman at St. Mary"; Long, *History of Jamaica,* 2: quotation on 449; Edwards, *History of the West Indies,* 2: 77. For comparison, see John Thornton, "African Dimensions of the Stono Rebellion," *The American Historical Review* 96, no. 4 (1991): 1101–1113.

24. First quotation in Lambert, ed., *House of Commons Sessional Papers,* 69: 217; Second quotation in Long, *History of Jamaica,* 2: 451. "Answers returned the 12th of April 1788 by Messrs. Fuller, Long, and Chisolme to the Questions put to them by their Lordships respecting the practice of Obeah in the Island of Jamaica," TNA, BT 6/10, 180–181; "Answer received from Mr. Fuller to the Question sent to him by their Lordships order on the 12th of April 1788," TNA, BT 6/10, 524–526. See also Diana Paton, *The Cultural Politics of Obeah: Religion, Colonialism and Modernity in the Caribbean World* (Cambridge, UK:

Cambridge University Press, 2015), 17–42; Jerome S. Handler and Kenneth M. Bilby, *Enacting Power: The Criminalization of Obeah in the Anglophone Caribbean, 1760–2011* (Kingston: University of the West Indies Press, 2013).

25. For comparison, see Thornton, *Warfare in Atlantic Africa,* 69–73; Manuel Barcia, *West African Warfare in Bahia and Cuba: Soldier Slaves in the Atlantic World, 1807–1844* (Oxford: Oxford University Press, 2014), 121–129.

26. Rucker, *Gold Coast Diasporas,* 95.

27. Rucker, *Gold Coast Diasporas,* 173; Long, *History of Jamaica,* 2: quotation on 447.

28. Rucker, *Gold Coast Diasporas,* 172–174.

29. Letter from Pemberton Valley, June 2, 1760, Ayrshire Record Office, Hamilton Papers, AA/DC/17/113.

30. Francis Treble to Caleb Dickinson, June 2, 1760, Somerset Record Office, Caleb Dickinson Letters, DD\DN/218.

31. "Letter from a Gentleman at St. Mary."

32. Jamaica House of Assembly, December 1760, TNA, CO 140/40, quotation on 232; Long, *History of Jamaica,* 2: quotation on 449.

33. "Letter from a Gentleman at St. Mary"; Long, *History of Jamaica,* 2: 448; Edwards, *History of the West Indies,* 2: quotation on 77.

34. Long, *History of Jamaica,* 2: 449–450.

35. "Letter from a Gentleman at St. Mary."

36. Long, *History of Jamaica,* 2: 450; Jamaica House of Assembly, December 1760, TNA, CO 140/40, 232.

37. Lambert, ed., *House of Commons Sessional Papers,* 69: 220–221.

38. Long, *History of Jamaica,* 2: 450.

39. Edwards, *History of the West Indies,* 2: 77.

40. Long, *History of Jamaica,* 2: 450; Jamaica House of Assembly, December 1760, TNA, CO 140/40, 232; Long, *History of Jamaica,* 2: 232; Map of Jamaica, TNA, CO 700/16.

41. Jamaica Council, April 10, 1760, enclosed in Henry Moore to BT, April 19, 1760, TNA, CO 137/60, fols. 296–297.

42. Jamaica Council, April 10, 1760, quotation on fol. 296.

43. Jamaica Council, April 10, 1760, fol. 296

44. Jamaica Council, April 10, 1760, fol. 296.

45. Francis Treble to Caleb Dickinson, Kingston, June 2, 1760, SRO, Caleb Dickinson Letters DD/DN/218.

46. Du Simitière, "Remarks on Uprisings of Negroes," 188.

47. Robert Graham to Nicol Graham, June 16, 1760, National Library of Scotland, Robert Graham Papers, Acc. 11335/177.

48. "Notice from Jamaica," May 8, *Cork Evening Post,* August 11, 1760.

49. Jamaica Council, April 10, 1760 and April 17, 1760, TNA, CO 137/60, fol. 297.

50. Jamaica Council, April 17, 1760.

51. Jamaica Council, April 17, 1760.

52. Lambert, ed., *House of Commons Sessional Papers,* 69: 217–221, quotations on 217, 221; Long, *History of Jamaica,* 2: 452; "Answer received from Mr. Fuller

to the Question sent to him by their Lordships order on the 12th of April 1788," TNA, BT 6/10, 525–528; Ray A. Kea, *A Cultural and Social History of Ghana from the Seventeenth to the Nineteenth Century: The Gold Coast in the Age of Trans-Atlantic Slave Trade,* 2 Vols. (Lempeter: Edwin Mellen, 2012), 1: 277; Robin Law, "Fante 'Origins': The Problematic Evidence of 'Tradition'," in Toby Green and Benedetta Rossi, eds., *Landscapes, Sources, and Intellectual Projects of the West African Past* (Boston: Brill, 2018), 128–129; Rebecca Shumway, *The Fante and the Transatlantic Slave Trade* (Rochester: University of Rochester Press, 2011), 138–141.

53. "Letter from a Gentleman at St. Mary."

54. "Letter from a Gentleman at St. Mary."

55. This region is the site of a descent known as Tacky Falls, which can be accessed "only via a very steep, slippery, heavily overgrown tract." Oral tradition holds that "at the edge of the ravine, there are caves under the huge rocks which lead to a clear cool underground lake ... where Tacky was able to hide from the British" and conduct his assaults. Joan Williams, "The Historic Tacky Falls," *The Jamaica Gleaner,* August 3, 2014: http://jamaica-gleaner.com/gleaner/20140803/arts/arts3.html.

56. Patrick Browne, "A New Map of Jamaica, In which the Several Towns, Forts, and Settlements are Accurately laid down as well as ye situations & depts. Of ye most noted Harbours & Anchoring Places, w:th the limits & boundarys of the Different Parishes as they have been regulated by Laws or settled by Custom; the greatest part Drawn or Corrected from actual Surveys Made by Mr. Sheffield and others, from the Year 1730 to the Year 1749" (London: publisher unknown, 1755). Downes's Cove, later called Forster's Cove when described by a geologist in the early nineteenth century. H. T. De la Beche, "Remarks on the Geology of Jamaica," *Transactions of the Geological Society* s2-2, no. 2 (1827): 143–194, Forster's Cove described on 148–149.

57. Letter from a Gentleman at St. Mary.

58. Long, *History of Jamaica,* 2: quotations on 457; "Letter from a Gentleman at St. Mary"; du Simitière, "Remarks on Uprisings of Negroes," 184.

59. "Letter from a Gentleman at St. Mary"; Long, *History of Jamaica,* 2: 451; Craton, *Testing the Chains,* 131; Edwards, *History of the West Indies,* 2: 361–362.

60. "Letter from a Gentleman at St. Mary."

61. "Letter from a Gentleman at St. Mary"; Long, *History of Jamaica,* 2: quotation on 457.

62. "Letter from a Gentleman at St. Mary."

63. "Letter from a Gentleman at St. Mary."

64. "Notice from Jamaica," May 8, *Cork Evening Post,* August 11, 1760; Long, *History of Jamaica,* 2: 457–458.

65. Du Simitière, "Remarks on Uprisings of Negroes," 184; Long, *History of Jamaica,* II, 458.

66. "Letter from a Gentleman at St. Mary."

67. Long, *History of Jamaica,* 2: 458; Manuscript insertion into Long's own copy of his *History of Jamaica,* BL, Add. ms. 12405, fol. 365r, cited in Miles Og-

born, *Freedom of Speech: Talk and Slavery in the Anglo-Caribbean World* (Chicago: University of Chicago Press, 2018), epilogue, n.19.

68. Jamaica Council, April 17, 1760, TNA, CO 137/60, fols. 297–299, quotations on 298.

69. Jamaica Council, April 17, 1760, TNA, CO 137/60, fols. 297–299, quotations on 298, 299, 299.

70. Cotes to Admiralty, April 19, 1760, TNA, ADM 1/235.

71. HMS *Marlborough* Lieutenant's Log, Thomas Hayward, April 10, 1760, NMM, ADM/L/M/48.

72. Master's Log for HMS *Marlborough,* Robert Thompson, Sunday, April 13, 1760, TNA, ADM 52/937; Also see Lt. John Leano, April 13, 1760, NMM, ADM/L/M/48; Thomas Hayward, April 13, 1760, NMM, ADM/L/M/48.

73. Jamaica Council, April 17, 1760, TNA, CO 137/60, fol. 298.

74. HMS *Lively* Lieutenant's Log, Lt. Thomas Hicks, April 24–25, 1760, NMM, ADM/L/L/157.

75. HMS *Port Antonio* Captain's Log, April 24–26, 1760, TNA, ADM 51/717.

76. HMS *Lively* Lieutenant's Log, Lt. Thomas Hicks April 26, 1760, NMM, ADM/L/L/157; HMS *Port Antonio* Captain's Log, Capt. John Lewis Gidion, April 30, 1760, TNA, ADM 51/717.

77. HMS *Lively* Lieutenant's Log, Lt. Thomas Hicks, April 26, 1760, NMM, ADM/L/L/157.

78. HMS *Lively* Musters, April 1, 1760 to May 31, 1761, TNA, ADM 36/6003, fols. 30–31.

79. For important revisions of the conventional view on women in slave revolts, see Thavolia Glymph, "Rose's War and the Gendered Politics of a Slave Insurgency in the Civil War," *The Journal of the Civil War Era* 3, no. 4 (2013): 501–533; Aisha K. Finch, *Slave Rebellion in Cuba: La Escalera and the Insurgencies of 1841–1844* (Chapel Hill: University of North Carolina Press, 2015); and Rucker, *Gold Coast Diasporas,* ch. 6.

80. I am grateful for the consultation of Emmanuel Akyeampong on the list of names, personal communication, May 25, 2016.

81. HMS *Lively* Musters, April 1, 1760 to May 31, 1761, TNA, ADM 36/6003, fols. 30–31; Trevor Burnard, "Slave Naming Patterns: Onomastics and the Taxonomy of Race in Eighteenth-Century Jamaica," *Journal of Interdisciplinary History,* XXXI, 3 (Winter 2001): 325–346.

82. HMS *Lively* Lieutenant's Log, Lt. Thomas Hicks, April 26, 1760, NMM, ADM/L/L/157; "A List of French Prisoners," HMS *Lively* Musters, April 1, 1760 to May 31, 1761, TNA, ADM 36/6003, fols. 29–30. For HMS *Lively*'s specifications, see "The Present Disposal of His Majesty's Ships and Vessels in Sea Pay," TNA, ADM 8/35.

83. "Notice from Kingston, Jamaica," April 19, *Pennsylvania Gazette,* June 5, 1760.

84. Du Simitière, "Remarks on Uprisings of Negroes," 183–184.

85. Rucker, *Gold Coast Diasporas,* 39, 156.

86. "Notice from Kingston, Jamaica, April 19," *Pennsylvania Gazette,* June 5, 1760.

87. HMS *Marlborough* Lieutenant's Log, April 18, 1760, NMM, ADM/L/M/48.

88. Diary of Mesopotamia, April 19, 1760, UA R.15.C.b.1 (3); Diary of Bogue, April 19, 1760, UA R.15.C.b.2 (1).

89. Du Simitière, "Remarks on Uprisings of Negroes," 184.

90. "Notice from Jamaica, May 8," *Cork Evening Post,* August 11, 1760.

91. Quotations in "Notice from Jamaica," May 8, *Cork Evening Post,* August 11, 1760; See also Du Simitière, "Remarks on Uprisings of Negroes," 184.

92. Du Simitière, Remarks on Uprisings of Negroes, 184; "Notice from Jamaica, May 8," *Cork Evening Post,* August 11, 1760.

93. Du Simitière, "Remarks on Uprisings of Negroes," 184.

94. First quotation, Francis Treble to Caleb Dickinson, Kingston, June 2, 1760, Somerset Record Office, Caleb Dickinson Letters DD\DN/218; Second quotation, "Notice from Jamaica, May 21," *Cork Evening Post,* August 11, 1760.

95. Edwards, *History of the West Indies,* 2: 79.

96. First quotation, Francis Treble to Caleb Dickinson, Kingston, Jamaica, June 2, 1760, Somerset Record Office, Caleb Dickinson Letters DD\DN/218; Second quotation in Long, *History of Jamaica,* 2: 458n.

97. Du Simitière, "Remarks on Uprisings of Negroes," 184.

98. Quoted from Long, *History of Jamaica,* 2: 458n.

99. Edwards, *History of the West Indies,* 2: 79.

100. Richard Price, "Dialogical Encounters in a Space of Death," in John Smolenski and Thomas J. Humphrey, eds., *New World Orders: Violence, Sanction, and Authority in the Colonial Americas* (Philadelphia: University of Pennsylvania Press, 2005), 47–65.

101. Lambert, ed., *House of Commons Sessional Papers,* 69: 219; Vincent Brown, "Spiritual Terror and Sacred Authority: Supernatural Power in Jamaican Slave Society," in Stephanie Camp and Edward E. Baptist, eds., *New Studies in the History of American Slavery* (Athens, GA: University of Georgia Press, 2006), 179–210.

102. "Notice from April 22," *Gentleman's Magazine 30* (June 1760): 294.

103. Moore to Sec. of State, Duplicate of a Letter sent April 24, 1760, TNA, CO 137/60, fol. 300.

104. "Notice from Jamaica," May 8, *Cork Evening Post,* August 11, 1760.

105. Francis Treble to Caleb Dickinson, Kingston, June 2, 1760, SRO, Caleb Dickinson Letters DD\DN/218.

106. "Notice from Jamaica, May 21," *Cork Evening Post,* August 11, 1760; quotation in Long, *History of Jamaica,* 2: 457.

107. Long, *History of Jamaica,* 2: 455.

108. "Notice from Jamaica, May 21," *Cork Evening Post,* August 11, 1760; Long, *History of Jamaica,* 2, 455; Henry Moore to Board of Trade, Spanish Town, June 9, 1760, TNA, CO 137/32, fols. 7–8; Minutes of Council of July 14, 1760, relating to the Rebellion of the Slaves, enclosed in Moore to BT, July 24, 1760, fols. 23–24; "Extract of a Letter from St. Thomas in the East, July 19," *Pennsylvania Gazette,* September 4, 1760; Zachary Bayly to Caleb Dickinson, Kingston, June 1, 1760, Somerset Record Office, Caleb Dickinson Letters DD\DN/218.

109. First quotation, Henry Moore to BT, Spanish Town, June 9, 1760, TNA, CO 137/32, fols. 7–8; Second quotation, Zachary Bayly to Caleb Dickinson, Kingston, June 1, 1760, SRO, Caleb Dickinson Letters DD\DN/218; Third quotation, Francis Treble to Caleb Dickinson, Kingston, Jamaica, June 2, 1760, Somerset Record Office, Caleb Dickinson Letters DD\DN/218.

110. Henry Moore to Board of Trade, April 19, 1760 and April 24, 1760, TNA, CO 137/60, fol. 294; John Morse to Caleb Dickinson, April 24, 1760, Somerset Record Office, Caleb Dickinson Letters DD\DN/218; Francis Treble to Caleb Dickinson, Kingston, June 2, 1760, SRO, Caleb Dickinson Letters DD\DN/218.

111. Quotations in "Notices from Kingston, Jamaica, 7, June 14, 1760 and July 24, 1760," and "Notices from St. Jago de la Vega, Jamaica, June 14, 1760," in *Pennsylvania Gazette,* September 4, 1760.

112. See, for example, Michael P. Johnson, "Denmark Vesey and his Co-conspirators," *WMQ* 58, no. 4 (2001): 915–976.

113. Long, *History of Jamaica,* 2: 455–456.

114. Long, *History of Jamaica,* 2: 457. Michael Craton repeats Long's error in *Testing the Chains,* 136. The first historical account of these events published in 1764 similarly conflates the subsequent uprising on Arthur Forrest's estate in Westmoreland Parish with the revolt in St. Mary's, although it does not collapse the timeline as egregiously as Long's account. See Various Authors, *The Modern Part of an Universal History,* 41: 456.

115. Long, *History of Jamaica,* 2: 457.

116. Also see Catherine Hall and Daniel Pick, "Thinking about Denial," *History Workshop Journal* 84, no. 1 (2017): 1–23, esp. 2–8.

117. "Notice from Jamaica, May 8," *Cork Evening Post,* August 11, 1760.

118. Vincent Brown, "A Vapor of Dread: Observations on Racial Terror and Vengeance in the Age of Revolution," in Thomas Bender and Laurent Dubois, eds., *Revolution! The Atlantic World Reborn* (New York: Giles, 2011), 178–210.

119. Long, *History of Jamaica,* 2: 455; Rucker, *Gold Coast Diasporas,* 155, 212, 213–215.

120. Long, *History of Jamaica,* 2: 455; du Simitière, "Remarks on Uprisings of Negroes," 187.

121. Minute of Council of the July 14, 1760, relating to the Rebellion of the Slaves, enclosed in Moore to Board of Trade, July 24, 1760, TNA, CO 137/32, fols. 23–24.

122. Elsa V. Goveia, *A Study on the Historiography of the British West Indies to the End of the Nineteenth Century* (Washington, DC: Howard University Press, 1980), 62.

123. Maria Allesandra Bollettino suggests that slaves responded to the immediate opportunities presented by the mobilizations of the Seven Years' War and by the disorder of the planters' responses to events in St. Mary's, raising the plausible prospect that that news of the insurrection inspired serial rebellions as it traveled through the island. See Maria Allesandra Bollettino, "Slavery, War, and Britain's Atlantic Empire: Black Soldiers, Sailors, and Rebels in the Seven Years' War," PhD diss., University of Texas, Austin, 2009, 191.

124. Zachary Bayly to Caleb Dickinson, Kingston, June 1, 1760, Somerset Record Office, Caleb Dickinson Letters DD\DN/218.

5. The Coromantee War

1. Long, *History of Jamaica,* 2: 193.
2. James Knight, "Natural, Moral, and Political History of Jamaica," Long Papers, Add. ms. 12420, fol. 22, British Library
3. Long, *History of Jamaica,* 2: 206.
4. Lists of Landholders, and Quantity of Land Occupied in Jamaica, about the year 1750, BL, C. E. Long Papers, Add. ms. 12,436, fols. 8, 23.
5. Knight, "Natural, Moral, and Political History of Jamaica," fol. 22; Long, *History of Jamaica,* 2: 192.
6. Long, *History of Jamaica,* 2: 204–205.
7. Knight, "Natural, Moral, and Political History of Jamaica," fol. 22.
8. Long, *History of Jamaica,* 2: 204.
9. Thomas Thistlewood diary, 22, May 25–26, 1760; Thomas Thistlewood Papers, James Marshall and Marie-Louise Osborn Collection, Beinecke Rare Book and Manuscript Library, Yale University; Weather, Thomas Thistlewood Papers, Box 7, Folder 46, 18.
10. Leonard Stedman to William Vassall, June 7, 1760, Vassall Papers, Houghton Library, b Ms. Am 1250, Folder 84; Francis Treble to Caleb Dickinson, June 2, 1760, Somerset Record Office, Caleb Dickinson Letters DD\DN/218; Thistlewood diary, May 26, 1760; Journal of the Assembly of Jamaica, November 27, 1760, TNA, CO 140/40, 232.
11. *Journal of the Commissioners of Trade and Plantations,* 58: 20–21; Copy of Moore to Holmes in his letter of June 27, 1760, enclosed in Holmes to Cleveland, July 25, 1760, TNA, ADM 1/236, fol. 60.
12. Francis Treble to Caleb Dickinson, June 2, 1760, Somerset Record Office, Caleb Dickinson Letters DD\DN/218.
13. Stedman to Vassall, June 7, 1760, Vassall Papers, Houghton Library, b Ms. Am 1250, Folder 84; Rebels Kill'd and Taken, Holmes to Cleveland, July 25, 1760, TNA, ADM 1/236, fols. 60–61.
14. Long, *History of Jamaica,* 2: 453.
15. Stedman to Vassall, June 7, 1760, Vassall Papers, Houghton Library, b Ms. Am 1250, Folder 84.
16. Francis Treble to Caleb Dickinson, Kingston, Jamaica, June 2, 1760, Somerset Record Office, Caleb Dickinson Letters DD\DN/218.
17. Holmes to Admiralty, June 11, 1760, TNA, ADM 1/236, fol. 41.
18. Francis Treble to Caleb Dickinson, Kingston, Jamaica, June 2, 1760, Somerset Record Office, Caleb Dickinson Letters DD\DN/218.
19. Leonard Stedman to William Vassall, June 17, 1760, Vassall Papers, Houghton Library, b Ms. Am 1250, Folder 85.
20. Slaves were customarily allowed three days at Christmas, two at Easter, and two at Whitsuntide. Long, *History of Jamaica,* 2: 491n. The reform law passed in the wake of the revolt stipulated that slaves would be allowed the usual holi-

days at Christmas, Easter, and Whitsuntide, but that "No two holidays shall be allowed to follow or succeed one after the other." CO 139/21, fol. 45. See also Nicholas M. Beasley, *Christian Ritual and the Creation of British Slave Societies, 1650–1780* (Athens, GA: University of Georgia Press, 2009), 39, 44–45.

21. Thistlewood diary, October 18, 1760; Burnard, *Mastery, Tyranny, and Desire,* 172. Willem Bosman noted that a shaved head was a symbol of mourning among Africans on the Gold Coast. See Willem Bosman, *A New and Accurate Description of the Coast of Guinea: Divided into the Gold, Slave, and Ivory Coasts* (London: Alfred Jones, 1705), 229.

22. Neither insurrection, in St. Mary's or Westmoreland, began on a Tuesday, the traditional Akan Sabbath. Smallwood, *Saltwater Slavery,* 132.

23. Long, *History of Jamaica,* 2: 205.

24. Vincent Brown, "Narrative Interface for New Media History: *Slave Revolt in Jamaica, 1760–1761*," *American Historical Review* (February 2016): 176–186.

25. Thistlewood diary, July 30, 1760.

26. Long, *History of Jamaica,* 2: 460.

27. Long, *History of Jamaica,* 2: 207.

28. Thistlewood diary, May 26, 1760.

29. Diary of Mesopotamia, May 26, 1760, UA R.15.C.b.1 (3); Burnard, *Mastery, Tyranny, & Desire,* 170–174.

30. Stedman to Vassall, June 7, 1760, Vassall Papers, Houghton Library, b Ms. Am 1250, Folder 84; quotation in Long, *History of Jamaica,* 2: 452.

31. Thistlewood diary, May 26, 1760.

32. Rebels Kill'd and Taken, Holmes to Cleveland, July 25, 1760, TNA, ADM 1/236.

33. Thistlewood diary, May 26, 1760.

34. Diary of Mesopotamia, May 27, 1760, June 3, 1760, UA R.15.C.b.1 (3). See also Diary of Bogue, May 31, 1760, UA R.15.C.b.2 (1); Diary of Carmel, June 2, 1760, UA R.15.C.b.2 (2).

35. Diary of Mesopotamia, May 28, 1760, UA R.15.C.b.1 (3).

36. Stedman to Vassall, June 7, 1760, Vassall Papers, Houghton Library, b Ms. Am 1250, Folder 84.

37. Thistlewood diary, May 26–27, 1760.

38. Thistlewood diary, May 28, 1760.

39. Thistlewood diary, May 28, 1760, as quoted in Burnard, *Mastery, Tyranny, and Desire,* 172.

40. Lists of Landholders, and Quantity of Land Occupied in Jamaica, about the year 1750, British Library, C. E. Long Papers, Add. ms. 12,436, fols. 80–81; Holmes to Admiralty, June 11, 1760, TNA, ADM 1/236, fol. 41; Map of Cornwall County, Jamaica, 1763, TNA, CO700-JAMAICA17.

41. Long, *History of Jamaica,* 2: 453.

42. Francis Treble to Caleb Dickinson, June 12, 1760, Somerset Record Office, Caleb Dickinson Letters DD\DN/218.

43. Long, *History of Jamaica,* 2: 453–454.

44. Francis Treble to Caleb Dickinson, Kingston, Jamaica, June 12, 1760, Somerset Record Office, Caleb Dickinson Letters DD\DN/218.

45. Thistlewood diary, May 29, 1760.

46. Thistlewood diary, May 30, 1760.

47. Diary of Mesopotamia, May 30, 1760, UA R.15.C.b.1 (3).

48. Diary of Carmel, June 6, 1760, UA R.15.C.b.2 (2).

49. Testimony of John Venn, December 3, 1760, TNA, CO 140/43.

50. Francis Treble to Caleb Dickinson, Kingston, Jamaica, June 12, 1760, Somerset Record Office, Caleb Dickinson Letters DD\DN/218.

51. Diary of Bogue, May 30, 1760, UA R.15.C.b.2 (1).

52. Minutes of Council of July 14, 1760, relating to the Rebellion of the Slaves, enclosed in Moore to BT, July 24, 1760, TNA, CO 137/32, fol. 23.

53. Henry Moore to Board of Trade, Spanish Town, June 9, 1760, CO 137/32, fols. 7–8.

54. Henry Moore to Board of Trade, Spanish Town, June 9, 1760, CO 137/32, fols. 7–8.

55. Holmes to Admiralty, May 22, 1760, TNA, ADM 1/236; HMS *Marlborough* Lieutenant's Log, 1st Lt. John Leano, May 13, 1760, NMM, ADM/L/M/48.

56. HMS *Marlborough* Lieutenant's Log, 1st Lt. John Leano, May 22, 1760, NMM, ADM/L/M/48.

57. Minutes of Council of July 14, 1760.

58. HMS *Cambridge* Lieutenant's Log, 3rd Lt. Nathaniel Davies, June 3, 1760, NMM, ADM/L/M/48.

59. HMS *Cambridge* Lieutenant's Log, 3rd Lt. Nathaniel Davies, June 3, 1760, NMM, ADM/L/M/48.

60. Marines Borne as Part of Complement, HMS *Cambridge* Musters, July 1, 1759 to February 28, 1760, TNA, ADM 36/5259, fols.169–178; Marines, HMS *Cambridge* Musters, December 1, 1759 to August 31, 1760, TNA, ADM 36/5260, fols. 243–250; and A List of Marines belonging to HMS *Cambridge* sent to HMS *Harwich,* June 2, 1760, HMS *Harwich* Musters, March to December 1760, TNA, ADM 36/5809, fols. 256–258.

61. HMS *Harwich* Master's Log, June 3, 1760, TNA, ADM 52/892; HMS *Cambridge* Lieutenant's Log, 3rd Lt. Nathaniel Davies, June 3, 1760, NMM, ADM/L/M/48.

62. Foord & Delpratt to Samuel Munkley & Co, June 12, 1760, Bristol Record Office, AC/MU/1(11)h.

63. HMS *Cambridge* Lieutenant's Log, 1st Lt. Thomas Prescott, June 4–6, 1760, NMM, ADM/L/M/48.

64. Holmes to ADM, June 11, 1760, TNA, ADM 1/236, fol. 41.

65. Thistlewood diary, June 5, 1760.

66. Holmes to ADM, June 11, 1760, TNA, ADM 1/236, fol. 41.

67. HMS *Cambridge* Lieutenant's Log, 1st Lt. Thomas Prescott, June 4–8, 1760, NMM, ADM/L/M/48.

68. *Voyages: Transatlantic Slave Trade Database,* http://www.slavevoyages.org/estimates/lCDVnVHA, accessed December 18, 2018.

69. HMS *Port Royal* Lieutenant's Log, May 31 to June 1, 1760, NMM, ADM/LP/231; A List of Soldiers belonging to the 49th Regiment Bourne by Orders

of Thomas Cotes, Esq., Vice Admiral of the White, May 5, 1760, HMS *Port Royal* Musters, September 1, 1759 to April 30, 1761, TNA, ADM 36/6417, fols. 140–142.

70. Thistlewood diary, June 2, 1760.

71. Long, *History of Jamaica*, 2: 454; Holmes to Admiralty, June 11, 1760, TNA, ADM 1/236, fol. 41; Rebels Kill'd and Taken, Holmes to Cleveland, July 25, 1760, TNA, ADM 1/236, fol. 60.

72. Thistlewood diary, June 2, 1760.

73. Holmes to Admiralty, June 11, 1760, TNA, ADM 1/236, fol. 41.

74. Leonard Stedman to William Vassall, June 7, 1760, Vassall Papers, Houghton, b Ms. Am 1250, Folder 84.

75. Letter to Robert Hamilton, Kingston, June 12, 1760, Ayrshire Record Office, AA/DC/17/113.

76. Letter to Robert Hamilton, Kingston, June 12, 1760, Ayrshire Record Office, AA/DC/17/113.

77. Leonard Stedman to William Vassall, June 7, 1760, Vassall Papers, Houghton Library, b Ms. Am 1250, Folder 84.

78. HMS *Viper* Lieutenant's Log, June 2–5, 1760, NMM, ADM/L/V/77; HMS *Viper* Master's Log, June 2–5, 1760, TNA, ADM 52/1493.

79. A List of Soldiers Belonging to the 49th Regiment of Foot, HMS *Harwich* Musters, March to December 1760, TNA, ADM 36/5809, fols. 253–255; Thistlewood diary, June 4, 1760.

80. HMS *Port Royal* Lieutenant's Log, May 31 to June 5, 1760, NMM, ADM/L/P/231.

81. HMS *Harwich* Lieutenant's Log, June 4–5, 1760, NMM, ADM/L/H/61.

82. HMS *Harwich* Musters, 1758–1761, TNA, ADM 36/5809; HMS *Harwich* Master's Log, June 8–9, 1758, TNA, ADM 52/892.

83. A List of Marines Borne as Part of Complement, HMS *Harwich* Musters, 1757–1760, TNA, ADM 36/5809, fols. 79–82; Marines Borne as Part of Complement, HMS *Cambridge* Musters, July 1, 1759 to February 28, 1760, TNA, ADM 36/5259, fols. 169–178; Marines, HMS *Cambridge* Musters, December 1, 1759–August 31, 1760, TNA, ADM 36/5260, fols. 243–250; and List of Marines belonging to HMS *Cambridge* sent to HMS *Harwich,* June 2, 1760, HMS *Harwich* Musters, March to December 1760, TNA, ADM 36/5809, fols. 256–258.

84. HMS *Harwich* Lieutenant's Log, June 4–July 3, 1760, NMM, ADM/L/H/61.

85. Cotes to Admiralty, July 21, 1760, TNA, ADM, 1/235; Holmes to Admiralty, May 22, 1760, TNA, ADM 1/236, fol. 37; Holmes to Admiralty, June 11, 1760, TNA, ADM 1/236, fol. 41.

86. Holmes to Admiralty, June 11, 1760, TNA, ADM 1/236, fol. 41; Holmes to Admiralty, July 25, 1760, TNA, ADM 1/236, fols. 53; HMS *Cambridge* Lieutenant's Log, 1st Lt. Thomas Prescott, June 22, 1760, NMM, ADM/L/M/48.

87. "Letter from a Gentleman at Savanna-la-Mar, June 10, 1760," *Gentleman's Magazine* 30 (1760).

88. List of Landholders in Jamaica, ca. 1750, BL, C. E. Long Papers, Add. ms. 12,436, fol. 68.

89. "Death of Lt Col Sprag at Richmond, Surrey 30 Dec 1766," *Gentleman's Magazine* 38 (1766): 47.

90. List of Landholders in Jamaica, ca. 1750, BL, C. E. Long Papers, Add. ms. 12,436, fol. 61.

91. HMS *Cambridge* Lieutenant's Log, Third Lt. Nathaniel Davies, June 5, 1760, NMM, ADM/L/C15; HMS *Renown* Lieutenant's Log, Lt. Henry Clear, June 5–6, 1760, NMM, ADM/L/R/77.

92. Thistlewood diary, June 6, 1760; Rebels Kill'd and Taken, June 27, 1760, in Holmes to Cleveland, July 25, 1760, TNA, ADM 1/236, fol. 60.

93. List of White People Kill'd, June 27, 1760, in Holmes to Cleveland, July 25, 1760, TNA, ADM 1/236, fol. 60.

94. Thistlewood diary, June 9, 1760; Long, *History of Jamaica,* 2: 205.

95. Stedman to Vassall, June 17, 1760, Vassall Papers, Houghton Library, b Ms. Am 1250, Folder 84.

96. Long, *History of Jamaica,* 2: 205; Stedman to Vassall, Jamaica, June 17, 1760, Vassall Papers, Houghton Library, b Ms. Am 1250, Folder 84.

97. Thistlewood diary, June 11, 1760.

98. Jamaica Council, December 3, 1760, TNA, CO 140/43.

99. HMS *Harwich* Lieutenant's Log, June 5–July 3, 1760, NMM, ADM/L/H/61; Jamaica Council, December 3, 1760, TNA, CO 140/43.

100. "Extracts of two letters from Montego-Bay in the Island of Jamaica, July 1, 1760," *Boston Evening Post,* August 11, 1760.

101. Stedman to Vassall, Jamaica, June 17, 1760, Vassall Papers, Houghton Library, b Ms. Am 1250, Folder 84; List of White People Kill'd, June 27, 1760, in Holmes to Cleveland, July 25, 1760, TNA, ADM 1/236, fol. 60.

102. *Gentleman's Magazine* 30 (1760): 393.

103. Rebels Kill'd and Taken, June 27, 1760, in Holmes to Cleveland, July 25, 1760, TNA, ADM 1/236, fol. 60.

104. Stedman to Vassall, Jamaica, June 17, 1760, Vassall Papers, Houghton Library, b Ms. Am 1250, Folder 84.

105. "Extracts of two letters from Montego-Bay in the Island of Jamaica, July 1, 1760," *Boston Evening Post,* August 11, 1760.

106. Thistlewood diary, June 20, 1760.

107. Stedman to Vassall, Jamaica, June 17, 1760, Vassall Papers, Houghton Library, b Ms. Am 1250, Folder 84.

108. Thistlewood diary, June 4 and 19, 1760; List of White People Kill'd, June 27, 1760, in Holmes to Cleveland, July 25, 1760, TNA, ADM 1/236, fol. 60.

109. Rebels Kill'd and Taken, June 27, 1760, in Holmes to Cleveland, July 25, 1760, TNA, ADM 1/236, fols. 60–61.

110. Thistlewood diary, July 17, 1760.

111. Thistlewood diary, July 17, 1760.

112. Thistlewood diary, August 14, 1760.

113. Consideration of the Conduct of Brigadier General Norwood Witter, Jamaica Council in Assembly, December 19, 1760, TNA, CO 140/43.

114. Consideration of the Conduct of Brigadier General Norwood Witter, Jamaica Council in Assembly, December 3, 1760, TNA, CO 140/43.

115. Thistlewood diary, August 21, 1760.

116. Thistlewood diary, October 6, 1760.

117. *Journals of the Jamaica House of Assembly,* Vol. 5, October 24, 1760, 186.

118. *Journals of the Jamaica House of Assembly,* Vol. 5, October 24, 1760, TNA, CO 140/40, 186.

119. *Journals of the Jamaica House of Assembly,* Vol. 5, November 19, 1760, TNA, CO 140/40, 215. For the relationship between compensation claims and slave resistance in another British Caribbean slave society see David Barry Gaspar, "'To Bring Their Offending Slaves to Justice': Compensation and Slave Resistance in Antigua, 1669–1763," *Caribbean Quarterly* 30, nos. 3–4 (1984): 45–59.

120. Consideration of the Conduct of Brigadier General Norwood Witter, Jamaica Council in Assembly, December 19, 1760, CO 140/43.

121. *Journals of the Jamaica House of Assembly,* Vol. 5, December 5, 1760, TNA, CO 140/40, 232–233.

122. *Journals of the Assembly of Jamaica,* December 17, 1760, TNA, CO 140/40, 246.

123. Consideration of the Conduct of Brigadier General Norwood Witter, Jamaica Council in Assembly, December 3, 1760, CO 140/43.

124. Thistlewood diary, September 27, 1760.

125. Trevor Burnard and John Garrigus, *Plantation Machine: Atlantic Capitalism in French Saint-Domingue and British Jamaica* (Philadelphia: University of Pennsylvania Press, 2016), 151; For Norwood Witter's dissent see Copy of eight points of dissent to the bill [in the Jamaica Assembly] signed by Norwood Witter, Edward Clarke and William Wynter, Rose Fuller Papers, The Keep, East Sussex Record Office, SF 20–21, 20/65.

126. Rebels Kill'd and Taken, June 27, 1760, in Holmes to Cleveland, July 25, 1760, TNA, ADM 1/236, fol. 60.

127. Maria Allessandra Bollettino, "Slavery, War, and Britain's Atlantic Empire: Black Soldiers, Sailors, and Rebels in the Seven Years' War," PhD diss., University of Texas, Austin, 2009.

128. *Journals of the Assembly of Jamaica,* December 10, 1760, TNA, CO 140/40, 238.

129. Diary of Carmel, June 2 and 4, 1760, UA R.15.C.b.2 (2).

130. *Journals of the Assembly of Jamaica,* September 1760, TNA, CO 140/40, 173.

131. Court Martial of Jeremiah Gardner, September 7, 1759, TNA, WO 71/45, 186–190.

132. Court Martial of Jeremiah Gardner, November 12, 1762, TNA, WO 71/48, 285–290.

133. Markus Eder, *Crime and Punishment in the Royal Navy of the Seven Years' War, 1755–1763* (Burlington, VT: Ashgate, 2004).

134. HMS *Port Royal* Lieutenant's Log, James Ayscough, June 3–4, 1760, NMM, ADM/L/P/231.

135. HMS *Cambridge* Musters, December 1, 1759–August 31, 1760, TNA, ADM36/5260, fol. 245.

136. Long, *History of Jamaica*, 2: 193.

137. Consideration of the Conduct of Brigadier General Norwood Witter, Jamaica Council in Assembly, December 3, 1760, CO 140/43. On the breeding of disease-carrying mosquitoes in plantation landscapes see J. R. McNeill, *Mosquito Empires: Ecology and War in the Greater Caribbean, 1620–1914* (New York: Cambridge University Press, 2010), 40–44, 48–60.

138. HMS *Viper* Lieutenant's Log, William Herne Younge, 2, 4, 8, 9, 13, and July 14, 1760, NMM, ADM/L/V/77; Sir Gilbert Blane, *A Short Account of the Most Effectual Means of Preserving the Health of Seamen* (London: publisher unknown, 1780), 4.

139. Consideration of the Conduct of Brigadier General Norwood Witter, Jamaica Council in Assembly, December 3, 1760, CO 140/43.

140. Francis Treble to Caleb Dickinson, Kingston, Jamaica, June 12, 1760, Somerset Record Office, Caleb Dickinson Letters DD\DN/218.

141. Moore to Board of Trade, August 20, 1760, November 7, 1760, TNA, CO 137/32, fols. 25–26, 31–32.

142. Burnard, *Mastery, Tyranny, and Desire*, 173–174.

143. Diary of Mesopotamia, July 4 and 11, 1760, UA R.15.C.b.1 (3).

144. Diary of Mesopotamia, June 22–23, 1760, UA R.15.C.b.1 (3).

145. Diary of Bogue, July 2, 1760, UA R.15.C.b.2 (1).

146. Diary of Bogue, June 4, 1760, UA R.15.C.b.2 (1).

147. HMS *Dreadnought* Lieutenant's Log, John Greenfield, June 22, 1760, NMM, ADM/L/D/229.

148. *Journals of the Assembly of Jamaica*, Vol. 5, December 1760, TNA, CO 140/40, 232; Minutes of Council of July 14, 1760; "Extracts of two letters from Montego-Bay in the Island of Jamaica, July 1, 1760," *Boston Evening Post*, August 11, 1760; Long, *History of Jamaica*, 2: 456.

149. Diary of Mesopotamia, June 10–28, 1760, quotations on June 10, 21, and 28, UA R.15.C.b.1 (3); Diary of Carmel, June 15, 1760, UA R.15.C.b.2 (2).

150. Thistlewood diary, June 22, 25, and 26, 1760, 1, and July 2, 1760.

151. "Notice from St. Jago de la Vega, Jamaica, July 12, 1760," *Pennsylvania Gazette,* September 14, 1760.

152. Thistlewood diary, July 3 and 6, 1760; "Notice from St. Jago de la Vega, Jamaica, July 12, 1760," *Pennsylvania Gazette*, September 14, 1760; Minutes of Council of July 14, 1760; HMS *Harwich* Master's Logs, June 27 to July 5, 1760, TNA, ADM 52/892.

153. "Letter from St. Jago de la Vega, July 12, 1760," *Pennsylvania Gazette,* September 4, 1760; "Extract of a Letter from St. Thomas in the East, July 19, 1760," *Pennsylvania Gazette*, September 4, 1760; Holmes to Cleveland, July 25, 1760, TNA, ADM 1/236, fol. 61; "Minutes of Council of July 14, 1760."

154. Holmes to Admiralty, July 25, 1760, TNA, ADM 1/236, fols. 53–54.

155. Thistlewood diary, July 11, 17, and 18, 1760.

156. Thistlewood diary, July 12, 29, and 30, August 3, 1760.

157. Thistlewood diary, August 16, December 4, and August 1, 1760.

158. Mary Barclay to Thomas Hall, August 31, 1760, Hall Family Papers, UCSD Special Collections, Box 1, Folder 55.

159. Mary Barclay to Thomas Hall, August 31, 1760, Hall Family Papers, UCSD Special Collections, Box 1, Folder 55; Thistlewood diary, August 16, 21, 24, 28, and 30, 1760.

160. Thistlewood diary, September 21, 1760.

161. Diary of Mesopotamia, September 25, 1760, UA R.15.C.b.1 (3).

162. Diary of Bogue, October 8, 1760, UA R.15.C.b.2 (1).

163. Thistlewood diary, October 23, 1760.

164. Diary of Carmel, October 21, 1760, UA R.15.C.b.2 (2); Diary of Bogue, October 21, 1760, UA R.15.C.b.2 (1).

165. Diary of Carmel, November 4, 1760, UA R.15.C.b.2 (2).

166. Diary of Bogue, November 4, 1760, UA R.15.C.b.2 (1).

167. Diary of Mesopotamia, October 23, 1760, UA R.15.C.b.1 (3).

168. The Hynes family is listed as owners of Anchendown, Boston Spring, and The Bogg on a list of 1739 and as owners of 8,453 acres in Westmoreland, ca. 1750. See Jamaica Sugar Estates, 1739, BL, C. E. Long Papers, Add. ms. 12431, fol. 154; List of Landholders in Jamaica, ca. 1750, BL, C. E. Long Papers, Add. ms. 12,436, fol. 33.

169. *Journals of the Assembly of Jamaica,* October 2, 1760, TNA, CO 140/40, 177.

170. *Journals of the Assembly of Jamaica,* October 3 and 7, 1760, TNA, CO 140/40, 178–180.

171. HMS *Port Royal* Lieutenant's Log, Lt. James Ayscough, November 19, 1760, NMM, ADM/L/P/231; A List of Soldiers Passengers Borne at 2/3 Allowance of all Species by Order of Charles Holmes, Rear Admiral of the White, HMS *Port Royal* Musters, November 1760, ADM 36/6417, fols. 219–224.

172. Thistlewood diary, November 18, 1760.

173. Diary of Bogue, November 30, 1760, UA R.15.C.b.2 (1).

174. Diary of Carmel, November 4 and 7, 1760, UA R.15.C.b.2 (2).

175. Diary of Bogue, November 30, 1760, UA R.15.C.b.2 (1).

176. Diary of Carmel, December 24, 1760, UA R.15.C.b.2 (2); Diary of Bogue, December 24, 1760, UA R.15.C.b.2 (1).

177. Thistlewood diary, January 24, 1761; Diary of Mesopotamia, January 26, 1760, UA R.15.C.b.1 (3).

178. Diary of Carmel, January 28, 1761, UA R.15.C.b.2 (2).

179. Thistlewood diary, June 4 and 19, 1761.

180. Long, *History of Jamaica,* 2: 456–457.

181. Consideration of the Conduct of Brigadier General Norwood Witter, Jamaica Council in Assembly, December 3, 1760, TNA, CO 140/43.

182. Patrick Browne, "A New Map of Jamaica, In which the Several Towns, Forts, and Settlements are Accurately laid down as well as ye situations & depts. of ye most noted Harbours & Anchoring Places, with the limits & boundarys of the Different Parishes as they have been regulated by Laws or settled by Custom; the greatest part Drawn or Corrected from actual Surveys Made by Mr. Sheffield and others, from the Year 1730 to the Year 1749" (London: publisher unknown, 1755).

183. List of Landholders in Jamaica, ca. 1750, BL, C. E. Long Papers, Add. ms. 12,436, fol. 23; Browne, "A New Map of Jamaica," 1755; Map of County of Cornwall, 1763, TNA, CO 700-JAMAICA17.

184. Thistlewood diary, June 19, 1760.

185. Knowles to Board of Trade, March 12, 1754, TNA, CO 137/27, fols. 146–147; Mark Hall to Rose Fuller, October 21, 1755, Fuller Papers, East Sussex Record Office, SAS-RF 21/35.

186. Thistlewood diary, October 3, 1760.

6. Routes of Reverberation

1. Thomas Thistlewood diary, April 17, 1761.

2. Thomas Thistlewood diary, April 13, 1761.

3. "State and Condition of His Majesty's Squadron at Jamaica, December 20, 1761," TNA, ADM 1/1787; J. K. Laughton, "Forrest, Arthur (d. 1770)," rev. Ruddock Mackay, *Oxford Dictionary of National Biography*, 2004; Sarah Markham, *John Loveday of Caversham, 1711–1789: The Life and Tours of an Eighteenth-Century Onlooker* (Salisbury, UK: M. Russell, 1984), 415. On the conquest of Cuba, see Elena A. Schneider, *The Occupation of Havana: War, Trade, and Slavery in the Atlantic World* (Chapel Hill, NC: University of North Carolina Press, 2018).

4. Nathaniel Bayly to Caleb Dickinson, August 26, 1760, Somerset Record Office, Caleb Dickinson Letters DD\DN/218.

5. Charles Holmes to John Clevland, May 22, 1760, TNA, ADM 1/236, fol. 37.

6. Thomas Cotes to Admiralty, July 21, 1760, TNA, ADM 1/235.

7. List of Ships and Vessels Under Convoy of His Majesty's Ship *Dreadnought,* Maurice Suckling, Commander, August 29, 1760, enclosed in Maurice Suckling to John Clevland, TNA, ADM 1/2474; John Greenfield, Lieutenant's logbook for HMS *Dreadnought,* June 22, 1760, NMM, ADM/L/D/229.

8. A List of Ships and Vessels under the Convoy of His Majesty's Ship *Edinburgh,* Capt. William Langdon, Commander, enclosed in William Langdon to John Clevland, October 16, 1760, TNA, ADM 1/2049.

9. John Staunton, Lieutenant's logbook for HMS *Edinburgh,* September 17, 1760, NMM, ADM/L/E/51.

10. Virginia shipping returns, October 26, 1760, TNA, CO5/1448.

11. Gregory E. O'Malley, *Final Passages: The Intercolonial Slave Trade of British America, 1619–1807* (Chapel Hill, NC: University of North Carolina Press, 2014), 22–23.

12. Virginia shipping returns, July 14, 1760, TNA, CO 5/1448.

13. Virginia shipping returns, August 29, 1760, TNA, CO5/1448.

14. South Carolina shipping returns, August 23, 1760, TNA, CO 5/510, fols. 83–84; Gregory E. O'Malley, personal communication, September 16–19, 2016.

15. James Lawrie to Col. Haldane, 1760, Grant Family Papers Concerning Jamaica, National Archives of Scotland, GD461/35; Robert Graham to Capt. James Lawrie at the Mosquito Shore, Kingston, July 14, 1760, Robert Graham Papers, NLS, 91–92.

16. Robert Graham to Nicol Graham, Kingston, June 10, 1760, Robert Graham Papers, NLS, 87–88; Robert Graham to Capt. James Lawrie at the Mosquito Shore, Kingston, July 14, 1760, Robert Graham Papers, NLS, 91–92.

17. The place named by the Assembly as Crooke-Cove, after James Crooke, the owner of the nearest estate, is listed as Cousines's Cove on the 1763 map of Cornwall County, TNA, CO 700-JAMAICA 17; *Journals of the Assembly of Jamaica*, December 5, 1760, TNA, CO 140/40, 233; "An Act . . . to Prevent Any Captain, Master, or Supercargo of Any Vessel Bringing back Slaves Transported off the Island, Jamaica," December 18, 1760, TNA, CO 139/21, 47. See also Long, *History of Jamaica*, 2: 455; and Rucker, *Gold Coast Diasporas*, 212–214.

18. Thomas Rothley, Bristol, October 11, 1760, Somerset Record Office, Caleb Dickinson Letters DD\DN/218.

19. Morse & Bayly to Caleb Dickinson, October 18, 1760, Somerset Record Office, Caleb Dickinson Letters DD\DN/218.

20. William Henry Lyttelton, Report on the Island of Jamaica, 1763, Huntington Library, Stowe-Brydges Papers, ST G Box 12 (18); Burnard and Garrigus, *Plantation Machine*, 179–180.

21. Copy of part of a Letter from Rear Admiral Holmes to John Clevland, Secretary of the Admiralty, March 18, 1761, TNA, CO 137/61, 23–25.

22. William Henry Lyttelton, Report on the Island of Jamaica, 1763, Huntington Library, Stowe-Brydges Papers, ST G Box 12 (18).

23. "An Act to Remedy the Evils arising from irregular Assemblies of Slaves and to prevent their possessing Arms and Ammunition and going from place to place without Tickets and for preventing the Practice of Obeah and to restrain Overseers from leaving the Estates under their Care on Certain Days and to Oblige all free Negroes Mulattoes or Indians to Register their Names in the Vestry Books of the respective Parishes of this Island and to Carry about them the Certificate and wear the Badge of their Freedom and to prevent any Captain Master or Super Cargo of any Vessel bringing back Slaves transported off the Island," TNA, CO 139/21, 45–47.

24. Various Authors, *The Modern Part of an Universal History, from the Earliest Account of Time Compiled from Original Writers*, 65 vols. (London: S. Richardson, 1764), 41: 457–458.

25. On the general climate of racial hostility see Burnard and Garrigus, *The Plantation Machine*, chap. 6, esp. 147–154; Brooke N. Newman, *A Dark Inheritance: Blood, Race, and Sex in Colonial Jamaica* (New Haven: Yale University Press, 2018), chap. 3. For Norwood Witter's dissent see Copy of eight points of dissent to the bill [in the Jamaica Assembly] signed by Norwood Witter, Edward Clarke and William Wynter, Rose Fuller Papers, The Keep, East Sussex Record Office, SF 20/65. On the 1761 Devises Act see especially Daniel Livesay, "The Decline of Jamaica's Interracial Households and the Fall of the Planter Class, 1733–1823," *Atlantic Studies* 9, no. 1 (2012): 107–123; and Livesay, *Children of Uncertain Fortune: Mixed-Race Jamaicans in Britain and the Atlantic Family, 1733–1833* (Chapel Hill: University of North Carolina Press, 2018), 66–89.

26. Jeremiah Meyler, Savanna-la-Mar, to Henry Bright, Bristol, June 20, 1760, UMA Bright Family Papers, Box 8, in Kenneth Morgan, ed., *The Bright-Meyler*

Papers: A Bristol-West India Connection, 1732–1837 (Oxford: Oxford University Press, 2007), 360–361.

27. Morse & Bayly to Caleb Dickinson, October 18, 1760, Somerset Record Office, Caleb Dickinson Letters DD\DN/218.

28. Jacob M. Price, "Credit in the Slave Trade and Plantation Economies," in Barbara L. Solow, ed. *Slavery and the Rise of the Atlantic System* (Cambridge, UK: Cambridge University Press, 1991), 293–339; Morse & Bayly to Caleb Dickinson, London, October 18, 1760, Caleb Dickinson Letters, Somerset Record Office, DD\DN/218.

29. Alexander Grant to Sir Archibald Grant, August 24, 1760, GD345/1166/4/57; Alexander Grant to Sir Archibald Grant, December 22, 1760, GD345/1166/4/90; Alexander Grant to Sir Archibald Grant, December 18, 1760, National Archives of Scotland, Grant Family Papers concerning Jamaica, 1751–1792, GD345/1166/4/91.

30. See, for example, November 3, 5, 8–9, and December 16, 1760, *Journals of the Assembly of Jamaica,* Vol. 5, TNA, CO 140/40, 195, 226–227, and 234–236, 245.

31. Long, *History of Jamaica,* 2: 462, 471.

32. Long, *History of Jamaica,* 2: 463–464, quotation on 464.

33. November 6, 1760, *Journals of the Assembly of Jamaica,* Vol. 5, TNA, CO 140/40, 199–200.

34. December 16, 1760, *Journals of the Assembly of Jamaica,* Vol. 5, TNA, CO 140/40, 245; Letters, etc., on [The Stamp Act's] administration in America: 1765–1766, BL, Add. ms. 33030, fols. 50–203. I am grateful to Peter Pellizzari for drawing this source to my attention. See also Lynne Oats, Pauline Sadler; and Carlene Wynter, "Taxing Jamaica: The Stamp Act of 1760 and Tacky's Rebellion," *eJournal of Tax Research* 12, no. 1 (2014): 162–184: https://ore.exeter.ac.uk/repository/handle/10871/16322.

35. Minutes of the Board of Trade, Jamaica, November 7, 1760, TNA, CO 391/68, 20–22.

36. Jack P. Greene, "'Of Liberty and of the Colonies': A Case Study of Constitutional Conflict in the Mid-Eighteenth Century British American Empire," *Creating the British Atlantic: Essays on Transplantation, Adaptation, and Continuity* (Charlottesville: University of Virginia Press, 2013), 140–207.

37. Jack P. Greene, "Origins of the New Colonial Policy, 1748–1763," in Jack P. Greene and J. R. Pole, eds., *A Companion to the American Revolution* (Malden, MA: Wiley-Blackwell, 2000), 101–111, quotations on 109; Greene, "1759: The Perils of Success" in *Creating the British Atlantic: Essays on Transplantation, Adaptation, and Continuity* (Charlottesville: University of Virginia Press, 2013), 208–225.

38. Humble Address of the lieutenant-governor, council, and assembly, December 15, 1760, *Journals of the Assembly of Jamaica,* Vol. 5, 244.

39. Minutes of the Board of Trade, Jamaica, April 1, 1761, TNA, CO 391/68, 199–202.

40. See Andrew Jackson O'Shaughnessy, *An Empire Divided: The American Revolution and the British Caribbean* (Philadelphia: University of Pennsylvania Press, 2000), esp. 95–96 on Jamaica's acquiescence to the Stamp Act of 1765.

41. Burnard, *Planters, Merchants, and Slaves*, 4, 179, and more generally 157–210; Burnard and Garrigus, *The Plantation Machine*, 167–173.
42. Laughton, "Forrest, Arthur (*d.* 1770)"; Markham, *John Loveday of Caversham*, 415.
43. *Voyages: The Transatlantic Slave Trade Database:* http://www.slavevoyages.org/estimates/EnFT8ZRi and http://www.slavevoyages.org/estimates/WJj5sg8F, accessed June 16, 2018.
44. Thistlewood diary, September 2, 1760.
45. Thistlewood diary, October 24, 1760.
46. William Henry Lyttleton to the Board of Trade, April 12, 1763, CO 137/33, fol. 28; *Pennsylvania Gazette,* June 9, 1763, Item #30984, dated Boston, May 30.
47. *Pennsylvania Gazette,* March 7, 1765. Item #35280, dated Providence, February 9.
48. Copy of Charles Hiern to Caleb Dickinson c/o Barnard Dickinson, November 12, 1765, Somerset Record Office, Caleb Dickinson Letters, DD/DN/221.
49. Moon phases for Kingston, Jamaica, 1765: https://www.timeanddate.com/moon/phases/jamaica/kingston?year=1765; "Extract of a Letter from Zach. Bayly, Esq; Custos Rotulorum of St. Mary's in Jamaica, to his brother, Nath. Bayly, of Lincoln's inn-fields; dated at Nonesuch Estate in St. Mary's the 27th Nov. 1765; received by the *Ruby,* Capt. King," *Gentlemen's Magazine* 36 (1766): 135.
50. "Extract of a Letter from Zach. Bayly," 135; Zachary Bayly to William Henry Lyttelton, November 25, 1765, Lyttelton Papers, Clements Library; Simon Taylor to Chaloner Arcedeckne, December 9, 1765, in Betty Wood, ed., *The Letters of Simon Taylor* (Cambridge, UK: Cambridge University Press, 2002), 29–30.
51. "Extract of a Letter from Zach. Bayly," 135; Simon Taylor to Chaloner Arcedeckne, December 9, 1765, in Wood, ed., *The Letters of Simon Taylor,* 30; Zachary Bayly to William Henry Lyttelton, November 25, 1765, Lyttelton Papers, Clements Library; Zachary Bayly to William Henry Lyttelton, November 26, 1765, Lyttelton Papers, Clements Library; "Report on Party I sent from the Cross came up with the Rebels a little distance from thence . . . they found four of them dead," Folio d. November 25, 1765, from Nonsuch, St. Mary. Signed Za. Bayley, Accounts of Slave Risings in the Parish of St. Mary, Jamaica, 1765, from various correspondents to Lord Lyttelton Governor of Jamaica, Sterling Memorial Library, English Miscellaneous Manuscripts Collection, MS 753, Box 5, Folder 2.
52. Accounts of Slave Risings in the Parish of St. Mary, Jamaica, 1765, Sterling MS 753, Box 5, Folder 2; *Journals of the Assembly of Jamaica,* Vol. 5 (August 1766), TNA, CO 140/40, 593–596; Long, *History of Jamaica,* 2: 465–475.
53. Examination of James Charles Sholto Douglas, *Journals of the Assembly of Jamaica,* Vol. 5, TNA, CO 140/40, 594.
54. Zachary Bayly to William Henry Lyttelton, December 14, 1765, Lyttelton Papers, Clements Library; Quotation in Zachary Bayly to William Henry Lyttelton, November 25, 1765, Lyttelton Papers, Clements Library.

55. Examination of James Charles Sholto Douglas, *Journals of the Assembly of Jamaica,* Vol. 5, TNA, CO 140/40, 595.

56. Examination of James Miller, *Journals of the Assembly of Jamaica,* Vol. 5, TNA, CO 140/40, 593.

57. An Account of what Negroes were concerned in the Late Insurrection as far as has been yet discovered and what became of them, enclosed in Zachary Bayly to William Henry Lyttelton, December 14, 1765, Lyttelton Papers, Clements Library, University of Michigan.

58. An Account of what Negroes were concerned in the Late Insurrection as far as has been yet discovered and what became of them, enclosed in Zachary Bayly to William Henry Lyttelton, December 14, 1765, Lyttelton Papers, Clements Library, University of Michigan.

59. Examination of James Charles Sholto Douglas, *Journals of the Assembly of Jamaica,* Vol. 5, TNA, CO 140/40, 595; Long, *History of Jamaica,* 2: 464.

60. Account of Examination of Cuffie a Negro man belonging to Ja.Ch.Sh.Douglas Esq. signed by Douglas in presence of William Cross, William Craigie, Sterling MS 753, Box 5, Folder 2.

61. David Miller to Brig. Gen. William Lewis, November 20, 1765, Lyttelton Papers, Clements Library, University of Michigan; William Lewis to William Lyttelton, December 5, 1765, Lyttelton Papers, Clements Library, University of Michigan.

62. *Journals of the Assembly of Jamaica,* Vol. 5, TNA, CO 140/40, 556.

63. Examination of William Craigie, *Journals of the Assembly of Jamaica,* Vol. 5, TNA, CO 140/40, 595.

64. *Journals of the Assembly of Jamaica,* Vol. 5, TNA, CO 140/40, 592.

65. *Journals of the Assembly of Jamaica,* Vol. 5, TNA, CO 140/40, 593; Long, *History of Jamaica,* 2: 470–471.

66. *Journals of the Assembly of Jamaica,* Vol. 5, TNA, CO 140/40, 592; See Lyttelton's sanguine report in William Henry Lyttleton to Board of Trade, December 24, 1765, TNA, CO 137/34, f. 48.

67. See especially Marjoleine Kars, *Blood on the River: A Chronicle of Mutiny and Freedom on the Wild Coast* (New York: New Press, 2020) and "Dodging Rebellion: Politics and Gender in the Berbice Slave Uprising of 1763," *American Historical Review* 121, no. (2016): 39–69.

68. James Grainger, *The Sugar Cane: A Poem. In Four Books: with Notes* (London: R. and J. Dodsley, 1766 [1764]), 122–123.

69. Joseph Maud to William Henry Lyttelton, October 7, 1765, TNA, CO 137/62, 154; "Narrative of the Publick Transactions in the Bay of Honduras from 1784 to 1790 by Edward Marcus Despard," TNA, CO 123/10, 105–106.

70. October 6, 15, and 31, 1766, and November 6, 1766, Diary of Carmel, Bogue, and Mesopotamien Estate, 1764–1776, Unitaetarciv, R.15.C.b.3.

71. November 6, 1766, Diary of Carmel, Bogue, and Mesopotamien Estate, 1764–1776, Unitaetarciv, R.15.C.b.3.

72. Long, *History of Jamaica,* 2: 471.

73. Steven Wise, *Though the Heavens May Fall: The Landmark Trial that Led to the End of Human Slavery* (Cambridge, MA: Harvard University Press, 2005).

74. Edward Long, *Candid reflections upon the judgement lately awarded by the Court of King's Bench in Westminster-Hall on what is commonly called the Negroe-cause, by a Planter* (London: T. Lowndes, 1772), quotations on 74, 54, 47–48.

75. Long, *Candid Reflections*, 48–49. On Long's general antipathy to interracial sexual liaisons see Trevor Burnard, "'Rioting in Goatish Embraces': Marriage and Improvement in Early British Jamaica," *History of the Family* 11, no. 4 (2006): 185–197. Although, in *History of Jamaica*, Long claimed to suspect that the offspring of black and white unions might be infertile, this stood in stark contrast to his fear of suffusion of "contaminated" blood in *Candid Reflections*.

76. Long, *History of Jamaica*, 2: 474.

77. Long, *History of Jamaica*, 2: 351–356, quotation on 354.

78. Long, *History of Jamaica*, 1: 503–504; Suman Seth, "Materialism, Slavery, and *The History of Jamaica*," *Isis* 105, no. 4 (December 2014): 764–772.

79. Stuart Hall, "Race—the Sliding Signifier," in *The Fateful Triangle: Race, Ethnicity, Nation*, Kobena Mercer, ed. (Cambridge, MA: Harvard University Press, 2017), 31–79.

80. David Brion Davis, *The Problem of Slavery in Western Culture* (Ithaca: Cornell University Press, 1966), 460–466; Roxann Wheeler, *The Complexion of Race: Categories of Difference in Eighteenth-Century British Culture* (Philadelphia: University of Pennsylvania Press, 2000).

81. Long's Collection for *The History of Jamaica*, BL, Add. ms. 18270, 44. I am grateful to Miles Ogborn for bringing this reference to my attention.

82. Joseph Conrad, *Heart of Darkness*, edited with an introduction by Owen Knowles (New York: Cambridge University Press, 2007 [1899]), 62; Sven Lindqvist, *'Exterminate All the Brutes': One Man's Odyssey into the Heart of Darkness and the Origins of European Genocide* (New York: New Press, 1997); Patrick Wolfe, "Settler Colonialism and the Elimination of the Native," *Journal of Genocide Research* 8, no. 4 (2006): 387–409.

83. Long's libel included the supposition that Africans mated with orangutans, a slander famously repeated in Thomas Jefferson, *Notes on the State of Virginia* in 1785. *Notes on the state of Virginia: written in the year 1781, somewhat corrected and enlarged in the winter of 1782, for the use of a foreigner of distinction, in answer to certain queries proposed by him respecting; 1782* (Paris, 1784–1785). Long's siege mentality has continued to resonate in white fears of black and brown demographic majorities. See especially Lothrop Stoddard, *The Rising Tide of Color Against White World-Supremacy* (New York: Charles Scribner's Sons, 1920); Margaret Thatcher, TV Interview for Granada *World in Action* ("rather swamped"), January 27, 1978: https://www.margaretthatcher .org/document/103485, accessed January 24, 2019; Patrick J. Buchanan, *Suicide of a Superpower: Will America Survive to 2025?* (New York: Thomas Dunne, 2011), esp. 123–161; and Jamie Miller, *An African Volk: The Apartheid Regime and Its Search for Survival* (New York: Oxford University Press, 2016).

84. Claudius K. Fergus, *Revolutionary Emancipation: Slavery and Abolition in the British West Indies* (Baton Rouge: Louisiana State University Press, 2013),

esp. 36–41; Katherine Paugh, *The Politics of Reproduction: Race, Medicine, and Fertility in the Age of Abolition* (Oxford: Oxford University Press, 2017). Also see J. R. Ward, *British West Indian Slavery, 1750–1834: The Process of Amelioration* (Oxford: Oxford University Press, 1988); and Caroline Spence, "Ameliorating Empire: Slavery and Protection in the British Colonies, 1783–1865" (PhD diss., Harvard University, 2014).

85. Darold Wax, "Negro Import Duties in Colonial Pennsylvania," *Pennsylvania Magazine of History and Biography* 97, no. 1 (1973): 22–44, quotation on 31.

86. Darold D. Wax, "'The Great Risque We Run': The Aftermath of Slave Rebellion at Stono, South Carolina, 1739–1745," *Journal of Negro History* 67, no. 2 (1982): 136–147.

87. Darold Wax, "Negro Import Duties in Colonial Virginia: A Study of British Commercial Policy and Local Public Policy," *Virginia Magazine of History and Biography* 79, no. 1 (1979): 29–44, quotations on 42.

88. Wax, "Negro Import Duties in Colonial Pennsylvania," quotation on 35.

89. Sarah Salih, "Putting Down Rebellion: Witnessing the Body of the Condemned in Abolition-era Narratives," in *Essays Marking the British Abolition Act of 1807*, edited by Peter J. Kitson and Brycchan Carey (Cambridge, UK: Cambridge University Press, 2007); Ramesh Mallipeddi, *Spectacular Suffering: Witnessing Slavery in the Eighteenth-Century British Atlantic* (Charlottesville: University of Virginia Press, 2015).

90. Vincent Brown, *The Reaper's Garden: Death and Power in the World of Atlantic Slavery* (Cambridge, MA: Harvard University Press, 2008), 152–156. Also see Trevor Burnard, "Slavery and the Enlightenment in Jamaica and the British Empire, 1760–1772: The Afterlife of Tacky's Rebellion and the Origins of British Abolitionism," *Enlightened Colonialism* (2017): 227–246.

91. J. Philmore, *Two Dialogues on the Man-Trade* (London: J. Waugh, 1760), 54.

92. David Brion Davis, *The Problem of Slavery in the Age of Revolution, 1770–1823* (New York: Oxford University Press, 1999 [1975]), 270–271; Davis, "New Sidelights on Early Antislavery Radicalism," *WMQ* 28, no. 4 (1971): 585–594; David L. Crosby, ed., *The Complete Antislavery Writings of Anthony Benezet, 1754–1783* (Baton Rouge: Louisiana State University Press, 2013); Jeffrey Glover, "Witnessing African War: Slavery, the Laws of War, and Anglo-American Abolitionism," *WMQ* 74, no. 3 (2017): 503–532; Christopher L. Brown, *Moral Capital: Foundations of British Abolitionism* (Chapel Hill: University of North Carolina Press, 2007), esp. 391–450.

93. *Boston Evening-Post,* 6 Feb. 1764.

94. James Otis, *Rights of the British Colonies Asserted and Proved* (Boston: J. Almon, 1764), 43; Peter Linebaugh and Marcus Rediker, *The Many-Headed Hydra: Sailors, Slaves, Commoners, and the Hidden History of the Revolutionary Atlantic* (Boston: Beacon Press, 2000), 222–227.

95. Perry Gauci, *William Beckford: First Prime Minister of the London Empire* (New Haven: Yale University Press, 2013), 107–136.

96. James Boswell, *The Life of Samuel Johnson, LL.D.,* 5 Vols. (London: J. Davis, 1831), 4: 388.

97. Bryan Edwards, "Stanzas, Occasioned by the Death of Alico, an African Slave, condemned for Rebellion in Jamaica, 1760," in *Poems, Written Chiefly in the West-Indies* (Kingston: Printed for author by Alexander Aikman, 1792), 37–39.

98. Bryan Edwards, "Ode, on Seeing a Negro Funeral," in *Poems, Written Chiefly in the West-Indies* (Kingston: Printed for author by Alexander Aikman, 1792), 46–47.

99. Bryan Edwards, *A Speech Delivered at a Free Conference between the Honourable the Council and the Assembly of Jamaica, Held the 19th November, 1789, on the Subject of Mr. Wilberforce's proposition in the House of Commons* (Kingston: Printed for author by Alexander Aikman, 1789), 67.

100. Bryan Edwards, *The History, Civil and Commercial, of the British West Indies,* Fifth edition, 5 Vols. (London: G. and W.B. Whittaker, 1819 [1793]), 2: 73–86, quotations in order of reference on 80, 70, 87, 74, 80, 83, 74, 84, 75.

101. Frank Cundall, *Historic Jamaica* (London: Institute of Jamaica, 1915), 307; Zachary Bayly: Profile and Legacies Summary, *Legacies of British Slave Ownership:* https://www.ucl.ac.uk/lbs/person/view/2146652013, accessed June 29, 2018; Bryan Edwards, "Inscription in the parish church of St. Andrew, Jamaica, Zachary Bayly," in *Poems, Written Chiefly in the West-Indies* (Kingston: Printed for author by Alexander Aikman, 1792), 59–60; Bryan Edwards, *The History, Civil and Commercial, of the British West Indies,* Fifth edition, 5 Vols. (London: T. Miller, 1819 [1793]), 1: 307–310.

102. Edwards, *The History, Civil and Commercial, of the British West Indies,* 2: 75.

103. Bryan Edwards, *An Historical Survey of the French Colony in the Island of St. Domingo: Comprehending a Short Account of Its Ancient Government, Political State, Population, Productions, and Exports; A Narrative of the Calamities Which Have Desolated the Country Ever Since the Year 1789 and a detail of the military transactions of the British army in that island to the end of 1794* (London: John Stockdale, 1797).

104. Long, *History of Jamaica,* 2: 430.

105. Edwards, *History of the British West Indies,* 3: 36.

106. Edwards, *History of the British West Indies,* 2: 74.

107. Margaret Cezair-Thompson, "History, Fiction, and the Myth of Marginality: Portrait of the Writer as a Young Woman," *SX Salon* 11 (2013).

108. See especially Walter C. Rucker, *Gold Coast Diasporas: Identity, Culture, and Power* (Bloomington: Indiana University Press, 2015), 98–99. Also see Paul E. Lovejoy, *Jihad in West Africa during the Age of Revolutions* (Athens: Ohio University Press, 2016), 136, 140.

109. As the political scientist James Scott explained about some political myths in early modern Europe: "We must not see the myths of the czar and peasant as an ideological creation of the monarchy, then appropriated and reinterpreted by the peasantry. These myths were rather the joint product of a historic struggle rather like a ferocious argument in which the basic terms (simple peasant, benevolent czar) are shared but in which the interpretations follow wildly divergent paths in accordance with vital interests." James C. Scott,

Domination and the Arts of Resistance: Hidden Transcripts (New Haven: Yale University Press, 1990), 100.

110. Edwards, *History of the British West Indies,* 2: 81.

111. Rucker, *Gold Coast Diasporas,* 1–6.

112. Anonymous, *The Koromantyn Slaves, or West Indian Sketches* (London: J. Hatchard and Son, 1823).

113. Kenneth M. Bilby, "The Kromanti Dance of the Windward Maroons of Jamaica," *New West Indian Guide* 55, nos. 1/2 (1983): 52–101; Bilby, "How the ýolder headsý talk: a Jamaican Maroon Spirit Possession Language and Its Relationship to the Creoles of Suriname and Sierra Leone," *New West Indian Guide* 57, nos. 1–2 (1983): 37–88. Also see Bilby, *True-Born Maroons* (Gainesville: University Press of Florida, 2005).

Epilogue: The Age of Slave War

1. John Lindsay to William Robertson, August 6, 1776, Letters concerning Jamaica (including the slave rising), 1776, National Library of Scotland (NLS), MS 3942, fols. 259–263. Also see Richard B. Sheridan, "The Jamaican Slave Insurrection Scare of 1776 and the American Revolution," *Journal of Negro History* 61, no. 3 (1976): 290–308; Edward B. Rugemer, *Slave Law and the Politics of Resistance in the Early Atlantic World* (Cambridge, MA: Harvard University Press, 2018), 193–199; and Jason Sharples, *The World that Fear Made: Conspiracy, Imagination, and Power in Early American Slavery* (Philadelphia: University of Pennsylvania Press, 2019), chap. 6.

2. Lindsay to Robertson, August 6, 1776, NLS, MS 3942, fols. 259–263, quotation on 259–260.

3. Governor Sir Basil Keith to Lord George Germaine, August 6, 1776, TNA, CO 137/71, fols. 227–231, quotation on 229.

4. Keith to Germaine, August 6, 1776, TNA, CO 137/71, fol. 229.

5. Lindsay to Robertson, August 6, 1776, NLS, MS 3942, fol. 262.

6. Eugene D. Genovese, *From Rebellion to Revolution: Afro-American Slave Revolts in the Making of the Modern World* (Baton Rouge: Louisiana State University Press, 1979), quotation on 35–36; J. R. Ward, *British West Indian Slavery, 1750–1834: The Process of Amelioration* (New York: Oxford University Press, 1988), 219; Michael Mullin, *Africa in America: Slave Acculturation and Resistance in the American South and the British Caribbean, 1736–1831* (Urbana, IL: University of Illinois Press, 1992); Richard D. E. Burton, *Afro-Creole: Power, Opposition, and Play in the Caribbean* (Ithaca: Cornell University Press, 1997), 13–46. On the geographical memory of resistance in Jamaica see especially Kenneth M. Bilby, *True-Born Maroons* (Gainesville: University Press of Florida, 2005).

7. Colonel Grizzell to Keith, July 27, 1776, in Keith to Germain, August 6, 1776, TNA, CO 137/71, fols. 268–269.

8. Keith to Germaine, August 6, 1776, TNA, CO 137/71, fol. 229; List of the impeached Estates in the Parish of Hanover & the number of Negroes on them,

enclosed in Letter from the Magistrates, July 20, 1776, enclosed in Keith to Germaine, August 6, 1776, TNA, CO 137/71, fol. 272; Colonel Grizzell et. al. to General Palmer, July 19, 1776, enclosed in General Palmer to Keith, July 10, 1776, enclosed in Keith to Germaine, August 6, 1776, TNA, CO 137/71, fol. 242.

9. "The Examination of Pontack a Negroe belonging to Bluehole in the Parish of Hanover," August 6, 1776, TNA, CO 137/71, fols. 276–278, quotation on 276.

10. Laurent Dubois, *Avengers of the New World: The Story of the Haitian Revolution* (Cambridge, MA: Harvard University Press, 2004); Julius S. Scott, *The Common Wind: Afro-American Currents in the Age of the Haitian Revolution* (New York: Verso, 2018), 52–53; David Patrick Geggus, *Haitian Revolutionary Studies* (Bloomington: Indiana University Press, 2002), chap. 6; Guillaume Thomas François Raynal, *Histoire philosophique et politique des établissements et du commerce des Européens dans les Deux Indies* (Genève: Pellet, 1780), vol. 3, book 11, chap. 24 as quoted in Laurent Dubois and John D. Garrigus, eds., *Slave Revolution in the Caribbean, 1780–1804* (New York: Palgrave Macmillan, 2006), 56.

11. David Geggus, "The Enigma of Jamaica in the 1790s: New Light on the Causes of Slave Rebellions," *WMQ* 44, no. 2 (1987): 274–299; Sara E. Johnson, *The Fear of French Negroes: Transcolonial Collaboration in the Revolutionary Americas* (Berkeley: University of California Press, 2012).

12. Minutes of the Proceedings of the Committee of Secrecy and Safety in the Parish of St. James, Jamaica, January 10, 1792, enclosed in Lt. Gov. Williamson to Secretary of State, February 12, 1792, TNA, CO 137/90, fols. 112–141, quotation on 114.

13. St. James Committee of Secrecy and Safety, TNA, CO 137/90, fol.139.

14. St. James Committee of Secrecy and Safety, TNA, CO 137/90, fol. 140.

15. For comparison see Ada Ferrer, *Freedom's Mirror: Cuba and Haiti in the Age of Revolution* (New York: Cambridge University Press, 2014), chap. 7.

16. St. James Committee of Secrecy and Safety, TNA, CO 137/90, fols. 129–130.

17. Examinations of Sundry Slaves in the Parish of Trelawny, Jamaica, respecting an intention to revolt, enclosed in Lt. Gov. Williamson to Secretary of State, February 12, 1792, TNA, CO 137/90, fols. 143–150, quotations on 148, 145.

18. Robert Charles Dallas, *The History of the Maroons, from their Origins to the Establishment of their Chief Tribe at Sierra Leone,* 2 volumes (London: Longman and Rees, 1803), vol. 1; Mavis C. Campbell, *The Maroons of Jamaica: A History of Resistance, Collaboration and Betrayal, 1655–1796* (Trenton, NJ: Bergin & Garvey, 1990), chap. 7, 209–249; Ruma Chopra, *Almost Home: Maroons between Slavery and Freedom in Jamaica, Nova Scotia, and Sierra Leone* (New Haven: Yale University Press, 2018).

19. Simon Taylor to Robert Taylor, October 24, 1807, Institute for Commonwealth Studies, Taylor Papers, I/I/44; Simon Taylor to George Hibbert, October 31, 1807, Institute for Commonwealth Studies, Taylor Papers, I/I/43. For the biography of Simon Taylor see Christer Petley, *White Fury: A Jamaican Slaveholder and the Age of Revolution* (Oxford: Oxford University Press, 2018).

20. Susan Eva O' Donovan, "William Webb's World," *New York Times,* February 18, 2011.
21. Conway to Moore, October 25, 1765, BL, Add. ms. 12440, fols. 7–8; Shelburne to Moore, September 13, 1766, BL, Add. ms. 12440, fols. 29–30; Shelburne to Moore, October 11, 1766, BL, Add. ms. 12440, fols. 31–32.
22. Frederick Cooper, *Colonialism in Question: Theory, Knowledge, History* (Berkeley: University of California Press, 2005), 19.
23. Walter Johnson, "On Agency," *Journal of Social History,* Vol. 37, No. 1 (Autumn 2003): 113–124; Walter Johnson, "Slavery, Reparations, and the Mythic March of Freedom," *Raritan* 27, no. 2 (2007): 41–67; Carole Emberton, "Unwriting the Freedom Narrative," *Journal of Southern History* 82, no. 2 (2016): 377–394; Francois Furstenberg, "Beyond Freedom and Slavery: Autonomy, Virtue, and Resistance in Early American Political Discourse," *Journal of American History* 89, no. 4 (2003): 1295–1330.
24. Barry Strauss, *The Spartacus War* (New York: Simon & Schuster, 2009).
25. Bryan Edwards, *The History, Civil and Commercial, of the British Colonies in the West Indies* (London: John Stockdale, 1801), 3: 36.
26. See especially Laurent Dubois, *Haiti: The Aftershocks of History* (New York: Metropolitan Books, 2012); Michel-Rolph Trouillot, *Haiti: State Against Nation: The Origins and Legacy of Duvalierism* (New York: Monthly Review Press, 1990); Joseph Guyler Delva, "Haitians Stage Protest, Mock Trump over 'Shithole' Comments," *Reuters,* January 22, 2018.
27. Frederick Douglass, *My Bondage and My Freedom,* edited by David W. Blight (New Haven, CT: Yale University Press, 2014 [1855]), 197.
28. Ruth Wilson Gilmore, "Fatal Couplings of Power and Difference: Notes on Racism and Geography," *The Professional Geographer* 54, no. 1 (2002): 15–24, esp. 16; See also Katherine McKittrick and Clyde Woods, eds. *Black Geographies and the Politics of Place* (New York: South End Press, 2007).
29. St. James Committee of Secrecy and Safety, TNA, CO 137/90, fol. 131.

Acknowledgments

Looking back, I guess that my upbringing in San Diego, California, pointed me toward the study of imperial war. Even though San Diego has never been a place as central to the popular imagination as New York, Washington, DC, Los Angeles, or even Atlanta, its role as one of the most potent military garrisons in the history of the world made it pivotal to the US geopolitics of the latter half of the twentieth century. From my hometown, soldiers, sailors, and pilots sallied forth to secure our freedom—or our right to consume tropical commodities, Middle East oil, or whatever. Born at the height of the Vietnam War and raised during the Cold War, I witnessed the flowering of American militarism close to the heart of its power but far from its battlefields. Friends joined the Navy or the Marines, returning from their tours of duty with descriptions of brothels in the Pacific or with snapshots of dead enemy soldiers in the Persian Gulf. Although they had been there, their stories always seemed displaced to me; their experiences remained far away and had little bearing on the shelter of home. It wasn't until September 11, 2001, that the barrier between there and here seemed to collapse for many Americans, who suddenly confronted a long interwoven history of unbecoming conduct, clandestine collaborations, and surreptitious homicides across the globe, and who have been furiously trying to recover their distance ever since. Maybe this book represents my yearning to keep that distance small and to keep that hidden history in mind, in order to dispel the myths of geographical disconnection—and the class, racial, cultural, and gender differences mapped onto them—that allow people to devour each other with so little hesitation.

This account of empires and insurgents is not an allegory, but readers will notice that it was written during a period of amorphous and seemingly endless global conflict. Another book on slave rebellion might have emphasized other themes and lighted on other details. If a previous generation's scholarship on slave revolt was marked by its engagement with civil rights struggles, anticolonial nationalism, or a resurgent liberalism, this study must wear the effects of the twenty-first-century Terror Wars.

And yet that is not the book's most immediate source. As I have researched and written the story, I have drawn more directly on the alliance, fellowship, and generosity of others, many of them strangers. It is perhaps an irony, but also a reason for great hope, that a book about war should arise from countless acts of love and kindness. So many, in fact, that the attempt to count or list them seems quixotic, but nevertheless necessary.

Of my many teachers, none has had a greater impact on the way I approach this topic than David Barry Gaspar. His Duke University seminar on "Slavery, War, and Revolution" in the mid-1990s was a formative experience. The example of his scholarship, added to his patient and wise counsel, has guided my entire career as a historian. More recently, I have had the privilege to study principles in geographic and cartographic analysis with Peter Bol and Kirk Goldsberry at Harvard University's Center for Geographic Analysis, and with Tim Stallmann and Pavithra Vasudevan in the context of the Countermapping Collective at the University of North Carolina–Chapel Hill. My introduction to cartography prompted me to seek out Molly Roy, who produced the maps that hold my narrative together.

Connecting the moving parts of this hemispheric story presented a difficult archival challenge, which put me at the mercy of heroically dedicated archivists at many repositories. I am grateful especially to those at the United Kingdom's National Archives, the National Maritime Museum, The Keep, the Bristol Archives, the Somerset Record Office, the National Library of Scotland, the National Records of Scotland, the Beinecke Library and Sterling Library at Yale University, Houghton Library at Harvard University, the John Carter Brown Library, the Huntington Library, the UCSD Special Collections Library, the William L. Clements Library at the University of Michigan, the Unitätsarchiv in Herrnhut, Germany, and the Jamaica Archives in Spanish Town, Jamaica.

I also received critical research assistance from Trevor Burnard, who generously provided his transcriptions of Thomas Thistlewood's diary for the years 1760 and 1761; Grace Gerrish, who organized files and transcribed documents; Katharine Gerbner, who transcribed and translated critical Moravian diary sources; Jovonna Jones, who assisted in the collection of images; and Nicholas Crawford, Ryan Fontanilla, Julia Gaffield, and Laleh Khalili, who went out of their way to send me materials requested on short notice. Many others answered my stray questions and made important introductions, often leading me in even more promising directions than I could have expected. Especially helpful were Emmanuel Akyeampong, Andrew Apter, Manuel Barcia, Maria Allesandra Bollettino, Christopher L. Brown, Charles Foy, Courtney Hodell, Walter Johnson, Kelley Baker Josephs, Wayne Lee, Philip Morgan, Susan O'Donovan, Miles Ogborn, Peter Pellizzari, Richard Price, Ty Reese, James Robertson, Randy Sparks, and John Thornton.

The project received critical financial support from the Mellon New Directions Fellowship, the John Simon Guggenheim Fellowship, the National Humanities

Center Fellowship, the David Rockefeller Center for Latin American Studies Research Grant, and the Harvard Academy Junior Faculty Development Grant.

Throughout the process of writing the manuscript, with its many false starts and sharp turns, I have depended on the supportive criticism of a writing group that includes Glenda Carpio, Rachel St. John, and Ajantha Subramanian. This is a squad so formidable that my work improved with every drill. I'm also grateful to the great many others who offered generous readings, comments, and critiques on the various talks, papers, and chapters that led up to this publication. These include the members of the Atlantic History Graduate Workshop at Harvard University, along with George Reid Andrews, Edward Baptist, Naor Ben-Yehoyada, Sarah Balakrishnan, Jonathan Booth, Kathleen Brown, Elizabeth Maddock Dillon, Dwayne Dixon, Richard S. Dunn, Anne Eller, Roquinaldo Ferreira, Malick Ghachem, Ruth Wilson Gilmore, Steven Hahn, Catherine Hall, Marjoleine Kars, Jessica A. Krug, David Kruger, Christian Lentz, Lisa Lindsay, Simon Newman, Miles Ogborn, Diana Paton, Marcus Rediker, Erik Redling, Nicholas Rinehart, Ed Rugemer, Claudio Saunt, Matthew Specter, John Wood Sweet, Mark Thompson, Sonia Tycko, David Wells, Natalie Zacek, and Nuala Zahedieh.

Audiences at several invited lectures asked hard questions and provided crucial feedback. For this I thank attendees of presentations at the following institutions (in reverse order of occurrence): University of Chicago; Muhlenberg Center for American Studies, Martin-Luther-Universität Halle-Wittenberg; Yale University; University of Pennsylvania; Duke University; Eisenberg Institute for Historical Studies, University of Michigan; Faculty Humanities Seminar, University of Richmond; John L. Warfield Center for African and African-American Studies, University of Texas–Austin; Massachusetts Historical Society; Scottish Centre for Diaspora Studies, University of Edinburgh; Mellon Sawyer Seminar in Comparative Global Humanities, Tufts University; University of Colorado, Boulder; W. E. B. Dubois Institute, Hutchins Center for African and African American Research, Harvard University; School of the Museum of Fine Arts, Boston; University of Pittsburgh; Brown University; Dartmouth College; Rutgers University; New York University; Massachusetts Institute of Technology; Washington University; Triangle Early America History Seminar, National Humanities Center; International Institute of Social History; and University of Virginia.

I have been privileged to collaborate with scores of colleagues who have given much to this project, whether they know it or not. Some who come immediately to mind are the members of the Watershed Collective (Kelly Baker Josephs, Alex Gil, Laurent Dubois, and Kaiama Glover), the team at Axis Maps (David Heyman, Ben Sheesley, and Andrew Woodruff), and also Amy Alemu, Lori Allen, Jeff Caldwell, Raoul Daruwala, Alejandro de la Fuente, Anthony Farley, Adrienne Fitzgerald, Graham Judd, Rebecca Ladbury, Mary Lewis, Robin McDowell, Cory Paulsen, Yezid Sayigh, Tommie Shelby, Katherine Stevens, Deborah Thomas, Mechel Thompson, Raechel Tiffe, Benjamin Weber, and J. T. White.

In the final stages of drafting, graduate students in my course on "Black Ops: Militias, Small Wars, and Insurrections in Africa and its Diaspora" gave vital feedback on the manuscript. Mafaz Al-Suwaidan, Camden Elliott, Ryan Fontanilla, Nathan Grau, Chelsea Green, Kirin Gupta, Luis Malik, Franco Paz, Hannah Pinkman, and Caroline Filice Smith all humbled me with their insights and made me feel blessed to be their coworker. I also received remarkably helpful suggestions for revising the manuscript from Randy Sparks and Laurent Dubois, two historians I admire enormously. I hope that this book repays the kindness of their critiques.

Finally, I'm grateful for the sharp eyes of editors for helping me to keep words from getting in the way of what I want to say. Beth Rashbaum, Carina Schorske, and especially Ursula DeYoung have all enhanced the clarity of this book. At Harvard University Press, Kathleen Drummy and Robin Bellinger helped me put it all together, and Julia Kirby managed the publication process. Joyce Seltzer, a pivotal figure in the historiography of Black America, shepherded this project from its inception. I hope the final product honors the legacy of her magnificent career.

This book builds on ideas discussed in my previous publications. Most relevant are the following: "Narrative Interface for New Media History: *Slave Revolt in Jamaica, 1760–1761,*" *American Historical Review* 121, no. 1 (February 2016): 176–186; "Mapping a Slave Revolt: Visualizing Spatial History through the Archives of Slavery," *Social Text* 125 33, no. 4 (2015): 134–141; "The Eighteenth Century: Growth, Crisis, and Revolution," in Joseph C. Miller, ed., Vincent Brown, Jorge Cañizares-Esguerra, Laurent Dubois, Karen Kupperman, assoc. eds., *The Princeton Companion to Atlantic History* (Princeton: Princeton University Press, 2015), 36–45; and "A Vapor of Dread: Observations on Racial Terror and Vengeance in the Age of Revolution," in Thomas Bender and Laurent Dubois, eds., *Revolution! The Atlantic World Reborn* (New York: New York Historical Society, 2011), 178–198.

My family has been my steadiest support and greatest inspiration; I thank Willie Brown, Manuelita Brown, V. Vasanthi Devi, and K. S. Subramanian. I have been nurturing this book nearly as long as my daughters Zareen and Anisa have been alive. They've said they want me to write a happy story next. I cannot promise them that, but I can assure them that spending time with them has been the happiest story I could have imagined, anyway. As to their mother: so far, so good, dear Ajantha. Your companionship during this odyssey has been my greatest joy.

Index

Page numbers in *italics* refer to maps and illustrations.